John Wilson Croker, Louis John Jennings

The Croker Papers - The Correspondence and Diaries of the late Right Honourable John Wilson Croker

Vol. II

John Wilson Croker, Louis John Jennings

The Croker Papers - The Correspondence and Diaries of the late Right Honourable John Wilson Croker
Vol. II

ISBN/EAN: 9783744721943

Printed in Europe, USA, Canada, Australia, Japan

Cover: Foto ©ninafisch / pixelio.de

More available books at **www.hansebooks.com**

THE CROKER PAPERS.

THE

CORRESPONDENCE AND DIARIES

OF THE LATE

RIGHT HONOURABLE

JOHN WILSON CROKER, LL.D., F.R.S.,

SECRETARY TO THE ADMIRALTY
FROM 1809 TO 1830.

EDITED BY

LOUIS J. JENNINGS,
AUTHOR OF 'REPUBLICAN GOVERNMENT IN THE UNITED STATES.'

IN THREE VOLUMES.—Vol. II.

SECOND EDITION, REVISED.

WITH PORTRAIT.

LONDON:
JOHN MURRAY, ALBEMARLE STREET.
1885.

LONDON:
PRINTED BY WILLIAM CLOWES AND SONS, LIMITED,
STAMFORD STREET AND CHARING CROSS.

CONTENTS OF VOL. II.

CHAPTER XIV.
1829.

The Last Days of Catholic Disabilities—Position of the Ministry—The Clare Election—Bishop Curtis and Wellington—Recall of Lord Anglesey from Ireland—Conversation between the Duke and Mr. Croker—Mr. Peel's Conversion to the Cause of Emancipation—Lord Lowther—Anxieties of the Government—Progress of the Emancipation Bills—The Duke of Cumberland—His Hatred of Wellington—The new Police Force—Correspondence between Peel and Croker—Advice upon a new Paper—The growing Power of Journalists predicted—Proposals for a new Edition of Boswell's 'Johnson'—Mr. Murray's Reply—Plan and Execution of the Work—Sir Walter Scott's Letters—Correspondence with Isaac D'Israeli, Sir Henry Ellis, Lord Eldon, &c.—The Work attacked by Macaulay—His own Disclosures as to his Motives—His elaborate Efforts to secure Revenge—Public Opinion and Mr. Croker 1

CHAPTER XV.
1830.

The New Agitation for Parliamentary Reform—Popular Excitement—Declaration of the Duke of Wellington—Penryn and East Retford—Mr. Croker's Advice to Peel—Illness of the King—Disturbed State of Politics—The Duke of Wellington and the Whigs—Theatricals at Hatfield House—Death of George IV.—The New King—"Black Sheep"—Lord Brougham and the Opposition—The General Election—Defeat of Mr. Croker for Dublin University—Revolution in France—Abdication of Charles X.—Death of Mr. Huskisson—Talleyrand in London—Dissensions in the Tory Party—Sir H. Parnell's Attack—Defeat of the Ministry—Mr. Croker resigns his Office at the Admiralty

—Lord Grey's Ministry—Lord Brougham and Lord Lyndhurst—Difficulties of the New Ministry—Mr. Croker on Party Consistency—Death of Sir Thomas Lawrence—His Pecuniary Troubles—Letters to Mr. Croker 50

CHAPTER XVI.

1831.

Mr. Croker's Opinions on the Reform Question—In Advance of his Party—His Disbelief in Reform as a "System"—Doubts about Public Opinion—Letters to Lord Hertford—Lord Hertford on Reform—His Distrust of Peel—Peel's Attitude on Reform—An Autograph of Talleyrand's—Sir David Baird and the Duke of Wellington—Rumoured Whig Dissensions—"Everybody distrusts Peel"—The Cry of Retrenchment—Reform Prospects—Lord Althorp's Budget—Growing Importance of Peel—Insult to the King—The First Reform Bill—Anomalies of the Measure—Discouragement of the Anti-Reformers—Letters from Sir R. Peel—Conversations with the Duke of Wellington—The Dissolution—Second Reform Bill—Mr. Croker's Speeches—Rejection of the Bill by the Lords—The Nottingham and Bristol Riots—Third Reform Bill—Literary Projects—Proposed Editions of 'Hume' and 'Pope' 92

CHAPTER XVII.

1832.

Last Stages of the Reform Discussion—Meeting of Parliament in 1832—Passage of the Bill in the Commons—Preparations for meeting the Hostile Majority in the Lords—Resignation of Lord Grey—Attempts to form a Tory Ministry—Mr. Croker's Record of the Negotiations—He refuses Office—Sir R. Peel on Consistency—Failure of the Duke of Wellington—And of the Speaker—General Correspondence—Appearance of Cholera in London—The Duke of Wellington sometimes Insulted—The Ultra-Tories—The Duke at a Levée—Peel's Sincerity Questioned—A new Tory Club (the Carlton)—Aberrations of Lord Dudley—Mr. Croker's Advice to the Lords—Letters from the Duke of Wellington—Dinner at the Duchess of Kent's—A gloomy Forecast—Mr. Croker urges Sir R. Peel to take Office—Peel's Reply—Prorogation of Parliament—Mr. Croker's Resolve to retire from Public Life—His Motives—The Duke's Opinion—Sir R. Peel on Battlemented Houses—Charles X. in England—The Library at West Moulsey . . 145

CHAPTER XVIII.

1833-1834.

The First Reformed Parliament—Diminished Strength of the Tories—The Name "Conservative" first used by Mr. Croker—"Paying Debts"—The Duke of Cleveland—Mr. Manners Sutton re-elected Speaker—"Finality" in Reform—An old Superstition—The Coercion Bill—Irish Debates—Disorder in the House—Course taken Peel—His Remarks on the new House—And on the Working of the Reform Bill—Probable Anticipations of Office—Estrangement from the Duke of Wellington—The Duke's Opinions on Politics—Giving Pledges at Elections—Peel preparing to accept Office—Lord Goderich created Earl of Ripon—The Malt-Tax—A Victory Reversed—Unpopularity of the Budget—The Royal Academy Dinner—Defeat of Sir John Hobhouse—Capture of Don Miguel's Fleet by Napier—An Unhealthy Season—Toryism of Sir Francis Burdett—Close of the Session—Dinner given by the King—A Ministerial Pamphlet—Notes upon it by Peel and Wellington—Sir R. Peel on the Landed Interest—Dinner given by the Duke of Gloucester—Conversations with the Duke of Wellington—Lord Grey's Resignation and Lord Melbourne's alleged "Dismissal"—Mr. Croker's Narrative—Sir Robert Peel's Ministry—Proffer of Office to Mr. Croker—Death of the Duke of Gloucester—The Tamworth Manifesto 197

CHAPTER XIX.

1835.

The Dissolution and the Elections—Combination against Sir Robert Peel—His Letters describing his Position—Lord Stanley's Refusal to join the Ministry—Mr. Croker recommends Mrs. Somerville and others for Pensions—Peel's Reply—The Rev. George Croly—Benjamin Disraeli and Mr. Croker's Speeches—Anticipated Contest on the Speakership—The Ecclesiastical Commission—Church Revenues—Peel's Reply to "Some of Our Tories"—Fears of another Dissolution—Defeats of the Government—The Malt-Tax—Dissenters' Marriages with Church Rites—Letters of Sir R. Peel—Sir R. Peel's Difficulties—Mr. Croker's Advice—Final Defeat and Resignation of the Ministry—The Premier on his Reverses—Summary of his Measures—The Academy Exhibition of 1835—Sir R. Peel on Wilkie's Painting of Wellington writing a Despatch—And on David's Painting of the Death of Marat—Suggests a History of the Reign of Terror—Illness of Sir W. Follet—The

Second Ministry of Lord Melbourne—Corporation Reform—Memorandum of the Duke of Wellington—Sir R. Peel and Dr. Pusey—The "Tyranny of Party"—Amendments to the Corporation Bill in the Lords—Works on the French Revolution in the British Museum—The Duke of Wellington on the State of the Country—And on Napoleon I. 251

CHAPTER XX.

1836-1838.

Mr. Croker's Literary Work in 1836—Article on Wraxall's 'Memoirs'—Letters from Lord Wellesley and Lord St. Helen's—Lord Aberdeen on Wraxall's Blunders—Sir Robert Peel on Lord Stanley's Position—Doubts as to his future Course—The Duke of Wellington on the Stamp Act—Sir Robert Peel as a Sportsman—Conversations with the Duke of Wellington—The Battle of Talavera—The Retreat from Burgos—His Power of Sleeping at Will—Opening of 1837—Death of William IV.—First Appearance of the "Bedchamber Question"—Sir Robert Peel on the Functions of the Monarch—Two "Coincidences"—Retirement of Mr. Walter from Parliament—Sir Robert Peel on Secular Education—Mr. Croker's Correspondence with the King of Hanover (Duke of Cumberland)—Lord Durham's Mission to Canada—The Duke of Cumberland on English Politics—The Wellington Memorial at Hyde Park—Disputes concerning a Site—The Duke on "Rheumatism" and "Libels"—An Inquiry after Shakespearian Relics at Wilton—Mr. Sidney Herbert's Reply—Lady Peel's Apiary—Sir R. Peel suggests a Cyclopædia of the Revolution—His Remarks on the State of the Country—His Pictures at Drayton—Notes of a Visit to Lord Sidmouth—Anecdotes of Burke, Pitt, &c. 287

CHAPTER XXI.

1839-1840.

Difficulties of Lord Melbourne's Government—Defeated on the Jamaica Bill—The Bedchamber Question—The View taken by Sir Robert Peel—Opinions of Mr. Croker—Letters from the King of Hanover—His Estimate of English Parties—Correspondence with Lord Brougham—Renewed Overtures to Mr. Croker to stand for Parliament—Lord Brougham on Public Affairs—Letters from the Duke of Wellington—Dr. Hook on the

Tractarian Movement — Sir James Graham's Fears of Democracy — The Queen's Marriage — Louis Napoleon's Raid on Boulogne — The Eastern Question in 1840 — The "Bloated" Armaments of Europe — Hostile Feeling in France towards England — Prospects of War — Letter to Bishop Philpotts on the Church Service for Sundays — Reply of the Bishop — Particulars concerning Mr. Perceval's Character and Opinions — Sir Robert Peel on the Events of 1830–32 — A misdirected Royal Letter . . . 339

CHAPTER XXII.

1841–1842.

Fall of Lord Melbourne's Administration — Dissolution of Parliament — Great Tory Gains in the New Elections — Sir Robert Peel's Second Administration — The Corn Law Agitation — Peel's Sliding Scale — His Account of the Debates upon it — Foreshadows a Tax upon Property — The Income Tax imposed in 1842 — Mr. Croker again defends Peel's Policy — Peel on the Necessity of a Liberal Tariff — England's Commercial Policy "on its Trial" — England must be made a Cheap Country to Live in — Peel's Defence of the Income Tax — Sir James Graham on the Corn Law Agitation; and on the Local Disturbances — Sir R. Peel on High Prices and Landed Property — Public Distress at Paisley, &c. — The United States' Boundary Question — Sketch of the Dispute — The Mysterious Map — The "Strong Red Line" — Lord Ashburton's Account of the Map — His Defence of the Treaty — The Second Map — Letters from Mr. Goulburn, Lord Aberdeen, Lord Ashburton, and Sir Robert Peel — Conversations with the Duke of Wellington — Last Letters from Theodore Hook — Birth of the Prince of Wales — The Queen's Attention to Business — Remarkable Duels — Church Music — The Prime Minister in Former Times and Now — Letter from Sir R. Peel — Visit to Windsor — Peel on the "Voracity" for titles — The "Distinction of an Unadorned Name" — The Tractarian Movement — Mr. J. G. Lockhart on the Rich and Poor in England — Sir R. Peel on the Price of Bread — Death of Lord Hertford — His Latter Days — Mr. Croker's Account of Lord Hertford's Death — Suspicions of Lord Hertford's Insanity — The Missing Packet of 100,000 fr. — Nicolas Suisse — Probable Nature of his Duties — Mr. Croker's Prosecution of Suisse — Suisse Retaliates — Trial and Acquittal of Suisse — Letter from Lord Hertford's Son — The Attacks on Mr. Croker by Macaulay — Their Manifest Injustice — Mr. Croker's Character in Private Life — Slanders published since his Death . 375

LETTERS, DIARIES, AND MEMOIRS

OF THE

RT. HON. JOHN W. CROKER.

CHAPTER XIV.

1829.

The Last Days of Catholic Disabilities—Position of the Ministry—The Clare Election—Bishop Curtis and Wellington—Recall of Lord Anglesey from Ireland—Conversation between the Duke and Mr. Croker—Mr. Peel's Conversion to the Cause of Emancipation—Lord Lowther—Anxieties of the Government—Progress of the Emancipation Bills—The Duke of Cumberland—His Hatred of Wellington—The new Police Force—Correspondence between Peel and Croker—Advice upon a new Paper—The growing power of Journalists predicted—Proposals for a new Edition of Boswell's 'Johnson'—Mr. Murray's Reply—Plan and Execution of the Work—Sir Walter Scott's Letters—Correspondence with Isaac D'Israeli, Sir Henry Ellis, Lord Eldon, &c.—The Work attacked by Macaulay—His own Disclosures as to his Motives—His elaborate Efforts to secure Revenge—Public Opinion and Mr. Croker.

THE defeat of Mr. Vesey Fitzgerald in Clare sounded the death-knell of Catholic disabilities. He had been a consistent supporter of the cause of Emancipation, but he went before his constituents as a member of the Government of Wellington and Peel, and that Government, so far as the people knew anything of it, was hostile to Catholic claims. The Duke had hitherto been inflexible, and every public act or speech which was identified with the name of Peel was antagonistic to concession. Peel, indeed, acknowledged that to the removal of Roman Catholic disabilities he "had offered, from" his "entrance into Parliament, an unvarying and decided opposition."* It does not fall within our province here either to recount the slow steps by which Catholic Emancipation was reached, or to discuss the course pursued by Sir Robert Peel; even a passing comment on the events of this period must be limited to a few words explanatory of the letters and papers now to be produced.

In the last chapter it was shown that great excitement had been caused by the Clare election, and by the speech of Mr. Dawson (Peel's brother-in-law) at Derry, in which a policy of surrender seemed to be hinted at. "The Clare election," as Lord Palmerston declared, "began a new era, and was an epoch in the history of Ireland."† Later in the year there happened another incident which caused renewed excitement. Dr. Curtis, the Roman Catholic Archbishop of Armagh, wrote a letter to the Duke of Wellington on the Catholic question, in reply to which the Duke observed that any present "settlement" appeared to be "impossible." Bishop Curtis sent a copy of this letter to Lord Anglesey, who, in reply, expressed his disapproval of the Duke's policy. Soon afterwards Lord Anglesey was recalled, and the Duke of Northumberland—an opponent of the Catholics—was sent to Ireland in his place. It was said at the time that Lord Anglesey had been removed solely in consequence of his letter to Archbishop Curtis, but this was not the version of the affair given by the Duke to Mr. Croker.

Memorandum by Mr. Croker.

January 9th, 1829.—I saw the Duke of Wellington, and he entered fully with me into all the affair with Lord Anglesey.

* Memoirs by Sir Robert Peel, i. p. 2.
† Sir H. Bulwer's 'Life of Palmerston,' Book VI.

He began by saying, "Well, Croker, here we are in another of these nine days' wonders!" He then went on more seriously to tell me as follows :—

Anglesey's recall is not at all connected with the correspondence with Dr. Curtis. It arose out of other circumstances, and would have equally taken place had that correspondence not occurred. The discussion began about O'Gorman Mahon and Steele, whose removal from the magistracy we thought it right to suggest, but which he was averse to. In the course of this correspondence, which was strictly confidential, I thought it my duty to observe on his intimacy with Lord Cloncurry as making a very bad impression on the well disposed, both here and in Ireland, and particularly on the King himself. Indeed, I had long had great difficulty in keeping him in his situation, as I could show you under the King's own hand. To my last letter to him on this subject, which was really written in private confidence, and all through dictated by private friendship towards him, and a great desire to prevent such an addition to our public difficulties as his recall could not fail to make, he wrote to me in a tone that, even as a gentleman, I could not put up with. He told me that though all my letters were marked *private*, yet that he knew I would make use of them if I should see an occasion for doing so, and that therefore he for his part *would make use of them*. This, both in the insinuation against me, and in the declaration of what he would do, was not to be borne. My first impression was to write to show him the impropriety, the moral impossibility, of his making public letters which involved not only the King's name, but H.M.'s personal views and feelings, but I was better advised, and made no answer, feeling that all confidence between us was gone, and that it would be lowering myself to appear to take shelter behind the King, or to endeavour to obtain by request or remonstrance what his own sense of honour and duty ought to lead him to.

I therefore waited till the Cabinet could be assembled, and on Wednesday the 24th I read to my colleagues the whole correspondence, (which no one but Peel had seen before,) and they were unanimous that such a state of things between the Prime Minister and the Lord Lieutenant could not continue, and that Lord Anglesey must be recalled. Accordingly on that day I wrote to the King to state these our opinions. His Majesty was unwell and unable to write to me, and desired to see me at Windsor on Saturday, the 27th, so that three days were lost by this accident. I saw H.M. that day, but was not able to get back to town in time to write by that night's post. I however wrote next day, Sunday. I addressed him as usual, 'Dear Lord Anglesey;' my letter was only a few lines, alluding to the circumstance of the cessation of our intercourse, and acquainting him that H.M. had therefore resolved that he should be relieved in the Government.* This letter, of course, he received on Tuesday, the 30th. Now you know his letter to Dr. Curtis is dated the 23rd, yet I cannot help suspecting that it is antedated, and that it was not really written till he had had my letter of recall.

Croker.—What, do you think he had the boldness to antedate his letter a whole week?

The Duke.—Why, there are circumstances that incline me to think so, though I admit there are difficulties as to *time*, which are in the way of that conclusion.

Croker.—It is very unlucky for Lord Anglesey that he wrote his letter. It has afforded a motive for his recall, which all the world, even his own friends, admit to have been sufficient.

The Duke.—Yes, 'tis all my good luck, my Fortunatus's cap [as he said this he touched his little red Cossack cap which he wears in the house in cold weather]. I never could have explained all the reasons which led to the recall. I could not have told the world the King's feelings. I must have thrown myself on the confidence of the country, but Anglesey has saved me all trouble about it, for every one now admits that after such a letter he must have been recalled. But I have no doubt that he had, as he threatened me, already made use of my former letters. I could detect traces of them—of the knowledge of them—in the speeches of the Association and in the *Times*. You, not knowing what I had written, could of course see nothing of this, but when a person knows a train of circumstances, as I did, he can easily see whether another person speaking on the subject is aware of those circumstances, and I am convinced that the Catholic leaders had seen some of my private communications to the Lord Lieutenant.

---

* [This letter is printed in the 'Wellington Despatches,' N. Ser. v. 366, where the whole correspondence relating to Lord Anglesey's recall will be found.]

This is the sum of what passed between us on this subject. His Grace seemed in excellent health and spirits, and interspersed our conversation with some droll comments and expressions, at which we laughed.

I forgot to say that he attached considerable importance to the change of the article "*a* settlement" into "*the* settlement." He said that Peel had come to speak to him about the letter when it appeared, and that his first impression on reading it in print was that he could not have written it; that it gave a different idea from what he had ever had in his mind. Upon calling for the copy of it he found that he had not said "*the* settlement which would," &c., but "*a* settlement which would"—if the latter word had been *should*, the Duke's meaning would have been still more clear. This I have since observed to him in a note; but even as it is, the printed letter talking of *the* settlement goes on to *assert* that it *would* be, *if* so settled, beneficial, &c., whereas the written letter expresses the Duke's wishes for such a settlement as should be beneficial.

Sunday, Jan. 11th, 1829.—The Duke of Wellington sent me Curtis's letter, to which his celebrated note was an answer.* It quite explains that answer in the sense I understood it, but still I must always think that his Grace's note had helped on the Catholic Question a great step, for he admits the *principle* of concession, and alleges only *temporary* objections. I called on him after I had returned the letter, and he entered into the Catholic Question. He said that he was satisfied he could propose a settlement of it satisfactory to all parties if they would but let him try; but that he found people so unreasonable and obstinate as to be quite unmanageable. One person,

---

* [The following is the text of the Duke of Wellington's letter :—

"My dear Sir, Dec. 11.

"I have received your letter of the 4th inst., and I assure you that you do me justice in believing that I am sincerely anxious to witness the settlement of the Roman Catholic Question, which by benefitting the State would confer a benefit on every individual belonging to it. But I confess that I see no prospect of such a settlement. Party has been mixed up with the consideration of the question to such a degree, and such violence pervades every discussion of it, that it is impossible to expect to prevail upon men to consider it dispassionately. If we could bury it in oblivion for a short time, and employ that time diligently in the consideration of its difficulties on all sides (for they are very great), I should not despair of seeing a satisfactory remedy."]

because, twenty years ago, and in a perfectly different state of affairs, he had given some note or other, now talks of his consistency, and will not see that everything has changed about him, and that his obstinacy makes him really inconsistent. This happens to people on both sides, and if neither party will yield anything, no step can ever be made. "For my part, I am harassed to death by the whole thing. The difficulties that arise on every side on every question are really distracting, and it seems as if all the world relied on me for settling questions to the settlement of which no one will lend a finger."

C.—You remember, Duke, what I once before told you, that you are like a young heir who succeeds to a great inheritance, but so encumbered on every side that he has not a guinea to spend.

D.—Yes, just so; and people expect me to pay off the debts that all my predecessors have accumulated as well as my own.

I never saw him so moved as he seemed to be on this occasion, or talk with so little confidence in his power of managing affairs, or with so much emotion. I have very inadequately noted what he said, but it was all in a strain of complaint, and chiefly that he had no assistance from any one, and particularly that he could get no encouragement or help towards settling the Catholic Question; and I certainly in the little I said gave him no great encouragement as to the opportunity—this seemed to me a juncture of circumstances as inauspicious as any that had occurred during the twenty-five years that I had been advocating that question. I had been all my life anxious to see the question settled on grounds of policy and, I even thought, justice; but that the late proceedings of O'Connell and the Catholics had now brought it to a point of intimidation, and that I for one was ready to vote against any concession to intimidation.

Parliament met on the 5th of February; but, a few days beforehand, Mr. Peel took the opportunity of communicating to Mr. Croker the change which had passed over his opinions. It is clear, however, from his own papers that the "conversion" had taken place some little time previously, though he had withheld it from the knowledge of the party which he was preparing to lead into a great and sudden change of policy.

From Mr. Croker's Diary.

January 31*st*, 1829.—Saw Peel. He announced to me his conversion to Catholic concession, and showed me the papers and letters between him, the King, and the Duke on the subject. I was in great difficulty what to say to him. I was glad of the arrangement of the question, though it comes too late for any good; but I fear he will individually lose some of the public confidence. He has written to place his seat at Oxford at the disposal of his constituents,—in my mind, and so I told him, a democratical and unconstitutional proceeding, and a precedent dangerous to the independence of the House of Commons.* On the whole I am almost equally surprised and dissatisfied with the whole affair. When I read his letter to the King, I really did not know what he had decided to do.

Feb. 2*nd.*—Saw Peel, to whom I felt it to be due to say that the greatest surprise of the public was not so much the concession to the Catholics, as his consenting to be the mover of it. I advised, or rather suggested, to him to see Lowther, and have some explanation with him. He begged of me to call on Lowther† and send him to him, which I did. Lowther called afterwards, and told me that Peel had shown him the papers, but had not convinced him.

Feb. 4*th.*—Dined at Peel's to hear the Speech. Every one came who was expected except Holmes, who feigned illness. I sat between Bankes and Hardinge; they say the former will resign; his conversation with me did not lead that way. The dinner was dull enough. I think we were forty-four. I made one or two verbal corrections in the speech. The

---

* [On this point Peel wrote ('Memoirs,' i. 312): "I will not seek to defend the resolution to which I came, by arguments drawn from the peculiar character of the Academic body, or from the special nature of the trust confided to its members. Still less will I contend that my example ought to be followed by others to whom may be offered the same painful alternative of disregarding the dictates of their own consciences, or of acting in opposition to the opinions and disappointing the expectations of their constituents."]

† [It must be remembered that Lord Lonsdale had enormous influence, and commanded many votes in the House of Commons, directly or indirectly—as Mr. Croker's list, previously given, partly shows. Great efforts were therefore made to prevent the downright secession of his son, Lord Lowther.]

conversion of Peel seemed to all so impossible, that I am told some of his guests did not believe it till they heard him read the speech.

Feb. 5th.—Lowther is in great doubt what to do. Holmes and I persuade him to do nothing—at least till events begin to develop themselves.

Went to the House; the thing went off very flatly—a very full House, which soon thinned. Peel only cheered by the Opposition, as Canning used to be in 1827. I said this great mystery had burst like a *bubble* and not like a *shell.*

Feb. 7th.—Dined at the Speaker's—full dress dinner. This, the Speaker's first dinner, consists of all Privy Councillors in the House of Commons holding office, and of the Lords and Secretaries of the Treasury, and the Attorney and Solicitor-General. The next day (generally Sunday) is for the Privy Councillors and leading men in Opposition. The third (the Saturday week) is for the official members, not Privy Councillors or only Privy Councillors in Ireland, and a few leading men of the Government side. I had dined nineteen years at this last dinner, and had almost survived all my first associates at it, who had been *called up* to the first dinner. General Phipps is, I believe, the only one left who had dined at this dinner in January, 1810. He is now alone, as I am come to the Privy Councillors' table. What an empty name is that of Privy Councillor, but as long as public opinion designates it as an honourable step, public men must consider it so too. I am an instance of this; I had formerly declined it, and at last I accepted it, fully aware of its inanity, only because people told me that not to be a Privy Councillor would look like degradation.

Our dinner was dull enough, and I was in bad spirits. I sat between the Solicitor and Dawson. Peel made a joke about old Collett,[*] who, not knowing Peel's conversion, had written to him to say that he was hastening up to support the good old Protestant cause. This gaiety shows that Peel is sincere and cordially converted, but in a moment he seemed to recollect himself, and looked very grave and almost discomposed at his own mirth, and sat silent and frowning the rest of the evening. The Attorney-General made a wry face at Peel's merriment. It is, it seems, doubtful whether he will not resign. I slept at the Admiralty.

[*] [Mr. E. J. Collett, M.P. for Cashel.]

Feb. 9th.—Saw Peel, who begged of me to insert in the *Courier*, as from myself, his letter to the Vice-Chancellor of Oxford; he was induced to do this by the report which had got abroad that his resignation was *conditional*, and, of course, liable to a suspicion of insincerity. I did so, and sent with it a few complimentary words, but in the character of the editor.

Cooke and Murray bring me accounts, from very different classes of society, of Peel's—and even the Duke's—loss of character, and the possibility of the measure failing after all.

Lowther is still very reluctant to stay in; he showed me a long explanatory letter which the Duke has written to the Duke of Rutland, and of which he had sent copies to the other grandees, and amongst the rest to Lord Lonsdale. Lord Lonsdale's answer was that he could not pledge himself. The Duke of Wellington's letter concludes by saying that, if the Duke of Rutland and the other great interests would not support him he would resign, " for he would not be left at the mercy of the *rump* of the Whigs and Mr. Canning." The last sentences are written in his familiar, not to say homely, style.

Feb. 10th.—Catholic Association Suppression Bill in the House; no great interest about it; more on the Kent Petition. Sir Ed. Knatchbull spoke moderately and, as I thought, fervently, in general for Peel, but he dropped a hint that it was a pity that the conversion had not taken place in Mr. Canning's time; this threw Peel into, or gave him occasion to assume, a fit of passion, in which he said that, once for all, he declared he would give no further excuse for his change.

Feb. 14th.—Dined at the Duke of Wellington's to meet the Duke and Duchess of Northumberland, with Lord, Lady, and Lady G. Bathurst, Mr. and Mrs. Peel, Mr. and Lady C. Greville, Mr. and Mrs. Arbuthnot, Lord Francis Leveson, Mr. Goulburn, Lord Hill, Lord Corry, the Knight of Kerry, Archdeacon Singleton (D. of N.'s private secretary), George Dawson, Sir George Hill, Gerard Wellesley, and Capt. Wellesley. I sat between Peel and the Archdeacon; for so great a dinner it was tolerably pleasant. Peel told me a most extraordinary story of the disappearance from South Shields of a young apothecary's boy, and of its being proved that Hare, the Edinburgh murderer, was at Shields at the time under the name of the *Country Bayman*.

From another Diary kept by Mr. Croker.

Tuesday, Feb. 10*th,* 1829.—I called on the Duke of Wellington relative to a point connected with the English transports which have brought the Portuguese emigrants back to Brest. Before I could enter on this subject, he began, " Well, Croker, here we are in another mess ! "

C.—I hope not. I think the present opposition to your proposal will not be serious, though its consequences may.

D.—Oh, yes; you may depend upon it—very serious even now. Why, what a situation we were in the other night in the Lords ! You in the Commons were better humoured, but in the Lords we were sullen and sour, and if the Opposition (I mean the old Opposition, the Whigs) had moved an amendment on any topic of the address—for instance, Portugal—the Government would have been in a minority, for a great body of our usual supporters would have voted with them. The Whigs themselves saw this, and Holland afterwards told Aberdeen that this was the reason that he did not push on the Portuguese question.

C.—I am very sorry to hear it; it is lamentable to be thus at the mercy of one's opponents; but this will not last long.

D.—I hope not; but I don't know. Depend upon it, we shall have a hard battle to fight.

I then proceeded to ask his Grace, for my own private guidance in the advice I might be called upon to give to a friend of mine (Lord Lowther),[*] whether it was true that his Grace had had a conversation with Lord Beresford, in which he had told that Lord (what Lowther had just written to tell me) that all persons holding office must vote with him or retire.

D.—Why, you ask me a great secret—a question that reaches the *sanctum sanctorum*; but I will tell you that what I said to Lord Beresford does not amount to what you state; but, even if it did, one's answer must depend on the kind of person who speaks to you. There are people who, if you allow them any loophole, will indulge their own vanity or prejudices to any extent, and if I were not to show a determined resolution where should I be? If those in my rear have any excuse for slipping away, how can I meet the

---

[*] [Lord Lowther was then Commissioner of Land Revenue. He did not resign, but voted against the Catholic Bill.]

enemy in front? Besides how am I to bring down my *household troops* if there is any wavering amongst a class of my official men? But Bankes could tell you that I acted to him, whom I knew to be quite sincere, in a different spirit from that attributed to me. I begged of him not to resign. I asked him to wait a little for events, to see what I meant to do, and what line other people might take. For God's sake advise your friend not to resign, and, at all events, not to do so without coming to me. I shall be glad to have the fullest explanation with him, but, at all events, let him not resign, and beg of him not to speak about his intentions. Men speak to their private friends or their mistresses, and get heated as they talk, and pledge themselves so deep that they create a new point of honour to be got over. No, no; he must not resign; send him to me—that is, advise him before he takes any step to come and talk to me, which in fairness he ought, I think, to do. People, I hear, complain most of the surprise; but how could I tell them what I did not know myself? how could I speak to any man till I was in possession of the King's final determination?

We then proceeded to talk of the Portuguese subject. Lord Aberdeen had come in during the latter part of the preceding conversation, and on the Portuguese question the Duke adopted his suggestions.

Feb. 16*th.*—I saw the Duke this morning in consequence of a letter I had just received from Lord H., which seemed to press Lord Douro's return for Aldbro'. As the Duke had several people waiting to see him, I hastened to put an end to my visit when I had said what I came to say, but he had a mind to talk to me, and twice called me back. The only thing in our chat, however, of any importance was his saying, "You see the Duke of Cumberland is come; this is an increase of my difficulties."

C.—It may be a little troublesome at Windsor, but can have no effect on the country.

D.—Oh, yes; at Windsor and everywhere we shall have these horrid libels in public and all manner of intrigues in private. In short, I assure you 'tis a great annoyance!

Tuesday, March 10*th.*—I called on the Duke of Wellington to show him an extract from the first speech he ever made in Parliament on seconding the address in 1793, and supporting the Catholic concession of that day. He seemed to have totally forgotten it, and Peel, to whom I showed it last night, had never seen it. As it supports the Duke's present course, and justifies his consistency, I mean to read it if I get a fit occasion in the course of these debates, and did not like to do so without apprising the Duke.

Mr. Croker to Lord Hertford.

February 2nd, 1829.

The information which I sent you three days ago is confirmed and now public. The King's Speech is to recommend the consideration of Catholic Emancipation. People in the streets say that they cannot believe this as long as Peel remains in office, and those who do not love him talk very harshly of him in the supposition of his consenting to stay after, they say, the reiterated pledges he has given to the contrary: but he will stay. I can say nothing as to *terms* and *conditions*, but they are of no consequence; "*il n'y a que le premier pas qui coûte,*" the first concedes all, and any securities or restrictions can have no effect, but to make the dose a little more palatable. You can have no idea what a hubbub it has made, and it will be ten times greater when it is known, as it will be to-morrow, that P. consents. Some say that his consent will not bind Goulburn. I have no such notion. P. would not stay if any man, high or low, goes out upon it; at least such is my opinion of his high sensitiveness to public opinion. I should not like to write to you how folks talk of his supposed conversion, but all minor difficulties and personal considerations will be lost in the magnitude of the question itself.

March 28th and 31st.

Old Eldon was four hours with the King one day last week under the pretence of presenting petitions. I know that this has given *great umbrage* to Ministers, but be assured it will and can come to nothing.

The Catholic Relief Bill was passed at 4 o'clock this morning—320 to 142, majority, 178, being, *pro ratione totius numeri*, the greatest majority we have had, though by a few the smallest in actual numbers. The debate was exceedingly dull. Wetherell was absurd as usual. The Duke of Newcastle's great Mr. Sadler * fell to nothing: the best speech of the night was our friend Vesey's.

* [Michael Sadler, M.P. for Newark—a violent Anti-Catholic.]

The Duke of Cumberland and the Duke of Wellington are irreconcileable—the former talks violently of the latter, who, though he does not *talk*, is not in his debt, I fancy, as to what he *thinks* of H.R.H. Something more than mere politics seems to have supervened.

The public ferment is subsiding fast, and, by the time you return, all will be quiet, except the exasperated feelings of disappointed politicians. The public will have forgotten the Catholics as completely as they have the Dissenters.

The hatred which the Duke of Cumberland had for the Duke of Wellington has been made known to the public of late years by the publication of the Wellington papers and other works. The Duke of Cumberland tried hard to set the King, his brother, against the Prime Minister, and insisted always upon calling him "King Arthur." "Between the King and his brother," wrote the Duke of Wellington, "it is next to impossible to govern this country." The King's shifty course in reference to the Emancipation Bill, which upon one occasion (the 3rd of March) led the heads of the Ministry to resign, was mainly instigated by the Duke of Cumberland. The Duke renewed his efforts to wreck the Wellington Ministry when the Bill was sent to the Lords, but without much success.

Mr. Croker to Lord Hertford.

April 9th, 1829.

The thing is over, and well over—a majority of 105 in the Lords has astonished friends and foes and will make Windsor as Popish as Downing Street. The Bill has gone through the Committee of Lords with two nights' debate, but without a single amendment, and on some bye-topics there were two divisions—135 to 64, and 113 to 14! Winchilsea has declared that he will never come into the House of Lords again, and the D. of C., I am told, declares that as soon as the Bill shall be law he will leave England *for ever*. The public mind is much more composed, and the mob are much more inclined to cheer the Duke and Peel than their antagonists.

I dined yesterday with the Lord Mayor, having previously attended Peel's inauguration as a freeman of London, in Guildhall; the thing looked handsome, but, literally, the room was better than the company—Lord Nugent, Joe Hume, and such like were, except office men, the most distinguished of the company. We are not yet quite right—our aristocracy still stands sullenly aloof—but things improve, and after Easter I think the Duke will have reunited the great body of his scattered forces.

April 16th.

The Emancipation Bill has received the Royal Assent. Till the Commission actually arrived, which it did not till near 3 o'clock, there was an expectation that the King would still refuse his assent, and the Whigs, so inveterate is that party in absurd speculation, were actually thinking that they were coming into office. I have, however, always told you how it would be. The K—— could do nothing but submit. But to show you how reluctant he was, I need only repeat to you what Peel said to me the day the Royal Assent was given—" Well, the Bill has now passed its *last* and *most difficult* stage."

May 7th.

Our only news since I wrote last was Anglesey's motion relative to his recall, by which, as the lawyers say, he took nothing. But there was a curious incident in the debate. A. stated that he had the King's authority to read his and the Duke's letters; the Duke, on the authority of H.M., contradicted this *point blank*. A. repeated it, and no one doubts how the fact was—but it was very awkward to have the King thus made a pivot for contradictory assertions. The D., however, was on velvet, for he had two or three witnesses on his side, viz., the Chancellor, and Lord Aberdeen, who, as well as one other person, were present when he received H.M.'s assurance. We hear that this vexes H.M., which is no wonder; but he is chiefly vexed with A. There are those who whisper that A. was set on by the Duke of Cumberland in hopes of embarrassing W. There can be no doubt that the two Dukes are *mortal foes*. I need not tell you which will be finally victorious—but H.R.H.'s unexpected stay here, and his now announced intention of bringing over his Duchess and his son, give some uneasiness.

We have had a division on East Retford, strong enough to

set us at our ease on that point. I cannot but think that we are in the wrong, and that the best way of averting a worse and wider reform would be to transfer the franchise to Birmingham, Manchester, and Leeds, as cases of flagrant corruption may arise in the small boroughs; but, involved as we have unluckily been, in this question, we have no option as a party but to go on. People in the street say that the D. of W. looks very ill—I see him too often to observe the change, if there be any.

The old Duchess of Richmond had a number of stuffed *rats* under glass cases on her drawing-room table, to which Her Grace affixed the names of all the apostates—and I forget whether I told you that some one, equally wise and witty, had conveyed a live rat into the House of Lords and let him loose during one of the last debates; but the pleasantry failed, for the poor little beast soon found a corner to hide himself in.

From the Diary.

March 4th.—The Ministers, that is the Chancellor, D. of W., and Peel, are gone down to Windsor to-day on a sudden summons which arrived very late last night. The King is in great perplexity about this Catholic question. He is, I have no doubt, sincerely distressed: he told me in 1810 that he was as good a Brunswicker (the first time I think I ever heard the word) as his father. His connexion with the opposition made the world believe that he had adopted their Catholic politics, but it is not so.

March 5th.—The Ministers came home last night *out of office*, but during the night more prudent counsels prevailed at Windsor, and a messenger arrived to-day with the King's acquiescence in the measure which, therefore, Peel will open this morning.

A member, presenting a petition from certain inhabitants of Dublin, alluded to the College, and Mr. North took him up, which obliged me to say something. I find that from want of practice or growing old,* or both, I have lost a good deal

---

* [There are other references in Mr. Croker's letters about this time to his growing old. He was only in his forty-ninth year, and had still twenty-eight years of life before him. As for his power of speaking, it was universally admitted that he never acquitted himself with so much credit as a Parliamentary debater as in the Reform debates of 1830-32.]

of my power of speaking. I do not see my arguments clear before me and I think I hesitate for a word, which I formerly never did. Nothing can be well done without *pains* and *practice*, and I neglect both. It is strange enough, but I have no ambition that way. I have remained too long in subordinate office to think of parliamentary eminence.

March 18*th*.—While I was at breakfast the Bishop of Ferns arrived on a visit to me. I am afraid he is come on the project, we have heard of, of the Irish Bishops' waiting on the King in a body to urge him to refuse his consent to the Commission. We battled a little good humouredly about the Catholic question, the time and manner of which I dislike as much as he does, but I am still more afraid of a dissolution of the great *Church and King* party, which is almost certain to follow any serious split on this unhappy occasion. I have been all my life friendly to Emancipation till this moment, when I fear it is too late to conciliate the Catholics, and is sure to alienate the Protestants; what was denied to reason and policy is surrendered to intimidation.

The only other public measure to which reference is made in the letters of this year was the formation of the new Metropolitan Police Force, upon the proposition of Mr. Peel. It is difficult now to believe that down to the year 1829 the public should have been contented with the guardianship afforded them by a few decrepit and broken-down parochial watchmen, swaddled up in great coats and endless capes, carrying with them a large lantern so that they could be seen from afar, and a thick stick to knock upon the pavement so that they could be heard, and passing the night, as a rule, in the seclusion of their own watch-boxes. The present generation know of the watchmen only from caricatures or scenes in old farces, and yet all London managed to get on with them as its sole police force—aided by the professional " thief-taker," of whom Jonathan Wild was a type—down to the approach of the Reform era. It is true that robberies multiplied, and that the streets were not safe after dark; but no system to supersede the employment of the parish watchman seems to have been suggested by any official or member of a Government until Mr. Peel established a day patrol, and followed it up by laying the foundation of our present police force. It was not till some time afterwards that the new policeman was seen in the metropolis or in the provinces, for at first the popular prejudice against the force was very great. Frequently when the constables made their appearance, they were hooted and insulted, mobs following them crying out "crusher," "raw lobster," "Bobbies," and "Peelers." The last-two nicknames were derived, of course, from the founder of the force, and they have probably done more to perpetuate the name of Peel in the popular mind than the measures by which he hoped to be remembered, the chief credit for which has since been popularly assigned to Mr. Cobden and Mr. Bright. For one person among the bulk of the people who thinks of Sir Robert Peel in connection with the Corn Laws, a thousand have his memory recalled, however faintly, by the familiar designation of "Peeler," which the policeman has never shaken off, and which is now applied to him in a friendly sense rather than in ridicule.

Mr. Croker took a hearty interest in the new project, and offered some suggestions to Mr. Peel with regard to the pay of the force and its dress. The uniform was at first intended to be of red and gold, but blue was fortunately chosen instead.

Mr. Croker to Mr. Peel.

September 28th, 1829.

DEAR PEEL,

Having my pen in my fingers to write an address to you, I cannot refrain from saying that I find a general opinion prevailing that your policemen are not paid sufficiently. Three shillings a day for men capable of even *reading*, to say nothing of *understanding* and *executing* the printed instructions seems wholly inadequate. Every artisan has five shillings a day, and can you expect to have higher and more laborious duties done for (considering the deductions) about one-half the rate of a common workman's wages? It reminds me of Lady Hervey's *bon mot*, when some one of her friends was complaining to her of the badness of servants, and enumerating the faults of a footman. "Why, my dear," said Lady Hervey, "the truth is that you expect all the virtues under Heaven for 20*l.* a year." If you resolve to stick to 3*s.* a day as a minimum, at least you should have a higher rate to which good service and good conduct might hope to rise. Suppose you said that every man who should serve five years with approbation should have 4*s.*, and he who should serve ten years 5*s.* a day. This would, I think, answer the double purpose of encouraging good conduct, and of enabling you to get trustworthy men at first, for men might be had at 3*s.*, with a prospect of 4*s.* and 5*s.*, who would not look at it without some such hope.

Your prospect of promotion by vacancy is not enough, because at most the promotion can be but *decimal*, even as to the sergeant's rank, and to the higher ranks the prospect must be so remote as to be almost ineffective. Baffen calculates that a chance of ten thousand to one is absolutely no chance *at all.* I do not know what the odds are against any individual constable rising to be an inspector, but I am satisfied it must be too remote to have any strong effect on minds so little susceptible of regulated and calculated feelings as those which you can hope to hire at 3*s.* a day. Let me add one other consideration. The carpenter or mason who earns 5*s.* a day does so by about *ten hours' work*, and with liberty to live where he pleases, with occasional holydays, the society of his family, the enjoyment of his club, the periodical and certain recurrence of his Sunday's recreation. Your 3*s.* a day man is to be on duty, that is, in requisition for duty, the whole twenty-four hours; *his duty* is in the night, and without shelter in bad weather, or society in fine; he must reside where he is ordered; he can have no recreation; in short, as they say of a broom that it is dirty to keep other things clean, your constable must live in a state of perpetual trouble, labour, and disquiet that other folks may enjoy their rest. Can this be expected from *competent* persons at 3*s.* a day?

I know that soldiers and sailors have but a shilling, but I will not waste our time by showing you how fallacious such an analogy is. Depend upon it, your present rate will not answer, and you must by some means or other contrive to improve your scale.

     Yours, my dear Peel, most sincerely,

            J. W. C.

  Mr. Peel to Mr. Croker.

         Whitehall, October 10th, 1829.

MY DEAR CROKER,

 Thanks for your suggestions in regard to the Metropolitan Police.

 When I fixed the present rate of pay, I fixed it under an impression that it might be necessary to raise it, but I felt quite sure that it would be much easier to raise than to reduce the rate of pay. I cannot say that the short experience I have hitherto had has confirmed my first impression. I will not as yet speak decidedly on the point, but I am very far from being prepared to admit that the improvement of the situation of a common police constable by the giving him more money, would increase the efficiency of the establishment.

 I have above 2000 applications for the appointment at the present rate of pay (this no doubt is a very bad test, if it were the only one). Every man who has been dismissed or has resigned, has with scarcely an exception petitioned for reinstatement. I do not again rely much upon this.

 I must first consider what is the class of man I want; and secondly, will the rate of pay maintain the proper respectability of that class?

 No doubt three shillings a day will not give me all the virtues under heaven, but I do not want them. Angels would be far above my work. Looking at the duties I want to be performed, I am not at all sure whether (all considerations of expense being put out of the question) three or four shillings a day will not ensure their performance in a much better manner then ten or twelve would. I have refused to employ gentlemen—commissioned officers, for instance—as superintendents and inspectors, because I am certain they would be above their work. They would refuse to associate with other persons holding the same offices who were not of equal rank, and they would therefore degrade the latter in the eyes of the men.

 A sergeant of the Guards at 200*l.* a year is a better man

for my purpose than a captain of high military reputation if he would serve for nothing, or if I could give him a thousand a year without entailing a fresh charge. For somewhat similar reasons, a three shilling a day man is better than a five shilling a day man.

After all, however, the real question is—how will three shillings a day support a man? I speak as yet hesitatingly; but I have good reasons for thinking that one of my police constables, if a single man, can find out of his pay of a guinea a week: (1) lodgings, (2) medical attendance, (3) very comfortable subsistence at his mess, (4) clothing; and can, after finding these, save out of his pay ten shillings a week.

Now, I think the policy of enabling him to save more is questionable. However, the impressions under which I am at present writing are liable to be varied by further experience.

I must add to the number of the police for the present district. I must say that it has worked much better in the first fortnight than I could have expected.

Ever most faithfully yours,
ROBERT PEEL.

Before passing from the subject of the New Police, it will be desirable to quote another letter, which helps to reveal an important side of Mr. Croker's character, little known or little regarded by his assailants. Even after this interval of time, there is an interest in knowing that his kind-hearted application was successful.

MY DEAR PEEL,

I was some months ago moved by a *tale of woe* to get a man (of whom I knew, and indeed still know nothing, but the said tale and repetition thereof) some employment, which produces him about 10s. a week. On this he and his wife and children have starved for nearly a year, and he has now asked me to recommend him for one of the places in the New Police. I told him point blank I would *not*, but since I did so, my heart has relented; and I have persuaded myself that I ought to endeavour to relieve the kind of misery, which I myself think the greatest of all, namely, that of a man of some education, and of *once* good prospects, reduced to penury.

The man has no more claim on me than I have on you; and I took him in hand from the same motive that may induce you to do him some good if you have a vacancy—*mere charity*; for, as I said before, I know nothing of him but his distress, and his decent appearance and conduct while struggling with poverty. His name is Frederick W—— —he is six feet one or two inches high—about thirty years of age—was a bookseller and is now a pauper. If you can place him in your Police, he seems to me fit to be useful in such a station—but if you have any difficulty, *say so at once*, for he has no hope that I should apply.

Yours ever,
J. W. C.

Mr. Croker became engaged this year in a literary project of considerable importance, to which more particular reference will presently be made. But he was also entreated to join in the effort to establish a new paper, and this drew from him a long and exceedingly practical letter. It will be observed that he hints at the suggestion that one member of a Cabinet should undertake to "instruct" the press properly. His predictions as to the power of journalism, in Parliament and out of it, have been more than verified.

Mr. Croker to Mr. J. Planta.

August 21st, 1829.

It is not everybody that can write for the newspapers: the latter is an art, perhaps I should better say a *knack*, which one man has in a greater degree than another, as one man will beat another at picquet, who, *en revanche*, will beat him at whist. If, as some critics say, it is harder to write a good epigram than an epic, why should there not be different powers required for writing a paragraph and a pamphlet? Believe me, the fact is so: the talent may be as small a one as you choose to call it, but it is one *sui generis*. Mr. Bayley's "Butterfly" is a mere trifle, but Southey could no more have written it than Bayley could have written "Thalaba." A short, terse, epigrammatic style, both of thought and expression, is what produces most effect in a newspaper, where people do not expect didactic or dialectic essays, and where indeed they will not read them. The style which I have heard called *coup de marteau* (not the hammering style) is, I think, the best; but clever men in this walk, as in others, have their own peculiar gait. When you have got a clever man, he will let you see his peculiar manner; but pray do not think that every writer can be a paragraph writer.

I now come to the great difficulty of all. I suppose you to have a good paper open to you, and a capital hand to work; how is he to be supplied with materials? He cannot make bricks without straw. How is he to know the line to be taken? You yourself will often not know. For instance, if *I*, an old, and as some of the gentlemen of the press used to think, a good hand, pretty high in office, not inattentive to the state of Europe, had been obliged to answer the article in the Morning Journal which you sent me, I should not have known what to say. As to England and France, I could perhaps have spoken pretty safely, but I have, upon my honour, not the most distant guess of what turn it might suit the position of our affairs to give to the observations on Spain, Portugal, Russia, Turkey, or Prussia. No one but a member of the Cabinet could do this safely and completely—not that if a Cabinet Minister were to hold the pen, he need tell State secrets, but he alone would thoroughly understand the case, and know what to avoid, what to hint, what to deny, when to leave folks in their errors, and when to open the real views of the Government. I have heretofore conveyed to the public articles written by Prime and Cabinet Ministers, and sometimes have composed such articles under their eye— they supplied the *fact*, and I supplied the *tact*, and between us we used to produce a considerable effect. In a Cabinet like ours, surely there might be one person who could find leisure for this sort of supervision, if not for some more direct co-operation. If anything of this kind were practicable, it ought to be done in the most profound secrecy, and every possible precaution against even a *suspicion*, should be taken, and the Minister who should undertake it, and you his *conveyancer*, as Junius calls it, should throw in here and there, such a slight mixture of error or apparent ignorance, as should obviate suspicion of its coming from so high a source.

But I fear it is impossible to hope that a Cabinet Minister could be permitted, or found willing to undertake this delicate task, though, *soit dit en passant*, the times are gone by when statesmen might safely despise the journals, or only treat them as inferior engines, which might be left to themselves, or be committed to the guidance of persons wholly unacquainted with the views of the Ministry. There is a prodigious change now in progress all throughout Europe in this particular; the French Journals are edited by Peers, Privy Councillors, and Deputies, and see the result—they are undoubtedly at this moment the best written and the most effective body of political literature that ever existed. Our papers are now very poorly done, by needy adventurers; yet in what a style they are written, and what effect do they produce? The example of France will soon be contagious, and we shall see men of high hopes and attainments conducting journals, and obtaining, at last, through their literary character, seats in the House of Commons. Depend upon it, all this is coming; and the day is not far distant when you will (not *see*, nor *hear*), but *know* that there is some one in the Cabinet entrusted with what will be thought one of the most important duties of the State, the regulation of public opinion.

When I used to write, as I did with some effect, for a few seasons, I lived altogether with my political friends; I knew what was doing, and what ought to be said—they helped me and some persons, by contagion, became writers, ay, and admirable ones too, who never expected to see a line of their penning in print. I had disciples who, like the pupil of Pietro Perugino, eclipsed their master. The success of that period, of which I was an humble though an active agent, was so complete that it turned the press—I mean the preponderating force of the press—right round; the Government had the voice of the Journals, and the Opposition (what had, I believe, never before happened in the history of English parties)—the Opposition complained loudly of the *licentiousness* of the press; which only meant that they were no longer able to wield it exclusively to their own purposes.

You may ask me why *I* cannot take up my old pen again? I answer, first because it *is* an old one, and that the hand that used to guide it is grown old too; and that the mind that used to prompt it is grown not only old, but indolent—not to say dispirited.

> "Solve senescentem mature sanus equum, ne
> Peccet ad extremum ridendus, et ilia ducat"—

that is the honest truth.

The project in which Mr. Croker actually embarked was that of producing a new edition of Boswell's 'Johnson,' first proposed in a conversation with Mr. Murray on the 8th of January, 1829. The idea was taken up and acted upon with business-like despatch. On the 9th, Mr. Croker unfolded his plans a little more in detail than he had been able to do by word of mouth, and when Mr. Murray received his letter, late at night, he sat down to answer it at "a quarter to twelve." He offered one thousand guineas for the work. In less than five days, Mr. Croker had gone into his task with his usual energy and heartiness, writing letters to all his friends who were likely to be of any service to him, and laying out all his plans on the most careful and comprehensive scale. The objects which he wished to accomplish are best set forth in his own words.

Mr. Croker to Mr. Murray.

January 9th, 1829.

DEAR MURRAY,

You received so warmly my hint about a new edition of Boswell's 'Life of Johnson' that I have given the subject a little more consideration.

Since Boswell's death, Mr. Malone has superintended two or three editions, and Mr. Chalmers one; but I must say that Malone has done little and Chalmers next to nothing. I made in one volume of Boswell's own edition near eighty queries on so many passages which seemed to me to require elucidation. On looking at those passages in Malone's and Chalmers' last edition, I found but one in which even an attempt at explanation was made. Anecdotes which we now know (*aliunde*) to relate to Burke, Sheridan or Langton, are left in the vague of "an eminent orator"—"a young gentleman," or "a respectable friend;" and I think I may say that hardly a note has been added to throw any light on the manners of the time, the state of society, or the character of persons; and, as Dr. Johnson himself said of the *Spectator*, a thousand things which everybody knew at the time, have, in the lapse of forty years, become so obscure as to require annotation. It is to be regretted that Mr. Malone did not apply himself to this line of explanation—*he* could have done, with little trouble, what will cost a great deal to any man now living. I know not whether there is any man who could now hope to do it well; but I am also satisfied that I should, *at this day*, do it better than any man, however clever or well informed, will be able to do it twenty years hence.

But there is another improvement of which I think a new edition susceptible. Boswell published after Sir J. Hawkins and Mrs. Piozzi, and was in enmity with both. He, therefore, was shy of them, and unwilling to borrow their information; and as Boswell's materials were chiefly furnished by his own annual visits, of a few weeks each, to London, his work naturally omits a great many curious and entertaining circumstances which occurred in the intervals of his visits, and it gives therefore an imperfect and desultory view of Johnson's social life and conversations; this might be remedied by introducing into their proper places, or under their proper dates, such extracts from Hawkins or Piozzi as may be worth preserving—they should form part of the text, with, however, a distinguishing mark. The anecdotical and journal-like form of Boswell's book renders such interpolations comparatively easy, and not in any degree injurious to the general style. I should not absolutely exclude all anecdotes from *other* sources; but I should admit any such with great caution. Boswell had examined Hawkins's and Piozzi's publications not merely with critical but with *hostile* accuracy, and we may be satisfied that whatever he did not contradict he believed to be correct, and I would admit no anecdote which should not be authenticated in a similar manner by the evidence or acquiescence of Johnson's personal friends and admirers.

Such is my general view of the way the new edition should be formed. I will add a word or two on the material or mechanical part. The last edition is in 4 vols. 8vo., of about

450 pages each—the additions and annotations I compute might extend to about 200 or 300 pages—it would be for you to decide whether you would add a fifth volume, or increase each of the four volumes by about 50 pages each.

As to *time*, I think I could engage to deliver the first volume by the 1st of March, and one volume every five or six weeks after, which is, I suppose, as fast as the printers could work, and would enable you to publish by the middle of June.

If, however, there be any of your literary friends whose greater leisure or better information would enable him to do the work earlier or more satisfactorily, you are quite at liberty to make use of my hints, and employ him to carry them into effect. I shall be glad to see the thing done, but I have no great desire to be the *doer*. So you are quite at liberty on that point.

Yours, dear Murray, very truly,

J. W. C.

Mr. Murray to Mr. Croker.

Albemarle Street, January 9th, 1829.
Friday Night, 11.45.

DEAR SIR,

Since writing to you in the afternoon, I have had time to read and to consider your obliging communication, respecting a new edition of Boswell's 'Life of Johnson,' with the attention which it deserves. I entirely agree with the admirable view which you take of this valuable work, and of the unsatisfactory way in which it has been edited, and I feel with you that if its omissions be left to a future age, it will be impossible to supply them. I assure you that I know of no person who could now supply what former editors have so carelessly neglected, so well as yourself. You must be aware that I have long known how much your attention and time have been engaged in the literary history of the period (amongst others) to which this work refers—an extraordinary production which grows more valuable as it recedes from the time in which it was first composed. I hope you will point out the value of this biography, and the necessity which there is for elucidating it now; the readers of the present day require this information, and it will be very useful to me in offering the work to the public.

With regard to the business part, I should prefer publishing (at least at first) the original work, with the insertions and notes as proposed by you ; and for these additions, notes, and editorship, I shall be happy to give, as something in the way of remuneration, the sum of one thousand guineas.

JOHN MURRAY.

Mr. Croker to Mr. Murray.

January 10th.

DEAR MURRAY,

In reply to your letter of last night, which I received this morning, allow me to say that your pecuniary terms are offered in the same spirit of liberality (I had almost said of prodigality) which has marked all your transactions of that nature which have come to my knowledge. I, in return, am bound to do all I can to make my work not unworthy of such liberality.

From the first moment Mr. Croker applied himself with tireless diligence to his new and interesting labours; and, as all the world now admits, he brought together a store of facts and elucidations which added much to the interest of Boswell's pages, and which, but for him, would never have been accessible to the public. A part of the treasure he had originally stored up was unfortunately lost by an accident in the course of transmission through the post. Lord Stowell, one of the few surviving contemporaries of Dr. Johnson, had permitted Mr. Croker to take down from his dictation a series of notes and recollections relating to his friend, and had also undertaken to answer any questions that might be referred to him. These notes were posted to Sir Walter Scott. The mail containing them was robbed, and they were never heard of again. The most searching inquiries failed to bring to light the least trace of the missing packet, and Lord Stowell had declined too much in health to be approached again on the subject. This loss was always deeply regretted by Mr. Croker. As he said in his preface to the book, no man alive had received and despatched more letters than he had done, and none had ever miscarried. But a vast mass of material still remained, for Mr. Croker left no stone unturned to find it. The descendants or connections of friends of Dr. Johnson, such as Bennet Langton, Sir Joshua Reynolds, and Dr. Strahan came forward with contributions; and Sir Walter Scott, Isaac Disraeli, Sir Henry Ellis, Lord Spencer, Lord Eldon, and many others offered their help. Sir Walter Scott's notes, especially to the 'Tour in the Hebrides,' were most valuable.

Sir Walter Scott to Mr. Croker.[*]

January 30th, 1820.

MY DEAR CROKER,

Your continued friendship and assistance on many occasions in life entitle you not to solicit, but to command, anything in my power to aid your wishes; and I am happy to express my readiness to do all in my power, regretting only that it is so much limited. I heard from Lockhart, who was down here for a week, of your intentions, and rejoice to learn from yourself that you are seriously set about adding to the charms of the most entertaining book in the world. I doubt my acquaintance with the most part of the book is too slight to furnish annotations. I was, when it was published, a raw young fellow, engrossing with the one hand and thumbing the Institutes and Pandects of old Justinian with the other; little in the way of hearing any literary conversation or anecdotes. My little knowledge of London folks began long after Johnson had gone to swill tea and speak sentences in the Elysian shades. Among those who remember him in full career, it might be worth while for you to speak to Northcote, the artist who enlivened the weary operation of sitting to him last spring by telling many anecdotes of Johnson, Goldsmith, Sir Joshua, and the original set. I may have made some remarks on the book, but I rather doubt it. It is now at Abbotsford, but I will soon get in the volumes and look over them with great satisfaction to take the chance of finding

---

[*] [This interesting letter is not in Lockhart's 'Life of Scott,' but many of the facts and anecdotes contained in it were used by Mr. Croker in his edition of Boswell's 'Johnson.']

anything useful. It occurred to Lockhart and me that your task would require you to reprint Boswell's 'Tour in the Hebrides,' for which I could find some curious illustrations. Meantime, that I may not send an empty letter, I jot one or two things down as they occur to me.

Miss Seward knew Johnson well, and mimicked him with great effect. There was a story she told me with great power, but I fear it will lose its zest by my decay of memory. It respected the Sage's marriage with the widow Porter, the mother of Miss Porter, to whom he was supposed to have paid his addresses in the first place. His own mother heard the news with utter astonishment, and exclaimed against the imprudence of the match. But Johnson chose to interpret all her surprise into wonder that Mrs. Porter had listened to his addresses, not astonishment that he should have paid them. Without allowing her to explain herself, he proceeded to assure her that he had been quite candid with the lady, and had pointed out to her all the disadvantages attaching to him. "I told her," he said, "that I was as poor as a rat, and destitute of any settled profession; that I was afflicted with a disease which had left its stamp on my countenance; that I was blind and ugly, and moroever of a family which was dishonoured by the execution of a near relative. She replied most candidly that all these drawbacks made no difference in her choice; that she was not much richer than myself, and she was religiously resolved to trust to heaven's blessing and my talents for a sufficient income; that if I was unsightly, she was no longer young, and it was not for my good looks that she gave me a preference. Finally, that, although she had not had an uncle who had been hanged, yet she enjoyed the relationship of more than one near relative who richly deserved it." Poor Mrs. Johnson, astonished to hear the match represented as much more [less?] unfavourable to her son than the widow Porter, was fain to abandon her maternal remonstrance. By-the-bye, the fate of this unhappy uncle, who seems to have been

> "The man to thieves and bruisers dear,
> Who kept the ring in Smithfield half a year,"

is said to have taken place at Dumfries circuit in Scotland. Old Dr. McNicol touches on the circumstance in his remarks on Johnson's 'Tour in the Hebrides.' He observes that the Doctor has said a tree is as great a rarity in Scotland as a horse in Venice. "I know nothing about this," says the Highland commentator, "as I do not know the numbers of the Venetian cavalry. But I am much mistaken if a near relative of the Doctor's at no remote date had not some reason given to believe that a tree was not quite so great a rarity." This story, if true, adds some faith to the report that Johnson's grandfather (like the grandfather of Rare Ben) was actually an Annandale Johnstone who altered the spelling of his name, euphoniæ gratiâ, or to Anglicize it. Do not you, however, go to establish this tradition if you are afraid of ghosts, for spirits can be roused; old Samuel will break his cerements at the idea of being proved a Scotchman.

Old Lord Auchinleck was an able lawyer, a good scholar, after the manner of Scotland, and highly valued his own advantages as a man of good estate and ancient family, and moreover, he was a strict Presbyterian and Whig of the old Scottish cast, videlicet a friend to the Revolution and the Protestant line. This did not prevent his being a terribly proud aristocrat, and great was the contempt he entertained and expressed for his son James for the nature of his friendships, and the character of the personages of whom he was *engoué* one after another. "There's nae hope for Jamie, man," he said to a friend; "Jamie is gaen clean gyte. What do you think, man? He's done wi' Paoli; he's off wi' the land-louping scoundrel of a Corsican; and whase tail do you think he has pinned himself to now, man?"—here the old judge summoned up a sneer of most sovereign contempt—"a *dominie*, man—an auld dominie. He keepit a schule, and caa'd it an acaadamy!" Probably if this had been reported to Johnson he would have felt it more galling, for he never much liked to think of that period of life when he was one of the educating individuals, as Sir John Sinclair calls them. Besides, he must have been fretted by Lord Auchinleck's Whiggery and Presbyterianism. These he carried to such an unusual height that once, when a countryman came in to state some justice business, and being required to make his oath, declined to do so before his Lordship because he was not a *covenanted* magistrate. "Is that a' your objection, man?" said the judge. "Come your ways in here, and we'll baith of us tak' the solemn league and covenant together." The oath was accordingly signed and sworn to by both, and I dare say it was the last time it ever received such homage. You may guess how far Lord Auchinleck, such as I describe him, was likely to suit a high Tory and Episcopalian like Johnson. I have heard that Bozzy, when he brought Johnson to Auchinleck, conjured him by all the ties of regard, and in requital of the services he had rendered him upon his tour, that he would spare two subjects in tenderness to his father's prejudices. The first related to Sir John Pringle, President of the Royal Society, about whom there was some dispute then current; the second concerned the general question of Whig and Tory. Samuel was not in the house an hour before both the deprecated topics had been touched upon. I have forgot what passed about Sir John Pringle, but the controversy between Tory and Covenanter raged with great fury and ended in Johnson pressing upon the old judge the question, What good Cromwell, of whom he had said something mitigatory, had ever done to his country, when, after being much tortured, Lord Auchinleck at last spoke out: "Why, Doctor! he gar'd kings ken that they had a *lith* in their neck." He taught kings they had a *joint* in their neck. Jamie then set to *staving* and *tailing* between his father and the philosopher, and availing himself of his father's sense of hospitality, which was punctilious, reduced the debate to more order.

At Glasgow Johnson had a meeting with Smith (Adam Smith), which terminated strangely. John Millar used to report that Smith, obviously much discomposed, came into a party who were playing at cards. The Doctor's appearance suspended the amusement, for as all knew he was to meet Johnson that evening, every one was curious to hear what had passed. Adam Smith, whose temper seemed much ruffled, answered only at first, "He is a brute! he is a brute!" Upon closer examination it appeared that Dr. Johnson no sooner saw Smith than he brought forward a charge against him for something in his famous letter on the death of Hume. Smith said he had vindicated the truth of the statement. "And what did the Doctor say?" was the universal query: "Why, he said—he said—" said Smith, with the deepest impression of resentment, " he said—' *You lie!*'" "And what did you reply?" "I said,'You are a son of a b——h!'" On such terms did these two great moralists meet and part, and such was the classic dialogue betwixt them.

Johnson's rudeness possibly arose from his retaining till late in life the habits of a pedagogue, who is a man among boys and a boy among men, and having the bad taste to think it more striking to leap over the little differences and courtesies which form the turnpike gates in society, and which fly open on payment of a trifling tribute. The *auld Dominie* hung vilely about him, and was visible whenever he was the coaxed man of the company—a sad symptom of a *parvenu*. A lady who was still handsome in the decline of years, and must have been exquisitely beautiful when she was eighteen, dined in company with Johnson, and was placed beside him at table with no little awe of her neighbour. He then always drank lemonade, and the lady of the house desired Miss S——h to acquaint him there was some on the sideboard. He made no answer except an indistinct growl. "Speak louder, Miss S——h, the Doctor is deaf." Another attempt, with as little success. "You do not speak loud enough yet, my dear Miss S——h." The lady then ventured to raise her voice as high as misses of eighteen may venture in the company of old doctors, and her description of the reply was that she heard an internal grumbling like Etna before explosion, which rolled up his mouth, and there formed itself into the distinct words, "When I want any, I'll ask for it," which were the only words she heard him speak during the day. Even the sirup food of flattery was rudely repelled if not cooked to his mind. I was told that a gentleman called Pot, or some such name, was introduced to him as a particular admirer of his. The Doctor growled and took no further notice. "He admires in especial your 'Irene' as the finest tragedy of modern times," to which the Doctor replied, "If Pot says so, Pot lies!" and relapsed into his reverie.

I do not think there is anything to be had at Auchinleck. The late Sir Alexander was a proud man, and, like his grandfather, thought that his father lowered himself by his deferential suit and service to Johnson. I have observed he disliked any allusion to the book or to Johnson himself, and I have heard that Johnson's fine picture by Sir Joshua was sent up-stairs out of the sitting apartments at Auchinleck. In these circumstances, he was not likely to write notes on the volume. Sir Alexander differed from his father in many particulars; he was a very high-spirited man, whereas in James's veins the blood of Bruce flowed faintly and sluggishly, though he boasted so much of it. Indeed, with the usual ill hap of those who deal in *mauvaise plaisanterie*, old Bozzy was often in the unpleasant situation of retreating from expressions which could not be defended. He was always labouring at notoriety, and, having failed in attracting it in his own person, he hooked his little bark to them whom he thought most likely to leave harbour, and so shine with reflected light, like the rat that eat the malt that lay in the house that Jack built. Our friend poor James was in some of his gestures and grimaces very like his father, though a less man. There was less likeness betwixt the elder brother and the father. Neither of them could remember much of their father's intimacy with Johnson, if anything at all. I will make enquiry, however, if you wish it, of some of the present young man's guardians: he is not I believe quite of age, though I am not sure.

Before leaving the biographer, I may mention two traits of his character; that he was very fond of attending on capital punishments, and that he used to visit the prisoners on the day before execution with the singular wish to make the condemned wretches laugh by dint of buffoonery, in which he not unfrequently succeeded. This was like the task imposed on Byron to "jest a twelvemonth in an hospital." In fact, there was a variation of spirits about James Boswell which indicated some slight touch of insanity. His melancholy, which he so often complained of to Johnson, was not affected, but constitutional, though doubtless he thought it a mark of high distinction to be afflicted with hypochondria like his moral patron. But Johnson, however indulgent to his own sinkings of the spirits, had little tolerance for those of his imitator. After all, Bozzy, though submitting to Johnson in everything, had his means of indemnification. Like the jackanapes mounted on the bear's back, he contrived now and then to play the more powerful animal a trick by getting him into situations, like the meeting with Wilkes, merely to see how he would look. The voyage to the Hebrides exhibited some tricks of that kind, the weather being so stormy at that late season that every one thought they must have been drowned. Undoubtedly Bozzy wanted to see how the Doctor would look in a storm. When wind-bound at Dunvegan, his temper became most execrable, and beyond all endurance save that of his guide. The Highlanders, who are very courteous in their way, held him in great contempt for his want of breeding, but had an idea at the same time there was something respectable about him, they could not tell what, and long spoke of him as the Sassenach *mohr* or large

Saxon. You will see by this time what my powers afford, nothing better I fear than trifles and empty bottles, but they shall be turned upside down whenever you will.

I cannot but think the plan of your book admirable, and your additions, corrections, and improvements likely to give new zest to that which is in itself so entertaining. You have only to tell me that the sort of trash which I have given you a specimen of can be made useful, and you shall have all that my memory can supply upon reading over the book, and especially the 'Voyage to the Hebrides.' By-the-bye, I am far from being of the number of those angry Scotsmen who imputed to Johnson's national prejudices all or a great part of the report he has given of our country in that publication. I remember the Highlands ten or twelve years later, and no one can conceive of how much that could have been easily remedied travellers had to complain. The love of planting which has become almost a passion—I wish the love of taking care of plantations bore any proportion to it—is much to be ascribed to Johnson's sarcasms.

Are you aware that the cleverest parody of the Doctor's style of criticism is by John Young, of Glasgow, and is very capital? I think it is mentioned in Boswell's life, but you should see it. I will lend it to you if you have it not.

A propos of Johnson and Reynolds, the last observed the charge given him by Johnson on his deathbed, not to use his pencil of a Sunday, for a considerable time, but afterwards broke it, being persuaded by some person who was impatient for a sitting that the Doctor had no title to exact such a promise. And once again à *propos;* ornamental illustrations are now so much the taste that I think, considering that all the principal personages in your work have been immortalised by Sir Joshua, you ought to give engravings from their portraits, which cannot but add a certain valuable interest to the volume. Mr. Watson Taylor had, if he has not the portraits which belonged to Mr. Thrale.

I will now, in nautical phrase, *haul taut and belay.* If you wish me to go on, I will endeavour to send you what I can recall to my recollection. Do not mutiny against my handwriting; I have chilblains on my fingers in this bitter weather which prevent me from writing, and my eyes are failing me most vilely.

Ever yours truly,

WALTER SCOTT.

Sir Walter Scott to Mr. Croker.

March 14th, 1829.

MY DEAR CROKER,

I answer your letter immediately because of that passage in which you bid me send back Lord Stowell's anecdotes. Now, my dear sir, I have never received any such, nor have I the least idea of the *intrepid lawyer* the which your query refers to. I have only received from you to my knowledge two letters about Johnson, the last dated 10th of March, 1829. As I left town on the 11th of March, another parcel may have since that period reached my lodgings there, in which case I shall get it safe.

Did you ever hear of Lord Elibank's reply when Johnson's famous definition of *oats* was pointed out first to him? "The food of men in Scotland and horses in England," repeated Lord Elibank; "very true, and where will you find such *men* and such *horses*?" The retort, I think, was fair enough.

I wish we may have no trouble here. One hot-headed person might do infinite mischief at this moment, but my comfort is there is no Lord George Gordon to be feared. The good sense of the upper classes has kept those of the lower quiet, but I wish it were all well over.

Yours very truly,
WALTER SCOTT.

Sir Walter Scott to Mr. Croker. Extract.

March 21st, 1829.

MY DEAR CROKER,

I am sincerely vexed about the packet, which never reached me. I waited a day after receiving yours to see if Anne, who was in town *gallivanting* it at some Caledonian ball, might bring intelligence of it; but she came yesterday, and brought none. I have written to the Secretary of the Office to make every inquiry possible. I have seldom lost a letter, though my name is a common one here. Sometimes the letters of Sir William Scott, of Ancrum, have been sent to me. If he had received mine he would have returned it instantly, as he would immediately see for whom it was intended, and that it brought no *Carlisle* news. I will make inquiry however.

The first edition of the 'Tour to the Hebrides' contains a sarcastic account of the mode in which they were received in Skye by Lord MacDonald. Peter Pindar alludes to the retrenchments:—

> "Who from McDonald's rage to save his snout,
> Cut twenty lines of defamation out.
> * * * *
> Let Lord McDonald threat thy back to kick,
> And o'er thy shrinking shoulders shake his stick."

We shall be all good boys here. I think the great majority of everything like sense, or talent, or even property is on the side of the Ministry, and though the roar may for a season be with the ultra-Protestants, it will be *vox et præterea*.

Always yours truly,
WALTER SCOTT.

I did not wonder at not hearing from you, knowing how busy the bustling time must have kept you all. In my own case I should have suspected a mis-address of the unlucky packet, but your habits of business are too correct for that; and, besides, unless it has sailed to "ape and monkey climes," it would have surely returned to you by this time.

Sir Walter Scott to Mr. Croker.

MY DEAR SIR,

I am afraid of not being able to solve your problem about Miss Dempster, being too little acquainted with the family. Dempster had a half brother, a captain in the Company's service, who wrote an uncommonly severe epigram on George's bad success in love and politics. Possibly Mrs. Dempster, of Skibo, Miss Dundas that was, could tell you something about it.

I am dying here like a poisoned rat, as the old Dean says, to see you all going to the devil so quickly. It is only necessary to give the Duke a good income tax and the country is clear, but a bank-note seems to terrify everybody out of their wits, and they will rather give up their constitution to Hunt and Cobbett than part with an Abraham Newlands to preserve it.

I cannot help saying, like a Scottish worthy in difficulty, "Woe worth thee, is there no help in thee?"

      Believe me, always yours,
         WALTER SCOTT.

The thorough and painstaking spirit which Mr. Croker applied to every detail of his work, and the unsparing industry which he devoted to it, may be partially, and only partially, understood by a glance at a few examples of the letters with which he sought assistance from all quarters.

Mr. Croker to the Rev Dr. Hall, Master of Pembroke.

         March 27th, 1829.

The Swinfens are a very old Staffordshire family, which still flourishes at Swinfen. Every kind of biographical information on any name that occurs will be of use to me. For any use that I shall have to make of the Prayers and Meditations the printed copy will suffice, and I need not trouble you with collating or copying. Your assistance is too precious to be thrown away on drudgery.

Whenever you have occasion to copy or note a classical quotation or allusion I would beg of you (when you happen to have them present to your memory) to mention the author, and the place where they are to be found. My library is so large that I have been obliged to distribute it in three different houses, and I have not always at hand the volume in which I should look for the passage. I ought to correct the foregoing by saying, not that my *library* is *so large*, but that, unfortunately, I have not in any of my residences space enough for my books, and so am obliged to divide them, which is very inconvenient.

To Mr. Alexander Chalmers.*

         August 20th.

All preceding editors, as well as Mr. Boswell himself, have, from obvious motives, gone on the plan of leaving many hints, allusions, and obscurities unexplained—perhaps I should

---

* [Editor of an edition of 'Boswell,' and of Chalmers' 'Biographical Dictionary.']

speak more correctly if I said that you had all left unexplained points which, by the lapse of time, are now growing obscure, but which, when your editions were published, appeared too obvious to require explanation. I am aware that this was inevitable, and that, take what pains I may, my own edition will, in thirty years, need another annotator. Nobody thinks of telling what everybody knows; and yet how soon does it happen that no one remembers what all the world knew a few years before? How many people are there in London who do not know where Rosamond's pond lay? Who knows what the game of the Mall was? The Northern roads are still measured from an imaginary standard of *St. Giles's Pound*, of which no trace is to be found in the memory of the inhabitants of the parish.

To Sir Walter Scott.

August 28th.

Dear Scott,

Can you give any reason why all the world seem to have maintained so absolute a silence on the subject of Boswell's Lady? All that is told of her is that she was *Margaret Montgomerie*. I have discovered by accident that she was "*Miss Peggy Montgomerie, of Lainshawe*"; and I think I recollect to have read that the Montgomeries of Lainshawe claimed a Scotch peerage—the name I forget—somewhat like Lisle.* Can you give me any account of her?

I cannot but think that Boswell's *original Diary* must be in existence somewhere. It clearly was not what was printed from. I suspect (indeed Boswell says so somewhere) that there are masses of manuscripts at Auchinleck. Who are the young Laird's guardians? or, how could we have inquiry made? It would be a pity that for want of taking a little trouble such a prize as the original journal would be, should escape me.

If you could direct me what line to pursue, I would use all diligence and apply in all quarters.

Yours most sincerely,

J. W. C.

* [*Vide* Croker's edition of 'Boswell,' p. 224. It was the peerage of Lyle.]

To Sir James Mackintosh.
October 15th.

Do you think that I have treated the question of *party* properly? If you and I can agree on such a point, we probably are right, as I had the misfortune for so long to be politically opposed to you; and it is one of my great regrets at the strange events of late years that the happy union which was at last accomplished, did not, so far as you were concerned, continue. I had for a long time, as you know, thought we might have been together, nor do I yet see why we should be separate.

To Thomas Moore.
November 24th.

MY DEAR MOORE,

Can you give me any account of *O'Kane*, the Irish Harper? He is mentioned in Boswell, and I should like to have a short note on him from *you*, in preference to one of my own.

To Isaac D'Israeli.
April 25th.

MY DEAR SIR,

Though not troublesome to you, I am not idle; but the printer has adopted a new plan, which has disabled me from sending you *proofs*. In a day or two I shall trouble you with two or three *revises*.

Where could I get a sight of Johnson's original *plan of his Dictionary*?

Can you tell me when, and to whom, George the 3rd talked of the *Giants of Literature*—see Boswell, sub anno 1750.

What can have become of Boswell's *original* Diary? It would be invaluable, and cannot, I think, have been destroyed.

Yours, my dear Sir, most sincerely,
J. W. C.

Mr. Isaac Disraeli—or D'Israeli, to adopt his own orthography, followed by his son for many years of his life—read some of the proofs of the new edition, and appears frequently to have communicated with Mr. Croker while the sheets were in the printer's hands.

Mr. Isaac D'Israeli to Mr. Croker.

Bloomsbury-square, January 28th, 1829.

MY DEAR SIR,

It is with pleasure I recognise your handwriting. Your awaiting my making "a sign" implies on your part a degree of watchfulness which is very flattering. Your correspondence is too agreeable an incident for me ever wilfully to occasion its extinction—and in future I shall know how to awaken its dormant energies by answering my own letter.

I now for ever bid "a farewell sweet" to that phantom, the Conway papers! I, who live more in the age of Charles the First than in my own, considered them of more importance than your account makes them. In the course of my researches I have traced several extraordinary documents, which, if not destroyed, ought to be in those collections—such as Lord Conway's journal concerning the Duke of Buckingham—Sir Henry Wotton's Diary of his Venetian Embassy—besides many papers of secret history, which rightly should have been deposited at the State-paper Office. One of the Lords Conway was a very eager collector of the fugitive pieces of the time, many of which floated in manuscripts. There must also be a copious assemblage of letters. I once read by your kindness the letters of Katharine, the Duke of Buckingham's wife, which led me to form another idea of the *man*. What an odd fate have these Collections met with! They were made with great care, by very careless persons, since better means were not taken to preserve them. And now having in part escaped the fury of cooks, the critical nibblings of mice, and the mould of time, they have found, as it was presumed, an Editor, so skilful and spirited as yourself—a publisher so active as Mr. Murray, and a possessor so liberal as Lord Hertford—all to no purpose! With such unexpected good fortune the Conway papers will probably never be seen by the world, and, what is more important, never be consulted by the historian.

I congratulate you, my dear sir, on having struck out a literary labour which will prove to be a most variable recreation—the editing of Boswell. You there have touched a vein which will flow, and I am all alive. It was one of the earliest books which fed my taste for literature and literary men. On its publication it raised a great disturbance, of which I could afford you many ludicrous instances. It was an act of juvenile heroism on my part, to have declared that it would outlast the delightful 'Ménagiana'* (Monnoye's edition), but people know little of such *ana* in that day. So many were displeased at themselves in those volumes; so many secrets were published; so many of the malcontents found themselves unnoticed—that nothing but abuse and reading the book was heard. My old friend Caleb Whiteford, who lived above me in my chambers at the Adelphi, assured me the conversations were not correct, some of his puns had not been immortalized. Peter Pindar once called Boswell in a letter to me, "Johnson's spitting-pot;" and the critical reviewer of my "Dissertation on Anecdotes," who proved to be Dr. George Gregory, after due commendation of the young author, anathematised him for his eulogy on Boswell; the anathema, being rather voluminous, probably will exhibit the condensed protests of all the Oppositionists. I can afford you one striking evidence of the fidelity of Boswell's circumstantiality.

My edition is the second—the author's own—I possess none of the modern editions, though Malone and the author's son edited them. Malone's notes are always useful, but dry. As the work itself is a heap of notes, will you not find some difficulty in contriving space to add your new ones? You will sometimes perhaps have to add, what in the present day we call illustrations, notes like essays. I have no marginal notes to send you, but I imagine I could Boswellise with you through a long summer's day. Whenever you consult me, I shall rejoice to aid you; but at present I have contracted a debt of honour with the public which I must satisfy. It is in vain I attempt to quit my Charles I., since he will not quit me.

Believe me, with great regards,
My dear sir, much yours,
I. D'ISRAELI.

From Mr. Isaac D'Israeli.

Athenæum, Tuesday, July 6th, 1829.

MY DEAR SIR,

I seize a hurried moment to acknowledge the receipt of your two notes. Believe me that the courteousness and the

* ['Ménagiana, ou les Bons Mots, etc., de M. Ménage,' par M. de la Monnoye. 4 vols. 1729.]

kindness of one will never be obliterated from my mind, and will ever form one of my most gratifying reminiscences.

I must now tell you how my literary affairs are situated. Although two months have passed among the workmen at my new residence, I shall not be able to enter till about the middle of August; meanwhile I shall reside in a cottage at the foot of my house. About seventy cases of books are then to be arranged. Without a command of my library and my manuscripts, I am nothing; and I do not like to answer to [for] the accuracy of facts by trusting to confused and imperfect recollections.

If, however, you will have the goodness to continue your communications, I will always do my best; and the first book I shall try to get at shall be Boswell's 'Johnson.' But the truth is, that this must be a chance, as I cannot know in what case it is to be found.

Of Mrs. Masters, the poetess, I once before sent you a note.* Is it Boswell himself who tells us that Johnson strengthened her lines? I once saw the volume of her poems, which appeared to be the usual echo of Pope's, when Pope reigned alone.

I dare not venture to guess at "the Peer" distinguished "for abstruse science," not knowing where to look for it at this moment in 'Boswell.' Could it be Hardwicke or Lyttelton? It might suit Lord Monboddo; but a Lord of the Sessions is no Peer.

I suspect that my "future address" may be lying under your table, and had slipped out of my letter on opening it. I once more enclose my card, and write it out, to prevent the same accident.

Allow me again to repeat the assurance of my sincerest regard, and that you will believe me to be, with entire devotion,

My dear sir, ever faithfully yours,

I. D'ISRAELI.

A few other letters relating to the same subject may be given.

---

* [Mary Masters published, in 1758, a volume entitled 'Familiar Letters and Poems.' The following is Boswell's note concerning her:— "Mrs. Masters, the poetess whose volumes he revised, and it is said, illuminated here and there with a ray of his own genius."]

Rev. Thomas Harwood * to Mr. Croker.*

Lichfield, August 23rd, 1829.

DEAR SIR,

I had hoped to have been able to send you some further memorabilia relating to Dr. Johnson's family; but, unfortunately, Mrs. Pearson either cannot find the papers or has inadvertently destroyed them. They were the Books of Accompt which Michael J. kept in the process of his trade. I much regret that they have not been preserved. This lady has sent me the following letter, which I copy :—

" To Mr. Johnson, Bookseller in Lichfield.

" Gresley, January 19th, 1729.

" SIR,

" I am amaz'd you doe not send me ye Milton and History of ye Royal Society I so long since wrote for. I desire you will not fail to get them as soon as possible, and also to send wth them Sir William Temple's Works, finely bound. Pray take care to get all these as soon as it is possible to have them, and send them to me with a bill.

" I desired our neighbour, Mr. Malbon, to call upon you, and tell you I wou'd not have Puffendorfe, as I once thought, but then did not guess he had been so Bulky, or so deep a Gent, as I since find he is, and am resolv'd not to have him. Y^e rest, y^t I have wrote for above, I shall take it ill if you doe not help to me wth all speed.

" Yo^{rs},

" MALLEYNE."

The first letter of the name seems to signify also the initial of the Christian name—as M. Alleyne.

The family of Alleyne had at this time a seat at Gresley in Derbyshire, fifteen miles from Lichfield, near Burton-upon-Trent. In the church of that village is a mural monument with a long inscription to the memory of different branches of this family.

To your question respecting the letter of Davies to Mr. Bettesworth, in which he calls Johnson " Dr.," I can only explain it by a reference to the date of the letter, the last figure of which is scarcely legible—indeed, the figure after 176- may be read as " 3 " or " 5 " or " 9." But the date

* [Author of a ' History of Lichfield,' 1806.]

in the title page of Bennet's book, if you have it, would accurately mark the date of the letter. I have never seen the book. Davies first calls him "Doctor," and afterwards writes MDr.—Dr. written upon Mr.; from which it may be conjectured that the designation of Dr. was not in general use. The letter referring to an intended advertisement of the book will sufficiently mark the time at which it was written.

Mr. Matthias never resided in Lichfield, but was a merchant in London, and a friend of Captain Porter. He was the father of the supposed author of the 'Pursuits of Literature,' and nearly related to, but not the father of, the present rector of Whitechapel.

I am in possession of the identical china saucer which was always used by Mrs. Johnson, and which Johnson carefully preserved. After her death the roll at breakfast was placed upon it every day, which he usually divided with his humble friend Levett.

I have the honour to be, dear Sir, your faithful and obedient servant,

THOMAS HARWOOD.

Sir Henry Ellis to Mr. Croker.

British Museum, October 29th, 1829.

DEAR SIR,

I understand from Mr. Murray that you are engaged upon a 'Life of Dr. Johnson.'

Are you aware that the Donation MS. in our house, No. 5994, Art. 2, contains Johnson's original memoranda for his 'Life of Pope.'

Mr. Cary, the Assistant Keeper of our Printed Books, tells me a very old edition (I think 1504) of 'Horace,' belonging to the Burney Collection, has a few notes in Dr. Johnson's hand. The same collection also has the first folio Shakspeare which was Johnson's, but, I believe, without notes though Burney complains of Johnson's ill-usage of it.

Boswell the elder, you of course know, deposited with us Johnson's own copy of the famous letter to Lord Chesterfield, which would look well in facsimile. Address is spelt in it twice, at least, with one *d*.

In a letter among Cole's MSS. I once read an anecdote, which I cannot find now, but of which I gave a copy to Mr. Jerdan, the editor of the *Literary Gazette*, who may possibly furnish it. It gave an account of a very rude speech of Johnson's con-

cerning the Scotch. Jerdan thought it too savage to tell of
the great man in his work, and therefore kept it to himself.

I do not find that Dr. Johnson was ever much at the
Museum. In 1761, however, "Mr. Sam. Johnson" is entered
as admitted to use our reading-room for six months. Several
of his friends used to come at that time, such as Dr. Percy,
Sir John Hawkins, and Bennet Langton; and "Wedderburne
Esq., of Lincoln's Inn." David Hume and Gray must have
been his fellow-students, with Dr. Robertson of Edinburgh.

I am, dear Sir, faithfully yours,
HENRY ELLIS.

From the Marquis Wellesley.

Regent's Park, November 8th, 1829.

MY DEAR SIR,

Johnson's Latin poetry has received the just condemnation
of every classical scholar. I confess that I am not disposed
to exempt the verses of his later years from that censure;
perhaps, however, his 'Insula Kenneth' might be spared from
the rod. It is certainly more tolerable than any other of his
compositions in Latin verse. I concur in your opinion
respecting the different readings in the 'Ode from Skye';
some of them are unintelligible, others absolute nonsense. I
do not, however, wish to have my name quoted as a censurer
of Johnson's Latin poetry. I feel that I have no just pretensions to the weight which you are so kind as to ascribe to
my opinions on such subjects; and I have so great a general
reverence for Johnson that I should be sorry to appear among
those who have censured any part of his works.

Believe me always, dear Sir, yours most sincerely,
WELLESLEY.

From Lord Eldon.

DEAR CROKER,

There are mistakes in the enclosed as to the *locus in quo*,
&c. When, by the kindness of Sir R. Chambers, I lived in
the house belonging to him as Principal at New Inn Hall at
Oxford, and was his deputy reading his Vinerian lectures, he,
Dr. Johnson, Sir Joshua Reynolds, and, as well as I can
remember, one or two other persons came from London to
Oxford. Walking in the garden at New Inn Hall, Sir R.

Chambers threw some snails over his garden wall. "Sir," said Johnson, "what you are doing is very unmannerly to your neighbour." Sir Robert said, jocosely, "Why, Dr., he is not a Churchman," or "he is a Dissenter"—I cannot at this distance of time be quite positive as to the words. "Oh," says the Doctor, laughing, "why then, throw away as hard as you can." This is the most accurate account my memory enables me to give you as to what passed more than half a century ago.

Yours, my dear Sir, with respect and kind regards,

ELDON.

It was a work conceived and carried on in this spirit, through two long years of toil, its pages enriched by hundreds of contributions from men who had access to all possible sources of information—it was this work that Lord Macaulay found it consistent with his sense of truth and justice to pronounce "a worthless edition of Boswell's 'Life of Johnson,' *some sheets of which our readers have doubtless seen round parcels of better books."*

To any one who has read Mr. Croker's 'Boswell,' or who has even taken the trouble to look through the notes, this judgment will appear so unfair and so unreasonable that a suspicion must inevitably be engendered that it was not arrived at by the legitimate exercise of the critical faculty, but must have been prompted by some personal and unworthy motive. The existence of such a motive was well understood at the time the onslaughts were made, and more recently it has been laid bare to the world by the publication of Macaulay's own 'Memoirs and Letters.' The attack defeated itself by its very violence, and therefore it did the book no harm whatever. Between forty and fifty thousand copies have been sold, although Macaulay boasted with great glee that he had "smashed" it; for readers of his letters will have observed that his appreciation of his own work was at least as high as that which the public of his day entertained for it. One review had "smashed" a book which has had a steady sale ever since; another put an inoffensive writer in the "pillory," from which he had vainly "begged" to be let out.* In the present day, it is usually felt that even if a man is able to produce such dire effects as these by his writings, it ill becomes him to show too keen a consciousness of his tremendous power.

The edition of 'Boswell' was not published until 1831. For some months previously in the House of Commons, there had been several sharp encounters between Croker and Macaulay in the debates on Reform. The two men, as it has been pointed out,† were to some extent "pitted" against each other, and more than once Mr. Croker gained a marked and telling advantage over his antagonist. He had greater felicity in ready reply than Macaulay, and on more than one occasion he utterly demolished an elaborately prepared and showy, but unsubstantial, speech of the "brilliant essayist." Macaulay, as it clearly appears from his own letters, was irritated beyond measure by Croker; he grew to "detest" him. Then he began casting about for some means of revenge. This would seem incredible if he had not, almost in so many words, revealed the secret. In July, 1831, he thus wrote: "That impudent; leering Croker congratulated the House on the proof which I had given of my readiness. He was afraid, he said, that I had been silent so long on account of the many allusions which had been made to Calne. Now that I had risen again he hoped that they should hear me often. *See whether I do not dust that varlet's jacket for him in the next number of the Blue and Yellow.* I *detest him* more than cold boiled veal."‡ He had long been waiting for his opportunity to settle his private account with Mr. Croker.

In the previous month of March he was watching eagerly

---

* Trevelyan's 'Life of Macaulay,' ii. 276.
† 'Quarterly Review,' July, 1876, p. 108.
‡ Trevelyan's 'Macaulay,' i. p. 239.

for the publication of the 'Boswell.' "*I will certainly review Croker's 'Boswell' when it comes out,*" he wrote to Mr. Napier—and considering the position of the two men, this notice must be regarded as an imperative command.* He was on the look-out for the book, not with the object of doing justice to it, but of "dusting the jacket" of the author. But as his letters had not yet betrayed his malice to the world, he gravely began the dusting process by remarking, "This work has greatly disappointed us." What did he hope for, when he took it up, but precisely such a "disappointment"? "Croker," he wrote,† "looks across the House of Commons at me with a leer of hatred, which I repay with a gracious smile of pity." He had cultivated his animosity of Croker until it became a morbid passion. Yet it is conceivable that he did not intend posterity to see him in the picture drawn by his own hand, spending his time in the House of Commons straining his eyes to see if there was a "leer" on Croker's countenance, and returning it with gracious smiles of pity.

The threat of revenge was made in July, immediately after the book appeared. On the 7th September, Macaulay wrote to Napier as follows: "I send off the *first part* of my article. The next will follow early in next week." It is quite clear from this that the threat preceded the writing of the article; the demand for the book was made in March, the threat in July, and the essay was not published till September. The animus with which the article was written was at once obvious to all fair-minded men. "It will be evident," remarked one journal,‡ "that the book has been taken up by one determined to punish the member of Parliament in the editor, and who . . . is determined to sacrifice truth to brilliancy"—an accusation repeated, and proved, many times

---

* 'Napier's Correspondence,' p. 110.
† 'Trevelyan's 'Macaulay,' p. 248.   ‡ The 'Spectator,' Sept. 1831.

since then. "Everybody is aware," remarked the chief literary newspaper of England,* "that the article was originally levelled less against Mr. Croker the editor than Mr. Croker the politician, and the abuse which may have been relished in times of hot passion and party vindictiveness, reads in our calmer days as so much bad taste and bad feeling." The American public were never for a moment deceived by Macaulay's vituperation. The book was held in esteem, and had a large sale, in the United States, and American writers have always done it justice. "Mr. Croker," says one, whose industry and ability are equally remarkable,† "deserves great credit for his excellent edition of 'Boswell.' We venture this assertion, notwithstanding the unaccountable attempt of Mr. Macaulay to depreciate the value of Mr. Croker's editorial labours." The "attempt," it has been shown, is not so "unaccountable" now as it was when these words were written. Macaulay has laid bare his entire process of wreaking vengeance—first, the peremptory notice to the editor, whom he practically ruled, that he intended to review the book; then the threat to dust the author's jacket, for the gratification of private malice; lastly, the article itself, laden with unsupported charges and gross mis-statements. If some obscure and wretched hack had been guilty of this conduct, slight indeed would have been the mercy shown to him in any quarter.

Public opinion has long ago redressed the wrong which was done. When a writer, however eminent, is proved to have committed an injustice for the express purpose of producing a "slashing article," or of satisfying a personal resentment, it sometimes happens that it is *he* who is seen standing in the "pillory"—not his intended victim.

* The 'Athenæum,' May 17th, 1856.
† Alibone's 'Dictionary of Authors,' i. p. 222.

CHAPTER XV.

1830.

The New Agitation for Parliamentary Reform—Popular Excitement—Declaration of the Duke of Wellington—Penryn and East Retford—Mr. Croker's Advice to Peel—Illness of the King—Disturbed State of Politics—The Duke of Wellington and the Whigs—Theatricals at Hatfield House—Death of George IV.—The New King—"Black Sheep"—Lord Brougham and the Opposition—The General Election—Defeat of Mr. Croker for Dublin University—Revolution in France—Abdication of Charles X.—Death of Mr. Huskisson—Talleyrand in London—Dissensions in the Tory Party—Sir H. Parnell's Attack—Defeat of the Ministry—Mr. Croker resigns his Office at the Admiralty—Lord Grey's Ministry—Lord Brougham and Lord Lyndhurst—Difficulties of the New Ministry—Mr. Croker on Party Consistency—Death of Sir Thomas Lawrence—His Pecuniary Troubles—Letters to Mr. Croker.

ONE dangerous cause of agitation was at last disposed of, but another, destined to produce even greater anxiety and confusion in politics, was rapidly taking a foremost place in the public mind. Catholic Emancipation was no sooner settled than the far greater question of Parliamentary Reform was revived. In some form or other, this question had been discussed over and over again for upwards of sixty years, and the necessity of some changes in the system of popular representation in Parliament had been frequently admitted since Lord Chatham made his well-known declaration that either Parliament would "reform itself from within, or be reformed with a vengeance from without." But the responsibility of dealing with so complex a problem was evaded by Whigs and Tories alike, and on the outbreak of the great wars there was business to be disposed of more pressing in its nature than the extension and readjustment of the franchise. It was not until 1829 that the dissatisfaction of various large communities on account of their exclusion from the suffrage became too earnest and too profound to be suppressed; riots were of frequent occurrence, political unions were formed, "mass meetings" were held; and once more an agitation was set on foot which the Ministers of the day were unable to resist. Yet the Duke of Wellington, unconscious of the real strength of the movement, or of his own weakness when opposed to it, declared in the House of Lords that not only was he not prepared to bring forward any measure of reform, but that he should "always feel it his duty to resist such measures when proposed by others." After this announcement, the return of the Whigs to power, at the end of a long and weary banishment, could not be delayed more than a few weeks, and as a matter of fact the Duke's Government fell to pieces, though not directly on the Reform issue, in less than a fortnight after he had run up the flag of "no surrender."

Reference has already been made to the disfranchisement of Penryn and East Retford on the ground of notorious bribery. It has been shown that Mr. Croker was always of opinion that it would only be just to bestow the seats thus rendered vacant upon constituencies of great and growing importance, and he believed that if this measure had been adopted in good season, it would have satisfied the demands made by the reasonable portion of the public, and allayed the popular excitement. These views, as we have seen, he urged upon Lord Liverpool in 1819. So early as 1822 he saw that the tide was fast rising, and he then addressed the following letter to Mr. Peel:—

February 1st, 1822.

DEAR PEEL,

I quite agree with you that the Government ought to look round and see what they can do on the three great points of diminution of taxation, of retrenchment, and of reform; and having made up their minds as to what it may be possible to do, they should take their final determination to stand or fall upon the ground they have taken. I wish to submit to you some views of mine on these points.

The cause of reform, it cannot be doubted, has made great progress—public opinion is created by the press or by public meetings, and by the numbers and weight of the advocates of a cause. Now, almost the whole press, and all public meetings, are loud for reform, and I believe I may say with truth that such is the apathy, or the timidity, on our side of the question that except an annual speech of Mr. Canning at a Liverpool dinner, and the occasional article of some obscure man of letters in the *Quarterly Review*, nothing is spoken or written to oppose the torrent of the reformers. To this must be added the accession of names which the reformers have acquired in some of the great Whig lords. Lord Fitzwilliam and Lord Darlington, two of the largest borough holders in England, have joined them—I care not with what reserves, mental or expressed. They have joined them to the public eye, and that is a junction for all effective purposes, for the reformers only want their names, and they want them not so much to add to their strength as to diminish ours, which it does doubly—first, in numbers (that I care little about), but secondly, in effect, which is very important; for if Lord Fitzwilliam, by all admitted to be a worthy, well-meaning, and amiable man, with 60,000*l.* a year, and eight rotten members, be not alarmed at reform, why should persons whose pecuniary interest is small compared to his, and who have no political power to lose? I know how beautifully Mr. Canning argues this point, and proves to the people at Liverpool that he is *pro rata* as much interested in it all as Lord Fitzwilliam; and I agree with him; but the question now is not what ought to be, but what is the effect of these desertions. In the humbler circle in which I move, I know that the effect is prodigious, and at tables, where ten years ago you would have no more heard reform advocated than treason, you will now find half the company reformers—moderate reformers, indeed, individually, but radical in the lump. One would extract the grey hairs and the other the brown, and our present parliamentary constitution would be left, after their several remedies, in a state of bald and defenceless nudity. If the existing course of things holds, I am confident that the result will be, what it always is with mobs or nations, that those who strut and look biggest and talk loudest will carry the day, and with the greater or less ease and celerity as they shall be more or less opposed. In this state of the public mind, nothing more is wanted than any unhappy vacillation or weakness in the Government, to break down the dykes and flood-gates, and lay the whole country under the wave of reform. What would rise out of that deluge neither you nor I nor any man can know or can guess, and having convinced myself that no human power can control the flood if once let loose, and that no human sagacity can foretell what are to be its consequences, I am obliged to say that we are bound to resist it altogether.

Here, therefore, is our first stand. We should not give an inch to parliamentary reform. Cases like Grampound will arise to embarrass us; we must deal with them when they occur, and on their individual grounds, and it is doubtful whether, well managed, they may not do more good than harm, for the redress of a gross abuse granted spontaneously, or at least naturally, and arising out of accidental causes, sometimes appeases the public mind, without giving it any higher idea of its own power. Some of our friends, I know, say that even Grampound they would not touch. Such men are safe in obscurity. I should like to see any man profess that doctrine in his place in Parliament. I would not touch it if I could help it, but, *si boire est tiré il faut le boire.* A Government oftener injures itself by attempting to defend abuses not its own, than by any other line of conduct I could mention. If a Government should be so absurd as to take up the defence of such a case with a high hand, it would lose itself, its object, and the country. It will require all our prudence to avoid, all our skill to parry, and finally all our force to meet this question.

I therefore conclude not to give an inch to parliamentary reform as a general measure, to oppose the slightest, the most harmless, the most alluring alteration which is proposed on *principle*—to remember that all the radical mover wants is a ποῦ στῶ; on the other hand, to take firmly whatever advantage we may be able to derive from the follies or criminalities of individuals, and burn Grampound to the ground rather than undertake its defence, or leave it to the enemy as a cover whence to assault us. I said in general that no one could guess what the consequences of reform would be. I should have said its eventual consequences, for the first step or two seem plain enough—the day which reforms the House of Commons, dissolves the House of Lords, and overturns the *Church.* Beyond that I cannot venture to guess. Temporary circumstances, the state of the army, and the personal character of the then King, would decide whether there would ensue a military despotism, another martyrdom at Whitehall, or another flight from Faversham.

Mr. Croker again, in 1830 (before the introduction and rejection of Lord John Russell's resolutions for enfranchising Leeds, Birmingham, and Manchester), tried to get the Government to lead and control the reform movement rather than be mastered by it. Whether this would have been possible in any case may, of course, be strongly doubted; but Mr. Croker's position was at the time quite reasonable; and at any rate it held out a fairer prospect of success than Peel's *non possumus* policy. Peel, however, was opposed to any extension of the suffrage. He said in Parliament, during the discussion on Lord John Russell's resolutions, that the question was "whether the popular voice was not sufficiently heard. For himself he thought that it was."

Mr. Croker to Mr. Peel.

February 24th, 1830.

My dear Peel,

A thought has struck me which (with some difficulties) has many plausible sides, viz. to resume the Grampound franchise from Yorkshire in general, and give one member each (like Higham Ferrars and Abingdon), to Leeds and Sheffield; and, in like manner, to divide East Retford between Manchester and Birmingham.

That would look something like a system and a principle, and might excuse a change of policy.

The great difficulty is the landed interest, which would

then get nothing on the present occasion, but as they got the last four seats, they might spare us these two; but above all, they must see that they will not be able to prevent a torrent if they refuse to pacify us by the admission of two drops.

Yours ever,
J. W. C.

The state of the King's health kept the Ministry in a constant state of uncertainty concerning their future course, for they had little expectation that a dissolution would strengthen their position. The course of events is clearly described in the following letters :—

Mr. Croker to Lord Hertford.

January 12th, 1830.

The King goes on well—the bleeding was, they say, *precautionary*, as he had some cough.

The Duke is resolved that there shall be no distress any where—" there is no distress—there can be no distress—there shall be no distress." I hope he may be able to bring the country gentlemen to his opinion.

Vesey gets on but slowly. There was, it is said, some kind of apoplectic seizure, and they begin to say that he will be never fit again for business. His notes to me don't look so serious—do they? I have my own opinion, which is that he shrinks from the responsibility of his office in Parliament, and makes himself as bad as he can, that he may go out with the more credit. That he felt it too much for his health and *spirits*, he has been telling me the last two months.

January 20th.

We have had frightful weather—quite an Arctic snowstorm. I do not know how we are to get through the funeral * to-morrow, which may, like the poor Duke of York's, be the fruitful parent of many funerals. This day three years Lawrence and I went down together, and walked side by side in that ceremony; and the only time I ever attended a funeral at St. Paul's—it was old Rennie's—Lawrence and I were paired together, and in the mists of the vaults people could

---

* [Of Sir Thomas Lawrence. See p. 87, *infra*.]

not distinguish, they said, which was which—he was about eleven years older than I am.

The country gentleman seems much out of humour, but Scotland, and some districts both in England and Ireland, are not dissatisfied. The King is mending of the remains of his inflammation of the body, but the mind is still not quite as Dr. Wellington would wish it.

April 22nd, 1830.

He [the King] was driving yesterday week in the great park when he met his hounds. He stopped to look at and talk about them, and alighted from his pony chair. On attempting to mount again he was seized with a spasmodic difficulty of breathing. These attacks, it seems, come and go. This is all that any one knows for certain, but people near him are very much alarmed. He himself looks at his situation very steadily and courageously. He once said to me, " I am very nervous, but very brave."

I myself incline to believe the danger to be more remote than the people in the streets, who are always greedy of bad news, and will have it.

April 26th.

We are all in the dark as to the disease. The wise ones say that it is certainly not *water*. Some imagined it was the hay asthma; and the medical people seem to think it arises from fat, or some supernatural clogging of the viscera about the heart or lungs. Public opinion is very gloomy about him, and I begin to fear that the thing looks serious. The Duke of Clarence has come to reside in town—rather unexpectedly it is said. Some say to avoid his usual attack, but it is a month too soon for *that*—others surmise that he thinks it right at this crisis to be at the fountain head of affairs; but I should have thought that if he were really alarmed about the King, Bushey, half way between Windsor and town, would have been the most convenient.

This topic absorbs all our conversation.

Mr. Isaac D'Israeli to Mr. Croker.

Bradenham House, High Wycombe,
March 11th, 1830.

MY DEAR SIR,

Weather permitting I hope to have the honour of dining with you on Saturday, 27th.

I will tear myself away from all the conspiracies and the conspirators of Charles I. Among "the grievances" of his unhappy reign I have discovered one hitherto unnoticed—viz., that Parliament has passed no Act that the historian should have his proofs dispatched by the post. This necessarily delays publication. I recollect that the editor of the *Literary Gazette* once whined over this distress of country authors, and held out a promise which Parliament never took into their consideration. Though the House has of late had some intimation about "dramatic writers," I suppose that no member will move for *us!*

Sometimes when I write, I recollect that it is possible that you may read me, and I endeavour to make my volumes amusing; but your 'Boswell' I suspect may prevent the world from finding any book afterwards sufficiently so.

Believe me, with great regard,
My dear Sir, ever faithfully yours,
I. D'ISRAELI.

Mr. Croker to Mr. Vesey Fitzgerald. * Extracts.*

May 3rd.

Sir Robert Peel has had a relapse, and Peel has gone down again to Drayton, leaving us not only without a general to lead us, but even without one fighting man; for he is himself *our host.* . . . I think the Duke of Wellington looks uncommonly harassed; but his spirits are as good as ever. You may depend upon it that, whether the King lives or not, there must be some political changes. We are incapable of doing our business in the House of Commons, and whence we are to get the needful help I cannot even guess.

The King is aware of his own situation, and contemplates it, as I learn, boldly. He received the Sacrament on, I think, Thursday. He sits bolstered up in bed, or in a chair, incapable of lying down; his head, they say, falls on his breast; his appetite is gone, and though neither speechless nor senseless, he is very torpid, and evidently fading rapidly away.

---

* [Mr. Fitzgerald was on the Continent, for the benefit of his health. Mr. Croker, it will be seen, kept him well informed concerning all that was going on.]

Such is the state which the accounts, of what seem the best authority, describe. If they be anything like the truth, the scene is about to close.

Now for politics. The Whigs are, I hear, taking a more *self-centered* attitude. They seem to think that they are capable of making an Administration; and if they co-operate cordially—that is, if Grey, Lansdowne, Holland, Brougham, Althorp, Burdett, and Graham could agree, they no doubt could do so; but could they stand? On the *present* principles of parties in this country, not a session! But who can say what change a new reign, and the prospect of a minority, might not operate? If to the Whigs were to be added—by the mediation of Anglesey and Carlisle—Goderich, Grenville and Seaford; Huskisson, Palmerston, and the Grants, they would have a very strong Government, so far as regards the filling of offices, and the speaking in Parliament; but unless the accession and character of the new sovereign should alter the opinions of the mass of the aristocracy, the gentry, and the people, I hardly think that even such a formidable coalition could eventually maintain itself. On the other hand, we have repeated declarations (former and recent) of the Duke of Clarence that he does not intend to change the Ministers he may find in power; the country at large has great confidence in the Duke of Wellington, and the House of Commons cannot, I think, fail to be impressed with the talent Peel has lately shown as leader. So much, then, we may look upon as settled for a *season*, at least; but what is to be done as to the subordinates? Murray must, it seems, move—of course into one of the military offices—and I have had a suspicion that the Duke had turned an eye towards *Goderich* to succeed him; that would do us no good in the House of Commons, and would rather do harm in the country—but less harm, I think, than any decided Liberal or Whig would do; for, depend upon it, there is hardly a man out of office whom the Duke could introduce—Lord Grey, Brougham, Huskisson, Stanley, Spring Rice—who would not occasion more eventual loss of strength than his accession would repay. I know that one or two partial tongues have whispered me as fit to replace Murray,* "me quoque dicunt—sed ego non credulus illis." Putting all other considerations aside, and God knows that they are many and weighty against such an

---

* [Sir G. Murray was Secretary for the Colonies.]

arrangement, I feel that all the Privy Councillors might fairly object to such a " passe droit." Calcraft, Beckett, Lord Francis Egerton, Leveson, Fitzgerald, Arbuthnot, and Hardinge *would* not, but *they*, like the others, reasonably might. Depend upon it, my dear Vesey, the thing is not feasible, and the most that could be done would be to move me to independent office, and there is no independent office at all so good, or that would be so agreeable to me, as my own, nor is there any probability of any of them being vacated.

I am quite aware of the extreme difficulty of going on in the House of Commons without help, but I much doubt whether Peel wishes for any. I say this advisedly, and I do not think he will change that feeling—for *such* it is, rather than an *opinion*—till he shall begin to feel the *personal* pressure of adverse debate. He has not yet been *attacked*, and his single speech has, every night, supported the whole debate on our side. This is a high and palmy state—resembling that of Mr. Pitt of yore—but when Brougham shall have lost all hope, and Huskisson all patience, Peel will find that he alone will not suffice, and that he must have people about him to take share in the risk and the responsibility.

I hear and see no symptoms of a change in the Chair—the Speaker looks and is, and what is more important, *says* he is, tolerably well, and with the present jealousy of pensions, I do not think that he, or if *he* were, that the Government would be, mad enough to risk a new embarrassment of that nature as long as he can be *kept in the chair*.

May 11*th*. The town is full of rumours of *intrigues* of which the *new Court* is already the object, and there are, to be sure, two or three strange facts on which such speculations are very naturally built. What do you think of Lady Jersey, who has never been on any terms of intimacy with the Duchess of Clarence, going down to Bushey—forcing the " consigne," and obliging H.R.H. to receive a long visit from her. The Duchess, it is said, received her very coolly, even to the extent of expressing some surprise at a pleasure so *new and unexpected;* but that is perhaps not so surprising as Anglesey's having gone down to the Duke of Clarence. He, I dare say, did not intrude quite so cavalierly as the Countess, and indeed I have heard that Lord Errol arranged the interview, but it is said with no more success than the other attempt. One thing only of the interview I have heard; that Anglesey, observing to H.R.H. the circumstances in which he would find himself at the King's death as to his personal residence—Windsor being out of the question till after the funeral, and St. James's having no accommodation for a King,—suggested his *visiting the ports*—Portsmouth and Plymouth—until Windsor should be ready to receive him. This seems in the last degree improbable, I might say insane; yet I have heard it from excellent authority, but with this observation, that Anglesey never dreamt of such advice being *taken*, but that it was a mode of reminding H.R.H. of his quarrel with the Duke of Wellington *about visiting the ports* two years ago, and a scheme to enlist his personal feelings against a continuance of the Duke of Wellington's power.

Peel does not come back to the House till Monday (17th). In the meanwhile poor Goulburn is obliged to make the whole fight, and there is really business enough for a month on the paper for the week. The votes of this morning give an account of 137 matters of business transacted yesterday, one of which was the Committee of Supply that occupied five hours, and it contains twelve notices for to-day. So great a mass of business I never before saw, and it seems to increase daily.

The bulletin to-day is that "the symptoms are not materially mitigated, but H.M. has had some sleep"; and I hear that the general state is not so bad as the rumours mentioned in the beginning of my letter represented it. However, you may depend upon it that hope is abandoned, and that it is a mere question of lingering a few days, or at best weeks, more or less. I forgot to mention one thing which shows some sensibility. He expressed a wish that his Ministers should in turn go down to Windsor, to pay their duty by inquiring after him. Accordingly Lord Bathurst and Melville went yesterday. They of course did not see him, but he was told that they were there, and they had a long talk with Halford, but came back knowing really no more than, if indeed so much as, their colleagues in town. This visit is very proper on many accounts, but it seems odd that the King should have himself suggested it.

The Duke of Wellington was down himself on Saturday, but did not see him, because (such is the assigned reason) if *he* had seen the King, *others* that were in the Castle could not be denied—meaning the Duke of Cumberland, whose visits are said to be peculiarly agitating, and therefore injurious; but the Duke of Wellington had seen him in the course of the week, and gave a good report of his spirits, appetite, and appearance.

May 14th.

The Duke of Wellington saw the King again on Wednesday, when he was a good deal struck with an alteration in his appearance for the worse—that is, he looked wasted and wasting; but his eye was lively, his hand cool and healthy, and his mind as clear and active as ever, and even his spirits were good; in fact, he showed strong vitality, and I dare say it will be with him as it was with the Duke of York, he will contest every inch with death, and exhibit all that tenacity of life which his family have constitutionally. The successor still talks, I hear, as he has always done, of his intention to continue to employ the Duke of Wellington,* but I also hear that besides the visit of Anglesey, which I before mentioned, he has seen Lords Grey and Holland, and many other persons, and the Whigs have certainly hopes of a change of that determination.

Some changes I am convinced he will make, and one of them will reach even as low as *me*. Such is my impression, and my present intention is to relieve the Duke of Wellington from all embarrassment on my account. Cockburn, I believe, feels and intends as I do; but all this is premature. I shall do nothing but by the Duke of Wellington's advice and approbation; but I am too fair not to make allowances for the feelings of H.R.H., and too honest, I hope, to allow my personal concern to risk a great public benefit. *Nous verrons.*

May 17th.

Peel saw the King yesterday, and was most agreeably surprised to find him so lively, intelligent, and strong. He talked of all Peel's private affairs, and of old Sir Robert's arrangements,† with all that astonishing knowledge of details for which he was always so remarkable. Peel stayed but half an hour, for fear of wearying him, but the King was reluctant to let him go. I myself am not led away by this gleam of amendment. I have seen too closely the progress of this disease, in

---

* [He did so; but the Duke was defeated on a motion to refer the Civil List to a Select Committee, November 15th; and Lord Grey took his place.]

† [Mr. Peel had succeeded to the Baronetcy on the death of his father on May 3rd.]

the cases both of my father and the Duke of York, to be deluded by these momentary rallies.

In the meanwhile, I think I may assure you that the Whigs have lately entertained more sanguine hopes than they at first did of being called on by the successor. I have heard that they have even already allotted the principal places.

I have not heard the name of Goderich whispered, nor Palmerston, nor the Grants; but the latter trio of course are included under the word Huskisson. They would certainly make a very respectable government in point of talent and station. In the Lords, Grey, Lansdowne, Holland, Melbourne, and Anglesey. In the Commons, Brougham (*if not Chancellor!*), Huskisson, Palmerston, the Grants, Mackintosh, Althorp, Graham, Stanley, Milton, Lord J. Russell and Rice, and, if the Duke of Cumberland be propitiated, some support from the Tories; many of whom hate Peel and our Duke even more than they fear the Whigs. With a dissolution, and the choice of a new Parliament in their hands, I think they would set off, as they did in 1806, with insolent majorities; but, as I believe I said before, I do not think the country would tolerate them a second session, because they must either offend public opinion by pursuing Whig measures, or forfeit it by abandoning their pledged principles.

May 18th.

The accounts of the King continue still to improve. I have not time to say more, though I have much to say. We threw out the Jews' Bill * last night, 228 to 163, after a very *faint* speech from Peel. He did not at all grapple with the real question, and seemed as if he wished to be beaten. What can this mean? Does he resent against the Church the rejection of Oxford? He last night *in principle* gave up the whole connection of Church and State.

May 21st.

As to what you are so kind as to think so important in this state of affairs, viz., my own position, be assured I shall do nothing hasty or vainglorious. I shall make no parade of disinterestedness, nor shall I give any handle, I hope, to public or private malignity; all I purpose is that the Duke of Wellington shall not be embarrassed, in the great arrange-

* [Mr. R. Grant's Bill for relieving Jews of political disabilities.]

ments he may have to make, by any private interests of mine. He was, you know, so deep in all our proceedings that he could not abandon us, but think what it would be to have the national destinies disturbed by private considerations and personal pledges. No; you would never advise me to be an active party to any such embarrassment; but be satisfied that I shall do nothing hastily, nor does any one but yourself know that such an idea has crossed my imagination—it would appear highly impertinent and presumptuous, and I shall carefully avoid all grounds or colour for such a reproach.

May 28th.

I must now tell you a story which I suppose we must not doubt, though it seems so strange that if it were not vouched by an ostensible witness it would receive no kind of credit.

A few days ago H.R.H. the Duke of Clarence sent for Sir William Hope to Bushey—so far is notorious. At this conversation, H.R.H. said he was quite satisfied with the Duke of Wellington, and indeed with Lord Melville, and meant to continue them both in office; but that with regard both to Sir G. Cockburn and Mr. Croker, his first act would be to send *them* to the right about. I thought myself highly honoured by so much of his personal kindness as the present King was so condescending as to allow me, but I certainly never expected the more important distinction of being marked as the object of the personal hostility of the Sovereign. I repeat you the story just as Sir William tells it in the streets. You recollect that Sir William was himself in early life, and indeed down to a late period, one of H.R.H.'s *bêtes noires*. True or exaggerated, the story puts an end to the idea I had mentioned to you. Any step on my part would now appear anything but disinterested or dignified, and I therefore shall certainly lie at single anchor to wait the turn of the tide.

The Whigs are certainly consolidating themselves. There was a meeting yesterday at Lansdowne House, but I have not heard what passed, nor even who was there; nor shall I in time for this letter, as I am obliged to send it to Mr. Fitzgerald before I go down to the House, and the day is so bad that I despair of any one's calling who is likely to bring gossip. We are curious to know whether Palmerston was there, as he certainly had some intention of being, and whether Lord Grey attended. This last circumstance is very important, as it would be quite a God-send to the Duke of Wellington, who is certainly hampered by some engagements with Lord Grey.

All the fashionable world has been for three days at Hatfield. The last day three farces were played. It all went off well. A translated farce by Hook, and an original one by Lady Dacre, were very successful; Mrs. Ellis and Mrs. Ellison were excellent; so were James Wortley and Charles Phipps; Lord Morpeth rivalled Liston. Francis Leveson was a Grand Duke in the 'Diplomati,' and very dull, as Grand Dukes usually are.

June 11th.

On Monday night, a friend, K. [Sir W. Knighton] sat up with him [the King], and frequently in that night thought him dying. On Sunday he sat up again. The King slept at times, but in the waking intervals he was as clear, as communicative, as agreeable, nay as *facetious* in his conversation as he ever had been Such are the vicissitudes of his state! Another friend (F)* saw him lately, and it was like an audience of final leave; but the King appeared to balance in his own mind the probabilities of life and death as almost equal. He talked successively of his journey to Aix-la-Chapelle, and his funeral procession to St. George's Chapel. I need not, however, point out to you that, however calmly and courageously he might talk in these alternations, the moment he admitted the fatal probability, the other must have been, even in his own mind, a very hopeless alternative. He told this friend, "Whenever you lose me, believe me you will lose one who has had a long, sincere, and undeviating regard for you." He asked whether the public took a great interest in his state, and being answered that they did, he seemed much pleased, and expressed his own conviction that it ought to be so, for he "had always endeavoured to do his duty," and had never willingly done harm to any one. This led him to talk of the *prayer* which is ordered to be read in the churches for him. He liked it, and said that "it was in *good taste*"—an odd

---

* [Probably Lord Farnborough, for whom the King expressed the greatest kindness and affection, and whom he named Keeper of the Royal Signet at his (the King's) decease. See 'Wellington Despatches,' New Series, vii. 66.]

expression on such a subject, but not, I think, an uncharacteristic one.

You will be glad to hear that although a decent silence is maintained on the subject, he is not negligent of the duties—perhaps I should now say the calls—of religion. The Bishop of Chichester, who is, I believe, the Clerk of the Closet, does not leave the house, and sees him frequently. The Duke of Wellington is astonished at his strength, both of body and mind, and says that it will rather surprise him if he is not alive in the autumn. Is it not strange and awful that one who has been represented as speculating on his [the Duke's] death, is likely to go before him?

June 27th.

On my return [from Ireland] I found the King grown weak and languid—that is dying! And in the night between Friday and Saturday, at a quarter-past three, after some hours of tranquil sleep, followed by a copious evacuation of blood, he expired. His last words were, putting his hands on the pit of his stomach, as if he felt a peculiar sensation there, "Surely this must be death," and it was so.

Then came all the bustle of a new reign, rendered more bustling by the contrast between the easy indolence of the last King, and the activity of the new one. Everybody seemed to be on the *qui vive*. There seem to have been strange delays and irregularities in the summonses or invitations to the Privy Councillors and others who attend, as you may remember, to proclaim the new King. I, who knew that such summonses must come, had dressed myself and made Cockburn do the same, and as soon as the summons reached us, we set off afoot through the park to St. James's, where we found half the Council already assembled; so that, near as we were to Whitehall, others must have had their notices more than half an hour before us, and I hear that some of the notices usually sent to some of the principal men in office, not Privy Councillors, were not sent at all. This I know, that Clerk and Hotham attended at the accession of George IV. and signed the proclamation, but were not invited on this occasion. However, a vast number of Privy Councillors, not less than ninety-three, were assembled by one o'clock, when the King came from his closet into the third drawing-room at St. James's, where we were all assembled, and made us his declaration, which you will see in the papers.

His voice faltered amiably at the mention of his brother, but he soon recovered that, and startled those of his Council who did not know him by exclaiming in a familiar tone against the *badness of the pen* with which he was signing the oath administered to him by the Lord President ["Damn the pen" *] but his deportment on the whole was decent and proper, polite to all, and kind to some.

We were all sworn again as Privy Councillors, and in turn kissed his hand. I supposed, after all I had heard, that his manner to *me* would be cold, if not something worse, but I was agreeably disappointed. When I took his hand to kiss it, he held mine longer than was necessary—"hoped I was well—was glad to see me—had not expected it—thinking that I had been in Dublin, but supposed that I had found the art of travelling by a balloon." This, with a gracious smile and a condescending manner, was much more than I could have hoped for, and makes me remember Louis XII., who forgot the quarrels of the Duke of Orleans. Cockburn, the other supposed black sheep, he treated with like civility, though perhaps in a somewhat cooler degree.

Before he came into Council, the *élite* of his Ministers went to him in a body—the Duke, Lord Chancellor, Lord President, Privy Seal, and two of the Secretaries of State. To them he made a little speech, to say that he would have been naturally indisposed to change his brother's Ministers, but that he was happy to find in office men in whom he personally had the greatest confidence, and that they might depend not only on his sincere confidence and good will, but on the most strenuous support that the King could give to his Ministers. After we had all taken the oaths, he and the Queen returned in their travelling carriage to Bushey, calling on Princess Sophia at Kensington in the way. There is some story of his having observed that he had no escort coming up, and that the escort was not ordered even for his return, till he had made the observation.

A curious and almost ludicrous circumstance occurred. Our friend Buller in swearing one batch pledged them to bear true allegiance to our Sovereign Lord King *George*—the King looked back quietly and emphatically, and said, "*William, if you please*"—the last three words I did not *hear*, as I was at

---

* [These words are inserted in the margin by Mr. Croker; much the same account is given by Charles Greville, 'Diary,' ii. p. 3.]

the other end of the table, but I am assured he said just what I have written. I myself heard Buller say "*George*," and the King say "*William*," but I lost "*if you please*," though I saw his lips moving. Something more curious is, that the Royal Chaplain, who this day officiated in the Royal Chapel of the Royal Palace of Kensington, prayed for "*King George.*" There was some delay (or blunder as I believe) about the Order in Council for the necessary changes in the Liturgy, and I suspect that if despatched *at all* last night, they were sent very irregularly, but no one could have imagined that a Court Chaplain should so far forget not the *rising*, but the *risen* sun, as to pray for the dead.

Sir Herbert Taylor is to be private secretary to the new King—a judicious appointment that will inspire public confidence, and has more effect than a more important pledge might have had. Macdonald, his deputy, succeeds to the Adjutant-General. I am glad of it for his sake, but it seems to me to be throwing away an appointment which might be usefully employed by-and-bye in smoothing political arrangements. I forgot to tell you that an unfavourable impression was made on the public mind yesterday by the King's having, in less than twelve hours from his brother's death, ordered the dress of the Guards to be altered. This looks strange, but it was in fact right, and was necessary to be done at the moment. A new and very expensive uniform had been ordered, and it was to spare the officers the expense of making up this costly dress that the King was advised to lose no time in countermanding it.

June 28th.

But I have no doubt that eventually the activity of his mind will bring him into collision with his Ministers. Here is an anecdote which I *know* to be true. Late yesterday a dragoon arrived at the Admiralty—a letter from the King to the First Lord! The letter—*a Holograph autograph* letter of the King—was to enclose to Lord Melville another letter from a midshipman which had been addressed *by mistake* to the Duke of Clarence as Lord High Admiral. This is an anecdote which would obtain applause as an instance of royal attention to humble merit; for my part I hope his Majesty may not wear himself out with minutiæ of this sort, and I think that a note from Taylor covering the middy's epistle would have been quite as well; particularly as the King's letter was accompanied by one from Taylor.

If his Majesty descends to these minutiæ, I do not know where he is to find time even for the small portion of sleep or aliment which he takes. They said yesterday that he had given his personal orders to a subaltern of dragoons on some subject connected with the escort, and that the poor boy was puzzled which to obey, the King or the adjutant.

As to our Parliamentary proceedings, the Cabinet have resolved to follow the precedent of 1820—to bring down a message to-morrow to announce a dissolution, and exhort the Commons to get through their business, to take a vote on account of the Civil List, and postpone the Regency to a new Parliament. We are run so close with the Sugar Duties (they expire on the 6th July) that all we can possibly do is to pass them *per saltum* in their present form. I conclude that we shall dissolve in about a fortnight or three weeks; but that time may be prolonged if the parties adverse to us *unite* to show their strength, which Brougham to-day gave us some intimation that we might expect, for he read the King and the public a short but pithy lecture on the text that without a certain and zealous majority in the House of Commons, no Government could get on. He added that no acquisition of talents and strength in another place (the House of Lords) would supply the defect of support in the Commons. This, it is supposed, alludes to some suspicion of a junction between the Duke and Lord Grey. But the upshot of all was that the Opposition would show the King that he could not do without *them*.

July 2nd.

If we do not get help somewhere, we shall become ridiculous. In the meanwhile, the Whigs have split. The Duke of Bedford and Lord Jersey voted with the Duke of Wellington on Wednesday against Lord Grey, and yesterday sent him a written remonstrance against his proceedings (and, *inter alia*, his concert with the ultra-Tories), and dissolved their political connections, and Lord Villiers is going down to stand in the Government interest for Rochester.

Nor is there more concert amongst our adversaries in the House of Commons. Huskisson told me last night that Brougham was in "a state of excitement bordering on insanity," and Sir Robert Inglis, who had voted in Brougham's train on Wednesday, quarrelled outright with him last night on the point whether drunkenness was a sin or only a vice.

In short, on a trivial, incidental point they showed a violent antipathy. This division, as long as it lasts, will save us, and it may last for ever; but I see clouds in other quarters big with storms, and I heartily wish that I were as you are, out of the vessel that is about to sail in such weather, on a, *to me*, wholly unprofitable voyage.

The General Election took place, and the result was unfavourable to the Ministry. Two of Sir Robert Peel's brothers were defeated, and his brother-in-law, Mr. George Dawson, whose speech had stirred up so much controversy the year before, was beaten in Ireland. Mr. Croker was also defeated in his appeal to his constituents of Dublin University, chiefly in consequence of a division in the party ranks created by Mr. North. Mr. Croker, however, speedily secured another seat, this time for Aldborough. Almost at the same moment there occurred the Revolution in Paris, and the abdication of Charles X. Louis Philippe, who afterwards was for many years in regular communication with Mr. Croker, ascended the French throne, while the deposed king sought refuge in England.

Mr. Croker to Sir Henry Hardinge.

August 19th, 1830.

DEAR HARDINGE,

Charles X. has assumed the incognito title of Count de Ponthieu. He is to have a temporary asylum in this country. I fancy he will establish himself at Lulworth Castle, on the coast of Dorset. It belongs, you know, to a mad Catholic gentleman, whom the Pope has made a Cardinal, and there is a Catholic chapel there, and the seat is surrounded by a Catholic population. So that nothing can be better.

My letters from Paris to-day state things as looking less settled. Cries from the wine-shops of " *Vive Napoléon II.;*" and what astonishes me, an expectation that Protestantism will be declared the religion of the State!

Folks begin to think that we shall soon have to find a *temporary asylum* for Louis Philippe!

> Yours ever,
> J. W. C.

On the 15th of September an event occurred which gave a great shock not only to the political world, but to the entire body of the community. It had been arranged that the Liverpool and Manchester railway should be opened with much show and ceremony, for it was justly felt that the occasion was destined to become memorable in domestic history. The Prime Minister (the Duke of Wellington), with the Home Secretary (Peel) and Huskisson, the member for Liverpool, were all present. By some misfortune, Mr. Huskisson stepped upon the line as the engine was approaching, and he received injuries from the effects of which he died a few hours afterwards.

Mr. Croker to Lord Hertford.

> September 18th, 1830.

I can think of nothing but the loss of poor Huskisson. There was no danger, no fear even; but he, not being quite so cool and active as we have seen him at Sudbourne, in attempting to get into his car, stumbled back a few feet, tripped, and fell, with his left leg and thigh just over the railroad, and that very moment the other engine passed and crushed the limb to jelly. It was an accident that might have happened any day in the Strand if one's foot had slipped at the edge of the kerbstone just as a stage-coach was going rapidly along; but the miraculous combination of circumstances is that he should fall where a fall seemed impossible; that he should fall within reach of the engine; that the member for Liverpool—that so important a person should, out of at least one hundred thousand persons, be the *only one* to suffer *any* accident; and finally, that it should have occurred just as he had shaken hands with (shall I say) his political antagonist,[*]

[* [The Duke of Wellington.]]

and reconciled, as it were, the only personal enmity he ever had. How many million of chances there were against such a catastrophe befalling him at such a moment! Had he not been member for Liverpool, he would not have been there; had he not quarrelled with the Duke of Wellington he would not have left his seat. In short, there is no end to the chain of circumstances that were linked to this most deplorable event.

Talleyrand was at this time in London as French Ambassador, and he was sometimes entertained by the Duke of Wellington. Mr. Croker describes one occasion on which he met the diplomatist.

Mr. Croker to Lord Hertford.

We had an exceedingly agreeable dinner. We were *twelve* at a round-table that should have held *eight;* but what we lost in elbow-room comfort, we made up for in being all forced into one conversation. Talleyrand is not at all changed since our "Conciliabule" fifteen years ago; and his mind seems as fresh as ever. He said two or three of his sly things. "Avant de partir," said he, "je conseillais au roi de faire *un grand acte.*" "And what was that?" was asked with a great deal of curiosity. "Mais," he replied, "*un grand acte politique,—d'aller passer trois jours à Neuilly!*" You know that the Citizen-King has not been out of Paris since his accession, and seems afraid of going beyond the barriers lest he should give umbrage to his good people of Paris.

The Duke asked him about la Reine. "La Reine," he said, was a "bonne femme—très bonne femme, et surtout *grande dame,* et c'est précisément ce qu'il nous faut dans les circonstances." You will judge by these two sarcasms what the old fox thinks of the *late* Revolution—observe, I do not call it the *last.* You would have been amused at the gravity with which, when some one talked of confiscation, he said, "Il n'y a plus de confiscation en France." I could not help whispering Alvanley, "except of France itself." For what has poor Charles X. suffered but a *confiscation?*

We hear that Talleyrand solicited this mission very anxiously, and he certainly is delighted to find himself here. The state of confusion and fear in Paris was, and is, much greater than we learn from the newspapers.

I begin to lose all hope of getting away again. Things seem to me to look blacker and blacker.

Yours ever,
J. W. C.

The prospect was, in truth, very dark on all sides. In July there had been the Revolution in Paris; it was evident that another was preparing in Belgium; and in England great disturbances had occurred in the agricultural districts, as well as in many of the large towns. Incendiary fires were once more of nightly occurrence. Wellington and Peel were both unpopular with their own party as well as with the country. Mr. Croker firmly believed that if the Ministry were overthrown, still greater evils would arise, and he was particularly anxious to restore something like harmony within the ranks of his political friends. It was with this purpose in view that he wrote the next letter.

Mr. Croker to Mr. William Blackwood.

October 29th, 1830.

Let me say a word or two to you on the tone your political articles have lately taken. If, as is, I suppose, the admitted right of all periodicals, you publish what you think likely to sell best, I have no more to say; but if you and your clever contributors feel a real interest in the matter, I would ask what good can be got by the continual attacks on the Duke of Wellington and Sir Robert Peel. I admit fully and frankly the causes of dislike which the old Tories have to both, and particularly the latter; and if there were any mode by which you could turn them out to make way for more congenial ministers, I am too old and, I hope, too fair an observer of the political world to make the slightest objection; such a course would be not only natural, but just and honest.

But can the mischief be undone?—(and I agree with you and your friends that great mischief was done; we only differ as to the compensatory degree of advantage). Because we have made one inroad on the Constitution, are we to lay *all* waste? For saving what we have, I see no other hope than keeping the Duke in power; if he were to go out, you would have revolutions in every State in Europe, England included perhaps; certainly *attempts* at revolution. There is no other public man who has character enough, either at home or abroad, to *ballast* the Cabinet in such a tempest and sea as are roaring round us. The one or two next to him in public weight are disposed to these very revolutionary principles. I know that when called to power they would abjure them, and do their best to keep their own present friends down; but then they would lose all consideration in the eyes of the public by what would be called apostasy.

Pray consider the few hints I have thrown out. They will lead to many ramifications, all tending to the one end, the *reunion* of the Tories under the Duke. Pray excuse this liberty, and believe me to be, very truly yours, &c.,

J. W. C.

Conflicts with the new police force continued to be of frequent occurrence, and in the House of Commons the attacks on the Ministry became more and more formidable. The end was nearer than Mr. Croker probably thought when he next wrote.

Mr. Croker to Sir Robert Peel.

November 3rd, 1830.

MY DEAR PEEL,

Barrow went up last night to Bond Street at nine o'clock, and gives me an account of the affair, formidable enough at the moment, but, I think, only accidental. It was all directed against the police, whose conduct was admirable; but he says that all through the town (that is, of course, as far as his way home led him) the rascally mob were pursuing the policemen, and maltreating them whenever they could get one alone.

For God's sake let them be supported; we are in no danger if we have amongst ourselves firmness and courage. Our House of Commons is a good one; we have a dozen talkers against us, and we must somehow contrive to have a dozen *for* us in the several branches of debate. For instance, Mr. Fitzgerald did very well last night on Ireland, and will do better when he gets confidence, for he still speaks under the restraint of recent Whiggism. It will be hard if you can't get declamation to answer Grant and Palmerston, who are really nothing but froth; and the great Brougham himself I firmly believe to be great only because we go on our knees to him. Let us get up. But we must not give them an inch, and we must maintain all our Institutions, and stand or fall *even* with the new police.

Yours,
J. W. C.

The Government was in such a position that the slightest reverse must necessarily have been fatal to it. The blow soon fell. It was necessary to readjust the Civil List, and the amount fixed was 970,000*l*. a year. This was considered too large by a considerable section of the House, although it was not so large as it had been in the previous reign. Sir Henry Parnell, a financial reformer of some weight and authority, complained that no change had been made in the disposition of the revenues of the Duchies of Lancaster and Cornwall, although there had been a promise in the King's speech that the hereditary revenues of the Crown should be placed at the disposal of the House. He brought forward a motion to refer the Civil List to a Select Committee; it was carried against the Government, and the Duke of Wellington resigned. Thus the Whigs came into power at last, under Lord Grey, and Mr. Croker resigned the office at the Admiralty which he had honourably filled for two-and-twenty years. Sir James Graham became First Lord, and to him Mr. Croker offered all the aid which his successor might desire.

Mr. Croker to Sir James Graham.

Dear Sir,   Admiralty, November 20th, 1830.

As there never has been an instance of the Secretary of the Admiralty being removed on a change of Ministry, it cannot be improper, though it may be superfluous, to acquaint you, who, I understand, are to be at the head of the new Board, that it is my intention to resign that office.

Permit me, however, to add that if there is any information or assistance which twenty-two years' experience may enable me to afford you in the outset of your arduous duties, I shall feel it my duty to do so, readily and frankly.

> I have the honour to be, dear Sir,
> Your faithful humble servant,
> J. W. C.

Sir James Graham to Mr. Croker.

> Grosvenor Place, November 20th, 1830.

DEAR SIR,

I am very much flattered by the kind spirit of your obliging note; and I can only express my regret that the Admiralty will no longer have the benefit of your brilliant talents and faithful services.

The offer of your assistance at the commencement of the arduous duties which I am about to undertake is very generous; and, even if I should not avail myself of it, I hope you will believe that it has gratified me as a proof that our political warfare has not deprived me altogether of your esteem.

> I have the honour to be, dear Sir,
> Your faithful servant,
> J. R. G. GRAHAM.

The events which led to this change in Mr. Croker's life are described in various letters now arranged in their proper order.

Mr. Croker to Lord Hertford.

> November 16th, 1830.

Our division of last night was 233 against us and 204 for —29 majority. We are therefore out! The Duke saw the King to-day. His Majesty was reluctant to part with his Government, but the Duke, I believe, showed him that it was inevitable, and tried to convince him that, though a present inconvenience, it would be of ultimate advantage.

The other Ministers are to be successively with His

Majesty, and all will hold the same language, except perhaps the Chancellor.* Up to two o'clock this morning he talked of resigning with his colleagues as a matter of course, but the knowing ones suspect that he will *rat*. I think not. Lord Bathurst, with breathless haste, filled up Buller's vacancy with his son William Bathurst, without the knowledge of the Duke or Peel, who were, and are, very angry. If we had stayed in, it would have been a new hare to hunt, and it may be so still; for it has been taken notice of in the House of Commons.

We have not yet heard that the King has sent for any one; but I suppose he will do so this afternoon. I see no one but Lord Grey; but *dreamers* talk of the Duke of Richmond and old Eldon.

When I saw the Duke, Arbuthnot and Hardinge were with him. Hardinge said the Whigs would endeavour to get the Duke to be Commander-in-Chief—a device which he *stigmatised* as disgraceful, in which the Duke seemed to assent.

The King has spent all the afternoon in seeing his Ministers, and is, or affects to be, much distressed at what has happened —but other people say that he talked with great indifference in expectation of it two or three days ago.

About half-past three His Majesty sent for Lord Grey, who came about five. What has passed has not yet transpired.

Peel in the House of Commons announced that Ministers had resigned, and only did the business till successors should be appointed.

Althorp has asked Brougham to put off the motion for reform which stood for to-night. Brougham seemed reluctant—said *he expected nothing from any Government*, and

---

* [There seems to have been no real cause for this suspicion, though it undoubtedly existed at the time. Lord Campbell wrote (November 16) in his Diary, "Copley will try to intrigue and keep the Great Seal" ('Campbell's Life,' vol. i. p. 488), and Mr. Charles Greville expresses himself to the same effect. Sir Theodore Martin remarks, with much greater probability of truth, that Lord Lyndhurst "would never have consented to do otherwise than follow the fortunes of his leader, for he was much attached to the Duke of Wellington, and knew himself to be too little in sympathy with the views of Earl Grey upon the question of Reform, to have accepted the Chancellorship under him, even if it had been tendered." —'Lyndhurst's Life,' p. 272.]

positively would put off the motion for no longer than the 25th.

So after twenty-two years of office I am about to be a free man. I wonder how I shall like it. Perhaps after a season I shall pine for my old green desk.

Yours ever,

J. W. C.

To Lord Hertford.

November 18th.

Lord Grey has made no progress as yet. Althorp at first refused office, but Grey said that if he persisted in that refusal he would throw up his mission. So Althorp submitted, and is, they say, to be First Lord of the Admiralty.* Lord Wellesley, too, is to get something—some say Lord Chamberlain, others the Board of Control; but I don't think that they will give any office of business to the most *brilliant incapacity* in England.† Lord Lansdowne ‡ and Spring Rice § will probably resume their old stations.

After some doubts, the Chancellor's resignation is certain. My Lady was all yesterday begging of Lord Durham to use his influence to save her lord—I believe without the least sanction from him. He seems to be quite fair, and steady to go with his friends; but who are his friends? There was a meeting yesterday at Peel's of forty official members of the House of Commons—he announced first that we were out, and secondly that he meant to retire to private life ‖—to give no opposition and not to lead the party—in short, to be his own unfettered man. We did not much like that; for it might suit him, but was not what we, going out with him, had a right to expect; for if he is at liberty to take his line, we are at liberty to take ours, and ours might be not to follow out one who, when we were out, would leave us to

* [He was made Chancellor of the Exchequer.]

† [He was not given a place in the Cabinet, but was subsequently Lord Steward, and then Lord Lieutenant of Ireland.

‡ [Lord Lansdowne was Secretary of State for the Home Department in Mr. Canning's Government (1827). He was now made President of the Council.]

§ [Mr. Spring Rice was made Secretary of the Treasury. He had held the post of Under Secretary for the Home Department in 1827.]

‖ [This was the second or third time Peel had talked of retiring to private life.]

shift for ourselves. However, on this reaching the Duke, he has announced that he means to keep the *party together;* not to oppose—nay, to support—the King's Government in all that may tend to the public safety, but to *observe* them, and if they attempt anything hostile to our institutions, to oppose. This, I hope, will warm the cold caution of Peel into some degree of party heat; but if he won't lead us there are others who will, at least, make the attempt. They said about town that the Duke had *abdicated* official life; but it is not so. He says he is essentially, and by his position and his duty, a public man, and will continue so as long as life and intellect last.

November 22nd.

To-night Peel, Goulburn, Murray, Herries, Hardinge, myself, and, in short, our whole party took the Opposition seats; and as O'Connell, Hume, and Co. have not gone over with the Whigs, it was very difficult to get a place, particularly as Sir Richard Vyvyan and some of the Ultras came to sit with us. The other side was comparatively empty, but as there are twenty at least out for re-election, that did not surprise me; but the *tone* of the House was decided opposition; for when Poulett Thompson's writ was moved for, and Lowther asked whether the honourable member had left the mercantile firm to which he had so lately belonged, there was a loud and general cheer, and O'Connell having made an observation on the number of retired Chancellors now existing (four), and saying that there would be soon two more, there was a general *mouvement de hilarité.*

The *burning* system is now turned to open *rioting* in Hampshire. So much the better; incendiarism cannot be got at, but *rioters* can. Indeed, I hear that one incendiary has been taken up with papers that will prove the case against him, and an account of 800*l.* spent by him in a tour through Kent and Sussex.

*Mr. Croker to Mr. Doyle.**

November 22nd.

My dear Doyle,

As you are, I believe, the man in the world who cares most about me, I wish you to hear from myself, and to

* [An old Dublin friend.]

approve of my having resigned my office. I suppose the new people would not have kept me, but I did not wait to know, as I at once determined to follow the Duke of Wellington. This will be a great release and comfort *for a time,* as I am really weary of eternal business, and am glad of a good excuse for retiring. How long that feeling may last I do not venture to promise, and public opinion seems to give the new Administration but a short tenure of power.

You will be glad to know that although the loss of income will *inconvenience* me, it will be only *inconvenience,* and that I shall be able to maintain my private and public respectability on a moderate scale of expense. My wife and girl are happy that I am out of office, and are quite contented with the more economical course of life which we must adopt.

Ever, my dear Doyle,
Affectionately yours,
J. W. C.

To Lord Hertford.

November 30th.

The new Ministry is at last completed in all its parts. I this morning left the office and the house in which I have spent twenty-two years. I left it with the kind of regret that one feels at hearing of the death of a very old acquaintance whom one was not very fond of. You are sorry to think that you are never to see *Jack* again, though you must confess that he was a *great bore.*

The Conservative party of observation under General the Duke of Wellington and Lieut.-Gen. Sir Robert Peel have taken their position, and will act if, and when, necessary. There is a great deal of turmoil in the country—audacity in the common people, and the most lamentable apathy and cowardice in the gentry; but it will be soon put down everywhere, for it has been checked where it began in Sussex and Kent.

The Duke gives a dinner on Saturday next to all who went out with him; I suppose we shall be near fifty.

I have just received your No. 1 from Lyons. You guessed right in supposing that *we wished to get out;* and we thought it safer for the country that we should go on a question of *form* (that is, of *confidence*), than on so vital a question as

Reform. I have long been of opinion that we could not go on, and, although there are few more financially inconvenienced by going out, no one can approve it more than I do. Peel is much more cordial and zealous than at first. He thought, it seems, there were some false brethren at the first meeting, which induced him to speak with so much caution.

December 8th.

Althorp is not only Chancellor of the Exchequer, but leader of the House of Commons. This looks like division. Palmerston,* however, is prompter to the puppet, and they will have talkers enough. They intend to reduce the salaries of all public officers sitting in Parliament; they will also now modify the Civil List, but I don't hear that they propose any saving—perhaps they will diminish the amount of pensions. I believe there was no question of Peel's neighbour, Lord Cassillis, for any office—out of sight out of mind! There is a promise of an attack upon the Duke for granting four pensions after he *virtually* was out. These four, one I hear to Black Billy [Holmes], and three Fitzclarences; the latter will probably save the former. There is nothing in its being done just at the moment; *that* is usual; but I doubt the right to grant at all before the Civil List has been settled.

Liverpool election is over; Ewart victorious by 29, after a poll of 6000. It has cost each, they say, 50,000*l.*; this seems incredible, yet I am assured it is true; Denison had a subscription of 15,000*l.*, but is himself in for 35,000*l.* The bribery was impudently flagrant. Three pilots who arrived from sea the last morning had each 150*l.* for their votes. What a commentary on Parliamentary reform!

Lord Grey's first offer to Brougham was Attorney-General. Brougham took the letter and quietly tore it in two and threw it under his feet; that was his whole reply. He then reiterated his notice for Reform, and Lord Grey took fright, and would have given him the Rolls, but the king, *forewarned*, would not do *that;* and so he became Chancellor. I forgot to tell you that we all dined with the Duke of Wellington on Saturday last—fifty in the great gallery—the most magnificent banquet I ever saw. We were all there except four or five. The Duke of Gordon gave the host's health, and said that he hoped he would soon give us the

---

* [Lord Palmerston was Foreign Secretary in this Administration.]

word of command "As you were!" to which the Duke of Wellington, in returning thanks, replied, "No, not as you were, but *much better;*" his meaning evidently being that our late situation was anything but comfortable; the dinner, however, was too fine to be lively.

December 14th.

We live in times when nothing surprises, else the scenes of last week were enough to astonish and alarm. I told you that a fellow, who certainly intended to assassinate the Duke of Wellington, was taken up on the 8th. While the Lords were discussing how he should be disposed of, the Duke stood up and said that he had a matter of much more consequence to notice. He wished to know of the new Ministers why they had suffered the king to be, as it were, besieged in his palace by an illegal assembly—a mob calling itself the Trades of London, many, many thousand strong. Melbourne answered he was aware of it, but thought it would have been imprudent to attempt to intercept them, and Brougham declared (in contradiction to the Duke), that the assembly was perfectly *legal;* upon this the Duke produced an Act directly prohibiting such processions under colour of address or petitions, and Brougham was put to open shame.

They say that there were 6000 or 10,000 men, and they stopped at St. James's till two hours after dark, insisting on seeing the King, and declaring they would not go away till they had. Whether it was the King himself, or (as I believe) Blackwood in his fine groom's coat, who appeared at the window to answer this call, is not certain, but the populace thought it was His Majesty; they gave three cheers, their bands struck up "God save the King," and they marched off in perfect military order.

This matter was noticed some nights after in the House of Commons, with the addition that the *tricoloured* flag had been carried in the procession, and this gave Lord Althorp occasion to pronounce a defence of that fact, and a panegyric on the tricoloured flag, which electrified the House, and has astonished the country.

The Ministers are going to increase the military force. Very right and proper; but it was chiefly their own violent declamations against the existing amount of force which has made this measure necessary. They will be obliged to eat all their pledges and promises in the same way.

During the year, Mr. Croker had occasion to write to a friend in reference to the duty which rested upon a public man of showing fidelity to his principles, and of preserving a consistent course in his policy. There can be no doubt that he attached much greater importance to these virtues than most people did then, or do now; and it was partly in consequence of that fact that he ultimately became estranged from Sir Robert Peel. "I am one of those," he wrote to his acquaintance, "who have always thought that party attachments and consistency are in the *first* class of a statesman's duties, because without them he must be incapable of performing any useful service to his country. I think, moreover, that it is part of our well understood, though unwritten, constitution that a party which aspires to govern this country ought to have *within itself* the means of filling all the offices, and I therefore disapprove of making a *Subscription Ministry*, to which every man may belong, without reference to his understood principles or practices." A memorandum on the same subject was drawn up by Mr. Croker at a previous period, apparently intended to be shown to Lord Goderich. There is, however, no note explanatory of the use which was actually made of it.

Memorandum by Mr. Croker. Extracts.

I will not here recapitulate the extraordinary and blameable lengths to which the Tory Opposition went, or were driven, in the reign of George I. and II., nor revive the obloquy with which they were assailed on their partial accession to power. For the next thirty years the fluctuations were frequent, but even in those days it did not quite pass without observation that the great Lord Chatham who, in the Tory Opposition, called the King's Electoral dominions a millstone round the neck of England, saw reason, when he came into his Majesty's councils, to consider that Hanover ought to be as dear to us as Hampshire. Mr. Charles Fox, a vehement member of the Tory administration, which maintained the right to tax America, was omitted from one of Lord North's treasury patents, and became immediately a vehement Whig, and when, after a change or two, Lord North himself was, on an ebb of the political tide, left on the strand, he rejoined his former friend Mr. Fox, and was as violent as the best, or as you and I would say, as the worst of them.

But these are obsolete instances, and belonged to a period in which the pursuit of place for the sake of place was considered more venial, and political consistency less of a public duty than in our days. Let me, therefore, look to better times and more illustrious examples.

Mr. Burke had attached himself to the Whig party from Whig principles, at a period when the Whigs professed attachment to the constitution as it existed in Church and State. Even in his earliest life, and even in the whirlwind of his opposition, Mr. Burke upheld the monarchical and aristocratical principle of our constitution; but the essential spirit of opposition was so strong that it often repressed or fettered those sentiments, and there was a time when Mr. Burke was as odious to the Tories as a Radical of the present day. But when the French Revolution had brought, not small questions of economy or reform, but the great fundamental principles of our constitutional and national existence into discussion, then Mr. Burke, not forgetting but overlooking and despising all minor topics, stifling all party feelings, severed all private friendships, and ranged himself on the side of the Constitution. This example was followed by the Duke of Portland, Lord Fitzwilliam, Lord Spencer, Mr. Windham; and although I heard and have read much abuse of these illustrious men for their junction with Mr. Pitt, I have never heard that any one ever censured Mr. Pitt (at least nobody of consequence ever did) for accepting their services in that hour of difficulty and danger.

The charge of inconsistency against himself and his friends was answered victoriously, not by denying that he had previously maintained Whig opinions on various subjects, but by asserting that these opinions, founded on principle, belonged to former times and circumstances, that they were not at enmity with the sentiments he had lately avowed, but rather (when well understood) the forerunner of such sentiments; and finally, that when men and measures had all changed around him, when the dangers to the constitution were not only different, but of an absolutely contrary character, it became his duty to fit himself to the new position in which he was placed. Mr. Burke had been an advocate for economical reform; and let me for a moment abandon the course of my argument to do him the justice of saying that in a short interval of power he endeavoured to redeem, and did to a certain degree actually redeem, his pledges to that effect—not by wild and slashing cuts at the Royal prerogative or the national defences, but by a sober and measured legislation propounded to Parliament in the most masterly, most prudent, and most eloquent discourses ever delivered.

Mr. Burke, I say, had been an advocate for *economical reform*, the Whig *cheval de bataille* of that day. He was accused of forgetting that great object in his energy against French principles, and for a vigorous war. Mr. Burke had no need, for the reasons I have just given, to defend himself against this charge, but with that expansive and comprehensive power of intellect which above all statesmen and most writers he possessed, he lays down certain general considerations which apply to the cases, and would justify the conduct of those who had not, as he fortunately had in some degree, the opportunity of redeeming such pledges.

After the authority of Mr. Burke, I shall now quote that which stands in my estimate, and I believe in your Lordship's, next to it—that of Mr. Pitt. But Mr. Pitt's example is even more authoritative on this point than Mr. Burke's, his pledges were more important, more clear of local and temporary limitations and considerations than Mr. Burke's; and although he so long held the helm of power, he not only did not redeem any one of those pledges, but was under heaven the instrument which delayed and defeated the attempts of others to carry them into execution.

Your Lordship is well aware that Mr. Pitt began life in opposition. He found Mr. Burke engaged in the pursuit of economical reform. It is the nature of an Opposition that men are there, as it were, at an auction for popularity; they bid against one another, and the boldest bidder carries off the prize—often worthless—always over-paid! This consideration seems to me to be of great importance with respect to the real character of the measures of Oppositions which are not under the control of some commanding genius. An Opposition as a body can be no wiser than its silliest member, who has always the power either to drag his friends after him, or else to usurp, over their reluctance, an individual popularity; we have seen abundant instances of this in our own days, but more particularly since the removal of Lord Grey to the House of Peers left the Opposition without an acknowledged and authoritative head.

It is not foreign to our subject to observe the converse of this proposition on the other side of the House. No administration is stronger than its weakest member. When a commanding genius like Mr. Pitt is present, his colleagues, however naturally weak or timid, are either emboldened by his courage or silenced by his supremacy. In cabinets of a more equal construction, and in the House in which the First Minister happens not to be, we have seen the scruples—often scruples of vanity or of timidity—of one, otherwise very unimportant, cabinet minister alter the whole course of enterprises of great pith and moment.

From this little digression (which, however, is not one in substance, though it may be in form), let me return to Mr. Pitt. Mr. Pitt, not content with supporting Mr. Burke in his efforts for economical reform, resolved, with the indiscretion of youth and the chartered licence of opposition, to shoot a bolt which should go higher and farther than even the Hibernian enthusiasm of Burke had imagined, and he evoked the spectre of Parliamentary Reform!

The political prescience of the *boy* who chose this theme would be wonderful if we did not recollect that he had but lately lost the advice of that shrewd and wily politician, but that original and daring genius—his father; he was probably the friend of parliamentary reform; he saw in it the seeds of a power over the democracy which would last when "Wilkes and Liberty" should have faded into oblivion; he saw in this question the means of uniting zeal for the rights of the people with apparent adherence to the true principles of the constitution; he was enabled to unite republicans, Dissenters, Jacobites, all those, in short, whose unvarnished hostility would have been treasonable, into a constitutional body, associated only for the restoration of the rights of the nation over its representatives. This mode of proceeding did not attack the Crown directly, nor the Lords; it was only a contest between the Commons and a person falsely styling himself their representative. The losers were not likely to be alarmed; while all the Whigs, or, to use a more popular and a more correct phrase, the ultra-Whigs, were for ever enlisted on the side of a question which included all projects of reforming every subject, and was not to be settled but by the establishment of universal suffrage, and such other concessions to the populace as would have made this country a pure, or, to speak more truly, an impure democracy.

But whether Mr. Pitt pursued this scheme by his father's suggestions or by the indiscreet and *out-bidding* spirit of a tyro at the auction for popularity; it is fortunate that he was soon called to other, and higher and happier, duties.

Can you and I, my dear Lord, or can any Tory bred up as we have been, you at the knees of Gamaliel and I with a distant but undeviating respect—can we say that because, as Lord Orford exclaimed in his rage, that "giddy boy" had juggled with this question of reform, he was therefore to be for ever excluded from the service of the Crown, and forbidden from the exercise of that matured judgment and that improved eloquence which (a providential boon in difficult times) enabled him to preserve the whole constitution from the attacks of his old followers, invigorated, and unimpaired by the friends of the French Revolution? Mr. Pitt's voice was the spear of Ithuriel; it wounded and it healed; but let us not concur in a doctrine which should establish as a maxim that no one who had wounded should ever attempt to heal; that the earliest false step must be persisted in by a succession of crimes to the death of the party and the ruin of the country; that no modification or change of opinion is to be allowed, and that all shall be brought at last to explosive violence, actual revolutions, and the extermination of one half the people—such would be the inevitable result of such a doctrine. I will only here sum up what I have to say to those Tory gentlemen who belong to what are called Pitt Clubs, that the two most formidable objects of their apprehensions, Parliamentary Reform and Catholic Emancipation, were the measures of Mr. Pitt; and if they tell me that he repented him of the first, and consented to postpone the second, I only ask for other noblemen and gentlemen who may have given countenance to these children of Mr. Pitt, that they may be allowed (if desirous of it), without undue prejudice, a similar *locus pœnitentiæ*, and equal allowance of time.

I conclude this theme by saying that if it be once introduced as an admitted principle that no man can take office without stipulating for the success of every question to which he may have given a support, however insolated or transient, and if every man in Government is to be bound to reject all concessions with those in whom he, on any point, has ever differed—I say then that the practical constitution of this country is overthrown; that we should have a few years of an almost despotic government succeeded by an anarchy and God knows what. According to our present practice, opinions are balanced, moderated, conceded; extremes on all sides are abandoned, and cabinets are formed, like all other human institutions, on an *average* of opinions—on those mutual concessions without which neither public nor private, national nor domestic affairs, the relations of husband and wife, parent and child, servant and master, landlord and tenant, could be conducted for a day.

The record of the year 1830 would not be complete without some reference to the death of an old and distinguished friend of Mr. Croker, who died on the 7th of January—Sir Thomas Lawrence. Mr. Croker had always been warmly attached to the great painter, and had rendered him many services, the necessities for which were constantly arising, for Sir Thomas Lawrence was never out of the hands of his creditors. No one could understand how it was that, notwithstanding his large gains, the President of the Royal Academy was invariably without a shilling to call his own. He was always in love and always in debt. He engaged himself to both the daughters of Mrs. Siddons, and they were both said to have died of disappointment—a termination of the story which probably had more of romance in it than of truth. It is indeed certain that he proposed marriage to each of the young ladies, and that each died; but it may well be that, as Allan Cunningham said, they "died much in the usual way, of disease and a doctor." He was afterwards implicated in the scandals which accumulated round the head of the Princess of Wales during her residence at Blackheath. The Committee of Inquiry exonerated him from all blame—perhaps not entirely to his own satisfaction, for apparently he took a pride in the reputation which he had acquired as a rake. With regard to his pecuniary affairs, there could be no room for doubt. In 1825 Mr. Croker had a conversation with the King (George IV.) on the subject. "He talked," Mr. Croker wrote in his diary, "a good deal of Sir Thomas Lawrence, and praised his portraits as to the countenance, but complained of his slovenly draperies and backgrounds, though he often imitated the last from old masters. 'He is a great deal too spotty and fond of colours in ladies' draperies. Cannot think what keeps him so poor. He ought not to be poor. I have paid him 24,000*l.*, and have not got my pictures. The Duke of Wellington is 2800*l.* in advance to him. All the world is ready to employ him at 1000*l.* a picture, yet he never has, as I am told, a farthing.'"

Sir Thomas had painted an excellent portrait of Mr. Croker, and he was still more successful with Miss Croker (Lady Barrow). Of this latter portrait, Allan Cunningham declares that "men stood before it in a half circle, admiring its loveliness, in the Exhibition." It was "all airiness and grace."* Mr. Croker was delighted with the picture, and felt desirous of giving proofs of his high regard for the painter. The following letters seem to show that he was not allowed to seek in vain for opportunities:—

Sir T. Lawrence to Mr. Croker.

December 14th, 1827.

I place reliance on a friendship that has always been zealous for me, and ask that service which is often so dangerous to friendship.

I would not, and will not, receive payment for that effort

---

* It was in the Exhibition of 1827, and Mr. Croker stated that "no portrait of the same size and of the same class ever produced so great an impression." An admirable engraving of it was produced by Samuel Cousins.

which was voluntarily offered by me as a just return for important kindness; but I am unexpectedly in want of that exact sum (150 guineas) to enable me to keep my word with a coarse man, whom I have appointed to-morrow at three o'clock to receive it. This note is written late on Friday evening, and will, of course, not reach you till the morning. If it be convenient to you to send it, I fear I must retain it for some days (possibly one of the latest) in the next month, no longer, not to one day.

My only and last request of this nature is made to you, and no weak pride will diminish my regard for you, though your acquiescence should confer on me an additional obligation. I hope I shall not suffer by it in yours.

Your obliged and faithful servant,
THOS. LAWRENCE.

[Endorsed by Mr. Croker: "Answered 15th, and enclosed a cheque for 150*l*."]

Russell-square, December 17th, 1827.

MY DEAR SIR,

Receive my sincere thanks for that exact, prompt answer, which you had full right to withhold, but which I expected from you.

I have additionally to thank you for an increase in the amount of my nephew's income, for, though the appointment may have been the act of another, the whole originated in your kindness.

Believe me ever, my dear Sir,
Most faithfully yours,
THOS. LAWRENCE.

There are frequent entries in Mr. Croker's books of loans made to the artist; none of any money being returned. There are two letters to Mr. Croker which do not touch upon the President's immediate necessities, and which possess an interest of their own, apart from the fact that they were written within a few months of Sir Thomas's death:—

Sir Thomas Lawrence to Mr. Croker.

Russell-square, May 7th, 1829.

MY DEAR SIR,

I cannot tell you what Sir Joshua's last prices were, because I know not if they were altered from what they were when I first came to town in 1787. As well as I remember (the memory of report only), they were then 200 guineas for the whole length, 100 for the half length, 70 for the kit-kat, and 50 [150 ?] for the three-quarters.

I have given away my catalogue for this year, so that I cannot at the moment send you the number of works exhibited; but it is between 1100 and 1200. In the first year, in 1769, it was 136.

Ever, my dear Sir,
Most faithfully yours,
THOS. LAWRENCE.

Russell-square, May 8th, 1829.

MY DEAR SIR,

Upon an average of the last ten years, the annual receipts of the Exhibition have been 5917*l*. The expenses have generally exceeded 1900*l*., so that the clear income has been about 4000*l*. per annum.

Deducting about one-third of the receipts for catalogues, it would appear that upwards of 70,000 persons visit the Exhibition during the ten weeks in which it is usually kept open.

THOS. LAWRENCE.

Russell-square, July 8th, 1829.

MY DEAR SIR,

It must be my excuse for not sooner answering your letter that I hoped to meet you at the Building Committee to-day.

I confess to you that I would rather you would NOT mention my prices, which, with all the allowance of increase in the value of money and expense of living, would still appear in too great contrast to those of Sir Joshua.

Speaking in entire confidence and sincerity, I think there may be one point in which I excel Sir Joshua, and it is that which has enabled me to be so fortunate in my progress.

I mean the knowledge of those forms and lines which constitute beauty, and in which I consider the power of rendering grandeur to be included. I would instance my Satan, Cato, Hamlet, and my picture of old Mrs. Locke in the present Exhibition as proofs to justify my assertion. The same power enables me to catch the quick, momentary *expression* of beauty (as in the portrait of Miss Croker), and is the cause of my present certainty in producing fidelity of resemblance. This is the *one advantage* that I possess. But then there is a charm in *the general practice* of Sir Joshua, as well as in his finest works, which we painters feel with the most sensitive enjoyment, and which makes comparison with *him* always more repugnant to me than it would be with any other painter. With this genuine and strong feeling, I cannot but deprecate public comparison between the proportionate reward of labours which in themselves are so dissimilar and unequal. Pray, therefore, *determine to omit it.*

Will you forgive me for recurring to another topic, and not think me indelicately pressing on your friendship? Commander of a Pacquet—in-door pensioner of Greenwich. Could one of *these* situations be procured for Captain Pogson? A wound in the head and the general result of severe service have really rendered him unfit for his former career of active employment, and he is obliged to look to humbler sources of profit for the comfort and sustenance of a most estimable wife and infant family.

From peculiar and painful circumstances, the obtaining this is an object of deep—of the deepest interest to me, and to obtain it I hardly know the sacrifice that I would not make.

Ever, my dear Sir,
Your faithful friend and servant,
THOS. LAWRENCE.

Mr. Croker to Lord Hertford.

January 12th, 1830.

Poor Lawrence died of an ossification of the heart. I suspect he was kept poor by great generosity to women. I know two or three to whom he was very liberal. I find that he lived a great deal more at home than I believed. He had *at least* two distinct societies, the individuals of each of which never met the other.

CHAPTER XVI.

1831.

Mr. Croker's Opinions on the Reform Question—In Advance of his Party—His Disbelief in Reform as a "System"—Doubts about Public Opinion—Letters to Lord Hertford—Lord Hertford on Reform—His Distrust of Peel—Peel's Attitude on Reform—An Autograph of Talleyrand's—Sir David Baird and the Duke of Wellington—Rumoured Whig Dissensions — " Everybody distrusts Peel " — The Cry of Retrenchment—Reform Prospects—Lord Althorp's Budget—Growing Importance of Peel—Insult to the King—The First Reform Bill—Anomalies of the Measure—Discouragement of the Anti-Reformers—Letters from Sir R. Peel—Conversations with the Duke of Wellington—The Dissolution—Second Reform Bill—Mr. Croker's Speeches—Rejection of the Bill by the Lords—The Nottingham and Bristol Riots—Third Reform Bill—Literary Projects—Proposed Editions of 'Hume' and 'Pope.'

It has already been shown that Mr. Croker was anxious to have the chief manufacturing towns enfranchised long before the majority of the party with which he acted could be brought to see the necessity of change of any kind in the old theory of representation. On this point he was for many years in advance of his party, just as he had been on the question of Catholic Emancipation. But he could not divest his mind of the fear that the great democratic wave which he saw advancing upon the country between 1829 and 1830 would do infinite harm, and eventually plunge the country in great disasters. He held, with Wellington and Peel, that the existing Constitution had worked well; that it had produced, in the main, a better government than other nations possessed; and that any attempt to reconstruct it throughout would be fraught with peril.*

No doubt he exaggerated the immediate effects which the Bill would produce. He thought that it would forthwith drag the country into the horrors of revolution. It must be borne in mind, however, that much was going on in the world at that time, although we have lost sight of it now, which tended to confirm the most gloomy forebodings. A dynasty had been overturned in France, the Continent generally was in a state of upheaval, and throughout England a spirit of turbulence and lawlessness was manifesting itself, and spreading universal misgivings or actual alarm. We look back from our present point of view, and see that no great or violent convulsion happened; that the world went on after the Bill pretty much as it had gone on before. But men who were passing their lives in the very midst of the turmoil and excitement could scarcely survey the scene with the same coolness. If they lived in towns, their peace was assailed by disorderly mobs and riotous processions; if their homes were in the country, the chances were that in the morning they would find a menacing letter from Captain Swing on the breakfast-table, and that in the evening the sky would be aglow with the light of their burning hay-ricks and corn-stacks. The cheap publications of the day reflected the violent passions which raged on every side, and the language of the popular spokesmen—of "Orator" Hunt, and others—

---

* "During one hundred and fifty years the Constitution in its present form has been in force; and I would ask any man who hears me to declare whether the experience of history has produced any form of government so calculated to promote the happiness and secure the rights and liberties of a free and enlightened people?"—SIR ROBERT PEEL on Reform, March, 1831.

was not calculated to convince calm and reasonable men that there was nothing to fear from the advancing force of democracy.

There was, of course, a large class whose sympathies were entirely with democracy, and who believed that the more the nation had of it, the better would it be. They anticipated without alarm the abolition of all limitations to the suffrage. Mr. Croker never had shared the opinions of this class, and he was not converted to those opinions by the events which ushered in the Reform era. He believed that to transfer power to the hands of the multitude would be to place the ancient institutions of the country in great jeopardy; that landed property would be assailed, the Church overthrown, the monarchy itself undermined. He looked forward, as he wrote to a friend on one occasion,* to a vast subversion, brought about " by a succession of events, each encroaching on the monarchy, till at last all authority, and therefore all security of persons and property, will be lost." It may be that if he were living to-day, he would contend that we are in the middle, not at the end, of the history; that the sequence of events must be watched till its close, before we can assume the right to decide whether or not the forecast of 1831-32 was based upon truth or error.

At the beginning of the struggle, Mr. Croker did not believe that the people at large were at all impatient for Parliamentary Reform; he regarded the agitation as having been artfully fomented by the Whig party. This point he dwelt much upon in his first speech of the Session (March 4, 1831):—

I find that, in the year 1821, 19 petitions only were presented in favour of reform. In the year 1822 the number was reduced to twelve. In the year 1823 the number was

* To Lord Dover, November 7th, 1831.

29. In the year 1824, there was no petition at all. In the year 1825, no petition; in the year 1826, no petition; in the year 1827, no petition; in the year 1828, no petition; in the year 1829, no petition; and even in the session 1830, only 14 petitions presented in favour of reform. Such, then, was the state of the public mind on this subject up to that date.

Then came the late dissolution of Parliament. The noble Lord and his political friends then sat on the side of the House from which I am addressing you, and they went from these seats to the elections, little dreaming that they should so soon change their situation to the other side of the House. They looked about for a political lever to move the Government of the day from its place, and then, from hustings and windows, and their different places of canvass, they instigated the clamours of the people in favour of reform; and the people, as the noble Lord boasts, responded to their call: 650 petitions have been the result of that appeal! Now, I will venture to affirm, that in all—no, I will not say all, for I have not yet looked through those which were presented in a mass on Saturday last—but that in the vast majority of them, the most prominent demand of the petitioners is, as I have just stated, for the abolition of tithes and taxes. The first object of the petitioners is, generally, reduction of taxation; the second is the suppression of tithes; and reform occupies most frequently, only the third place in the prayers of the petitioners.

The same view is expressed in the first letters which he wrote this year.

Mr. Croker to Lord Hertford.

Mistley,* January 3rd, 1831.

My date will tell you that I cannot give you the latest London news, but I believe there is little to tell. I hear that the Cabinet sits four and five hours at a time, and agrees upon nothing. On Reform I know not how they can agree, and all other objects are inconsiderable compared with that. I do not believe that the country is as yet much interested in the question. If the Tories could be united and well led, I think they are strong enough, in the House and in public

* [Mistley Hall, near Manningtree, was at this time occupied by the Speaker. It once belonged to a family named Rigby, and descended by marriage to Lord Rivers.]

opinion too, to defeat *any* plan of reform. Whether they will unite, and how they will be led, is more than I can answer.

The Cabinet has, they say, been feeling the pulse of Burdett and Hobhouse (sage advisers), and that these worthies will be content to have the qualifications for voting raised to 10*l.* Whether as a *general* principle, including freeholders, or limited to householders, my informant did not know, he only knew that a proposition relative to that sum had been well received by Burdett. Their first thought was to disfranchise a number of the smaller boroughs; to that project I fancy they still adhere. But it is more easily said than done, for I should like to know why a place like Dunwich, against which neither bribery nor perjury can be charged, should be disfranchised, while Liverpool, and Newcastle in the Potteries, are to be preserved as samples of purity of election?

The Ministers have committed another blunder, which may be serious in its consequences. They have, by an order of a Committee of Privy Council, without any mention of the King, ordered *a form of prayer* to be used on account of the disturbed state of the country. We can recollect neither precedent nor principle on which a Committee of Council can do such an act, and yet it seems impossible that they can have been such dolts as to do it absolutely without precedent. Now my solution is this, that on the two last occasions on which occasional prayers were ordered, namely on account of the sickness of George III. and George II., *ex necessitate rei*, the Lords of the Council ordered prayers for them, of course without their presence in Council, the malady that kept them from Council being the very evil to be prayed against; and I suspect that in turning back to the books they found these precedents, and did not advert to the difference of the cases.

I have been here these three or four days, no other stranger but Sir William and Lady Elliott (of Stobs). He is a dull and rather oddish sort of man, she a granddaughter of old Boswell, and as zealous a Tory as he was, but withal ladylike and pretty. She and I agree wonderfully, and she entertains me prodigiously with her zeal and her *naïveté*. She, in face and person, is a little like Miss Raikes, but perhaps all this while you know her better than I do. We shoot every day, Sir William, the Speaker, his two sons and I; but it is rather for air and exercise than sport.

Drayton, January 11th.

I am here on a visit to *Peel*. I cannot flatter myself that I have been invited as any great political character, yet I think I see that nothing but politics has brought us here. C. Ross and Clerk were here last week; and Sir G. Murray, Herries and Holmes are coming next week (the house not holding more than three or four at a time), so that it looks very like *planting* a party and building up an opposition, though our host's visible and avowed occupations are planting trees and building a house. I hear less and less every day of the Duke and the House of Commons; men begin to look *exclusively* to Peel. The A's* talk of the Duke as willing, nay anxious, to be again at the *head*; others who are almost as likely to know (H. H.† for instance), seem to think he is *not*, and will, even in the event of a victorious change, only take the H.G. I learn that Bucks, Cottesmore, Belvoir and Althorp are cordial and zealous, and engage that their friends shall attend *constantly* and *closely*— ditto old Pow.‡ (*your* old friend Pow.), ditto Alnwick, and they seem to say that all these incline to look to Peel as *caput*.

We hear that the *reform plan* of the Cabinet is something like this—members to half a dozen great towns; in *all* boroughs and towns, extend or confine (as the case may be) the right of voting to resident householders, and give copyholders votes in the counties. To the first and last I should have no objection at other times and in other circumstances, but it seems to me that any alteration whatsoever at this moment will involve everything, and that there is no safe course but to say—that against a *system* of reform we are pledged and fixed; that any step, however otherwise innocuous or even beneficial, which is part of a *system*, must be opposed as such— *principiis obsta*; and finally that the question is not *reform*, but in fact *revolution*.

I myself have no object. I am perfectly happy and content as I am. I hear that they mean to overhaul the pensions, even those on the Consolidated Fund granted by Act of Parliament. I can hardly suppose it; but you guess what the consequences would be—*n'importe*. Ireland is in a most diabolical state, and Anglesey is the most unpopular Lord

---

* [The Arbuthnots.] † [Doubtless Sir Henry Hardinge.]
‡ [Lord Powis.]

Lieutenant that has ever been there. I gave him five weeks to accomplish that degree of honour, but he has done it in three. Hussey Vivian vacates Windsor to let in Stanley,* and in return is appointed Commander-in-Chief in Ireland. I have no objection to this, for if it comes to blows, as it must, I shall be glad to see a man of decision there.

The reply to this letter shows that Lord Hertford thoroughly distrusted Sir Robert Peel, and that he would have preferred joining Lord Grey to acting with a man whom he regarded as deficient in the first qualities of leadership—firmness and energy. It will also be seen that Lord Hertford's opinions on the great question at issue were not so extreme as those which were entertained by many of his political friends.

Lord Hertford to Mr. Croker.

Naples, January 31st.

DEAR CROKER,

With regard to reform, I agree with you, as I did with Canning, that if it could be resisted *entirely*, it would be the preferable course; but is it not wise also to consider what hope now remains of being able to do so, and whether it is not well to give up a part to save some part? In your letter, which I received long ago, you agreed with what I guessed, as must have guessed every person acquainted with the list of the House, that it was preferred to go out on a point of *form* rather than upon *reform*.

Is not the plain English of it this: that twenty-four hours later the Government expected to be beaten on the question that some reform was expedient, and that you all proposed sliding out on the Civil List, to not being able to support the extent of the Duke's declaration, which is precisely Canning's formerly, and yours now? Then what hope can exist of your being able in February, and in opposition, to do what you could not *in government* do in November?

---

* [Mr. Stanley, the late Lord Derby, then Colonial Secretary, was defeated at Preston on seeking re-election after taking office. He was returned for Windsor.]

My idea on reform is to save as much as may be, and even, if I were in London, and saw an evident desire on the part of Ld. G. [Grey] to throw over his Radicals, I should try to be to him as quinine, to strengthen him to throw off his impurities. To the plan you mentioned, Sir F. B. having agreed to it, of 10*l.* and copyholders, I see no objection. I see none to a few large towns, even if the indefensible boroughs of Gatton, Old Sarum and Midhurst were to be got rid of on Lord John Russell's plan of compensation, *more Hibernico*—the plan of householders only in boroughs could not be acted on, as it would disfranchise the voters by servitude, as in Evesham, Aldborough, &c.

With regard to attendance, to restore *the Duke*, I am willing to ask of my friends any degree of attendance and fatigue, but it must be well understood that it is for the Duke, because I think in these times the worst Tory Government possible would be one under Sir Robert Peel. Without the European consideration of the Duke's name, Peel is at least as unpopular among the Tories. Under him all would be shipwrecked in some sudden typhoon. He has neither the energy of the Duke nor of Lord Grey; he did not reanimate the yeomanry, smothered but not extinguished by Lord Lansdowne; he suffered the army to be frittered down. Lord Grey, much to his praise, is raising both, and I honour him for it. Sir Robert Peel has a taste for reform without measuring his power.

I wish for the Duke's restoration to power, and I then hope he would throw over his lumber, and persuade Lord Grey to throw over his Radicals, and then if he brought together Sir Robert Peel, Fitzgerald, yourself and Hardinge, and Lord Grey and Palmerston, the Grants, &c., we should have what we most want—a strong Government.

In my humble judgment, if we unfortunately lost the Duke by death, or by his choosing to retire, I should prefer a Tory junction with Lord Grey, and saying to him, as *we* agreed together in London, would in such a case be best:—" You are now sure of your power, and no longer obliged to truckle to the Radicals; prove yourself a supporter of our ancient institutions, and of *your order*." I think he would then be a good Tory.

All I wish is to preserve to the King his crown, to myself my coronet and estate, burthened with a large property tax which I should swallow as easily as any of Hawkins's black doses. But I am sure an unremitting opposition, for the purpose of making so weak a government as in these times one would be under Sir Robert Peel, would drive Lord Grey into radical measures and to dissolution, which might now dissolve the country, while a year hence it might be innocuous.

A friend from Barcelona says a great person said confidentially, "These people if out would risk all; in, they will do as little harm as they can, and their measures of strength and security will be supported by *my* late government." This is much my creed; the late Government could (perhaps) not have augmented the army, the yeomanry, or ballotted the militia. What immense advantages may not accrue? If I wore a party button, it should be W. and G.* or G. and W., and if I were umpire I would bid them toss up for Premiership. For their union I hope; in it I see our only hope of security. Which will be wise enough to make the first overture, I know not; perhaps in these days of blindness, neither.

And so I have said my say, which after all is worth nothing, because one cannot tell what may have happened. If the retirement of the Duke occurred, what but revolution could follow so weak a Government as the Tories could form under Sir R. Peel if some chance gave them a momentary majority?

Mr. Croker to Lord Hertford.

January 19th.

The last day I was in the House I had some serious talk with Lord Blandford † in the vote office, and I took leave of him with a "good-bye, *Citizen Churchill*." How men of rank and fortune, and above all, those who have nothing but rank and fortune, can lend themselves to a faction that seeks to annihilate them, passes my comprehension. To do Citizen Churchill justice, however, he seemed to me to be alarmed and inclined to train off.

Lord Lyndhurst has finally accepted C. B.‡ I regret. I

---

* [Wellington and Grey.]

† [The Marquis of Blandford was in favour of Parliamentary Reform, and had brought forward several schemes of his own, among them one for the payment of Members.]

‡ [Chief Baron of the Exchequer.]

liked him as a private companion, and looked to him as of public importance in the other house. All that is over.

Drayton was very agreeable, the host more cordial and communicative than usual. Little shooting, but various and wild. I shot a *bittern*, the only one ever seen in those parts, and one day a couple, and the next day a single wild duck; some partridges and hares, but no pheasants. He [Peel] is going to build a good old English house. They say he has 20,000*l.* a-year in land, and as much in Consols and B. Stock; say 15,000*l.* in each, and it is pretty well. I wanted him to pledge himself, like the Duke, against all Parliamentary Reform, but though he will oppose anything, he will pledge to nothing. He said, good-humouredly, that he was sick with eating pledges, and would take care to avoid them for the future.

January 24th.

Is it not *retribution* that Anglesey, who exhorted the Irish to *agitate—agitate*—should be now prosecuting and persecuting the agitators, and may be, to-morrow, hanging and sabring them? In England several of the militia regiments (amongst others the Warwick) are ordered out for training; and they say that half a dozen will, when trained, be kept on for Irish service.

They talk of the Duke of Northumberland getting Buckingham House in exchange for his; his to be then converted into I know not what public offices. If L. [Lansdowne] does not prevent me (and he is very persuasive), I shall oppose this tooth and nail. B. H. may be good or bad taste, and the exact site may be unlucky, but it is a site fit only for a palace, and it is a farce to think of a royal family's *residing* in St. James's. His Majesty, I am told, finds the Pavilion too small in every way, and is to lay out 100,000*l.* in adding to that overgrown toy a large extent of bedrooms, offices, stables, &c. Nay, I am told, his Majesty has lately expressed some regret that he is too old to begin building at Kew, which is what he would most like.

I go to Strathfieldsaye in a day or two for a week to finish the pheasants, and begin with politics. I must tell you an anecdote of old Talleyrand. Murray wanted an autograph to engrave. S.E. benignantly consented, and taking a *long sheet* of paper, wrote his name. You guess where—at the very extreme top of the page, *so close* that the French lady, who wrote with a feather from the humming-bird's wing, and dried it with the dust of the butterfly's wing, could not have squeezed in an I.O.U.

Mr. Croker to the Duke of Wellington.

January 23rd.

A friend of mine and an admirer of your Grace's * is employed in writing the life of Sir D. Baird, under the direction of Lady Baird. He finds that Sir David made, and her Ladyship makes, a great grievance of his having been superseded by you in the command of Seringapatam, after the capture. He suspects that this was no real grievance, but a *querelle d'Allemand*, and that Baird was relieved in that command at his own request; but as Baird distinguished himself in the taking the place, it looks at first sight hard that he should (after being appointed to the command) have been deprived of it in favour of a junior officer. Could you give me any explanation of this point that would enable our friend to put this matter in a less objectionable view?

The Duke of Wellington to Mr. Croker.

London, January 24th, 1831.

MY DEAR CROKER,

I have received your note, and shall be happy to see you on the day that you have fixed.

I have often heard of Sir D. Baird's dissatisfaction on my appointment to take the command at Seringapatam, when he had commanded the successful storm of the town on which I was not employed, having been appointed to command the reserve in the trenches. Of course I had nothing, I could have nothing, to say to the selection of myself, as I was in the trenches, or rather in the town, when I received the order to take the command of it, and instructions to endeavour to restore order.

Baird was a gallant, hard-headed, lion-hearted officer; but he had no talent, no *tact*; had strong prejudices against

---

* [Theodore Hook. The 'Life' was published in 1832, and Lady Baird presented the author with a diamond snuff-box, which had been the gift of the Pasha of Egypt to her husband.]

the natives; and he was peculiarly disqualified from his manner, habits, &c., and it was supposed his temper, for the management of them. He had been Tippoo's prisoner for years. He had a strong feeling of the bad usage which he had received during his captivity; and it is not impossible that the knowledge of this feeling might have induced Lord Harris, and those who advised his Lordship, to lay him aside.

However, of course I never inquired the reason of his appointment, or of Baird's being laid aside.

There were many other candidates besides Baird and myself, all senior to me, some to Baird. But I must say that I was the *fit person* to be selected. I had commanded the Nizam's army during the campaign, and had given universal satisfaction. I was liked by the natives. It is certainly true that this command afforded me the opportunities for distinction, and thus opened the road to fame which poor Baird always thought was, by the same act, closed upon him. Notwithstandnig this, he and I were always on the best terms, and I don't believe that there was any man who rejoiced more sincerely than he did in my ulterior success.

Believe me, ever yours most sincerely,
WELLINGTON.

Mr. Croker to the Duke of Wellington.

January 25th.

I hear from London that our successors are at loggerheads, not on one, but on every measure; that Althorp insists on the redemption of all pledges, and that it is expected that we shall be sent for (I use the phrase used to me) before the 3rd of February. God forbid! *La poire n'est pas mûre.* Poor Lord Grey is, they say, harassed to death.

I hear also that France is in a very volcanic state. How can it be otherwise? If a palace had been built on the Island Sabrina the day after it was thrown up from the depth of the Atlantic, should we wonder at seeing it cracking —tottering—tumbling?

In England the Whigs erected their administration on three legs—non-intervention, retrenchment, reform; they are, I believe, at this moment as deep in *intervention* as any Government ever was. Instead of retrenching, they have increased all our establishments, and granted some flagrant pensions; and on the only question at all bearing on reform (that of Evesham) they attempted a corrupt job.

Memorandum by Mr. Croker.

Strathfieldsaye, January 28th.

The Duke is in very low spirits about politics. He believes that the King, from pique or fright or folly, will consent to some sweeping measures of reform, and when the Crown joins the mob all balance is lost. I said that surely Lord Grey, who, besides having so recently declared that he would stand by his order, has himself so large a stake in the present system, cannot seriously consent to anything revolutionary. Lord Rosslyn said :—" If that is all your reliance, we are in a bad way, and you know nothing of Grey's character; for with all his high airs he is as timid and irresolute as any man I ever knew, and more under the influence of people about him than you can imagine, and those are the very people who are now for the most violent measures—Lambton, Ellice, and the like. I remember him once infatuated with Wilson,* and thinking him not merely a good active soldier, but one of the ablest men in Europe."

Mr. Croker to Lord Lowther.

January 26th.

DEAR LOWTHER,

Your letters are all my consolation. There is a story of a Frenchman who absented himself from his mistress only for the pleasure of the letters she used to write him; but much as I like your letters, I shall be glad to have some of your company again.

I cannot believe that the Ministers are so utterly discordant as you hear. Depend upon it they will, they must, all concur in Brougham's proposition about *reform*. He goes far enough to satisfy Althorp, and not so far as to frighten Palmerston. I speak advisedly when I say that Palmerston was disposed to go great lengths in that line; so, I believe, is Charles Grant. Who then is to differ? Goderich? Richmond? And if agreed upon *reform*, all the rest is mere

---

* [Sir Robert Wilson.]

questions of establishments and *ways and means* to pay the increased force, upon which the House will probably differ from the Cabinet, but surely not the Cabinet with itself.

Wetherell never can be Chancellor—I say this, *even* though Brougham *is*. If we are to wait for the Ultra-Tories till *that* day, *bon soir la compagnie!*

They tell me from Paris that Lafitte is a bankrupt; but that he will retire with above a million of francs after all is paid; as Burke said of Plunkett, "Pretty well for a failure."

I am astonished at the support which I hear reform is to have. I see even the *Quarterly Review* talks for *moderate reform*. Moderate gunpowder!

To Lord Hertford.

February 1st.

I am just returned through a deep snow from Strathfieldsaye. Our party was the Arbuthnots, Goulburns, Hardinges, male and female, Aberdeen, Ellenborough, Herries, Alava, and, the last day, Rosslyn, Planta, and Black Billy. The *other* leader (Peel) was asked but could not come; *alleging* his wife's illness and business with his architect and gardener. My own private notion is that he would not venture to what would look like a political *re-union*. Every one seems to mistrust him—I do not; but I am convinced that he wishes to stand alone, and that this is the *mot de l'énigme*.

We were very easy and gay, talked eternal politics, but without any precise object, just as we should have done at Sudbourne. There has been a rumour that the host would go to the Horse Guards again; but it is not true; there has not even been a colour for such a report. He indignantly rejects the very idea of such a degradation. A dinner to which he was invited last week at a house in Sussex where you and I used to dine, has given rise to the renewal of this *on dit*. He is very well in health, high in spirit, and very zealous. We shot three days, the two first killed little, though in woods at Silchester which had not been shot for three years. Yesterday, eight guns killed about eighty pheasants. I had intended to have come away on Sunday, but I was actually embargoed by his kindness, and kept till to-day, when I was nearly blocked in by the snow. I was obliged to have four horses from Bagshot to Egham, and then could not get on above five miles an hour; I have not seen so thick a fall of snow for years.

February 8th.

I have been confined to my room ever since my last with a cold which is still very troublesome; and, although a few good-natured fellows look in upon me, they bring me no news, except of that kind which you will have received long ago. The affairs of Belgium are the most important, or at least the most urgent. The election of the Duke of Nemours is a sad affront to our diplomacy, and indeed to our national influence. They tell us that King Philippe will not allow him to accept; that, though it may stave off general hostilities for a season, it would only make the insult to *us* the greater, as it would show that the Belgians were spontaneous, nay zealous, against our interests, even without any instigation from France. Our Ministry professed to be all for non-intervention, retrenchment and reform; now, lo! they have intervened in the most direct way, and not only without success, but with disgrace.

Their retrenchment will be an increase of our military establishments, rendered indispensable by their blundering intervention, and a series of legal jobs and pensions such as James II. would not have ventured on; and, as to *reform*, the only question which touched that point was Evesham, in which they attempted a most corrupt job for Maberley, and Liverpool, where they actually prostituted office to the electioneering objects of Denison.

The Government has determined to let the pensions stand, reducing the amount in future to 75,000*l.*; the senior 75,000*l.* to stand on the Civil List, and to be filled up as they fall in; the juniors to be placed on the consolidated fund, and to die off. Thus the King, who gives up so much in appearance, will really give up much less than you would suppose; for the senior 75,000*l.* will die off very fast, all of which he will be entitled to fill up as they fall. This seems to me fair, for why should pensions granted *only* for the *lives* of George III. or IV., be maintained to the utter exclusion of the exercise of a like power by William IV.? which would be the case if some such arrangement as that proposed be not made.

Our friends are quite triumphant, that on the very point on which we went out the new Government has substantially adopted our course, only that of our ten classes they call the first five Civil List, and the other five Consolidated Fund, but without any alteration (except as to the pensions, and that only in prospect) either in amount or Parliamentary check. Reform stands for the 1st of March. I hear that it is by no means so popular a question as it was, and there are strong hopes that we may beat it. I hope so; if we do not, I am as convinced that a revolution of the widest nature will follow, as I am that the discharge of my gun will follow the pulling the trigger. What damage may be done by the discharge is another matter, and more to be guessed at than calculated. I myself am satisfied that it would end in a republic, and after an agony, more or less bloody, would revert to another restoration.

February 17th.

I am glad to say that common sense seems to be regaining ground, and Parliamentary Reform has within the last fortnight shown symptoms of weakness. The Duke of Wellington was with me the day before yesterday. He thinks that we shall beat Parliamentary Reform on the general grounds. In the meanwhile we hear that your quiet * is *up;* that —— (but I must play *Tacitus*) is very feverish, and that indeed there seems to be a general bubbling of the great caldron. This alarms J[ohn] B[ull], but for that very reason, not *me.* If that worthy takes fright, I shall take courage.

The Ministers opened a budget last Friday that was the first step to confiscation.† In defiance of public faith, for which they did not care, and in the teeth of the Act of Parliament which I believe they had not read, they tried the experiment of a *little* transfer tax, half per cent. on the funds. It raised a tempest; on the Sunday Althorp called all hands on deck at his house to consider what was to be done; ninety or a hundred Whigs attended. Two or three opposed the tax as a violation of faith, and on Monday Althorp came down and *ate* his proposition, and will be obliged to give up, I think, all the rest of his budget. The tax on seaborne coals is gone, a remission chiefly for the benefit of Lords Londonderry and Durham; but how Althorp is to provide for the deficiency I do not see.

* [The quiet state of Europe had been referred to in one of Lord Hertford's letters.]

† [Lord Althorp's Budget provided for the repeal of the duty on seaborne coals and other commodities, and for levying a duty of ten shillings per cent. on the transfer of real or funded property. The scheme provoked great hostility in the City and elsewhere, and was suddenly withdrawn.]

I am still confined with what sounds like the whooping-cough, which I remember you had a few years ago; but I had it when I was ten, and I do not think that this attack is it; but it is very like it. Peel has been twice to see me. So have Goulburn, Herries, Hardinge, &c., but they know nothing of the details of Parliamentary Reform.

February 21st.

There was a meeting at Peel's last Sunday. They, on the whole, incline to allow Parliamentary Reform to make its first appearance without serious resistance. Many will concur to turn it out, who are not ready to shut the door in its face. The Government every day more and more divided and undecided in the House of Commons, Cabinet Ministers pulling different ways.

March 1st.

I write because it is my stated day, and because, though the vital question is to come on to-night, no result can be expected, as we mean to allow the Bill to be brought in. There is great doubt whether it will not be beaten on the second reading. People on both sides give out that *we* shall have a majority of *sixty*; but when I see some of the steadiest old country gentlemen ratting over to Reform, I am alarmed. On the other hand, the Ministry is in itself so damaged that *its* recommendation of the measure is, with a large portion of the public, an additional objection to it. I put my trust in the manifest impossibility of satisfying those who ask for Reform, and the hope that between those whom nothing will satisfy, and us whom anything alarms, the half measure of the Ministers may founder.

I have not been yet out of the house, indeed not out of two rooms; but *coûte que coûte*, and in defiance of conjugal and medical advice, I am going down to raise my broken and ineffectual voice against the Revolution. I never before wished seriously for Parliamentary weight and power.

For the last week every one, Court, City, Ministers, Tories, all agree that the Government holds its seat at the mercy of *Sir Robert Peel*; and there can be no doubt that, if he had a good hand of cards, and would play them out, he would win the game. On the sugar duties, he alone saved the Ministry, and Chandos was at first very angry with him for doing so. But how else could he have acted? Until Reform is disposed of, and until some plan for replacing them be matured, or at least feasible, it would be madness to dislodge the present Ministry.

I am told that in any case I shall have offers. In your absence I shall act to the best of my judgment. I shall put myself into Wellington's hands, and do as he desires. I am by no means anxious for office, indeed just the reverse. I have lowered my scale of expenses, and if I am left as I am, I have nothing to desire, and I feel an inward quiet and satisfaction that I have been for twenty years a stranger to; so that I shall really rejoice if either *no offer*, or Wellington's opinion, should save me from renewed trouble and worry, and allow me, with my friends, my books—

> "Somno et inertibus horis
> Ducere sollicitæ jucunda oblivia vitæ."

W. R. [the King] is not quite well, a little more lethargic; but he has been these some years inclined to doze. He, good easy man, will submit to anything for a quiet life, nay, for a quiet day, though the morrow should look ever so alarming. The King and Queen, I regret to say, were pelted coming home from the play the other night. The Ministers have brought Shiel in to oppose O'Connell; he was intended for *Saltash*, but the Saltashers would not have a Papist, and so Crampton, the new Irish Solicitor, who was to have had Milbourn Port, exchanges with Shiel.

The measure referred to in the last letter was the first Reform Bill of 1831, introduced by Lord John Russell, then Paymaster of the Forces. It proposed to disfranchise sixty small boroughs, and to deprive forty-seven other boroughs of one of their two members; to give forty-two additional members to the metropolis and large towns, fifty-five to the counties, five to Scotland, three to Ireland, and one to Wales. It established a 10*l.* household franchise, under which, it was estimated, upwards of half a million persons would be added to the register. When the list of boroughs with the fatal mark against them was read, there were shouts of laughter, and had a division on the Bill been taken that night, it would probably have been thrown out. This was the general opinion of the time, and it is recorded in the following letter.

Mr. Croker to Lord Hertford.

March 15th.

The first night the proposition was met with shouts of derision, and if we had shortened that preliminary debate and divided, as I thought we should have done, against the introduction of the *principle*, we should, I am confident, have carried its rejection by a considerable majority; but the first symptom of that terror (of which you will, I fear, see but too many subsequent proofs) was that Lord G[ranville] S[omerset] and men of that calibre over-persuaded our leaders that we ought not to venture to oppose so popular a measure *in limine*. After this (which would have been plausible, at least, had the proposal been a half measure) we persevered in the same timid policy, when the scheme was opened upon us in all its violence; and, would you believe it? the same class of men, *now*, give the same kind of reasons why we should pass the second reading, and reserve our opposition for the Committee.

The Bill was full of anomalies, and some of them were brought to the notice of the House by Mr. Croker in his speech of the 4th of March. He said:—

Now, Sir, it appears that, while Calne, with 4612 inhabitants, is to return *two* Members, Bolton, with 22,000 inhabitants, is to return but *one*; while Knaresborough, with 5280 inhabitants, is to nominate *two* Members, Blackburn, with 22,000 inhabitants, is to be limited to *one*; Bedford, with 5466, and Tavistock, with 5482 inhabitants, are still to be favoured with the *double* representation; while Tynemouth and Brighthelmstone, with each above 24,000, are to be put off with *one*. Thus, to recapitulate, four small and now close boroughs, and which in the new system may become still closer, containing about 20,000 inhabitants, are to have the undiminished number of eight Members; while four great cities, I may call them, containing 94,000 inhabitants, are to be insultingly restricted to four representatives.

But let us give the noble Lord the full advantage of the

largest and most comprehensive view of his plan—what is the result?—eighteen of the old boroughs which his arbitrary line includes, containing about 80,000 inhabitants, will send thirty-six Members to this House; while eighteen new boroughs, with a population of about 280,000, are to have barely eighteen representatives: in the former case, one representative for every 2300 souls; in the latter, one for every 16,500.

This speech, and others which followed it, made a great impression at the time, and certainly tended to convince the House that the Bill as it stood ought not to pass. It will be remembered that in the month of April the Ministers were defeated by a sort of side blow, and that a dissolution followed. A House of Commons was then returned which was disposed to insist on much more sweeping measures of Reform than either party had ever contemplated. The calculations of Mr. Croker and most of his political friends were thrown into chaos. But they still entertained some hopes of controlling the Reform movement, even if they could not altogether turn it aside.

The Duke of Wellington to Mr. Croker.

London, March 16th, 1831.

MY DEAR CROKER,

I had read the Report of your speech in the newspapers; and I read it again last night with great satisfaction.

It is a most able view of the plan of Reform; and dissects admirably some parts of the measure.

We have still much to do, however, to expose it to the public as it ought to be exposed. I dislike it on account of its false pretences more than even for its internal faults.

I am very sorry that you still suffer. There is nothing like change of air for such a cold as yours has been.

Believe me, ever yours most sincerely,

WELLINGTON.

Mr. Croker to Lord Hertford.

London, March 22nd.

A week ago we reckoned a majority of 40, say 285 to 245. Twenty defections brought these numbers to a level, and two or three absentees will, I now fear, throw the majority the other way. The Government are moving *hell and earth*. They have been tampering even with the *little* household officers. Mark, of the Lord Chamberlain's office, was sent to Seymour, Henry Meynell and others to say that they must vote with Ministers or resign. They consulted a friend at H. P. C. (Duke of Wellington), who advised them not to resign. The great Duke of Devon himself then sent for them, and told them that they must either resign or vote. They answered that "they would do neither," so that they must dismiss them.

The Duke of Gloucester is against the Bill, and so is, I understand, everything royal, except the Duke of Sussex, whose influence with the King is very great just now. He and Herbert Taylor support the Ministers. The King's letter, of which so much has been said, was written by Henry Taylor, who is supposed to be quite a Whig.

The day after I spoke, I had what I have not had for two years, a command to dinner and much civility; but all this is of no avail. He that should feel most, feels nothing, or at least, shows nothing. He had a good opportunity last week of saving himself and his people from this frightful combination, but there was no old *Marquis of Buckingham* (vide 1783) to suggest it.

The Ministers after some infamous shuffling were beaten on Friday on the timber duties—236 to 190. Here was a fine occasion to have got rid of them, but it was missed, and they hope to cover all minor defeats in the great triumph of Parliamentary Reform. God knows I am in no degree personally interested in wishing them out; for my own private resolution (subject always of course to the wishes of the friends I love and respect) is never to be in public office again. Except for this fatal Bill, I never was so happy as I now am, and have no desire to change domestic peace for official turmoil.

Peel comes to me very often and kindly. He is sore perplexed. I suppose his conscience tells him that he is the primary cause of all the mischief. I learn that Ministers consulted Anglesey as to a dissolution; he replied that it would throw Ireland into anarchy, and that, with the new writs, they must send him 20,000 men. This staggered them; and they begged him to withdraw that letter. He answered that he could not, for that every hour increased his original conviction. They have therefore, in two Cabinets held Saturday and Sunday, determined *not* to dissolve till the last extremity. They realise the old Greek superstition that the deadliest poison in nature is contained in the hoof of an ass. Except in the matter of Parliamentary Reform, they are the weakest, most ridiculed, most despised Ministry that ever was in England.

March 29th.

Have I ever told you that the Duke of Gloucester has left the Whigs on the Reform question, and thought it his duty to remonstrate with His Majesty on the danger to the Crown? They *attribute* to H.R.H. a good thing. He is reported to have told the King that the result of the measures must be to deprive him of the Crown; and on the King's saying pettishly, "Very well, very well," the other added, "But, sir, your Majesty's head may be in it."

To Sir Walter Scott.

April 5th.

I say nothing about the revolutionary Reform, but I think of nothing else. If it be carried, England, no doubt, may be still great and happy; but it will be under a *different* form of constitution and administration from that which has raised her to her present greatness and happiness. No King, no Lords, no inequalities in the social system; all will be levelled to the plane of the petty shopkeepers and small farmers; this, perhaps, not without bloodshed, but certainly by confiscations and persecutions. 'Tis inevitable, and this is to be perpetrated by a set of men like Lambton and Johnny Russell, whom a club in Regent Street would not trust with the management of their concerns.

To Sir Robert Peel.

April 12th.

DEAR PEEL,

I have always thought that if we once get into the Committee, numbers being so close, Ministers will be ready

enough to make small sacrifices to secure their great system—
a system which every day and hour the more persuades me
will end, even perhaps in our own short time, the monarchy of
England; but before they get to the Committee there is a
question of the Speaker's leaving the chair. It was in that
stage that, I think, some former Reform Bill was strangled—
one of Mr. Burke's, I believe. Why should we not try to
bring our 301 to the post again on that general question? If
Holmes thinks well of it, I am sure that it would be in other
respects better than reserving our varieties of impotence for
the Committee; but as this is a question of *numbers*, I cannot
see how any of the 301 can go off on this, and I think some
of the 302 would be glad to stay away; but, after all, Holmes
must be here the judge.

Sir Robert Peel to Mr. Croker.

April 15th, 1831.

MY DEAR CROKER,

I discussed the point you mention with Holmes. He is
very fearful of the result.

If we go into the Committee with a minority of 20 or 30,
instead of a minority of *one*, we shall have the appearance of
an ebbing tide.

Our object must be an early majority if possible. I
prevailed on His Majesty's Ministers last night to promise
positively to treat us to a division on this simple question:
"While the number of Irish and of Scotch Members is
increased, shall the number of English Members be reduced
to the extent of 30 or 40?"

I think we shall beat them on that question. We must
have a meeting in the course of Sunday, I think. Give us
another month and there is an end of the Bill, positively an
end to it. It never could be carried except by the dread of
physical force. One sentence of a speech of Hunt is pregnant
with a most important truth. He said the night before last
in substance, "Physical force is fast awakening from its
dream. It finds that it is to be disfranchised, and it desires
that if there is to be exclusive privilege, that privilege may
be exercised by the upper classes of society, and not by the
vulgar 10*l.* householder class—the class just above physical
force, which has no quality attracting respect, whose arro-

gance is at all times intolerable to those immediately below it, and will become ten times more so, when it is inflamed by the possession of a novel and exclusive privilege."

This is the fatal error of the scheme. One month hence, if the Bill is still in suspense, there will be an enforced natural union between aristocracy and disfranchised population—against a vulgar privileged " Pedlary," as in a letter I have this morning received, a farmer, trembling for the fate of the Corn Laws, calls the new voters.

Ever yours,
ROBERT PEEL.

Mr. Croker to Lord Hertford. Extract.

April 19th.

I cannot doubt, therefore, that even if Gascoyne's motion * be carried, the Ministers will still persevere, and will be all the better for it; for they will have thirty-one bank-notes (as Lord Carnarvon pithily said in your house) to buy votes with; and, indeed, why should they abandon the Bill on the motion of *one* who, like Gascoyne, professes himself to be a friend to some *parts* of it. Depend upon it the real cause of the success of this fearful measure is that our leader neither has, nor *chooses to have*, the command of his army.

I hear the Ultra-Tories had a meeting on Sunday in which the majority objected to enlisting under our leader, who seems *as* little desirous of having them as followers; but with forces so divided, and, I will say, hostile to each other, how can we hope for victory? I, in my heart, believe that the old Homeric cause of the woes of the Greeks may be applied to our state from the $M\hat{\eta}\nu\iota\varsigma\ \Pi\eta\lambda\eta\iota\acute{a}\delta\epsilon\omega$ down to $\delta\iota\alpha\sigma\tau\acute{\eta}\tau\eta\nu$ $\mathrm{'}A\tau\rho\epsilon\acute{\iota}\delta\eta\varsigma\ \ddot{a}\nu a\xi\ \dot{a}\nu\delta\rho\hat{\omega}\nu,\ \kappa a\grave{\iota}\ \delta\hat{\iota}o\varsigma\ \mathrm{'}A\chi\iota\lambda\lambda\epsilon\acute{\iota}\varsigma$.

W. R. is not so far gone as he appears to be. Lord Grey asked him whether he might threaten a dissolution if Parliamentary Reform should fail. The answer was " No," and the Gaffer has been obliged to unsay what his followers had said on this subject. W. R. complained also that the ministerial press, and *nommément* the *Times*, had attacked the Queen,

---

* [The motion of General Gascoyne, on which Ministers were defeated, namely, that the number of Members for England and Wales should not be diminished.]

and desired it might be stopped. The very next day the *Times* spared the Queen indeed, but attacked the King.

The King had a great dinner of the 1st Guards yesterday. The Duke of Wellington was there, and sat next W. R., who was exceedingly civil, and talked to him with the greatest apparent openness and affection upon every subject in the world, except only domestic affairs. At the Opera on Tuesday night it was observed that neither the King nor Queen spoke to the Duke of Devon, who stood like a post behind them, but that they both appeared to chat familiarly with Lord Howe; some persons fancy that there was a spice of politics in this. Poor Wilson* has been assailed by his constituents, who call upon him to resign his seat, and call him rat, apostate, &c. If there be a dissolution, he will hardly find his way back. Lowther is just come in, who says that the King will neither accept the resignation of Ministers nor allow them to dissolve, but urges them to go on with the Bill.

Sir Robert Peel to Mr. Croker.

Drayton Manor, Fazeley, May 28th, 1831.

MY DEAR CROKER,

I left London early on Friday morning (the day after Cobbett's affair), and therefore know nothing that has passed since in London. I have been engaged much more agreeably here with Smirke.

I see that the *Standard* takes the same line that, I presume from your letter,† the *Albion* does. The *Standard*, or rather the people that write for the *Standard* and support it by their purse, insinuate that I am desirous of office, and ready to join *O'Connell in office*. God help him! The real ground of hostility is just the reverse; that I detest the thought of office, and am *not* ready to join O'Connell in effecting my return to it.

If the Tory party is gone to pieces, I doubt whether the new Parliament is to blame for the "Labefactation," as Dr. Johnson has it. I apprehend there are two parties among those who call themselves Conservatives—one which

---

* [Sir R. Wilson, subsequently defeated at Southwark, through supporting General Gascoyne's motion.]

† [The letter here referred to is not among Mr. Croker's correspondence.]

views the state of the country with great alarm; which sees a relaxation of all authority, an impatience of all that restraint which is indispensable to the existence, not of this or that, but of all Government; which is ready to support monarchy, property, and public faith, whenever and although the Ministers may be their confederates. There is another party, and that by far the most numerous, which has the most presumptuous confidence in its own fitness for administering public affairs (a confidence hardly justified by any public proof of capacity for the task); which would unite with O'Connell in resisting the Irish Coercion Law; which sees great advantage in a deficit of many millions, and thinks the imposition of a Property Tax on Ireland and the aristocracy a Conservative measure; decries the intemperance of the police; thinks it treachery to attack a Radical, or rather to defend yourself against a Radical, provided that Radical hates the Government; and which, never having yet dreamt of the question how they could restore order, prefers chaos to the maintenance of the present Government.

Now to this latter section I do not, and will not belong. I will not play that game, which, played by the Ultra-Tories against us, is the main cause of present evils.

A Radical and a Republican avowed are dangerous characters; but there is nothing half so dangerous as the man who pretends to be a Conservative, but is ready to be anything, provided only he can create confusion.

Is it not strange that men will not see so far (no very great distance) as the answer to these two questions? How are thirty offices to be vacated, filled with efficient holders, and the return of those holders secured? If this cannot be done, what will happen?

Ever affectionately yours,
ROBERT PEEL.

Memoranda of Conversations with the Duke of Wellington, in May and September, 1831.

The Duke.—"When I was ambassador in Paris after Waterloo, the French had a mind to pick a quarrel with me, right or wrong. Lord Wellesley had obtained as augmentation to his arms a lion or leopard bearing a tricoloured flag. So the

Demisoldes sent round a report that I had on my ambassadorial state coach an insulting representation of the British lion trampling on the French national colour. This was reported to me, and so seriously that I exhibited my coach panels to whoever chose to see them, to show that there was no pretence for this lie; but, unluckily, in the Duchess's arms, which were placed by the side of mine on the coach, there happened to *be an eagle*, and this then became a topic of offence, and my coach was in danger of being torn to pieces. It was not worth while to make a serious matter on my part of so ridiculous though malicious a misrepresentation, and I accordingly had the Duchess's arms omitted from the coach, and the affair was soon forgotten."

Walmer, May 24*th.*—This morning before 7 A.M. a courier arrived with a despatch for the Duke. This was soon known through the House, and when I came to breakfast Cooke, Alava, and Lord Douro all began to question me about it, as if I was likely to know. I had not heard of it, but after breakfast I saw by Arbuthnot's manner that something unusual had occurred, and both Lord Douro and General Alava were exceedingly curious to know what it could be. I myself did not feel the same curiosity about the matter, but, while we were amusing ourselves with all manner of guesses, the Duke sent for me into his room to tell me *sub sigillo* that the messenger had brought him a letter from Lord Howe,* soliciting (by the King's own command) his Grace's advice about a very impertinent paragraph in the *Times*, as to a letter written by Sir H. Taylor, by the King's order, to Lord Howe "to rebuke him for chattering," says the paragraph, "about the Reform Bill." There *was* a letter written by Sir H. T. in the King's name to Lord Howe to request him to regulate his opposition to the Bill, so as not to compromise the King or Queen; but this letter was known only to the King, Taylor, Lord Grey, and (of course when it reached him at Gopsal on Saturday) Lord Howe himself. As the paragraph appeared in Monday's *Times*, it was clear that Lord Grey must have communicated the information to the *Times*, or to some one who had communicated it to the *Times*. Lord H., who meanwhile had come back to town, hurried to the King and complained that what was, he thought, known only to

* [Lord Howe's letter, and the Duke's reply, are given in the 'Wellington Despatches,' New Series, vii. 443.]

the King and himself should be thus made known to and perverted by the editor of a newspaper, and his first movement was to resign his office on the spot. This exhibition of Lord Grey's indiscretion and his connection with the *Times* (which has been extraordinarily violent and offensive) produced a great effect on the King, who *wept* at the situation in which he found he was placed, and entreated Lord Howe not to resign nor to take any step in this embarrassing and extraordinary affair *till he had consulted the Duke of Wellington,* and this was the occasion of the messenger. The Duke answered him in an excellent letter (such as, agreeably to a suggestion of Lord Howe's, might be shown to the King), in which, after expressing his regret at this new sign of the connexion of the Ministers with the revolutionary press, and their disregard, not only of all delicacy, but of their duty towards the King, he advises him not to resign, which is, perhaps, the object of the informant of the *Times,* but to leave it to His Majesty's own discretion and sense of his dignity to vindicate himself from a continuance of such proceedings. The letter is long and calculated to open the King's eyes to the alarming signs of the times, even if, as may be gathered from Lord Howe's letter, His Majesty were not already alarmed on the subject.

I told the Duke in return that I had heard before I left town that Lord Howe was *en butte* to the Ministers, and that there would very soon be a trial of strength on the part of Ministers to get rid of him; that I had been informed that the Queen had told the King that she was well aware of the intrigues of his Ministers to get rid of Lord Howe; that she at least never could consent to part with him on such grounds as they alleged; that, if His Majesty pleased to dismiss him, she, of course, would submit, but in that case she hoped His Majesty would allow her to do without a Chamberlain altogether, which in these times of economy, would hardly be objected to by the Ministers, if she had no objection. I told the Duke that I had heard all this ten days ago, with the intimation that Lord Howe would be the pivot on which the fate of the Ministry would turn as far as Windsor was concerned.

The Duke was very much struck by the circumstance of the King's advising Lord Howe to consult *him*, and he made a forcible use of this topic in his answer to Lord Howe, as showing the King's false position when he was obliged to seek council against his Ministers from their political antagonists.*

Alava told us one morning at breakfast (the Duke being present and listening to the whole story as quietly as if it related to another person) of a very different kind of breakfast which the Duke and he had had the morning of the battle of Salamanca. The Duke had been very busy all the morning, and had not thought of breakfast, and the staff had grown very hungry; at last, however, there was a pause (I think he said about two) near a farmyard surrounded by a wall, where a kind of breakfast was spread on the ground, and the staff alighted and fell to; while they were eating, the Duke rode into the enclosure; he refused to alight, and advised them to make haste; he seemed anxious and on the look-out. At last they persuaded him to take a bit of bread and the leg of a cold roast fowl, which he was eating without knife from his fingers, when suddenly they saw him throw the leg of the fowl far away over his shoulder, and gallop out of the yard, calling to them to follow him. The fact is, he had been waiting to have the French *sighted* at a certain gap in the hills, and that was to be the signal of a long-meditated and long-suspended attack. "I knew," says Alava, with grave drollery, "that something *very serious* was about to happen when *an article so precious as the leg of a roast fowl was thus thrown away.*" Alava had told this story in all its little circumstantial details, and with all his usual liveliness and action, and he really brought round the catastrophe very dramatically and to our great amusement, while the Duke sat by with his head inclined, quite silent, but with a quiet smile which seemed to say that the narration was a good deal pleasanter than the reality had been.

Walmer, May 25th, 1831.—"To show you to what a state of terror Buonaparte had reduced all Europe, when I was in Zealand, and after I had won the little battle at Kioge, there was a Danish gentleman—one, indeed, I believe of the Ministers, or who had been in office—a Count Rosencrantz, who had a country house in that neighbourhood. I met him by accident one day, and when he told me his name I almost felt that he was an old acquaintance, and might have asked him for our old friend Guildenstern; but, seriously, I found

---

* [There is no allusion to this in the Duke's letter, but there is in Lord Howe's reply.]

him a well-bred and very sensible man; and, as we seemed mutually pleased with our conversation, we walked together in a wood for above two hours, talking of the state of Europe. When we were about to part, I told him that I would not ask him to dine with me, as I was in a wretched inn with no household nor any means of giving him a dinner; but that, if he would allow me, I should go and dine with him. He said no; he had rather be excused. Even this accidental walk in a wood might perhaps, he said, be reported at Paris with its exact duration, and he would be called upon to report every word of it, or at least as much as he pleased of it and as would *fill up the time,* and that, if he were to receive me at dinner, the consequences might be serious. He added that he would call and pay me a visit of ceremony, and that when I came to return that visit he would take care to be in the way, and we then might have another conversation, but that anything like an intimacy would compromise both himself and his sovereign; and he therefore begged of me as a private favour to avoid any appearance of it.

"When I was about to attack Kioge, which had a ditch and wall, and might have given me trouble, I detached—what was his name?—Linsingen with a couple of regiments of German cavalry to pass the river by a ford some way on my right to turn the town and alarm the enemy from his communications, and so force my attack; but he was afraid of risking his cavalry, and remained on the bank of the river, and, though I repeated the orders by several messengers, he could not be got to move. If he had done so, the thing would have given no trouble; but he was afraid. However, we took the place, for the Danes made but a poor resistance; indeed, I believe they were only new raised men—militia."

He then gave us an account of the battles of Roliça and Vimiera, and defended the Convention of Cintra as being at the time a prudent and advantageous result of his two victories. Not that he defended all the details, and two or three unlucky expressions, but the substance and spirit were right. "The French had not only the capital, but they had Badajoz, Elvas, Almeida, and Santarem—all places that would have required sieges, as also Peniche and the forts St. Julien and Cascaes, without the possession of which our ships could not enter the Tagus; the season of bad weather was fast approaching, and these places must have been regularly invested; and, on the whole, the entire evacuation of the forts, the strong places, the capital, and the kingdom was all that the most sanguine could have desired; and I am disinterested in giving this opinion, for *I* had nothing whatsoever to do with the terms of the Convention. I had signed the armistice indeed, but had no more to do with the Convention than any other general officer in the army. When I heard what was going on, I took the liberty to advise against one or two points, particularly the allowing the French to make stipulations for the Russian fleet, and doing so without consulting our admiral; but I found that my superiors disregarded my advice, and so I had no more to say.

"The French came on at Vimiera with more confidence, and seemed to *feel their way* less than [smiling] I always found them to do *afterwards*. They came on in their usual way, in a very heavy column, and I received them in line, which they were not accustomed to, and we repulsed them there several times, and at last they went off beaten on all points, while I had half the army untouched and ready to pursue; but Sir H. Burrard—who had joined the army in about the middle of the battle, but seeing all doing so well, had desired me to continue in the command now that he considered the battle as won, though I thought it but half done—resolved to push it no further. I begged very hard that he would go on, but he said enough had been done. Indeed, if he had come earlier, the battle would not have taken place at all, for when I waited on him on board the frigate in the bay the evening before, he desired me to suspend all operations, and said he would do nothing till he had collected all the force which he knew to be on the way. He had heard of Moore's arrival, but the French luckily resolving to attack us, led to a different result. I came from the frigate about nine at night, and went to my own quarters with the army, which, from the nearness of the enemy, I naturally kept on the alert. In the dead of the night a fellow came in—a German sergeant, or quartermaster—in a great fright—so great that his hair seemed actually to stand on end—who told me that the enemy was advancing rapidly, and would be soon on us. I immediately sent round to the generals to order them to get the troops under arms, and soon after the dawn of day we were vigorously attacked. The enemy were first met by the (50th?), not a good-looking regiment, but devilish steady, who received them admirably, and brought them to a full stop immediately, and soon drove them back; they then tried two other attacks, as I told you, one very serious, through a valley on our left; but they were defeated everywhere, and completely repulsed, and in full retreat by noon, so that we had time enough to have *finished them* if I could have persuaded Sir H. Burrard to go on."

[N.B.—In speaking of Sir H. Dalrymple and Sir H. Burrard, the Duke always called them the *Gentlemen.* "The *Gentlemen* lately arrived"; "the Gentlemen who were discussing the matter"; "the Gentlemen who thought enough had been done."]

"Sir B. Spencer gave evidence before the Court of Inquiry, that he had seen a reserve of French strongly posted on the heights of Torres Vedras, so I said to him, 'Why, Spencer, I never heard of this reserve before. How is it that you only mention it now?' 'Oh,' said he, 'poor Burrard has so large a family!' I had no desire to give pain or trouble either to Burrard or Spencer, who was a very odd sort of man, and I did not urge any questions on this point before the Court.

"Spencer was exceedingly puzzle-headed, but very formal; he one day came to me, and very slowly said, 'Sir, I have the honour of reporting that the enemy has evacuated Castello Bono.' It was not Castello Bono, but [Carpio], as, indeed, we could all see, and his aide-de-camp whispered him the right word, upon which Spencer began again as slowly and solemnly as before, 'Sir, I have—the—honour—to report,' &c., ending once more with '*Castello Bono,*' and, though he made three several attempts, he never could get rid of *Castello Bono.* He would talk of the Thames for the Tagus, and so on, eh, Cooke?" *Cooke:* "Yes, sir; it was to me he talked of the Thames. He told me one day to get my horse and just trot down to the Thames, and see what they were doing there! I told him that I wished with all my heart I could."

Mr. Gleig mentioned "*Buonaparte's plans of campaign.*" " Pooh!" said the Duke, " he had no general preconceived plan of a campaign, as indeed he owned. In one of his campaigns (that of 1809), General Wrede, the Bavarian, commanded the army which Buonaparte was assembling until his arrival. When he came, Wrede expressed a hope that the measures he had taken might be found to fall in with His Imperial Majesty's plan of campaign. B. immediately said that he never had a general plan of campaign; that he collected his forces together as well as he could, and then acted *pro re nata* as he thought best, adding that Wrede had done exactly what he could have wished by concentrating the army as much as possible, and handing it over to him to be employed according to the circumstances of the moment. This," said the Duke, "I had from Wrede himself."

May 26th.—[Here, unluckily, my note was somehow interrupted.]

Walmer, Sept. 21st.—We found the Duke with only Cooke, whom his Grace had asked to meet me, but he had come down on Thursday.

I find the Duke well in health and I may say in *spirits*, though he is very grave. Some of this seriousness, which is remarkable, is no doubt attributable to the death of the Duchess; but it is also considerably increased by, and deducible from, his anxiety about public affairs. He looks upon the result of the general election as decisive in favour of the Ministers' Reform Bill, and in that Bill he sees, as I have always done, nothing but revolution. His opinion is that the Bill may be considered as passed, and that the revolution has already begun its march, and will be accomplished, whether a little sooner or later, without violence or bloodshed, unless, indeed, there happen to be one or two assassinations, as of himself or Peel, which he thinks not improbable. He tells me that he had a few days ago a letter from a man who gave a name and date, apprising him that it was intended on the meeting of Parliament to attempt to shoot him from a crowd which would be assembled in Palace Yard. This letter he thought it right to send to Sir Richard Birnie, who had that very day returned a very flippant answer, making light, or rather, nothing of the matter, and saying that, if anything were intended, the Duke would not have been forewarned. The Duke answered him gravely that he must know that the last observation was not correct; that Cato Street and the intended proceedings on Lord Mayor's Day had (as well as some other attempts) been made known by anonymous information; but, at all events, that as the man gave a name, *Will. Sidmouth*, and a date, *Cheapside*, Sir Richard should have at least inquired whether there was any such person before he had sent such an offhand answer. This letter he wrote on Wednesday, and has not yet had an answer. He went on, in reference to the revolutionary aspect and prospect of the times, to say that, in the general state of disorganization and contempt of all authority which the Ministers had excited and kept up to secure their party triumph, there was no doubt a danger that they might be suddenly overborne by the irregular power they had called into action; but the great body of the nation was sound enough, he thought, to prevent any immediate violence. As the revolutionists are now all with the Ministry and enjoying a common triumph, I think this ferment will pass away; but its effects will remain, and grow gradually and quietly more and more destructive of our old constitution. First, all reverence for old authorities, even for the House of Commons itself, has received an irrecoverable shock, and then the composition of the new House of Commons, which will only change to become worse, will render government by royal authority impracticable. So it will go down step by step, quicker or faster, as temporary circumstances may direct, but the result will be that at last we shall have a revolution gradually accomplished *by due form of law!*

Lord Hertford to Mr. Croker. Extract.

April 8th.

DEAR CROKER,

Now to answer your question. I have always liked in the general sense of public advantage, and disliked in the sense of personal disadvantage, the Income Tax. But I would not confide such a tax to a government which I opposed. My notion of it has always been that it might remedy the great error of the Resumption of Cash Payments Bill, by being so arranged as to give incomes derived from land, professions, and trades, many deductions and allowances, and fall on funded and fixed money incomes with such force as a little to rectify this old error. But I must have real confidence in a government to entrust it with this screw, which, by turning a little more or less, squeezes sometimes 5, sometimes 10 or more per cent. A property tax, valuing what you possess like the Legacy Tax, is a detestable mode of raising money, and purely revolutionary, for the collector could walk into Sir R. Peel's house and ask him to pay a percentage on the pictures with which he has adorned the country, and into Lord Londonderry's and ask for one on the diamonds with which he has enriched it.

Lord Hertford to Mr. Croker.

Milan, May 15th.

DEAR CROKER,

I was entirely prepared for the bad news, from never having expected any other from the moment the passions of the people were supported by the K. and inflamed by his Ministers. I well remember how difficult it was for George III. and Mr. Pitt to stem the revolutionary torrent; had either given way, our revolution would have run as many races, and rung as many changes, as the French. I regretted the Duke's sweeping denial of all change, not as bad in itself, but as unwise and unnecessary, as it did not even secure the rejunction of the Tories, as was declared by the Lord of Scone before I left London. Perhaps they are sorry now, when it is too late. You blamed my regretting the D.'s speech. Was I wrong? I am glad Aldborough and Orford * die quietly in their beds, and with their old bedfellows, and am grateful for the trouble you have taken about them. I should have liked to see you regain the Dublin College, and was sorry you did not make the attempt. The newspapers talked of the D. of Northumberland and his county, and of others subscribing 20 and 30,000; these matters I felt were too late, even before I received your letter or met Lord Mulgrave at the Opera, *rayonnant*. The Duke had incapacitated himself from leading a moderate reform, and I fancy very few felt entire devotion to any other Tory chieftain. And so we fall. From the moment the K. and his Government adopted the Radical scheme, resistance might be creditable, but must be useless.

When we meet we will talk of Orford. I thought the united parishes would have much exceeded what you mention; if they did, however, I should have no hope, as justice could not be expected, even if Aldborough passed Calne or Tavistock by a thousand.

I have nothing local to tell you. The country is quiet and happy, and in the Roman states, all bless the Austrians for saving them from murder and pillage; for there revolution begins and continues by such brave acts; and even now, if an Austrian soldier falls asleep, somebody sticks a knife in his back, and if he awakes, a dozen run away; this happened at

---

* [These pocket boroughs of Lord Hertford's were to be disfranchised.]

Bologna while I was there. Thirty scoundrels made the revolution and formed themselves into a government one day; the next day, eight were frightened, and betrayed the remaining twenty-two. But we are negotiating amnesties and favours for these people.

I have proposed to the Pope to take an Irish brigade from the starving Catholics of the West of Ireland, and to send the Monks of St. Patrick, whose shamrock I sent you two years ago, to beat up for recruits. I proposed it to the Cardinal Legate in conversation; I find it is now seriously thought of.

The new Parliament met in June, and everybody must, by that time, have seen that the battle of Reform was practically over. The popular demand for the Bill had increased to such a point that there could no longer be any reason for supposing that the people were apathetic with regard to it; and the Government was armed with a majority in the Lower House against which it was useless to contend. Yet the Opposition by no means relaxed its efforts, and there were many of its members who did not despair of final success. The second Bill, which varied in no essential particular from the first, was introduced, again by Lord John Russell, on the 24th of June. It remained in Committee until the first week in September. Mr. Croker spoke on several occasions, and always with effect. Sir Robert Peel referred to one of his speeches as "unanswerable and matchless," and similar tributes of praise came from many other quarters.

The Earl of Elgin to Mr. Croker.

Leamington, July 15th.

MY DEAR SIR,

I am extremely sorry that during the few days I could stay in London, I could only have one passing shake of your hand, and no other opportunity of seeing you than that in the House of Commons. From no speeches during the progress of the Reform Bill has more satisfaction been felt by those who are well-wishers to their country and the Constitution than from yours. The analyses you have presented of its main bearings have been distinctly appreciated; and from the reasoning, with all your powers, on the clear data which your industry disclosed, the character and tendency of the measure has been much better understood, and its dangers and shameful partialities more generally felt. With these impressions, and the most anxious apprehensions from the intentions of Ministers, I greatly regret that it was not in my power to see you in town; and though I have no wish to involve you in discussions with me on anything that may occur to my thoughts, I am much inclined to mention to you one or two suggestions, to which I attach a good deal of importance.

Allow me, then, to call your attention to a consideration which I have not yet seen duly adverted to, and which, I think, bears powerfully on the attempt to make the census of 1821—or, indeed, any existing state of the population—a solid foundation on which to erect a new and permanent system for this country: I mean the recent improvements in conveyance on railways. I do not know whether you have seen that between Liverpool and Manchester. It is the only one on that scale yet in operation, yet as there are proposals for several others before the present Parliament, connecting Liverpool with Hull, and these extremities with the many important manufacturing districts in the intervening space, besides various other railroads known to be in contemplation, the Liverpool and Manchester one may be fairly taken as a criterion, after nearly a twelvemonth's experience. And in it we see so much extraordinary velocity, such regularity and power, that the efficacy of the discovery cannot fail to be reckoned upon. If so, can it for a moment be doubted that the land adjoining to such railways will be very soon covered with the population flocking from the crowded streets of the manufacturing towns, or attracted from all parts of Great Britain and Ireland? The value of land between Liverpool and Manchester, in the direction of the railway, is already excessively enhanced.

In the same way, can it be foreseen what capabilities may now be opened up—such, for instance, as valuable falls of water, to which there may not hitherto have been available access, iron, or copper, or lead mines, which an easy supply of fuel would at once bring into work, &c., &c.? Whenever such attractions may come to operate, will there not ensue a dislocation of population wholly unprecedented? In a word, if this matter has not yet been under your notice, I think you will find it worthy of your best attention, and an element of a very formidable nature against the system of the present Bill.

But the deepest regret with me in all this business, is the departure of our friends from (one may call it) the Constitutional establishment of an organized Opposition. Complaints are continually heard of the want of a combination of measures and well ordered discipline in your proceedings. The last glaring instance was on Tuesday last, when (be the object right or wrong in itself) Opposition was exhibited to the country dwindling down to thirty or forty, while at the same moment no diminution appeared in the numbers of Government; and Lord Milton, though evidently intent on pressing a suggestion of his own, openly abandoned it at the desire of his party. But though the most obvious inconvenience in this is the excessive injury it does to our cause, and the corresponding advantage to Ministers in Parliament, yet throughout every part of the country has the evil been quite incalculable to us, both during the late election, and indeed ever since the question of Reform has been before the public. For there has been no standard around which the disapprobation and apprehension felt by individuals towards the proposed measure could rally, none to give advice or encouragement, nothing to prevent the feeling, however right and valuable, of isolated parties from being left to evaporate from want of support or means of union. Contrast this with the tactics of our opponents, and see what formidable odds this alone furnishes against us. With them the Whigs, the Reformers, the powerful press, act as one concentrated body. Their every influence is exercised with the force of a well-sustained combination. The impressions they wish to convey, and the misrepresentations they choose to recommend, are counteracted by nothing in any degree corresponding with the able means they employ.

    Adieu, and believe me, ever
       Yours most faithfully,
          ELGIN.

It was in the course of these debates that there arose the controversies between Mr. Macaulay and Mr. Croker which have already been referred to; but no just cause of offence was ever given to Macaulay. His statements—many of them characterised by that love of the "picturesque" which led him to denounce Pitt's military administration as that of a "driveller," and to describe Swift and Stella at Sir William Temple's as if they were footman and scullery-maid carrying on a flirtation—his statements were refuted, but nothing was said to wound his vanity, which nevertheless *was* wounded, and an undying resentment stirred up in his mind in consequence. The following passage may be taken as a fair example of the way in which Mr. Croker dealt with his opponent:*—

I say, Sir, that I admit the learned gentleman's eloquence, and feel it peculiarly, not only from the admiration it excites, but from the difficulty it imposes upon the humble individual whose fortune it is—*haud passibus æquis*—to follow him. But I am relieved, in some degree, by the reflection that, as from the highest flights men are liable to the heaviest falls, and in the swiftest courses to the most serious disasters, so, I will say, is the most brilliant eloquence sometimes interrupted by intervals of the greatest obscurity, and the most impassioned declamation defeated by the most fatal contradictions; and I must assert that the speech of the learned gentleman had points of weakness which no imprudence or want of judgment ever surpassed, and carried within itself its own refutation beyond any other speech I almost ever heard. The learned gentleman seemed, sometimes, to forget that he was addressing the House of Commons; or, aware that a voice so eloquent was not to be confined within these walls, he took the opportunity of the debate here, of addressing himself also to another branch of the Legislature, in, as he no doubt thought, the words of wisdom taught by experience. Not satisfied with those vague generalities, which he handled with that brilliant declamation which tickles the ear and amuses the imagina-

* [From his speech in the House of Commons on the Reform Bill, Sept. 22nd, 1831.]

tion, without satisfying the reason, he unluckily, I think, for the force of his appeal, thought proper to descend to argumentative illustration and historical precedents. But whence has he drawn his experience? Sir, he drew his weapon from the very armoury to which, if I had been aware of his attack, I should myself have resorted for the means of repelling it.

He reverted to the early lessons of the French Revolution, and the echoes of the deserted palaces of the Faubourg St. Germain were reverberated in the learned gentleman's eloquence, as ominous admonitions to the Peerage of England. He sees that that frightful period—the dawn of that long and disastrous day of crime and calamity, bears some resemblance to our present circumstances, and he thinks justly: but different, widely different, is the inference which my mind draws from this awful comparison. It were too much for me to venture to charge the learned gentleman with intentional misrepresentation of the transactions to which he thus solemnly refers, but I must say that he seems to me to labour under strange forgetfulness, or still stranger ignorance. He tells us that he was but young when these events happened; but there are some of us, not much older than he, who witnessed that period with a childish wonder, which ripened, as the tragedy proceeded, into astonishment and horror; and, after all, it requires no great depth of historical research to be acquainted with the prominent features of those interesting and instructive times. I am, therefore, 'I own, exceedingly surprised, not that the learned gentleman should have thought the illustration both just and striking, but that he should not have felt that the facts of the case would lead any reasonable and impartial mind to conclusions absolutely the reverse of those which he has deduced from them. He warns the Peers of England to beware of resisting the popular will, and he draws from the fate of the French nobility at the Revolution the example of the fact and the folly of a similar resistance. Good God! Sir, where has the learned gentleman lived,—what works must he have read,—with what authorities must he have communed, when he attributes the downfall of the French nobility to an injudicious and obstinate resistance to popular opinion? The direct reverse is the notorious fact,—so notorious, that it is one of the common-places of modern history. . . .

Did the nobles, on that vital occasion, show that blind and inflexible obstinacy which the learned gentleman has attributed to them? Did they even display the decent dignity of a deliberative council? Did they indeed exhibit a cold and contemptuous apathy to the feelings of the people, or did they not rather evince a morbid and dishonourable sensibility to every turn of the popular passion? Was it, Sir, in fact their high and haughty resistance, or was it, alas! their deplorable pusillanimity, that overthrew their unhappy country? No inconsiderable portion of the nobility joined the *Tiers Etat* at once, and with headlong and heedless alacrity;—the rest delayed for a short interval,—a few days only of doubt and dismay; and, after that short pause, those whom the learned gentleman called proud and obstinate bigots to privilege and power, abandoned their most undoubted privilege and most effective power, and were seen to march in melancholy procession to the funeral of the Constitution, with a fallacious appearance of freedom, but bound in reality by the invisible shackles of intimidation, goaded by the invectives of a treasonable and rancorous press, and insulted, menaced, and all but driven by the bloody hands of an infuriated populace.

But was this all? did the sacrifice end here? When the *Tiers Etat* had achieved their first triumph, and when, at last, the three estates were collected in the National Assembly, was the nobility deaf to the calls of the people, or did they cling with indecent tenacity to even their most innocent privileges? The learned gentleman has appealed to the decayed ceilings and tarnished walls of the Faubourg St. Germain, where ancient ancestry had depicted its insignia, but which now exhibit the faded and tattered remnants of fallen greatness. Does the learned gentleman not know that it was the rash hands of the nobility itself which struck the first blow against these aristocratical decorations?

The learned gentleman attributes to the obstinacy and bigotry of the French clergy the ruin of the Church; but who in truth gave, in those early days of confiscation and usurpation, the first flagrant example of the plunder of the property, and the invasion of the power, of the Church?—A Cardinal Archbishop! Who first proposed the abolition of tithes?—A noble and a prelate! and on principles, too, let me observe *en passant*, so extravagantly popular, that even the patriot Abbé Grégoire, of Jacobin notoriety, could not countenance them. And in that celebrated night, which has been called the "*night of sacrifices*," but which is better known by the more appropriate title of the "*night of insanity*," when the whole frame

and order of civilised society was overthrown in the delirium
of popular compliance, who led the way in the giddy orgies of
destruction ?—Alas ! the nobility ! Who was it that, in that
portentous night, offered, as he said, on the altar of his
country, the sacrifice of the privileges of the nobility ?—A
Montmorency ! Who proposed the abolition of all feudal and
seignorial rights ?—A Noailles ! And what followed ?—We
turn over a page or two of this eventful history, and we
find the Montmorencies in exile, and the Noailles on the
scaffold !

One advantage, however, Macaulay had which was of incalculable value : he was on the winning side. The immense
power which was at the back of the Ministry was not
properly appreciated by the Opposition, or it would have
accepted the Bill on its second presentation, without incurring the risks of exasperating the public, and of having a
still more obnoxious measure forced upon it. It is true that
the House of Commons did pass the Bill, on the 22nd of
September, but the House of Lords threw it out, and then
came the melancholy events of the autumn—the riots at
Nottingham, and the still more serious outbreaks at Bristol.
These events were dwelt upon by Mr. Croker in his speech of
the 16th December :—

Whether the learned gentleman [Macaulay] meant to defend
the Government, or to abandon them, he (Mr. Croker) would
ask, not the learned gentleman, but the House and the
country, whether his Majesty's Ministers had exhibited any
spirit or any firmness on any of those points ? Let Bristol
speak for itself ; let Derby, let Coventry, let Nottingham bear
witness to the facts. Ministers possessed neither firmness
nor vigour ; and, so far from protecting others, they had
not shown even the power of defending their own dignity—
their own houses. Their privacy had been assailed at mid-
night by the delegates of political unions. They had been
publicly insulted by combinations of persons who declared
their resolution to pay no more taxes. Even when his
Majesty had been advised to issue a proclamation against

the societies to which his Ministers had previously truckled, these societies were induced *by negotiation* to yield obedience to his Majesty's proclamation. That was what the learned gentleman probably meant by putting the law into vigorous execution.

Had the royal authority been upheld here? An attack was made on the gaol at Derby, and the courage of one man saved it, and probably that great town from destruction. In Nottingham, a mob collected, which, if he was rightly informed, gave some hours' information of their intentions; that mob proceeded and burnt the castle of a noble person,* close to that town—not a place in which he personally resided, but one which his liberality had assigned to the purposes of charity. The castle was burnt in broad day, in the face of a great town, in the presence of magistrates, and within the reach of his Majesty's troops, who were doomed, by the inactivity of the authorities, to remain motionless spectators of the tumult. But Ministers had not thought it worth while to institute any inquiry into so extraordinary an event—the noble owner was only a Tory—that circumstance excused all! The impunity of this crime encouraged the reforming mob to one of the most atrocious violences that ever in a civilised country was inflicted upon a respectable and peaceful family. An attack was made upon the house of a gentleman—not an anti-reformer, nor connected with politics or party in any way. The mob marshalled themselves without interruption, and proceeded the distance of two or three miles to the scene of their intended mischief—they burst into the house, deliberately plundered it, destroyed everything they were unable to carry away, and finally set it on fire. The master of the house was absent; his lady in delicate health,† was forced from her couch to a precipitate flight; led by her young daughter—another Antigone—to a distant part of the grounds; they both remained for hours on the damp earth, the daughter supporting the mother's head on her bosom, and both concealing themselves under a laurel tree. He observed a smile come over the countenance of a noble Lord opposite

* [The Duke of Newcastle.]

† [Mrs. Musters, wife of Mr. John Musters, of Colewick Hall, celebrated by Lord Byron as Miss Chaworth. This lady died on the 5th of February, 1832, from the consequences of the fright which she had sustained in the attack upon her house above referred to.]

(Lord Nugent). It could, he supposed, not be a smile of approbation of the atrocities he was relating. He hoped the noble Lord did not smile at the afflicting story, but only at his imperfect manner of relating it. The story, however, was not yet concluded, for so profound was the terror of these unhappy ladies, that for hours after the wretches had quitted the grounds, the servants sought for their mistress and her daughter in vain. And at last when they found them in the situation I have so feebly endeavoured to describe, half dead with cold and terror, there was no apartment, no couch, no bed of that so lately splendid residence fit to receive them, and they were carried inanimate to the only place which had escaped the incendiaries—a groom's bed, over one of the stables. What was the conduct of Ministers on these afflicting and disgraceful occurrences? Was any step taken, or any reward offered for the apprehension of the offenders? Was a Special Commission held to inquire into these excesses? No. If there had been, could any man believe that the atrocities at Bristol would have taken place—atrocities which, though more extensive, did not exceed in cruelty that which he had just described?

To Mr. John Murray.

Brighton, October 9th.

I shall be in town at noon to-morrow, and hope to-morrow or next day to be able to talk with you and Lockhart (from whom I have had a kind letter to-day) about the political article of the next *Quarterly.* My own impression at present is to take a cautious line as to the *future,* tolerably decided as to the danger of a reform on any general *principle,* but giving no opinion on piecemeal reform. When I see every speaker in the Lords admitting the expediency of some degree of reform, I must be wilfully blind if I do not see that it is inevitable, unless some great change is operated in the public mind, and I do not think that we have any man at once great enough as an orator, a statesman, and a leader of a party to work that change. Pitt might, or Fox, or perhaps Canning; but no one now on the scene.

Yours ever,

J. W. C.

To Sir Robert Peel.

Kensington, November 11th.

MY DEAR PEEL,

I have not heard to-day what the accounts of cholera are. I only know that if that plague does not ravage the whole empire (and I do not much fear it) it will not be the merit of the Ministry; only think of their putting the colliers from Sunderland which convey *coals* (one of the most efficient of the preservatives against the disease) into quarantine, and allowing twenty stage-coaches to convey persons, for aught they know infected, north, south, east, and west; and all this *after warning.* The Board of Health in town had not seen the medical reports from Sunderland *at noon yesterday.* They had been, forsooth, sent up to Lansdowne House, that my Lord might read them before he left town for Bowood, whence he had come not for Cabinet, nor for cholera, but to dine with the Radical Lord Mayor—at least such is the story which I hear and believe!

As to Parliament, it must, I think, meet; the gravity of the circumstances seems to require it. The real misfortune is that its meeting will increase, instead of diminishing the danger, and the Ministers will call us together not, as in old times, to help the Crown against the mob, but in obedience to, and in encouragement of the mob. We shall have a dreary task to perform, and I heartily wish that I had any honourable escape from political life. I thought I had been released from my long thraldom on the 16th of Nov. last, but I have only shifted to a more anxious slavery.

I agree in all you say,[*] and participate in all you feel, except on one point. *Counter-associations* would only be more certain and earlier destruction. In the first place, it would sanction a principle of associations independent of the Crown, which would legitimatise the Radical National Guard, and end us at once. Secondly, when it becomes a matter of association and counter-association, it is a mere affair of numbers, and eventually of physical force. I need not say that, in the present state of excitement and insanity, we should be overpowered in both. I see no field for any exertion on *our* part but Parliament—our speeches there, as long as they will permit us to speak, may have some effect,

---

[*] [If this was said in a letter, the letter is missing.]

and may perhaps bring round a few, and at last more and more of the country gentlemen and of the country; but that seems to me to be the only hope—a forlorn one, I admit —we have. The four M's, the Monarch, the Ministry, the Members, and the Multitude all against us. The King stands on his Government, the Government on the House of Commons, the House of Commons on the people. How can we attack a line thus linked and supported? Your house is plundered by a mob; you appeal to the Ministers; the mob are their allies and friends; your complaint is laughed at. You arraign the Ministers for this offence in Parliament; again you appeal to friends and accessories, the majority will hoot you down, perhaps send you to the Tower. You finally appeal to the King; the King will tell you that you are a disloyal subject to complain of *his* people, and *his* faithful Commons, and *his* devoted Ministry; and he may perhaps strike you out of the Privy Council, too happy if at last you are not tried at a Special Commission for having broken the peace—the King's peace—by locking the doors and barring the windows of your house at the approach of the mob. Things of this kind, but even wilder and more absurd, happened in France from 1789 to 1793.

Sir Robert Peel to Mr. Croker.

November 12th.

MY DEAR CROKER,

I am very sorry you have sent so unsatisfactory a proxy, instead of taking your seat at seven to-day. We are quite alone here, and I am sure we could have defied cholera spasmodica by long walks after partridges.

I kept mine till late in the season, and have enough to have been enabled to kill with my single gun thirty-six partridges the day before yesterday. Pretty well for the 8th of November. I read the progress of our moral contagion with the utmost disgust and indignation. I will not say indeed the utmost, because I suppose they are in some degree abated by the absence of all surprise, by the foresight that what is happening must happen, as the inevitable consequence of a King and Government hallooing a ten-pound mob against the House of Commons, in the stupid belief that they could have the hunt to themselves.

It seems to me that counter-associations for the purpose

of defence must be formed, if Sir Francis Burdett and other supporters of the Government are allowed to organise armed clubs for the purpose of attack.

That the purpose is attack—attack upon life and property—cannot be doubted, and the only safety is in preparation for defence. What I chiefly desire is timely notice.

Perhaps you will still come with Herries, Dawson, and Holmes about the 16th.

Ever most faithfully yours,

R. PEEL.

Drayton Manor, November 13th, 1831.

MY DEAR CROKER,

Associations formed with any ostentation or parade, that should profess to be independent of royal control, and that should offer the least provocation, would be manifestly unwise. They might be justified by the bad precedent which seems about to be established, but still the pleading of such a precedent by a minority which has property to be assailed would not be prudent.

But I certainly, if the necessity arises, shall form, and shall counsel others to form, quiet, unostentatious associations for the sole purpose of defence against unprovoked aggression.

Association may be too grand a phrase. What I mean is a select cohort of persons on whom I can thoroughly depend, who may constitute an armed garrison for my protection and that of my family in case of actual attack—such attacks as have been made, and are threatened.

I am sure nothing could be more mischievous than to abandon property without defence, and it is well to be prepared before the hour of danger actually arrives. I am sure also that nothing could equal the effect of even a single instance of desperate and successful resistance against the armed vagabonds of a town.

A small band of steady men, backed by the law, and by the sympathy of property, would do much against ten-fold their numbers, attacking from any distance, ignorant of the *locale*, and with halters round their necks.

To form associations for resistance to the bill, or any vague indefinite object, would be madness; but I see no hope of salvation but in the most strenuous *and concerted* resistance to any aggressive demonstration of force on the part of reforming mobs.

I shall remain here until shortly before the meeting, and shall be very glad to see you at any time before then.

Ever yours,
ROBERT PEEL.

November 19th.

DEAR CROKER,

Dawson and Herries are here, and we thank you for your news. As the King repeatedly said to me (perhaps being the only poetry he ever made)—

> "I consider dissolution
> Tantamount to revolution,"

I have no belief that when the hour of trial comes he will resist the making of Peers.

How can he recede? Who ever did retrace his steps, having once begun the facile infernal descent? Who, at least, except such men as Lord Strafford and Mr. Pitt?

I shall still hope to see you and Holmes. I wish Aberdeen on his way from Scotland may meet you in his adverse carriage, as Mr. Barbour has it.

Ever yours,
R. P.

Drayton Manor, November 23rd, 1831.

DEAR CROKER,

I did not hear from Lord Wharncliffe until this morning. I then received a very vague letter as to the probable intentions of the Government.

My fixed determination is to keep myself wholly unfettered in regard to any measure of Reform brought forward by the Government, and to decline all communication, direct or indirect, with the Government upon that subject. I have many reasons for this. If I had no other than recent public declarations on the part of every Minister who has made any public declaration on the subject of Reform, that alone would be an insuperable bar to my negotiating or conferring with them respecting Reform.

Very truly yours,
ROBERT PEEL.

Mr. Croker to Lord Hertford.

There can be no longer any doubt that the Reform Bill is, what Hume called it, a *stepping-stone* in England to a republic, and in Ireland to separation. Both *may* happen without the Reform Bill, but with it they are inevitable.

I find that those who some months ago derided my alarms are now at least as much frightened as I am. I do not feel, like Peel, that the fright goes off by habit. Mine is only confirmed by experience.

To Lord Hertford.

London, December 12th.

The Duke has been confined by a bad cold, caught, I believe, by travelling in that miserable open britchska of his, which laid me up twice this year when I travelled with him. He is better, however. Let me now bring forward the history of the negotiation between the Moderates and the Whigs, of which I gave you some early particulars. It was, as I told you, all off; but last week (Friday and Saturday) it was unexpectedly revived thus. About ten days ago, Chandos went to Brighton to see, if possible, whether he could have any influence upon the King. He was civilly received, listened to, invited to dinner, greatly fêted by all the ladies, and, in short, was much pleased with his visit, though it produced nothing to build any hopes upon.

However, in the middle of last week he was surprised by a communication from Taylor, by the King's command, to desire him to call on Palmerston, and open to him the views which he had before expressed. Chandos at first demurred, till he was assured that Palmerston was prepared to receive him by the King's command. He then went; but the interview was, I hear, confined to making an appointment for himself, Wharncliffe, and Harrowby, with Grey, for Saturday. They attended, and found Grey and Althorp, and towards the latter end of the visit, Brougham, but no Palmerston. Brougham took little part, Althorp none. Grey was dry and haughty, offered nothing, would concede nothing, and, in short, nothing was done, and they separated, Harrowby saying that all that had passed confirmed him in his former opinion.

December 13th.--The Bill was brought in last night, and is in its great principles just the same as before; but in its details it is a great triumph for me and for our party, for there is not one of my points on which we divided in the Committee which is not conceded. For instance, the parish and the borough are no longer reckoned together. This condemns Calne and Morpeth, as well as Appleby and Saltash. Houses and amount of assessed taxes are adopted as the criterions; this I advocated in a long speech and ample details in the cases of Guildford, Dorchester, and Sudbury, and we had three divisions. I complained that Horsham was preserved entire, while Bolton, with 40,000 inhabitants, was to have but one Member. Horsham is now curtailed, and Bolton increased. I made a strenuous fight, and divided the House on separating Chatham from Rochester, and was beaten; but lo! it is now conceded. I battled against encumbering Whitehaven with Workington; they are no longer to be united. We all objected to the destruction of the Corporations. The corporate rights are to be preserved for ever, and even the new boroughs are to be made corporations. In short, never was there such a defence of, and indeed eulogy on, our efforts in the Committee as the new Bill makes; but you see that this is nothing, not worth a pin, except as empty glory, for it leaves the great objection just where it was; nay, by removing anomalies and injustice, it makes the Bill more palatable, and therefore more dangerous.

I am sorry to say that it was evident in the House that these alterations blind many foolish people to the deformity of the principle. Lord Clive *almost* pledged himself to support the second reading, and even Chandos seemed shaken. If Peel and I cannot show in the debate of the second reading (which begins on Friday, 16th instant) the futility as to the great object of all these alterations, we shall, I fear, cut a poor figure in our division. We shall, however, do our best; and I think that I shall be able to show that the new Bill is vastly more democratic than the old, for as the old numbers of the House are to be preserved (we were dissolved, you will recollect, for voting that on Gascoyne's motion), but as all the additions are given to town representation, the proportions against the aristocracy will be enormously increased. As to the Ministers, only Russell and Althorp spoke. Palmerston came in late, and seemed to go to sleep. Charles Grant never came at all. Robt. Grant sat in the gallery. Stanley was there, and Graham; and they, though they did not speak (nor was it necessary they should), seemed zealous for the Bill.

Mr. Croker's attention was not entirely taken up by politics, even in this exciting year. He had one or two literary projects in contemplation, upon which he had made proposals to Mr. Murray; but neither of these projects was brought to completion, although considerable preparations were made for a new edition of Pope. His notes and other documents were afterwards handed over to Mr. Elwin, for that complete, and probably final, edition of the poet's works which was undertaken at a later period.

Mr. Croker to Mr. Murray.

March 26th.

Dear Murray,

So far as your *terms* are an ingredient in the proposition you state, I need only say that I consider them as extravagantly liberal.*

I confess I had never thought of editing Hume's 'History of England;' and I should like to know the *principle* on which you would wish to see such an edition prepared. I can easily comprehend the making Hume the groundwork of a large embroidery of comment and elucidation; but I doubt, however well that employment might suit me, whether the result would be likely to suit *you*. Perhaps, however, you mean something more popular and marketable. Let me therefore know your views. I confess I feel a great wish for, not to say the necessity of, steady literary employment. My mind has been so long busy that idleness would be irksome and injurious, and I therefore shall engage willingly in any work which you may think me capable of performing to the satisfaction of the public, or, which is the same thing, to your own fair advantage as a publisher.

Ever, my dear Murray,
Most faithfully yours,
J. W. C.

* [Mr. Murray's letter (if the proposition was made by letter) is not among Mr. Croker's papers.]

To Mr. Murray.

I am ready and willing to undertake Hume, but before I tie down your liberality to so large an engagement I should like to be satisfied that it is likely to answer *your* purpose as well as it would answer *mine*. Think of it in this light, and if you see your way, I am ready to set out upon mine. I only hesitate on your account; for having so often chidden you for extravagant liberality, I do not like to become a *particeps criminis*.

But there is a *small* matter which I have been for years thinking of, and which John* tells me you also have lately thought of. I mean a new edition of Pope. None of our poets has been so often and so badly edited. Notes upon notes, commentaries on commentaries, tell you *all*, except just what one wants to know. Warburton has given us razor-edged disquisitions, fine and false, in the Divine Legation style, which are much more difficult to be understood than the text itself. Joe Warton has emptied into his notes all his classical commonplace books, and tells us a great deal about the literature and manners of every age except just Pope's own. Bowles has done little but scent out the taints of Pope's private character; and Roscoe tells nothing, because he knows nothing, beyond what he found before his eyes in former editions. But towards making the author as intelligible to posterity as he was to contemporaries, and putting the reader of 1831 into anything like the position of the reader of 1731—*that*, none of them have done, nor (what I complain of) even *attempted* to do.

Then what *bookmaking!* Pope was a poet. Yet every line of poetry he ever wrote might be contained in the first volume of Bowles's ten, in the same type and form that he has given. All the rest is taken up with notes which explain nothing, commentaries which no one reads or could understand, and letters from most of the ladies and gentlemen of the literary circles of the reign of George I. This is all very well in its own way; that is to say, the letters are, for the *notes* and *commentaries* are really waste paper; but it is not what an edition of Pope for common use ought to be.

If you ask me what I would have, or, if I undertook the work, what I should do, I answer *generally*, endeavour to put the reader of 1831 back into the place of the reader of 1731;

---

* [Then Mr. John Murray, junior: the present head of the house.]

leave the brilliancy and beauty of Pope's poetry to speak for itself, and only try to exhibit the persons and the *facts*, on which the poetry employed itself, and without some knowledge of which we can no more understand the poetry than the folks in the gallery do the Italian opera without the help of the book.

A few critical notes might be admitted when they tended to explain the meaning; and *all* the notes on the Dunciad, because they are all either explanatory or part of the fun. For the same reason, I should not be disinclined to add the memoirs of P. P. and of Scriblerus and some other small prose pieces.

Yours ever,

J. W. C.

To Mr. Murray.

April 19th.

DEAR MURRAY,

I undertake Pope with alacrity, and at whatever pecuniary terms you yourself please to name.

As to the *text*, I shall print from Warburton's E. E., as they say in counting-houses; but in fact all the texts since Pope's death are the same, except as to the errors of the press. All the editions give variations. I shall not, except where the variation connects itself with the personal history of the writer on the subject, as in the case of Atticus and Addison.

I shall omit all the commentaries in which the metaphysical adulation of Warburton endeavoured to give Pope "a meaning which Pope never meant"—which nobody now reads, and which, if they did, they would be likely to exclaim: "Egad, the interpreter is the harder of the two."

Of the *notæ variorum*, I shall reject all that do not directly illustrate the text; and as they are but a small part of what are now appended in every edition of Pope, and as they go but a small way in the real object of notes, viz., *elucidation*, I suppose I shall have to add a considerable number of notes of my own—more, I guess, than I shall retain of those former editors'.

I shall refrain as much as possible from polemics. Bowles and Roscoe offer abundant food for criticism, but my object will be *Pope*, and not his annotators.

Yours faithfully,

J. W. C.

CHAPTER XVII.

1832.

Last Stages of the Reform Discussion—Meeting of Parliament in 1832—Passage of the Bill in the Commons—Preparations for meeting the Hostile Majority in the Lords—Resignation of Lord Grey—Attempts to form a Tory Ministry—Mr. Croker's Record of the Negotiations—He refuses Office—Sir R. Peel on Consistency—Failure of the Duke of Wellington—And of the Speaker—General Correspondence—Appearance of Cholera in London—The Duke of Wellington sometimes Insulted—The Ultra-Tories—The Duke at a Levée—Peel's Sincerity Questioned—A new Tory Club (the Carlton)—Aberrations of Lord Dudley—Mr. Croker's Advice to the Lords—Letters from the Duke of Wellington—Dinner at the Duchess of Kent's—A gloomy Forecast—Mr. Croker urges Sir R. Peel to take Office—Peel's Reply—Prorogation of Parliament—Mr. Croker's Resolve to retire from Public Life—His Motives—The Duke's Opinion—Sir R. Peel on Battlemented Houses—Charles X. in England—The Library at West Moulsey.

THE Reform Bill had been read a second time, by the decisive majority of 162, before the adjournment of the House for the Christmas holidays. On the 17th of January, Parliament again met, and the consideration of the Bill was resumed without delay. By that time it was clear that all heart had gone out of the Opposition in the Lower House. The debates were carried on in the lifeless manner which is inevitable when everybody feels that the result is practically decided beforehand. On the 22nd of March the Bill was read a third* time, and on the following day it finally passed without a division. Thus had the longest and hardest part of the struggle come to an end.

It then became necessary to decide how the Opposition in the Upper House was to be frustrated, and the expedient of creating peers in sufficient numbers to carry the Bill was once more discussed, and not only discussed, but pressed earnestly upon the King by Lord Grey and Lord Brougham. But on the 7th of May an unexpected incident occurred. Lord Lyndhurst moved to postpone the clause disfranchising the condemned boroughs, and this resolution was carried by a vote of 151 to 116. The Cabinet decided at once to recommend the King to call into existence fifty new peerages; the King declined, and the Ministers resigned. For a brief period there seemed a probability that the Tory party might regain power on the basis of moderate reform. Lord Lyndhurst was sent for by the King, and he at once applied to the Duke of Wellington, who in his turn consulted with Sir Robert Peel, Mr. Croker, and Mr. Goulburn. They all declined to take office. Sir Robert Peel, as it appears from the highly interesting memorandum left by Mr. Croker, attached much importance to the necessity of public men retaining a character for consistency, and he contended that this character would be forfeited, so far as he was concerned, if he went a second time through the part he had played on the Catholic question. In expressing this opinion, he did but anticipate the all but unanimous judgment which was pronounced upon his conduct in 1846, after he had revealed his conversion on the question of the Corn Laws.

The Duke was not long in discovering that he could not form a government, although he appears to have believed

---

* The second reading was carried in the Lords by a majority of nine, the strength of the Opposition having fallen from 199 to 175 votes.

that the Speaker (Manners Sutton) might succeed. But while the Speaker was at work, Mr. Baring made the avowal that the resignation of the late Ministry was a great calamity, and he offered to take no part against them if they would return to office and carry on their Bill. This, as Mr. Croker states, was at once looked upon as securing the return of the Whigs, and so highly did Sir R. Peel still value political consistency that he accepted this alternative with pleasure, rather than see the Duke make the slightest compromise with principle. Mr. Baring's announcement paralysed the efforts of his political friends, and the Speaker's proposed administration scarcely served as a subject of gossip for twelve hours. Lord Ebrington was once more at hand with a motion of confidence in the late Ministry, and it was carried by a majority of 80. Then petitions were poured in by hundreds; there were fresh disturbances; threats of riot; great clamour in the House and out of it; and in the end the Duke went to the King and advised him to recall Lord Grey. At the same time, he undertook to withdraw from active opposition to the Bill. It was all so arranged, and the Bill passed through the Lords, and became law on the 7th of June.

Mr. Croker's account of the attempts to form a Tory Ministry is much more full and accurate than that which Greville and other writers have given, for he was in the midst of the negotiations, and evidently made his notes carefully, in a separate memorandum-book, day by day. This book bears a little label outside, on which is written, "Notes of what passed about a change of Ministry, May 1832."*

---

* "From the 9th to 15th May took place those anxious consultations among the Tory party, the full record of which would be worth a mine of gold."—This remark is made in a review of Lord Lyndhurst's 'Life,' by Mr. T. E. Kebbel. See the 'Fortnightly Review,' January 1884. Mr. Croker's Diary includes this period, and contains a more complete record than we are now likely to obtain from any other source.

The important part which he took in the various negotiations sufficiently appears from the following documents, and it is evident from other sources of information that his services were highly valued by the party leaders. "It is, I think, *absolutely necessary*,"* wrote Lord Lyndhurst to the Duke of Wellington, "that Croker should consent to be a Member of the Cabinet. I think with his assistance the House of Commons may be managed." It will be seen, however, that Mr. Croker firmly refused to enter Parliament again or to take office.

Mr. Croker to Lord Hertford.

January 17th, 1832.

The Tories flatter themselves that all is not yet lost. They build on His Majesty, in whom I have no faith at all.

The Duke of Wellington is quite convalescent; I walked with him yesterday, for two hours, up and down Rotten Row, in a warm sunshine, which seemed to do him a great deal of good. He was in good spirits and very chatty; but, *au fond*, he thinks every day worse and worse of public affairs. So do I, although I think the danger *narrowed*. The danger was some months ago from the people, excited as they had been by the King and ministers. I now think the danger is from the King and the ministers alone; that is, that they will endeavour to revive the frenzy which is cooling in the public mind, and by that, or by any means, to pass the Bill; and the Bill once passed, good-night to the Monarchy, and the Lords and the Church. I really believe that if the King were to-morrow to send for the Duke of Wellington and make him First Minister, we should not have even as much of riot or disturbance as we had on the rejection of the Bill by the Lords. The *Bill* has no friends out of office. All England is divided into two great parties: those who want *more*, and those who want *less* than the Bill, and these are the real parties in the contest.

* See the 'Wellington Despatches,' viii., 307. The date of the letter is May 12, 1832. The words "absolutely necessary" are in italics in the original.

January 24th.

In the first place, the discussion is very flat; neither side mustering two-thirds of their former little following; no great zeal, except always in the office-holders, who are zealous enough to keep their places; but I see symptoms of a different result next time, in the Lords. John Wortley would not vote against Schedule A, nor Lord Sandon, nor Lord Eastnor, so that I suppose their noble fathers mean to allow the Bill to be read a second time. But all these oppose Schedule B, but with so little effect, that we divided last night worse on Schedule B with their assistance, than we had done on Schedule A without it.*

The little politicians of the Clubs are very busy with rumours of dissensions of the Cabinet; of differences between Downing Street and Brighton, and even between the King and Queen; on the two former points I know no more than I told you in my last, and I believe all such rumours, if they have any foundation at all, are much exaggerated, and will come to nothing.

February 14th.

Cholera has arrived in London, and is in full speed along the banks of the river. On Saturday, one case at Ratcliffe, and next morning one on the opposite bank; from Sunday noon to Monday noon, eight more cases, all or nearly all of which were fatal; for, in this early stage, death is the notice and sign of the peculiar disease. What the consequences may be 'tis hard to foresee. We hope that the mortality is not likely to be great, and the slowness of its progress prevents any sudden panic; but its secondary consequences, in the stagnation of trade and consequent distress of the lower orders, appear to me to be very alarming. I presume all the ports of Europe will put the river Thames in quarantine, and that would put near half a million of souls out of the means of earning their daily bread.

The Reform Bill still drags along. It will certainly pass our House, and they say be read a second time in yours. Harrowby is sincere, but timid and over critical; Wharncliffe is intriguing for power. The Bishops, they say, will not be so numerous, nor so steady, and on the whole some wise

* [Schedule A contained the list of boroughs to be disfranchised; schedule B the boroughs which were to lose one member out of two.]

men begin to think that it would be the safest plan to give the Bill the go-by in the Lords by proposing against it certain resolutions of moderate reform; but this is, I believe, at present, no more than a floating idea of some subalterns; for I have no reason to suspect any change in the policy of the chiefs.

Lord Grey made a strong speech in favour of Irish tithes the other day, and in Committee in the Lords proposed that the *public* should pay the clergy their arrears and take on themselves the collection from the peasantry to repay the Treasury its advance. This has set all the Papists and Radicals furious with Lord Grey and the Bear,* and Howick and Durham very cunningly appear as furious as they, and say that they will quit Lord Grey if he does not retract; which I have no doubt he will. In the tithe Committee in the Commons, Duncannon opposes Stanley point blank; the Ministry, in short, not divided amongst themselves, it would seem at first sight, take opposite sides for the purpose of consolidating opposite parties and keeping their majority together. Lords Grey and Stanley endeavour to manage the moderates, and Duncannon and Ellice to keep well with the Radicals. Meanwhile Ireland progresses in barbarism, and *rents* are in many counties as hard to obtain as *tithes*.

Mr. Croker to Lord Hertford.

Feb. 21.

I went down to dinner at Strathfieldsaye on Friday and came back on Sunday. The Duke is very much improved in health; he hunts every day, at least he did all last week. I thinks he begins to dislike London, where he can neither walk nor ride without being occasionally insulted, or, at least, hearing disagreeable expressions. It is remarkable with what respectful, I should say *increased* attention he is received by every well-dressed person, and even by a vast majority of the lower orders; but occasionally a blackguard hoots or says something gross, and this, I think, induces the Duke to prefer Strathfieldsaye, where he can take the exercise that is necessary for his health more at his ease. But his spirits are very low. He sees everything *en noir*, at least as much as I do; and I cannot but suspect that, besides his alarm for the public welfare, he is mortified that these events should have

---

* [The Rt. Hon. Edward Ellice was generally known as "the Bear."]

happened in his time, and *par suite*, though not perhaps *in consequence*, of his own measures. Yet, on the other hand, he ought to console himself by thinking that if some of those measures had not been taken, we might have been in a worse state. Catholic Emancipation, no doubt, led to the rupture of parties which led to the Grey Ministry and Reform : but who will say what the effects of the Revolutions of Paris and Brussels might have been in Ireland, if Catholic Emancipation had not been granted ? I believe there would have been an Irish rebellion, and perhaps a Reform ferment in England also. Be it as it may, our Duke is sadly dispirited; and his sagacious mind is looking out, not for a prospect of salvation, but to guess what shape the misfortune will first take.

Peel, on the other hand, though, talking confidentially with me, he admits the danger to as great an extent, almost, as the Duke or I see it, yet *feels*, or *seems to feel* it, infinitely less. It does not affect his *spirits*, though I think it does his *judgment*. He is very reluctant to attend the House, and anything like a bold course he entirely rejects; when he does attend and speak, it is ably and firmly; but somehow he does not appear what is expressively called *hearty*.

Then, again, the ultra-Tories are but a hollow support. A few of them—Wetherell, Inglis, Lord Stormont (and I suppose his father)—are very cordial ; the two first sincerely actively, and usefully so. But the Duke of Cumberland, who affects to be the head of the party, old Eldon, and in our House Sir R. Vyvyan, Lord Encombe,* Kenyon, and a few of the Irish, though they vote with us, are evidently a different party, and will never, I think, be reconciled to Peel, unless, what will never happen, he should swear allegiance to the Duke of Cumberland.

Nor are our opponents more comfortable. Philosophers say that if it were not from the pressure of the atmosphere everything on the face of the earth would fall to pieces and fly off. So nothing but the pressure of Reform keeps the ministerial majority for an hour together. Nay, even as it is, they are kept together with the greatest difficulty and by every kind of trick and intrigue. They themselves see all this, and the ministers know that their present reign must be short, but they think that, having by the details of their Reform Bill secured to themselves whatever is left of Parliamentary influence, they must be in the long run and

* [Grandson of Lord Eldon.]

eventually the prevailing party. They are assuredly mistaken; but such is their blind and wicked calculation.

There was a meeting of Tory Peers at the Duke of Buckingham's yesterday, to consider how to meet the Bill. The defection of Wharncliffe and Harrowby (the latter of whom *canvasses* for votes on the second reading with great zeal) renders it doubtful whether they could beat it on the second reading, even now, and of course a small creation of peers would become irresistible. They therefore, as I hear, think of meeting the Bill by a resolution for *moderate Reform*, and this, I believe, was the general sentiment in Pall Mall yesterday; but I was in the House of Commons from four till two this morning fighting the Bill, and had no opportunity of hearing details.

February 28th.

Revolution progresses, and so does cholera; but so slowly that we have got accustomed to both, and no one is alarmed. At present cholera seems to thrive most on the south bank. We have had less frost this year than I ever knew, and no snow at all; the day or two I was at Strathfieldsaye were positive summer—hot sunshine, yet dry under foot; latterly we have had fogs; raw but dry; but it has hardly rained these six weeks. In short, I never saw such a winter. I suppose we shall pay for it in spring, and some doctors think that we are now paying for it in cholera.

At the levée the other day, the Duke of Wellington had two anti-Reform addresses to present; and, fearing that if handed in in the usual way to the Lord-in-waiting, the King would never see them again, the Duke made an abstract of them, and, to the great astonishment of the King and his attendants, read His Majesty the abstracts in full levée. This very much vexed the ministers, and did not much please the King, though he listened at the time graciously enough, and was civil in asking after the Duke's health; the Duke preferred doing this to an audience in the closet, first because it was bold and above board; but secondly, as he himself told me, that if he went into the closet he might be asked for advice which he did not like to give till at least the Mutiny Bill should be passed.

March 6th.

Things are, to my judgment, in the most unaccountable state. Duke of Wellington is gone down to his country house alone or with the Arbuthnots; and although we see so much intrigue and defection going on, he seems to abandon the field. *Tout cela me passe.* His natural good temper is very much altered. Mortification and alarm at the state of public affairs affect him deeply. Peel is quite the reverse; he seems very stout-hearted and in good health, and makes every now and then a display against the Bill; but, I know not how it is, he too seems inclined to consult his own personal ease, and people are not satisfied of his sincerity, but I really believe it is only the weariness of being eternally defeated, and the conviction that no good is to be done.

I myself am very much wearied and dispirited. I think I was yesterday as "low," as they call it, as I ever was in my life; and it certainly all arises from my constant anxiety and labours in this barren vineyard. But I shall go through with it, irksome, nay painful as it is, with the consolation that I am doing my duty towards my friends and my country, with gratitude and sincerity.

Peel and Charles Ross are founding a Tory Club,* to which I do not think I shall belong, if, as at present intended, it fixes its abode in the retirement of Carlton Terrace, where they are treating for Lord Kensington's House. I have retirement enough at my own Kensington.

From Mr. Croker's Diary.†

Monday, 7th May.—Ministers were beaten in the House of Lords by 151 to 116 on the question of postponing the disfranchisement clause of the Reform Bill.

Tuesday, 8th May.—Lords Grey and Brougham went down to Windsor to submit to his Majesty the unanimous advice of the Cabinet "that a number of peers sufficient to carry the Bill unaltered should be, made." In conversation (with Sir H. Taylor) Lord Grey talked of fifty, but Lord Brougham said sixty, and the King seemed ready to make twenty, but these were only *explanations*—the *proposition* was "an adequate but indefinite number." The Ministers came back with an impression that the King would *not* consent, but the final determination was postponed to next day.

---

* [This was the Carlton Club. The present building was not completed till 1856.]

† [Labelled "Notes of what passed about a change of Ministry, 1832."]

Wednesday, 9th May.—The King came to town to his weekly levée. He had made up his mind not to consent to an indefinite number of peers, upon which the Ministers resigned. The King saw them successively. He intimated to Lord Brougham and the Duke of Richmond a kind of wish to retain *them*, founded as to the latter on a notion that he was adverse to the creation; but they were both resolved to go with their colleagues. The King then sent for Lord Lyndhurst, who had been his Chancellor, and who, now holding a judicial situation, might be expected to give him the most impartial advice, and he desired Lord Lyndhurst to consider what was fit to be done, and authorised him to make overtures to any person whom he might think likely to undertake the Government with success; and he asked Lord Lyndhurst whether he should stay in town; Lord Lyndhurst advised him to return to Windsor, which he did. That evening Lord Ebrington, who had, on the rejection of the Bill last autumn, moved a vote of confidence in the Ministers, gave notice of a similar one for the next day.

Thursday, 10th May.—I received, at Molesey, a letter from Goulburn to desire me to come to town to attend a meeting at Lord Stormont's to consider how Lord Ebrington's motion should be met. I arrived in town about eleven, and was going to see the Duke of Wellington, when I met Goulburn, who told me that the Duke and Lord Lyndhurst were just gone down to Peel's, whither he was also going, and wished me to come, but I did not think it proper to do so on his suggestion. At half-past twelve I went to Lord Stormont's in Jermyn Street, where I found Peel, Goulburn, Herries, Murray, Hardinge, Cockburn, Clerk, Ch. Wynn, A. Baring, Sir J. Walshe, Sir R. Vyvyan, and about thirty others of our party. I was so deaf with a cold that I did not hear much of what was said, and said little myself. The question was whether to meet Lord Ebrington's motion by a direct negative or by the order of the day. I saw little difference, and proposed that Peel should, when he heard Ebrington's speech and motion, decide *on the spot* what course to take. This was approved, Baring consenting to take the lead. While this was going on, Peel whispered me not to go away without him; so when it was over, which was about one, he took my arm and begged me to walk with him to the Duke of Wellington's, who, he told me, had a similar meeting of our friends in the Lords to consider what was to be done, and wished to see us after it should be over.

When we arrived at Apsley House we found the Lords dispersing, and did not think it right to go in just as they were all coming away, so we took a turn in the park, and then went to the Duke, just preceded by Lord Lyndhurst. When we (four) were seated, Lord Lyndhurst told me—I supposed (as was the fact) that he had already told the others—what had passed between him and the King, and the extent of his mission, and began to discuss what should be done. By the way, he said that he was a good deal struck by the firmness and discrimination of the King, whose style of talking on business he thought very much improved since he had been in office. His Majesty showed, he said, considerable adroitness and practicability. When he had done this explanation, which had been chiefly addressed towards me, I asked him, "Whom do you mean to put at the head?" He made a significant motion with his hand towards Peel and said, "*That* Peel must answer." Peel then said, with a tone of concentrated resolution, that he could not and would not have anything to do with the settlement of the Reform Question, and that it was evident that it must be settled now, and on the basis, as he understood, of the present Bill. Lord Lyndhurst said (what he had not before mentioned in my presence, but had, it seems, told them in the conversation in the forenoon), that the King had not fixed that the new Government was to be formed on the specific engagements to carry *Schedules A or B*, but that his Majesty having thrown out something to *that effect*, Lord Lyndhurst had objected that none of the Tories could consent to swallow these schedules in the lump, upon which his Majesty varied his phrase, and said, "Well, then, an *extensive* reform," and that "an *extensive reform*" was therefore the basis of his lordship's mission.

Peel said, "It was all the same in his view. *He* was peculiarly circumstanced—he had been obliged to arrange the Catholic Question by a sacrifice of his own judgment, and he would not now perform the same painful abandonment of opinion on the Reform Question." He talked of "the advantage to the country that public men should maintain a character for consistency and disinterestedness, which he would for ever forfeit if, a second time, he were on any pretence to act, over again, anything like his part in the Catholic Question."

I said that I agreed that on the principle of carrying the

Bill, I did not think that either Peel or the Duke would be in an honourable position, and that it seemed to me that Lord Harrowby* was the natural person to undertake the Government on such a basis; I said I was aware of his state of health, and his known reluctance to take office, but as he was the person who had brought us all into the difficulty by having concurred in the second reading (but for which, the Duke's or Peel's course would have been clear), I thought that as a man of honor *he* ought to come forward to cure—as far as it might be curable—the mischief he had made. All seemed to agree in my reasoning, but Lord Lyndhurst declared that he *knew* Harrowby would not consent. I insisted that he ought at least to be sounded and pressed, and immediately. The Duke opposed this. He said he was to have a meeting of Tory Lords next day, and that he was afraid that they never could be persuaded to support Lord Harrowby, but at all events it would not be safe to make Lord Harrowby any proposal till he had felt the pulse of those Tory Lords. I said that I was afraid Lord Harrowby might take advantage of the delay in applying to him, and shelter his real reluctance under a plea of offended dignity, in not being sooner apprised of what was expected from him. All I could say, however, was overruled by the Duke, and it was resolved to do nothing till after the meeting at Apsley House to-morrow. It is scarcely worth while to mention that I stated to Lord Lyndhurst that his Majesty's pledge to Schedules A and B rendered it impossible that *I* could take any share in his Government, and that therefore my advice and opinions were only those of a disinterested friend. I walked away with Peel, and he suggested the Speaker as Premier. Soon after this I left town for Molesey, and having stayed there five minutes (to see Mrs. Croker, who was very ill), I rode back to town, and got to the House of Commons about eight.

I did not feel inclined to speak, as I had not heard the early part of the debate, and was not very well; nor had I, indeed, an opening, except after Macaulay, but as I had happened to reply to him on five different occasions, I thought it would

---

* [Lord Harrowby was one of the leaders of the party in the House of Lords known as the "Waverers." They voted against the second reading of the Bill as originally introduced, and for the second reading in its amended state, while objecting altogether to the principle of the measure. The "Waverers" materially helped to secure the passage of the Bill.]

look too much like *pitting* myself against him; and as it had happened three times that I had interposed between him and Wetherell, I on this occasion remained silent. I was afterwards sorry I had done so, for I did not much like the tone of the debate, which I thought rather *low* on our side. Indeed, I observed in the meeting in the morning that people looked grave and anxious, and not at all like a victorious party. The appearance in the House was of the same cast, but we made a good division, 208 to 288. Lord Ebrington's similar motion in October had been carried by a majority of 131. The announcement of the numbers was received with cheers on both sides. *We* thought it a good division—they affected to think it so for them, but the Ministers looked, I thought, *abattus*, and when Althorp got up to answer a very foolish flourish of Wetherell's on the mode of presenting the address, he looked quite pale with agitation, but whether with vexation at the division, or anger against Wetherell I cannot decide.

Friday, May 11th.—I returned to Molesey early in the morning. In reconsidering the state of affairs, I could not but see that if a Tory government of some shade or other were not formed, and if the Whigs were allowed to return triumphant over the King's scruples, the revolution might be looked upon as *consummated*, for bad as the aspect of affairs now is, such a triumph to the agitators would render them intolerably audacious and too strong even for the Whigs themselves to manage; I therefore wrote Peel a strong letter urging him to take the Government—even on the King's terms, if there was no other resource or alternative. I afterwards learned that Lord Lyndhurst went down to Windsor to report that the only advice he could give His Majesty was that he should come up to town, and send for the Duke of Wellington; and he brought back His Majesty's commands that the Duke should attend him at St. James's at one o'clock, to-morrow.

Saturday, May 12th.—I came early into town and called on the Duke; he said, "Well, we are in a fine scrape, and I really do not see how we are to get out of it." He told me that Lord Harrowby had absolutely refused (I never heard the particulars of the communication with Lord Harrowby). He also told me that Lord Lyndhurst had had a communication with the Speaker, to induce him to put himself at the head of the Government; but that also had failed. He then said that the meeting of Lords yesterday had agreed to support the King's Government even in passing the present Bill with some amendments: and then he told me that if no one else would, he would himself undertake the Government. He said that he had passed his whole life in troubles, and was now in troubles again, but that it was his duty to stand by the King, and he would do so; for "what," he added, "could I say to those gentlemen who met here yesterday, and who consented at my suggestion to forego all their private feelings and interests for the great object of preventing a revolution, but that I would not myself hesitate to undergo all the odium and all the danger which might attend our attempt?" However, when I told him that I had written to urge Peel, and was about to go to him to entreat him verbally to undertake the Government, his Grace encouraged me to do so, and authorised me to say to Peel that he was ready to serve with him or *under him*, or in any way that he should think best for the common cause. I said that I did not like to carry a message, but that my advice should be founded on that hypothesis. He then said, "I am particularly pleased with the advice you give Peel, because it leads me to hope that you mean to act on the same principle yourself, and to help me in this great emergency." He spoke doubtingly, as if he knew that I had expressed a contrary intention, as I had, indeed, ever since we left office in 1830; and I had repeated it to Lord Lyndhurst in the first of three discussions, on the 10th, in the Duke's hearing, and I have no doubt that he had not forgotten it. I replied by begging His Grace to recollect that I had apprised him verbally and in writing, soon after we left office, of my firm resolution never again to enter into it, happen what might; that that resolution I had maintained all along, and by that I must now abide; but I said that exclusive of that, there were reasons which must have obliged *me* to decline taking office under present circumstances. I had neither birth, nor station, nor fortune; nothing but my personal character to hold by, and I would leave him to judge what would be thought of *me* if, after the part I had taken, I should be found supporting schedule A, and accepting a high office and salary as the price of that support. I should lose myself and do the cause more harm than good; whereas, out of office and independent, I should be at liberty to adapt myself to the new circumstances of the case, and my opinions might have some weight in the House and in the country, when it was seen that they were at least disinterested, and that I had no private or personal object in the support which I might be able to afford the King's Government; but I assured him that these considerations, though primary in *principle,* were only secondary in point of *time,* because my mind had been made up, as I had often apprised all my friends, private and political, at Christmas, 1830, never again to enter upon official life; and I had so early made my resolution known, at a time when it almost seemed presumptuous and idle to suppose such a case, in order that one might not, if such a crisis should ever arise, be supposed to refuse through any dissatisfaction either at what might be offered, or from what hands.

He acquiesced in what I said; rather, I thought, more readily than I expected, but still with an air of pique and disappointment. He then told me that he was going to the King at one o clock, and would tell His Majesty that, happen what would, he (the Duke) would stand by him and endeavour to extricate him from the difficulty in which he was placed. "A difficulty, however," he added, "created altogether by his allowing the delusion as to his real opinions to have committed the House of Lords, as well as the country at large, to the principle of the Reform Bill."

I then went to Peel, with whom I found Goulburn and Holmes. Peel had answered my letter, and read us the answer, which I afterwards put in my pocket. Then began a discussion in which I pressed upon him—as a last resource, and if every other scheme should fail—the duty of saving the King, the country, and the world, from the obvious consequences of the re-establishment of the revolutionary Government, and he dwelt on the same topics as before, in reply. I persisted so long, and urged points so strongly, that Holmes and Goulburn (who, however, were of my opinion) interfered, and said that I had done all that could be done, and that they thought I should push it no farther. Yet I think I shook Peel's resolution for a moment. I certainly tried his temper. After they went, I stopped, and we recovered our good humour thoroughly, and were about to sally out to stroll through some of the exhibitions, when it struck us that it would hardly be decent, when it was known that the King was come to town on a subject so serious, and in which he and I were in some degree involved, that we should be seen ostentatiously parading our indifference to the crisis in the exhibition rooms. This seemed rational, and so I went away alone. I looked in at the new Club, and there heard that the Duke had been at St. James's and had *kissed hands* as First Minister, and also that he had been hurrahed by the mob as he left St. James's; I thought the fact *impossible* after all that had so lately passed, and that no communication had or could have passed since he had authorised me to press Peel to accept the first place. About 4 o'clock I returned to Peel, with whom I found Lord Fitzgerald. I told Peel the rumour of the Duke's having kissed hands as a thing impossible. He said he thought it might be true, and then went on to tell me that about ten minutes after I had left him he was summoned to the King; that His Majesty invited him into his service without saying in what post, or who was to be his First Minister, and that he had shortly but firmly declined, on the same reasons he had before given me.

He did not seem to think that the King was *very* pressing, and he by no means corroborated Lord Lyndhurst's report of his dexterity and *savoir faire;* on the contrary, he thought him awkward and confused. He began by saying that it "was eighteen months since they had met in conversation;" Peel assented. Then followed two or three similar observations, to which Peel also assented, "and then," said His Majesty, "I recollect you said that some degree of reform was desirable." To this Peel could not assent—" he recollected nothing like it, though it was possible that something might have passed which at such a distance of time might have left that impression on His Majesty's mind—for instance, he might have told His Majesty that he expected that the House of Commons of that day would pass some resolutions of reform; but that, so far from approving or conceding anything to such resolutions, he was prepared to leave office if they were carried." His Majesty also said that he had parted with his late Ministers with the "*greatest regret,*" and spoke of them in terms that showed that he either did not feel or did not estimate the extent of the insult and peril which he had resisted; in short, he seemed to have taken his stand where he did, without being well aware of the whole importance of the case, or of the spirit which must have actuated his late Ministers. He concluded the interview by saying that "he hoped the refusal to enter his service was not to be understood as applying to all future times, and that he hoped to see him again on some more favourable occasion."

DIFFICULTIES OF THE TORIES.

When Peel left the King, the Speaker went in, and he afterwards called and told Peel that the King had desired him to come into his official service as *leader of the House of Commons;* that when the Speaker in return asked him who was to be Minister, he looked confused, or, as the Speaker termed it, *flabbergasted,* and stammered out "The *Duke of Wellington."* The Speaker then declined, though the King offered to do all that was in his power to compensate him for abandoning his present claim to the peerage and pension usually bestowed on retiring Speakers. It was this which made Peel believe the rumour that I had discredited, of the Duke's having kissed hands, for it was thus clear that he was already first Minister when the King had sent for Peel and the Speaker; and moreover Peel understood that he had the day before nominated Hardinge to Ireland, and had in two or three other points acted as the *Prime Minister* only could do. I then told Peel of the message which I had been authorised to deliver in the morning, and which seemed absolutely at variance with the Duke's having accepted a situation which I understood from him he wished to see filled by either Peel or Sutton, or even Lord Carnarvon, in preference to himself. Lord Fitzgerald said it was clear there was some serious misunderstanding somewhere. I myself suspect that the Duke thought the King was offering Peel and Sutton successively the *first place,* while the King was, in fact, only offering the *second.* The facts appear clear as to Peel and Sutton, and I must believe that the mistake was His Majesty's.

I dined at Lord Lonsdale's, and sat next to Lord Ellenborough, who confirmed me in what I had before guessed, that the Duke had *not* kissed hands, and was still only considering what arrangement could be made. This makes all clear and consistent.

After dinner I called and sate late with Peel. He still supposed that the Duke was to be at the head of affairs, and augured ill of the success of the Administration, although he thought Sutton might have succeeded. I afterwards learned that at the very time when Peel and I were thus talking, Sutton was with the Duke, and that, after a conversation of some hours, finding that the Duke persisted in thinking that he himself should be at the head of the Government, the Speaker declined to undertake the lead of the House of Commons, because he felt, as he had already told the King, that his utility, "such as it was," consisted in his being "wholly unpledged on the Reform Bill, and that therefore the amendments he might offer would be received with no personal disfavour, whereas that, with the Duke at the head, His Grace's avowed antipathy to *all* reform would afford an Opposition a colourable ground for suspecting all their propositions." So the Speaker considered the thing as ended with regard to himself.

Sunday, May 13*th*.—As I was going to Molesey for all day, I thought it right to look in at Apsley House, and ask whether his Grace had any commands for me. I found Goulburn and Wynn waiting to see him by appointment, but as I was in a hurry to get away, the Duke saw me first, that is, he really pulled me into his room, for I told him that though I had called to pay a visit, I had really nothing to say to him. He again pressed me, and much more strenuously than before, to take office, and a little surprised me by saying "that in such a crisis as this, if a man put himself on the *shelf*, it might not be so easy to take him off the shelf when he perhaps might desire it." I told him at once rather sharply that "such an observation could not apply to me; that I had recorded with *him*, as well as with other friends eighteen months ago, my fixed resolution never to take office again; and that, besides all other reasons, I really felt that my health could not stand the worry of business; that it was with nervous reluctance and the most painful sensations that I went to the House at all; that nothing but an imperious sense of duty drove me there, and that I was quite sure that if I were to undertake the double duties of minister and debater, I should knock up in a couple of months; and I repeated that besides all these, which were immediate and insurmountable objections, I felt that I never could lend a hand to any Reform Bill of the kind which was in contemplation, though I might support it when it should come to us if it appeared, as, no doubt, it would, the *lesser of two evils*." The Duke acquiesced in the reason arising from my state of health, but seemed, I think, a little, though *but* a little, annoyed. He then asked me what I thought of Wynn. I said that he would be of great use to an administration of moderate reformers. He then mentioned some other persons, of whom I said what I thought, which was favourable, and I particularly urged the advantage which Baring would be of. I mentioned Lord Wharncliffe, but said that I did not suppose he would take office. "I am sure," said the Duke, "they would be unlucky who should take office with him."

When I came out, Goulburn went in, desiring me to wait for him, which I did. When he left the Duke, he walked with me to Knightsbridge. He told me that the Duke had again pressed him to take office, but that though he was personally willing to help the King in such a crisis, Peel's refusal had rendered it impossible for him who stood in a situation exactly the same as Peel, to take a line that would expose him not only to all the taunts of political adversaries, but to the bitter reproach of a comparison with Peel. The Duke had before told me (when I had mentioned Herries) that he had positively declined—(Ellenborough had said the day before that he made no difficulties). The Duke told me that he, Herries, also had come to a resolution *never* to accept office; this a little surprised me.

On getting to Molesey, and revolving all that had passed, I thought that the negotiation with Sutton must have failed from some misunderstanding, and I therefore wrote to Ellenborough to advise that it should be explained. I said I thought that with Sutton and Baring in the Cabinet, *and the Duke at the Horse Guards*, a moderate Reform Bill might be satisfactorily carried, but I also suggested that if all other modes should fail, I thought the Duke, in resigning his mission into the King's hands, should inform his Majesty that, to save him from the personal mortification of making peers after having spontaneously refused to do so, he and his friends would withdraw their opposition, and thus render it unnecessary to create the number of peers against which his Majesty had pledged himself.

I do not know the details of what passed during the remainder of Sunday, but I suspect, from what Wynn said to me in the Duke's ante-room, that he also was disinclined to accept, and I afterwards heard that *no one* had been willing but Hardinge and Murray, who, from motives of personal devotion, were ready to follow the Duke, though I fancy with little hope of ultimate success. In the course of the day, however, it became clear to the Duke that *he* could not succeed, and I afterwards learned that he sent to desire to see the Speaker, who called on him about 4 o'clock, and then the Duke informed him that he found he could not make a Government, of which he was to be at the head, but that he had no doubt the Speaker could, and offered to serve with or under him, and also informed him that he had Baring's authority to say that he would take office under the Speaker, though he had not appeared willing to accept under the Duke. The Speaker asked time to consider of it. Lyndhurst, who was by, pressed for an answer that night, but the Speaker would only promise one next day. Next day the Speaker consulted Fitzgerald and Peel, and both advising him to accept, he wrote a note to the Duke to say that he wished to see him once again before the matter should be *finally* arranged, but that so much he would, even then, say, that under all circumstances he felt it to be his duty to undertake the task.* I know not what circumstances prevented the Speaker's seeing the Duke in the morning—perhaps he was inquiring what support he could have; but it was settled that after the House, if it rose before one in the morning, he would go up to Apsley House.

There was a large meeting at Brooks's to consider how the Whigs should act; there was a great difference of opinion. Stanley spoke for, I hear, near an hour. Some were for joining Hume in a motion for stopping the supplies, and taking other violent steps; but the ministers advocated more moderate measures, and Hume's project was given up. Several others were still more moderately inclined, and would not even pledge themselves to oppose the new Government.

May 14*th.*—I came early to town. Having so positively refused to take office myself, I now felt that my going unbidden to the Duke might look like idle curiosity, so I did not call at Apsley House; but I met Ellenborough in the

[* The Speaker's letter is given as follows in the Wellington Despatches:—

Palace Yard, 14th May, 1832.

MY DEAR LORD DUKE,

I am most anxious to have a personal interview with your Grace before the whole matter, as far as I am concerned, is concluded: and I would therefore have come to you this morning, if I could have found the time. But as I am now forced to prepare for the House, and cannot anticipate how long we may sit, I will now say with reference to the proposition made by your Grace yesterday, that if *no other* arrangement *can* be made, I must give way, though with fear and trembling. . . .

Ever, my dear Lord Duke,
Your most faithful and obliged,
C. MANNERS SUTTON.]

park, who told me how matters stood with the Speaker, but that it was to be kept a profound secret, as he wished—Ellenborough did not know why—to take the chair that evening without any suspicion of his intentions getting out. He also told me that Baring would take office with the Speaker, and that all looked very prosperously. But why this delay?

I saw Peel twice, who told me that he had seen a memorandum on the part of the King, of what had passed with the late Ministry about the creation of peers—that it was very confused, but that it was obvious that His Majesty's case was a bad one; that he had consented to the principle of a creation to carry the bill, that he had even offered 41 (the number of the former majority), and that, therefore, it was a mere question of degree, and that really between 41 and 50, or even an indefinite number, the difference was not broad enough for the stand which the King had so tardily resolved to make. We walked together to the House about half-past four, a good many people lining the streets, and the police keeping the way clear. In the House, on the occasion of a petition from the City, a debate grew up which must have a great effect on the whole affair. The Whigs, led by Lords Ebrington and Milton, and supported by Macaulay and T. Duncombe in clever and very bitter speeches, branded the Duke by anticipation with every mark of political bad faith, if he should accept office on the basis of passing the bill against which he had made so remarkable a protest on the 16th April. Ebrington said it would be "public immorality," Milton hinted at "the caprice of a fickle individual," Macaulay talked of "infamy and place," and Tom Duncombe made a violent but clever and amusing speech, in which he likened the Duke's change to a crane-neck carriage, and worked out the allusion wittily and well; but they all declared (as did Althorp, who said a few words with more warmth than usual) that they should accept *whatever* bill the new Ministry should offer, but would not, beyond that, give them any credit or confidence; nay, they hinted that they would only take such a bill as a *step* to any further demands that they might see occasion to make. In reply to all this, Hardinge got up to defend the Duke of Wellington from the injurious hypotheses on which the Whigs were condemning him. This was well enough; but Baring unluckily got up, and, though disclaiming any official character, yet spoke certainly with a kind of Ministerial authority, in defence of the supposed Administration, and, what with replies and explanations, kept up a very damaging debate for several hours; towards the close of which things took a turn as short as Tom Duncombe's crane-neck could have made, for Ebrington, having dropped something like a regret that the Ministers had not known how much the Opposition would have conceded, as they would then, perhaps, not have insisted on the peers, Baring said that he contemplated the resignation of the late Government as a *great calamity*, and that if they would consent to return and carry the Bill, as it now seemed they might do, without swamping the House of Lords, he, for one, would not consent to form an Administration to replace them.

Ebrington (whose proposition seemed very unpalatable to Ministers) was obviously put up by them to *retract*, saying that the time for such a compromise was *irrevocably* passed; upon which Hume and the Mountain shouted "No, no," and Burdett and Hume enlarged on this point; and the debate was adjourned to the next day, for the avowed purpose of affording an opportunity for such a reconciliation with his late Ministers as might "*replace* His Majesty in the affections of his subjects," although Althorp expressed an opinion that no such arrangement could be made.

Peel went home to dinner at half-past nine, before the debate was over, and I followed him, when Hume got up. There dined Peel, Wm. Peel, Hardinge, Dawson, Goulburn, and Lord Stormont. We all agreed that Baring had been indiscreet, and that the proposition which he had made must end in the return of the Whigs, which Peel declared he thought better than that the Duke of Wellington should lend himself to passing the Reform Bill in any shape. What seemed to all of them the most important feature in the debate was that Sir Robert Inglis, whose opinions were, of course, those of Oxford and the Church, had reluctantly, as it seemed, but forcibly, denounced the loss of character and confidence which must attend the Duke's undertaking office for the purpose of passing the Reform Bill. Inglis spoke so low that I did not well hear what he said, but Peel considered it *fatal*, and conclusive against any Government to be formed of any class of anti-Reformers.

The House rose about half-past eleven, and the Speaker came at twelve in his coach to take Peel and Hardinge to the

Duke's. I having withdrawn myself from the whole affair, was unwilling to accompany them, but Peel insisted on my coming also. The Duke had already heard from Baring what had passed, and every one was clear that the aspect of affairs was entirely changed—so much so, that the Speaker's intended Administration was dropped in silence. It was hardly alluded to, although this very meeting had been originally appointed for the purpose of finally settling that matter. After a good deal of conversation, it was agreed, on Peel's proposition, that the Duke should tell the King that after what had passed in the House, and the temper shown, it was impossible to hope to form a Tory Administration on the basis of passing the Reform Bill, and that therefore His Majesty must take his own course. The Duke was to add that, in order to save His Majesty's personal honour as to the creation of Peers, he himself would, as far as depended upon him, remove all pretence for such a creation by withdrawing his opposition.

We got home very late. I suppose it must have been near three in the morning.

May 15*th.*—I saw Peel, who seemed pleased and relieved by the resolution of last night, and thought it a most fortunate result for the honour and character of the Duke. Lord Ellenborough came in and told me that the Duke was gone to the King, where he seems to have remained a long time. I went, as I had promised last night, to the Speaker, who told me in detail all that had happened. The only thing I did not know already was, that the first day Lord Lyndhurst had been to him and made the appointment for his seeing the King next day, and at that time seemed to give him the option of being Premier—which, however, the King did not next day confirm, and His Majesty told the Speaker he disapproved of having the First Minister in the House of Commons. Mrs. Sutton, who came in towards the close, on my telling the Speaker not to halloo till he was out of the wood, for that if Lord Grey were to be obstinate and imperious he might yet be called on—Mrs. Sutton, I say, tried to persuade me to accept Cabinet office if the Speaker should be forced to do so; but, having refused the Duke, I had no difficulty in resisting her entreaties. I went down and slept at Molesey.

May 16*th.*—On coming to town I found the Whigs confident that all was settled, and the Tories believing that the

King held out. Certain it was that His Majesty was in communication with Lord Grey, and that all the underlings said everything was arranged, and that they had not been hard on the King.

I dined at Macleod's, where there was the Duke of Argyll, who told me that he understood all was arranged. I went afterwards very late to Lady Salisbury's, where I heard that there were still doubts, or rather that nothing had been declared; but the Whigs were in spirits, and the Tories in despair. I found some of the Tory ladies, and even a few of the gentlemen, were angry with me for not having been ready to take office. These good people never consider —1st, my position as to the Reform Bill, and, above all, as to Schedule A.; 2nd, that not having been in the old Cabinet, the old Cabinet have no claim on me; and 3rd, that it would be impossible for me, even if I wished for office ever so much (the contrary being the fact), to take such a step without the concurrence of those political friends (Lord Hertford in particular) with whom I had hitherto acted. What might not Lord Hertford say if, on his return to England, he found the Member for Aldborough advocating Schedule A.? It really would be a dishonourable breach of trust, besides being a base surrender of my own opinions.

May 17*th.*—I called on Peel. He had not heard that anything had been done. We talked over what had passed, and were glad that the Duke was relieved from the pain of proposing the Reform Bill in any shape. Some one had told Peel that I would have come in with the Speaker. I asked him how he could have listened to such an absurdity; that I never had been asked, for Mrs. Sutton's idle talk, vague as it was, referred to future contingencies; and that I had never spoken to any one but himself on the subject of the Speaker's Administration; that if I would not serve with him or the Duke, how could he imagine for a moment that I could serve with any one else?

Hardinge came in and told us the Duke would make an explanation. Peel said he disliked explanations. Hardinge told us what the Duke might say, or rather what he would, if called upon, say for him in our House, which would admit that he had resolved to support the Reform Bill. I saw no necessity for such an admission. Why say what he would have done, when he never had been able to form a Cabinet to consult with? I advised all that to be left in the vague, and merely to say that the Duke had not accepted office, but had only undertaken to try whether a Government could be formed on a principle consistent with the King's engagements and the sentiments of those who might be called to office; and finding that that could not be done, he had resigned his mission back into His Majesty's hands. To this both Peel and Hardinge objected that such was not the true reason, because Sutton and Baring were merely to have redeemed the King's pledges, but that they broke down from the want of support in the House of Commons;—to which I rejoined that my view was the really just one, for although *two*, or even *four*, gentlemen had been willing to come in on that basis, all the rest of the principal people had held off, and it was really because neither Peel, nor Goulburn, nor Herries would consent to take any share in the Reform Bill, that the Duke's mission had failed.

In the House the Ministers came in all together, evidently from a Cabinet. They looked very sullen. Althorp stated that the negotiation was going on, and 'that he hoped and believed it would be satisfactorily terminated, but did not like to speak too confidently. It is clear that the King stickles for *some* changes, for Althorp dwelt on his pledge that no *essential* changes would be conceded. Ebrington said a few, but very strong, words to encourage the Ministers to be resolute in insisting on the bill unaltered. It is obvious that they are in great perplexity, and even Sir James Graham had laid aside that saucy sneer which seems habitual to him.

The rest of this affair, I suppose, will be better told in the newspapers than by me, who am now quite out of the secret, if there be one.

May 18*th*.—Mrs. Croker continuing very ill, and rather worse, I remained at Molesey, and was surprised at finding that a body of workmen from Manchester (who had been marched up, it seems, to intimidate the King and the new Government, but were stopped and ordered back in consequence of the restoration of the Whigs) had quartered themselves in this and the neighbouring villages, and were, like sturdy beggars, insisting on getting food and money. Two of them came to my gate and made some noise, and I could hardly get rid of them. Each carried a small skein of cotton yarn, which they pretended to sell; but when I showed them the absurdity of such a pretence, the value of all they had not sufficing to pay Hampton ferry, they confessed that they had come up *many thousands* to carry the

Reform Bill, which was to put down machinery, and enable the poor man to earn a livelihood. It seems that they were halted while the change was pending, and that they were dispersed, either to diminish alarm, or to procure food and lodgings for so great a body. They wore a kind of workman's uniform—a flannel jacket, trimmed with narrow blue ribbon. One was an Englishman, and civil; the other an Irishman, and very much inclined to riot and rob. But his companion listened to reason, and when he heard that there was a lady dangerously ill in the house, he half forced away his troublesome comrade. I have no doubt that they were part of a body which have been brought up from Birmingham and Manchester to help the Whigs. I thought it right, however, to apprise Lord Melbourne, Secretary of State for the Home Department, of this migration of the northern hives. I could not make out any details of their numbers or march, but they said they were many thousands, and in the three or four villages within the circumference of a mile there were, they said, about forty.

Mr. Croker to a Friend.   March 26.

Our poor friend Lord Dudley, in Park Lane, is ill to a degree to excite some alarm. His absences and oddities have become so marked, that Halford, who witnessed some of them, *intruded* his advice and ordered bleeding, cupping, &c. He had music and a dance on Wednesday, but never took any notice of his guests, but sat in an arm-chair all night in an ante-room. He had a dinner on Friday, and allowed the Duke of Sussex to sit at the lowest place at table, as he had gone to dinner without him, and there was no place vacant except one at the bottom. The Duke of Wellington and Lord Rosslyn came in a little late from the House, and had to dine at a side table, and his whole conduct was so strange that Halford, who dined there that day, volunteered, as I have told you, his interposition.

April 3rd.

Lord Dudley invited last week the Duke of Wellington and Lord Lyndhurst to meet Lord and Lady Holland;* *bien assortis, n'est ce pas?* But he saved himself all trouble in amalgamating such discordant materials; for when they

---

* [Lord Dudley had quarrelled with Lady Holland, and had not spoken to her for many years previously.]

arrived at Dudley's they found that my Lord dined out! On a certain Wednesday he told Mr. Murray, the bookseller, to advertise his library for sale, and next day he consulted him about buying a larger additional one. In short, he shews every mark of harmless derangement.

During the progress of the Reform discussions in the Lords, Mr. Croker was requested by Lord Haddington to explain what course he would advise the Upper House to pursue in reference to the Bill, short of rejecting it altogether. He was asked, in fact, to place himself in the position of a moderate Reformer, who had voted for the second reading of the Bill, and who now desired to "diminish its danger to the constitution and the monarchy," by such amendments as might seem practicable. In reply to this request, Mr. Croker wrote a letter, which was privately printed, containing essentially these propositions:—That enfranchisement should not be carried beyond the limits proposed in the first Reform Bill; that disfranchisement should go no further than might be required for enfranchisement—"if you want forty Members, rather take one each from *forty* boroughs, than wholly annihilate *twenty;*" instead of a 10*l.* franchise, admit everybody who paid rates and taxes. This letter, of course, had no practical effect, and it bears evidence upon every page that its author never supposed it would have any; but it attracted a good deal of attention, at the moment, among the persons who saw it. It was first read by the Duke of Wellington, and the correspondence respecting it has already been published in the 'Wellington Despatches.'

The Duke of Wellington to Mr. Croker.

London, April 7th, 1832.

MY DEAR CROKER,

I return your letter, which is a very able production. But we are living in times in which, and among men with whom, it is necessary to be very cautious. These men are responsible for more than they are aware of. Their defection from the good cause may occasion its ruin. If they had not left us, we should have had a majority of not less than sixty, with all the gentlemen of England at our back against the Bill. We might have dictated our own alterations. As things are, they have ruined themselves and us.

Believe me to be ever most sincerely yours,

WELLINGTON.

Mr. Croker to the Duke of Wellington.

Saturday evening, 14th of April.

MY DEAR DUKE,

I send your Grace the letter, but I cannot send you the other papers before Monday, as my materials are in the country.

I have just had Haddington with me. He is confident of killing the bill; and Ellenborough, who called while he was here, seems equally confident.

I own I do not see how Lord Grey can keep the bill anything like what it is but by *a Creation*. Ellenborough seems strong for an instruction, but the policy of that must depend on the *Combination* which would support that mode rather than the same thing moved in Committee.

Yours ever most attached,

J. W. CROKER.

*The Duke of Wellington to Mr. Croker.**

London, April 24th, 1832.

MY DEAR CROKER,

Since I wrote to you yesterday I have seen Lord Lyndhurst. He is very anxious to have some conversation with you. He is turning his mind to an alteration of the Reform Bill.

Will you settle a time to see him?

Ever yours most sincerely,

WELLINGTON.

* ['Wellington Despatches,' New Ser. viii. 271.]

Mr. Croker to the Duke of Wellington.

West Moulsey, 27th April, 1832.

MY DEAR DUKE,

I have finished my letter and sent it to the press, but what use we shall put it to, your Grace shall determine when you have read it. . . .

I shall call on your Grace on Tuesday morning; and if you would allow me to suggest whether I might not meet Lord Lyndhurst and Lord Ellenborough with your Grace on that day, to talk over the matter, I shall hold myself disengaged to obey your commands all day.

In reading my letter your Grace will recollect that it is written for the Waverers; but I think the practical part we should all agree on.

Yours, my dear Duke, most faithfully,

J. W. CROKER.

*The Duke of Wellington to Mr. Croker.**

Strathfieldsaye, April 29th, 1832.

MY DEAR CROKER,

I am going to town to-morrow, and I shall be very happy to see you at half-past ten on Tuesday.

I will apprize Lord Ellenborough and Lord Lyndhurst of your desire to see them with me. If they should fix any earlier or later hour on that day I will send you word to Kensington Palace.

I have not altered my opinion respecting the expediency of any publication by you, or by any of those who belonged to the late Government in particular, or are connected with the Conservative party.

The whole world is too ready to throw upon us the entire responsibility for what is going on; perverting every fact, and inventing lies of all descriptions, to prove that we are the cause of the mischief. If you or any of us publish anything, they will have too good cause for making similar assertions.

I intend to do my best to amend the Bill. But I shall take every opportunity of protesting against every part of

* ['Wellington Despatches,' New Ser. viii. 289.]

the system which it is proposed that it should carry into execution.

I will not take the course of proposing alterations to make the system worse in my sense than it is. I will try to improve the Bill in my sense; but still protesting against it, and intending to vote against it upon the third reading.

I cannot think that it would be consistent with this course for me to recommend the publication of a pamphlet containing a system of improvement of the Bill.

Ever yours most sincerely,
WELLINGTON.

London, May 1st, 1832. 9 A.M.

MY DEAR CROKER,*

I received your two notes† last night. I will wait here till four this afternoon in case you should come to town.

In case you should come to-morrow morning, let it be by nine o'clock, and apprize me this day of your intentions, in order that I may have Lord Lyndhurst and Lord Ellenborough here.

I should doubt our being able to go so far as you propose in the matter of franchises and large towns. However, we can talk over details hereafter.

The important point now is the publication, or rather the completion of the printing, and the circulation to some of the Waverers, viz. Lord Haddington, of your work.

We are very awkwardly situated in relation to the Waverers.

They are an object of detestation and jealousy to our friends and supporters. They are so with great reason. We communicated cordially with them previously to our leaving town. What do you think of Lord Wharncliffe communicating with Lord Grey on Saturday last; and this, notwithstanding that he was warned by Lord Lyndhurst, at my request, of the inconvenience of this course?

Both parties being more or less involved in the pursuit of the same object, we cannot quarrel without great public

---

* ['Wellington Despatches,' New Ser. viii. 292.]

† [These two notes referred to a change in the appointed day of meeting, rendered necessary by the illness of Mrs. Croker.]

inconvenience; and we must continue to communicate to a certain degree. But our communications must be very guarded, and we must keep to ourselves anything of which it is desirable that our opponents should not have a knowledge.

This being the case, conceive what an advantage would be taken of such a document as your work, which must be our brief.

I think that a proper time for publishing the work will come. It is but fair and just by you that it should be published. But I am convinced that it would be a very false step to publish it at the present moment, or to do what is as bad, to give it into the hands of the enemy.

Secrecy is of much more importance than men are aware of in all transactions, and particularly in political transactions, and in the management of a public assembly. I wish just to refer you to the advantages derived by our opponents on the same subject by the secrecy in which they involved their measure till the moment at which it was opened in Parliament.

We had previously determined not to oppose the first reading, and we could not alter our course after the measure was produced. But if we had known what the measure would be, we should have opposed it; and our opposition would have been successful.

Believe me, ever yours most sincerely,
WELLINGTON.

Sir Robert Peel to Mr. Croker.

Whitehall, April 23rd.

MY DEAR CROKER,

I approve the general principles of your letter. I see nothing left, now that the House of Lords has approved the principle of the Reform Bill, but a strenuous concerted effort on the part of all those who deprecate such a reform as that which it involves, to mitigate the evil of it. Both Lords and Commons have now by their votes so far discredited the system of Government under which we have lived, that it seems to me inevitable to try another.

That other had better, in my opinion, be the result of

amendment to the present Bill, than of a new scheme of Reform, proposed by Anti-Reformers, who would be themselves disparaged by their own proposal.

The original Bill of the Government, *wherever it is less mischievous* than the present, is a good document to appeal to; but there are no doubt many amendments of detail introduced into the present, which ought not to be rejected.

I think you should not go too much into detail in your letter. The patience of our forces in Committee will soon be worn out in the Lords; proxies will not tell; the more, therefore, the fire is reserved for important points the better.

Ever yours, my dear Croker,

R. PEEL.

The allusion at the close of the first paragraph of the next letter was prompted by Mr. Croker's fixed belief that the days of the monarchy were numbered.

Mr. Croker to Lord Hertford.

April 17th.

I dined on Saturday at the Duchess of Kent's, with a large Conservative party—four Dukes and three Duchesses, and the rest of thirty people in proportion. I was the only untitled, and almost the only undecorated guest. The little Princess ceases to be little. She grows tall, is very good looking, but not, I think, strong; yet she may live to be plain Miss Guelph.

I forgot to tell you that the speaking in the Lords * was admirable—particularly our friends Ellenborough, Lyndhurst, and the Bishop of Exeter the most effective; but the Duke of Buckingham was *very good* indeed; part of Lord Mansfield very fine; and Lord Bristol acute, polished, and brilliant. Lord Tenterden spoke with great weight. On the other side Lord Grey's first speech was feeble, and his reply furious. Lord Shrewsbury ranted Popery of Bloody Mary's day, and Lord Durham beat Billingsgate hollow. Brougham was able, moderate, cautious—much more for the *seals* than for the Bill.

* [On the second reading of the Reform Bill.]

We now come to the letter written by Mr. Croker to Sir Robert Peel during the negotiations for the formation of a new Government after the resignation of Lord Grey. It is referred to, as the reader will have noticed, in the Journal already printed in this chapter. It has frequently been maintained that Sir Robert Peel might have taken the management of the Reform question, and secured his party a long lease of power, by accepting office in 1832. Mr. Croker's persuasions were doubtless prompted by this belief. And considering the events of later years, and the attitude in which the two men were placed by those events, it is curious to observe the pains taken by Mr. Croker to remove from Sir Robert Peel's mind his dread of being thought inconsistent. It will be remembered that Charles Greville expresses a suspicion that Peel was not sorry for the dilemma in which the Duke was placed—"Nothing can be more certain than that he is in high spirits in the midst of it all, and talks with great complacency of its being very well as it is, and that the salvation of character is everything; and this from him, who fancies he has saved his own, and addressed to those who have forfeited theirs, is amusing." *

Mr. Croker was careful to intimate that he expected no reply to his letter, but Peel answered it the following day, and did not fail to afford strong reasons for his views.

Mr. Croker to Sir R. Peel.

West Moulsey, Surrey, May 11th.

MY DEAR PEEL,

The more I think of the situation of affairs, the less satisfied I am with the line which you seem inclined to adopt. I think your *feeling* a little obscures your *judgment*. Allow me, therefore, who feel for your honour and happiness, all that any man can feel for another, but who am a more

* 'Diary,' ii. p. 301.

impartial judge than you can be in your own cause, to offer you some considerations which have grown up in my mind.

I fully admit the embarrassment to any man of having to countenance a measure which he has opposed and still disapproves, and I admit also (though not in the degree you seem to feel it) the peculiarity of your personal position in reference to the unhappy Catholic question; and I carry perhaps still higher than you do, my knowledge of the difficulties of office at this conjuncture. All *that* premised and conceded, I still think that it may be your positive duty, as a man of honour, to take office, just as it might be to fight a duel—a duty both painful and perilous, but, if honour requires, indispensable.

I further agree that you are the last man who ought to undertake the Government at this moment; but if at last it comes to be you or nobody, the very fact decides the question. Every effort should be made to get Lord Harrowby or Lord anybody to consent to take the helm for the moment; but if there should be ultimately no alternative (which seems to me most probable) but Lord Grey or you, can you doubt what the public advantage and your private honour alike require of you?

If Lord Grey returns, see what must happen—the King enslaved, the House of Lords degraded, the Bill passed, the Revolution, I may say, consummated. And what will be your consolation then? The poor and negative one that you have maintained an apparent consistency in not having touched, even with a view of diverting it, the fatal instrument of the mischief. But the consistency will be only apparent; the real consistency would be that, as you did all that was possible to avert the danger, so now, when it is inevitable, you should exert every effort to mitigate and diminish it. A man easily finds, or rather fancies, colourable reasons for not doing what he has no mind to. You have no desire to be Minister. You are disgusted, if not dismayed, at the prospect, and you permit your dislike and dread to array themselves in the self-deluding garb of consistency and contempt of power. You are now quite sincere. The natural and peculiar delicacy of your mind gives substance and weight to the shadows—for they are no more—which you imagine might cloud your character; but be assured you will not long, and the world will not for a moment, be so deceived; and if the King and Constitution sink under your eyes, without your having jumped in to attempt to save them, your prudence and consistency will be called by less flattering titles in that black-edged page of history which will record the extinction of the Monarchy of England.

"But you may fail." You may; probably will; I do not deceive you or myself with any confidence of success. But what then? We shall not be worse off with the Whigs triumphant after an interval of a month, than after one of a week. Nay, we must be better off. We shall have restored the Monarch to his proper station, and even a month of Royal dignity and authority will do some good. See some of the effects already. Lord Ebrington's motion last year was carried by a majority of 131; last night by one of 80; and that majority of 80 would, I firmly believe, melt totally away before a Ministry which should consent to some, nay to *great* sacrifices, to save what might remain of the Monarchy. Is it without a pang that one lightens the ship, in the last hour of danger, by throwing overboard its treasures, or its guns? But who would not do so rather than let her founder under you?

Honour! character! Yes, the greatest, the only moral treasures of our nature; but they must be allied to courage and self-devotion! What but *disgrace* can result to the whole party, if, after having committed the House of Lords, and encouraged the King, to this violent rupture, they are to be abandoned, and thrown upon the tender mercies of their exasperated enemies? If the Whigs are allowed to get back without a struggle on the part of the Tories, and of you personally, *en dernier ressort*, depend upon it, instead of honour and character, we shall have only degradation and contempt. We shall be despised as fellows who had not courage to take advantage of the events they had prepared, and to which they had instigated others. This reproach will fall most heavily on Lord Harrowby, if he should decline to take his share in the danger; but it will eventually revert to you and the Duke, if you also should, on any pretence, evade the responsibility with which your stations, your talents, your former conduct and principles, and your recent combinations and arrangements, invest you in the eyes of all mankind.

Pray ponder over all this. I give it to you not dogmatically, however strong my expressions may be, but only as materials for your own consideration—as hints of what

I think the opinions of the world will be in the premised cases. It is easy enough to say, "I will have nothing to do with it," but *you* must have something to do with it, for your very refusal is a very important and responsible *something*.

Yours affectionately,

J. W. C.

P.S.—This requires no answer—only your own serious thoughts. I shall see you to-morrow. What an anniversary is this for such a letter. Was Mr. Perceval's task more difficult in 1809 than yours would be now? I think it was not, but I think also he would not have declined it were he now in your position, and that no one else could be found to undertake it.

Sir Robert Peel to Mr. Croker.

Whitehall Gardens, May 12th, 1832.

MY DEAR CROKER,

If I could be a *waverer* as to the course which I should pursue in such a crisis as the present, I should by the very act of wavering prove that I was unfit for the crisis.

I foresee that a Bill of Reform, including everything that is really important and really dangerous in the present Bill, must pass. For me individually to take the conduct of such a Bill—to assume the responsibility of the consequences which I have predicted as the inevitable result of such a Bill—would be, in my opinion, personal degradation to myself.

Read the following—one of a hundred declarations to the same effect made by me, in the melancholy anticipation that some such event as that which has now occurred would occur:—

Sir Robert Peel.—" Dissolve Parliament if you will,—I care not much whether I am returned again; but if I did feel any anxiety on this point, I would go to my constituents with your Bill in my hand, and I would put forward as my especial claim for a renewal of their confidence, my determined opposition to its claims.

" If the people of England still insist on the completion of this measure, I shall bow to their judgment, but my own opinions will remain unchanged. To all the penalties of maintaining those opinions—the incapacity for public service, the loss of popular favour, the withdrawal of public confidence—I can and must submit. The people have the right and the power to inflict them, but they have neither the power nor the right to inflict that heavier penalty of involving me in their responsibility. I feel that it has ceased to be an object of fair ambition to any man of equal and consistent mind, to enter into the service of the Crown."

I look beyond the exigency and the peril of the present moment, without diminishing the extent of the danger, and I do believe that one of the greatest calamities that could befall the country would be that utter want of confidence in the declarations of public men which must follow the adoption of the Bill of Reform *by me* as a Minister of the Crown. It is not a repetition of the Catholic question. I was then in office. I had advised the concession as a Minister. I should now assume office for the purpose of carrying the measure to which, up to the last moment, I have been inveterately opposed as a revolutionary measure.

If I am to be believed, I foresee revolution as the consequence of the Bill. What is your advice? That I should be the author of a more remote but certain revolution, in order to avert an immediate one? But the very adoption of the Bill by me is revolution—it is a concession, against my conviction, to a popular demand. There is as much of violence in it as in the making of Peers.

[No signature].

Mr. Croker to a Friend.

May 29th.

When the King proposed, as the basis of a new Administration, the Bill (substantially) of the old Ministers, it was evident that no Conservative Government could be formed, and that the attempt would perhaps accelerate rather than retard the Revolution, which, in either case, was inevitable, and so the Whigs returned to *place*—but not the *same* place. Their position seems to me materially changed. It is no longer "the King and *his Ministers.*" It is no longer King, Ministers, Lords and Commons, united in one principle. It is quite clear that each of these four parties have a different and (in essentials) contrary object. In short, all have taken off their masks. The King turns out to have been a reluctant reformer all through. The Ministers are avowedly the tools of the mob. The House of Commons is so divided that (except on some question of reform, or one connected with it) I do not think the Tories or the ultra-Tories, the Whigs, the ultra-Whigs, the English Radicals, or the Irish Radicals, could carry any one measure through the House. The Lords are affectedly busy in the lamentable farce of passing with considerable majorities a Bill which everybody knows there is a large majority against; and finally, but most important of all, the mob has thrown aside the mask of loyalty, and all pretence of respect for the present form of Government. The King, the Queen, and the Royal Family are libelled, caricatured, lampooned, and balladed by itinerant singers hired for the purpose, to a degree not credible. They are constantly compared to Charles and Henrietta, and to Louis and Antoinette, and menaced with their fate; and the Attorney-General declares in Parliament that he thinks no libeller should be prosecuted, if only he happens to be sincere in his opinion; and when in the Lords the impunity of all this treason (for it has gone beyond sedition) is charged against Ministers, they exhibit a violent indignation—against the libellers and traitors?—No; but against the Lords, who complain of their atrocities.

Depend upon it, our Revolution is in a sure, and not slow, progress; and every legitimate Government in Europe will feel its effects. We have been for half a century the ark which preserved in the great democratic deluge the principles of social order and Monarchical Government. We are now become a fire-ship, which will spread the conflagration.

In the month of August, Parliament was prorogued, and Mr. Croker took the decision, from which he never afterwards could be induced to swerve, to retire altogether from public life. There was no difficulty whatever about his obtaining a seat in the new Parliament. Dublin University was now prepared to return him at any time, as is sufficiently proved by the letters he received throughout the years 1832 and 1833. Other constituencies invited him to represent them, and the interest of private friends, notwithstanding the Reform Bill, was more than strong enough to provide a place for him in the House, had he been willing to accept it. But his resolution was immovable. Even the opinion of the man whose judgment he trusted most—the Duke of Wellington—had no influence over him, so far as this subject was concerned. The reasons which rendered him so steadfast to his determination are set forth in the following letters :—

Mr. Croker to the Duke of Wellington.

Sudley Lodge, Bognor, August 11th, 1832.

MY DEAR DUKE,

I think it right to inform your Grace that I have to-day declared, what I had all along resolved, that I would not offer myself for the new Parliament. I believe, in my conscience, that *that* Parliament will substantially be as complete a *usurpation*, leading to as complete a subversion of our ancient Constitution, as the Long Parliament. My sitting in it would be an acknowledgment of its legality, my soliciting a seat would be an admission of its beneficial tendency. I must, perforce, obey its decisions, but I am not bound to concur in making them, or to assist in enforcing them. I shall, in my humble station, dutifully submit to what is *de facto* established, but I will not spontaneously take an active share in a system which must, in my matured judgment, subvert the Church, the Peerage, and the Throne—in one word, the Constitution of England. Many men whom I love and respect, younger, of more sanguine temper, of high station, and greater abilities will, I believe, take a different course. I regret it; because I fear that their countenance—perhaps I should better say their acquiescence—will diminish, or at least delay, the chance of an early return to something like our old system of Government. But *they* do what they conceive to be their duty. I do mine.

One only contingency could have altered this determination; I have received so many—indeed, such general assurances of support from the University of Dublin, accompanied with such apprehensions of approaching danger to all our institutions—that I was afraid I should receive a formal requisition calling upon me, as one who had three times in better days solicited the honour of representing them, to accept *now* the trust as one of difficulty and danger. Such a call I felt that I could not in honour decline. The more disagreeable, the more dangerous, the more I should have felt bound to accept it; and, as in all cases of personal character and honour, the suggestion of private judgment and political principle must have been rejected. But although I am assured that I should be unanimously elected, I am no longer apprehensive that any such honourable *claim* and call will be made upon me, and I therefore feel myself perfectly free to follow my original and conscientious determination. I had had an invitation from Ipswich, and a more formal and very weighty requisition from the City of Wells, but could of course have no difficulty in declining both, though at Wells, I suppose, I should have been pretty sure of success.

J. W. C.

The Duke of Wellington to Mr. Croker.

London, August 14th, 1832.

MY DEAR CROKER,

I have received your letter. I am very sorry that you do not intend again to be elected to serve in Parliament. I cannot conceive for what reason.

Ever yours most sincerely,
WELLINGTON.

Thus the Duke, having received, and doubtless carefully considered, Mr. Croker's letter, briefly tells him that he cannot conceive "for what reason" he declines to re-enter Parliament. This significant comment on the reasons so minutely set forth by Mr. Croker expressed what must be regarded as the strictly common-sense view of the matter. It never can be wise for a man to give up public life altogether because some measure has been passed of which he happens to disapprove. Even on the highest grounds of conscience or principle, it is his duty still to use his influence on what he believes to be the right side, and to endeavour to avert the evil which he foresees or fears. What Jeremy Taylor said of life generally, may certainly be applied to that part of life which is passed upon the political stage—one is bound to play out the game. "We are in the world like men playing at tables; the chance is not in our power, but to play it is;

and when it is fallen, we must manage it as we can." Not thus, however, did the question present itself to Mr. Croker's mind. He felt very strongly that he could not honourably take any part in a system which he had denounced as dangerous and wrong, and towards the end of August he wrote to another friend, even more fully than he had written to the Duke of Wellington, in support of his views.

Mr. Croker to Lord Fitzgerald.*

The Grange, August 28th, 1832.

I am very sorry to find that all my political friends (unless Peel, who has given no opinion except by taking a different course) disapprove of my determination. They say that "admitting that all were hopeless, it is my duty to continue my resistance to the Revolution even 'to death in the last ditch'; but all is *not*, say they, hopeless. The Parliament will be a better one than the present. Much may be done, everything ought to be attempted." I believe they are utterly mistaken; a great fuss is made of some dozen or two of places which, contrary to all expectation, show a desire to return Conservatives. It surprises us, and therefore makes an undue effect; for, when all is done, I do not believe it possible that above 150 Tories should appear on the new arena; and "what are they among so many?"

It is, in truth, a miserable delusion to consider the agricultural interests as essentially Conservative. No doubt the county gentlemen are, as they always have been, Tories—that is, adverse to change. So they were in 1642, in 1688, and so again in 1830. But how did they succeed? and if they were not able to resist the populace then, when they really composed so great a proportion of the constituency, what can they do now, when to the 40s. freeholder are added tenants at 10l. 20l., 50l. per annum? But what is it that is in danger? The Church, and the Peerage, and the Crown! Will the agriculturists "die in the last ditch" to maintain the parson's right to his tithe, or the landlord's rent? In short, I believe the county constituency will be just as bad as that of the towns,

* [Mr. Vesey Fitzgerald succeeded to the Barony of Fitzgerald and Vesci on the death of his mother, in January 1832.]

for the question of *tithe* will unite them all, small farmers and great gentlemen, in the common assault upon the whole social system. But all this, however important, has nothing to do with my personal conduct, because it is only a *result*, while I must act on the present circumstances; and seeing, as I clearly do, that to solicit, or even to accept a part in a system created by usurpation, and pregnant with confusion, would be a participation in the guilt, I will, I repeat, have nothing to do with the new Parliament.

As I hinted before, all my political friends are very angry with me. The Duke seriously so. He is here,* and I doubted almost whether he would speak to me; however we are very cordial, and though I undergo the attacks of the whole house all day long, it is all in good humour and compliment. Lady Sandwich, to whom I said yesterday that I was about to write to you on the subject, desires me to give you her remembrances, and say that she is quite sure that you will partake her *indignation* at my *desertion*. I dare say you will at first, because you would like to see me with this fine feather in my hat; but on consideration I think you will agree that, *happening to be ashore*, I am right in not embarking again in a new voyage in which I can gain nothing, and indeed do nothing, and am invited by no better inducement than that the ship must founder. The metaphor is, I see, a bad one, for I am in the ship, and must founder with her, and the real question is, whether I shall voluntarily involve myself in the moral and political responsibility of the inevitable catastrophe? Must I not only be lost, but must I sacrifice my principles, my character, my comfort, and my happiness? I say nothing of health, though that too, I believe, would break down long before the general catastrophe; and so, heaven be praised, ends that odious chapter of self.

Now for the rest. Lord Grey has privately refused the Speaker his peerage, and I hear the King, grateful to Sutton for his readiness to accept the Government last May, is resolved that he shall be his first peer.† Lord Grey gave Sutton to understand that he was in some embarrassments about peerages, but that they might not have been unsur-

---

* [At "The Grange," the residence of Mr. Croker's old friends, Lord and Lady Ashburton.]

† [Mr. Manners Sutton was made a Knight of the Bath in 1833, and created a peer in 1835, with the title of Lord Canterbury.]

mountable, if Sutton had not been so determinedly hostile. This was touched very gently and remotely, but if Sutton had taken the hint, and said, "Why should you anticipate my hostility?" the matter might have been arranged; at least, that is Sutton's opinion and mine, but though he might for so great an object as the enlisting Sutton, and in so peculiar a case as a resigning Speaker, have ventured on the creation, we know that he would have had great difficulties in satisfying certain other individuals.

Next come two questions, which will surprise you as they did me. It is mooted whether he ought to come into Parliament, and if he does, whether he should strenuously refuse to be elected to the chair. The Duke of Wellington (as he, Sutton, tells me) is clear in advising him to come in and not to take the chair. This seems to me incomprehensible. I should have decided both questions the other way. I cannot conceive how a man who has for sixteen or seventeen years sat in that chair, and who has had precedence of all the Commoners of England, can descend to be called to order by Spring Rice (their reported Speaker), and to yield the *pas* in society to old Newport. But connected with this matter there was a little plot. I hear, from a most confidential source, that the King (if not at the suggestion, at least with the knowledge of the Duke of Wellington) intended, at the last levée, which the Speaker necessarily attended, to offer Sutton his seat for Windsor. I need not suggest to you the motives and obvious results of such an offer. Whether it was made or not, Sutton did not tell me; in fact, it was not from him that I learned anything about the exact object. He only told me that, "The Duke urged him to come into Parliament, and that when I met his Grace here he would explain to me his views and *all about it*." But having myself retired from politics, and knowing the Duke's disapprobation of my doing so, I could not venture to broach such a subject with him, and therefore I cannot tell you whether the King did or did not make the *actual* offer.

Well, Ned Ellice is out. People ask why? No one can tell. Yet I think I can guess. He was so liberal of his promises and pledges to pass the Bill, that he is actually bankrupt, and runs away to escape the importunity of his political creditors.

Sir Robert Peel was in the meantime at Drayton, thinking

very little of politics, as he caused it to be understood, but very much of the new Drayton Manor which he was then building. Instead, therefore, of discussing the Reform Bill or the prospects of the new Parliament, he sent to Mr. Croker a short treatise on battlemented houses.

Drayton Manor, August 10th, 1832.

My dear Croker,

Notwithstanding your retirement, and my supposed immersion in politics, *your* letter was the first communication I have received since I left London which related to elections or reminded me of politics. I feel as if I had done with them—at least for a long season—and read of the House sitting till three o'clock, and abortive attempts to amend the Reform Bill in the present session, with no feelings but those of satisfaction that I am a hundred miles from the scene of contention.

I am not going to have battlements, and I am not going to have labels to the windows of the main body of the house; and I feel quite confident I am right. The parapet, or ornamented balustrade, was in use in the time of Elizabeth and James, and not the battlement. The battlement was of an earlier date.

The great authorities extant in domestic architecture of the times of Elizabeth and James, are Hatfield, Audley End, Blickling, Ingestre, Aston Hall, Warwickshire, Burghley, (Lord Exeter). Add: Beaudesert, Losely Hall, Surrey; Kentwell Hall, Suffolk; Bramshill (Sir John Cope's), built for the Prince of Wales, son of James I. I could add many others. In not one of those above mentioned does a battlement appear. There is uniformity, and without an exception a parapet, either plain or enriched, in the place of a battlement, and the courses are almost as uniformly as they have been placed in my house. There is scarcely a window in any one of the houses above named with a label. There is not one where the course is so near the top of the window as it is in mine.

I am in a strange state—with one house rising before the windows of another. The stone turns out to perfection, and they are roofing in the body of the house.

Ever most sincerely yours,
My dear Croker,
Robert Peel.

I forgot to say that I did not buy the Hobbemas,* nor did I attempt to buy them; but I did buy what I could not find on the osier-pool or by the brook-side:—1st. The original Portrait of Dr. Johnson by Sir Joshua; 2nd, The Bust of Pope by Roubiliac †; 3rd, The Bust of Dryden by Scheemaker; and 4th, A beautiful Portrait by Dobson, an English portrait-painter whom Vandyke introduced to the patronage of Charles the First. The two first are truly valuable; but people were buying gilt chairs and old China, and let me quietly buy my portraits and busts for 300*l.*, altogether.

Mr. Croker to Sir R. Peel.

Sudley Lodge, Bognor, August 15th, 1832.

MY DEAR PEEL,

I give you joy—Pope—Dryden—Johnson—for 300*l.*! I am as poor as you may live to be; but I should have given 300*l.* for Pope alone. It is, to my taste, the finest bit of marble which I ever saw; and if I were to have one costly work of art, it should have been *that*, if I could have compassed it. When I heard Lord Hertford was going to Erlestoke, I was just about to advise him to bid for that, which I estimated at 500*l.*; but he has such a disposition to make one a present of anything one happens to admire, that I was afraid he might offer it to me, and so I luckily held my peace. I forget the Dryden. The Johnson, if it be the picture—as I believe it is—which I saw twenty-six years ago at Mrs. Thrale's, is invaluable. So again I give you joy, if, in the storm-portending times in which we live, the gewgaws of art or literature are worth a thought.

You, I think, *mistake*, and therefore, as we say in Pandemonium, *mis-state*, what I said about "battlements" and "labels." I did not mean to rest the battlements on authorities, but merely on beauty. There are authorities both ways, and the weight of authority *may* be with Smirke and you; but there is enough on the other to justify what I only advocated as an

---

* [At the sale of Mr. Watson Taylor's pictures. The portrait of Dr. Johnson was painted by Sir Joshua Reynolds for Mr. Thrale, and is now in the National Gallery.]

† [The original clay model of this bust is in the house of Mr. John Murray, at Wimbledon.]

embellishment. There is a class of parapets which are as handsome, perhaps more so, than embattlements; but they are expensive; and, as well as I remember, your parapet is plain *upright*, in preference to which, even in the teeth of authority, I should like a battlement. As to the *labels*, *I did* quote authorities, because you once quoted authorities against me. Now I insist that authority is against *you*. Observe, I am not speaking of the great windows, as you seem to think, which are protected by the string-courses, but of the smaller windows (as my drawing showed), which, by some internal accident, depart from the general size and external character of the great windows. These I assert ought, according to the best authority, and that best of authorities, *reason*, to have labels to protect their upper frames. So much for architecture.

Now for a little politics, a subject that will soon be dried up as between *us*, but which I think it right to trouble you with, for, I hope and believe, the last time. You are aware of my reluctance to come into the new Parliament.* . . . I well know the sacrifice I make—not of the vanity of being re-elected for that place—in other times that would have been something—but of that private society and intimate intercourse, which in our habits cannot exist without political connexion, or at least without living in the same political atmosphere. I shall lose the society of those with whom I have lived the intelligent half of my life, and I shall have, not the pleasure, as Lucretius calls it, but pain of seeing them tost on a tempestuous sea, while I stand—perhaps not out of danger, but out of sight—on the shore. But, under all circumstances, believe that I shall be, my dear Peel,

Your most sincere and affectionate friend,
J. W. C.

The Duke of Wellington to Mr. Croker.†

Walmer Castle, September 28th, 1832.

MY DEAR CROKER,

I have received your note of the 26th, and I shall be happy to see you on Saturday the 6th.

---

* [Mr. Croker here repeats the arguments used in his letters to the Duke of Wellington and Lord Fitzgerald, *supra*.]

† ['Wellington Despatches,' new series, viii. 415.]

I am inclined to believe that the retreat of Charles X. from Edinburgh was a measure of prudential anticipation, on his part, of a course which he conceived was to have been prescribed to him in a short period of time. He saw clearly that he had no hope of protection from the Ministers, and he anticipated the *invitation* which they would receive from home to send him away.

When he went, they treated him and his family in a very scurvy manner. The Duchesse d'Angoulême, in London, was unnoticed, excepting by a private visit from the Queen. They did not even give her a Government yacht or steamboat; or to the King one of King William's vessels to carry him away. Her Royal Highness went in the common passage boat to Rotterdam, His Majesty in a trader to Hamburgh.

Yet I know, and they know, that when the family came here, there was nothing about which King Louis Philippe was more anxious than that they should be received and treated with respect and attention, and everything done to provide for their accommodation.

This want of respect and attention to them, therefore, is to be attributed to an innate desire to court the Radicals, and to manifest a contempt (however cowardly) for fallen greatness

Believe me, ever yours most sincerely,

WELLINGTON.

In October, Sir Robert Peel sent a pressing invitation to Mr. Croker to pay him a visit at Drayton ; and the reply to this conveyed a somewhat melancholy account of Mr. Croker's thoughts and feelings at the moment. There can be no doubt that he greatly missed his old employment, and that the prospect of never again being heard in the House of Commons, although it was a sentence voluntarily pronounced upon himself, depressed his spirits. The fit however passed off, and his letters soon recovered their usual tone.

Mr. Croker to Lord Hertford (in the form of a journal).

October 21*st.*—I dined at Kew, as you know. His Royal Highness * asked me when *you* were to leave town. I said

* [The Duke of Cumberland.]

"Next morning." He then asked, "Early?" I said, "I suppose about ten." He said, "That's too early, else I should go in to see him. If I had known that he was in town I should have called on him to-day." They are in great alarm for Prince George; though his accident was so slight its consequences are, out of all proportion, formidable. *Sight* is they say, irrevocably gone, and even *life* is in danger. I observed an instance of Royal *confidence*. I, who had heard from some people of the family that matters looked very ill, avoided the subject; but the Duke of Dorset, who came in after me, asked after Prince George. "Oh," said the Duke of Cumberland, "he's quite recovered—quite well; *in high force.*" At that moment he was in imminent danger.

October 22*nd to* 27*th* I spent at Drayton with Goulburn, Herries, and Holmes. Our host really in "high force," and thinking, better than any one I have yet met, of the *probabilities* of salvation. It seemed to me, however, to be rather the confidence of his temper than his reason; but either way it was cheering, though I regret to say not catching. He builds a good deal of hope on the Dutch war bringing people to their senses. I doubt that there will be war, and if there is it will awaken no great degree of public feeling, and it will have the effect of uniting the Government and the Radicals, who are every hour separating.

November 1*st.*—I went up to town to attend a meeting of persons desirous of testifying regard for Sir Walter Scott.* You had been written to, but I have not heard whether you consented to lend your name; the general wish seemed to be to rescue Abbotsford, its library, and collection of curiosities, from the hands of the creditors, and settle them as heirlooms in the family; but I doubt the success of the scheme; it would require a subscription of 50,000*l.*, and I do not expect half the sum, indeed I doubt the public's liking that object— a monument, a statue, or even a pillar, I think, will be readily provided for; but buying a large estate; and paying off trading debts, is quite another matter.

November 3*rd.*—Brougham is ill, some say *very*. He did not receive the Judges the first day of term, nor the new Lord Mayor. Lord Tenterden resigns, and Denman, triumphant from the acquittal of the Bristol magistrates, is, it is said, to be *Chief Justice*—'tis the birthright of his station. I

---

* [Sir Walter Scott had died on the 21st of September.]

should not be surprised if Brougham longed for that *permanent* place himself, and his illness may not be unconnected with some design of that kind.

I am glad *to hear* that Prince George is better; they feared last week effusion of blood on the brain; but it seems that apprehension is vanished, and he is constitutionally so much better, that he walks out in the garden, but he is, I fear, still blind of both eyes, and likely to remain so. When the Duke of Wellington was at Sudbourne, he told us that the Conservative registries had been so neglected in Hampshire that Lord Devon would withdraw. I now hear that they turn out better, and he is to stand. They have a story, that at one of the late Conferences, when hostile measures by France and England were actually decided upon, Bulow got up, took his hat and walked off, and I hear to-day that Lieven has also retired from the Conference; but I was long enough in the secret to learn to doubt street reports of such matters.

The acquittal of the Bristol magistrates has made a good deal of sensation. The public call it a *conviction* of the Government, and Denman prosecuted the business as if he thought it would bear that interpretation. I believe the Ministers are much mortified at the result, which certainly does fix the blame on Colonel Brereton, who was acting under their orders.

November 5th.—How prophetic the above has been! On my arrival in town to-day, I find that poor Lord Tenterden is dead, and, wonderful to say, I find in everybody's mouth a rumour that, agreeably to my foregoing guess, Brougham means to be Chief Justice himself. Nothing is too strange for that man, and I believe he could even do this, but his colleagues will not allow him. What would they do for a Chancellor? Westminster Hall says that Denman is the man. The Clubs talk of Lord Lyndhurst, and Denman to be Chief Baron. This would be the best arrangement for the law, and I think the best for the Whigs, for it would remove Lyndhurst from politics. In his present position he is always a *point d'appui* for the formation of a new Government.

November 9th, London.—I came in here to attend a meeting for promoting a subscription to purchase Abbotsford and its collections out of the grip of creditors, and to entail them as a monument—a kind of literary Blenheim, on Scott's descendants. We had a good meeting of Whigs and Tories, but no Radicals. I do not think we shall be able to raise anything like enough to fulfil our object. Lord Mahon moved, and Burdett seconded one set of resolutions, and I moved, and the Socinian Bishop Maltby seconded another; but, like all coalitions, I fear we shall fail in our ultimate object.*

Mr. Croker to Sir Robert Peel.

West Moulsey, November 15th.

Having a little paper to spare, let me say a word about the *tower*. Don't think I sent you the sketches of Rhine towers as *authorities* (though I might, for they are probably of the age we call Norman). I only sent them as hints and specimens of how the thing would look, and indeed chiefly to correct the slight error I had made in talking to you on the subject, as well as to explain *how slight* that error was. But if you want *authorities*, they are all through England and Normandy. I have no fine books, and cannot refer you to many examples, but the other day at the Scott meeting at Bridgewater House, Smirke began to speak to me on the subject, but we were immediately interrupted by the business of the day; as I walked away, having been thus reminded of the subject, I happened to look at the front of St. James's Palace, and there I found the square base resolving itself into the octagon tower as they do at Burleigh. I am almost sure there is something of the same kind at Warwick. As to the turret or belfry on a tower, there are abundant examples. There are, I think, at Warwick two *turrets* on one tower. *Belfries*, as applied to castles, are of a later date, but don't be deterred from having a utility like a belfry by the want of authority. Utility and common-sense are, as I think I once before said to you, the best authority; and to please the eye is the next; and as your tower is an ornamental expense, I should, if I were you, have the belfry to it, and should give it the most agreeable form, in spite of all the authorities in the world, even if they could be produced against me.

Yours affectionately,
J. W. C.

---

* [The library was purchased by the friends of Sir Walter Scott, and made over to the family. It remains at Abbotsford as the original owner left it.]

P.S.—I have received to-day a formal invitation to stand for Nottingham, and, if I should decline, to recommend a candidate. I have declined in three words, and have taken no notice of the latter proposition. I have at last retired into my pretty den here, and am as happy as one can be with the prospect of seeing little of the friends of my early and better days.

I wish you could see my library here. I think it a model for a book-drawing-room; it is but just finished, and all in the very cheapest way; but every one who has seen or sat in it is delighted with it. It is rather odd, and would frighten poor Smirke by its angles and irregularities; but it is warm and comfortable, and holds 3000 volumes without diminishing the size of the room, and without having, I think, any of the sombre formality of a library. I have besides a little den which holds 1000 volumes more, and in which I *work*. In short, with the drawbacks which I have mentioned, I am as happy in my mind, as satisfied with my very moderate fortunes, and as contented with my humble location and still humbler avocations as it is possible to be.

Mr. Croker to Lord Hertford.

November 21st.

The devil to pay amongst the Whigs and Radicals. Burdett and Hobhouse have found out that they are Whigs, and so have their old supporters, and have set up Colonel Evans against Hobhouse, because Hobhouse's stomach has taken a squeamish turn since he has lived so much at Whitehall, and cannot digest *pledges*. Now as he used to swallow pledges like strawberries, the Radicals are suspicious that so great a change in his taste must proceed from a constitutional indisposition, and they mean to send him travelling for the benefit of his health. On this Burdett takes alarm, and publishes a letter against pledges somewhat *stronger* in language than perhaps Peel might use, but in the most Conservative direction, and concludes by telling his *quondams* fairly that he had rather be turned out with Hobhouse, than returned with Evans. In short, the proposition of "*enfranchising his close borough*" of Westminster "*takes away his breath.*" If the cause were not so serious, all this would be laughable. If candidates and money could be found to oppose them, the

Ministerialists would be everywhere beaten; but as it is, they will get in most of their office men. Palmerston certainly for South Hants, Spring Rice probably for Cambridge, Althorp and Russell for their two counties; the rest is more doubtful. Then, *I hear* that Lord Grey becomes more and more anxious to escape; he has set fire to the mine and wants to run away from the explosion.

December 11*th.*—The Metropolitan elections are all over quietly, and (with one exception) to my satisfaction. The Radicals are everywhere beaten by the Whigs; but unluckily in London the only *Tory*, Lyall, is defeated. In Marylebone, Finsbury, &c., the Radicals made no muster at all. There was no Tory candidate, and the Government Members have come in, and so, I believe, they will generally.

December 13*th.*—The elections are going as badly as possible for the Tories as a *party*. Of about 150 returns they have only about 44. Peel is in, so are Manners Sutton, and Goulburn for Cambridge, Herries for Harwich, &c. Tom Duncombe is in the most ludicrous misery for his defeat. Folks think that he must join Brummell. He says that it has cost Lord Salisbury 14,000*l.*, and that for half the money he would have retired; the extent of bribery is—I repeat it—enormous, and will decide all.

CHAPTER XVIII.

1833-1834.

The First Reformed Parliament—Diminished Strength of the Tories—The Name "Conservative" first used by Mr. Croker—"Paying Debts"—The Duke of Cleveland—Mr. Manners Sutton re-elected Speaker—"Finality" in Reform—An old Superstition—The Coercion Bill—Irish Debates—Disorder in the House—Course taken by Peel—His Remarks on the new House—And on the Working of the Reform Bill—Probable Anticipations of Office—Estrangement from the Duke of Wellington—The Duke's Opinions on Politics—Giving Pledges at Elections—Peel preparing to accept Office—Lord Goderich created Earl of Ripon—The Malt Tax—A Victory Reversed—Unpopularity of the Budget—The Royal Academy Dinner—Defeat of Sir John Hobhouse—Capture of Don Miguel's Fleet by Napier—An Unhealthy Season—Toryism of Sir Francis Burdett—Close of the Session—Dinner given by the King—A Ministerial Pamphlet—Notes upon it by Peel and Wellington—Sir R. Peel on the Landed Interest—Dinner given by the Duke of Gloucester—Conversations with the Duke of Wellington—Lord Grey's Resignation and Lord Melbourne's alleged "Dismissal"—Mr. Croker's Narrative—Sir Robert Peel's Ministry—Proffer of Office to Mr. Croker—Death of the Duke of Gloucester—The Tamworth Manifesto.

WHEN the new House of Commons assembled, it was found that the changes in its composition were not nearly so great as most people had anticipated. Most of the well-known Members on both sides were safely back in their seats, although a few familiar faces had disappeared from the scene —among them, that of Sir C. Wetherell, one of the most active, and sometimes one of the most amusing, of all the opponents of the Reform Bill. On the other side, Orator

Hunt was defeated at Preston. The general result, however, was that the Tories, who had already been much weakened in 1831, suffered a further diminution of their strength. They mustered only 149, against 509 Whigs and Reformers. The fortunes of Toryism have never since then been reduced to so low a state. Even in 1880, after the great reverse which fell upon the party, there were still 237 Members of the House who professed its principles.

The Radicals, although numerically weak—not exceeding fifty—were active and determined, and Mr. Croker foresaw that they were destined to exercise a great, it might even be a preponderating, influence. "The only one of the three parties that can be reckoned upon," he wrote to a friend on the 6th of January, "is the Radical. The Conservatives, a few by pledges, many by professions, will find themselves obliged to vote for popular measures. So will the Ministerialists; and, to say the truth, I have more hope from the *latter* than from the Conservatives, who, I fear, will not be able to exhibit a compact and certain body of above forty or fifty." It will be observed that Mr. Croker here adopts the word Conservative instead of Tory. The name was then just coming into use, Mr. Croker himself having first introduced it in 1831, in an article in the *Quarterly Review*. It crept slowly into general favour, although some few there were who always held out against it, encouraged by the example of the late leader of the party, Lord Beaconsfield, who was not at all likely to extend a welcome to anything which came with Mr. Croker's mark upon it.

The programme of the Radicals was large and comprehensive—vote by ballot, universal suffrage, abolition of Church Establishments, formed a part, and only a part, of it. Great demands, and great professions, were made on all sides; but after all, the measures which chiefly tend to render the year

1833 noteworthy, were the abolition of slavery in English colonies, and the Bill of Lord Ashley for regulating the labour of children in factories. But before this or any other business was done, the Ministers had, as Mr. Croker said, to pay their debts.

Mr. Croker to Lord Hertford.

West Moulsey, January 25th.

The Ministers, like honest men, have been paying their debts, but, unlike Alvanly, they seem to give some creditors a preference. Lord Stafford is Duke of Sutherland, and the modern Harry Vane, Duke of Cleveland. When I told Francis Leveson, six months ago, that his father was a reformer in hopes of being a Duke, he laughed at me, and assured me that the poor old man had no such thoughts, but was frightened at the idea of losing his present titles and estates, and supported the Ministers out of mere cowardice and dotage. When Cartwright, on the hustings at Northampton, prophesied that Cleveland was to be a Duke, the patriot peer was indignant, and actually obliged Cartwright to unsay what he had said; and lo! in a few weeks the *Gazette* fulfils my rejected guess and Cartwright's disavowed assertion. Then they have made Western a peer, because he was beaten in Essex by Baring. This last stroke has been peculiarly designed to show how cordially the King is with them; for surely if there were any peerage which His Majesty might and ought to have refused, it was this particular one; for besides the obvious indecency of making a man a peer only because he was rejected by a *reformed constituency*, there was this peculiarity in the case, that Baring was the man to whom the King owed and professed great obligation for his readiness, in May last, to sacrifice his own comfort and his private feelings for His Majesty's service. And what do you think is the excuse that the King has condescended to give the Tories for this strange act? Why, forsooth, that he wanted to have another friend to the agricultural interest in the House of Lords. *Risum teneatis?* Yet his favourite society is Tory; and all his verbal civilities and attentions at Brighton are for the Tories. He promised, it is said, Sir H. Neale the command at Portsmouth, *vice*

Foley, dead; but his Ministers would not consent, and His Majesty submitted, but consoled his own dignity by inviting Neale to spend a week at Brighton, and to dine with him every day, " to *show the fellows* and the world his real sentiments." Is not that capital?

On the last day of the year there was a small party at the Pavilion. When the clock struck twelve, everybody got up from the card table and went and kissed the Queen's hand, and made the King a bow, and wished their Majesties ". a happy New Year;" upon which the King started up in great spirits, and insisted on having a country dance to dance in the New Year. Lady Falkland sat down to the piano, struck up a lively tune, and everybody took out their partners; and who do you think the King took out? Lord Amelius Beauclerk. You know Lord Amelius, and you think I am jesting. No, by all that's nautical, quizzical, clumsy, monstrous, and masculine, Lord Amelius was His Majesty's partner; and I am told by one who saw it, that the sight of the King and the old Admiral going down the middle, hand in hand, was the most royally extravagant farce that ever was seen.

Lord Munster has been lately at Brighton, and has had even better luck than Lord Amelius; for his father gave him last Tuesday 2500 sovereigns, with which he made the best of his way to Petworth, in hopes, I suppose, that Lord Egremont would take the royal hint, and imitate so laudable an example. One word more, and I have done with Royalties for the present. Wharncliffe is at Brighton, and the King asked him the other day if he could tell him "who the new Bishop of Waterford was to be?"

January 30th.

Well, our friend Sutton was elected Speaker yesterday— 241 to 31—Morpeth proposing, Burdett seconding, and Littleton crying " Nolo Speakerari;" in spite of which, Hume, O'Connell, Cobbett (who sits on the Treasury bench), Faithfull of Brighton, Beauclerk of Surrey, and Warburton, spoke for Littleton, as being " in unison of opinion with the House and the country," whereas Sutton, being a Tory, his re-election would " be a Tory triumph." Burdett seems to have become a zealous Conservative. The only important thing which occurred was Althorp's explanation as to the *finality* (a word which I coined, and which is now in great vogue) of the Bill, by which it appears that they have hit on a device to keep well with all sides. He agreed with Hume that the Bill was only a means towards an end, and that he expected progressive improvements from its having passed; but on the other hand, as related to our representative system, he looked upon the Bill, and trusted the House would do so too, as *final*. This means, we see no necessity for altering the Reform Bill, which has produced us so great a majority; but we are ready and willing to alter everything else. This is my commentary; but I know not what other folks may think.

Are you fond of a bit of superstition? One day last week, at A. Baring's, I told them at breakfast that I dreamt a tooth had dropped out, and that, of course, I should hear of the death of a friend. So we looked at the newspapers for a couple of days with some kind of interest, but no bad news came, and we were about to give up our superstition, when lo! two days after, I read an account of the death that very same night of my dear old friend Lord Exmouth, who with his dying breath sent me a most affectionate message.

You will be anxious to hear how the new Parliament goes on. The debate on the Address lasted four nights, O'Connell and all the Irish opposing the Government with a violence of which there has been no example; but it must be confessed that the Speech foreshadows measures of coercion against Ireland of which there is no example, and we hear that the measures themselves are to be of a character and rigour that no Tory Minister would have ever dared to hint at.[*] Absolute power in the Lord Lieutenant to suspend the Habeas Corpus; to proclaim any parish, barony, county, province, or the whole country, under military law, and liable to Courts-Martial; and, even when the ordinary criminal process is resorted to, to enable the Government to change the venue for trial to Lancashire, Cheshire, or Wales. Such is the rumour, and such, I have no doubt, were the first intentions

---

[*] [The Whig Coercion Bill of 1833 gave the Lord-Lieutenant power to proclaim disturbed districts, substitute martial law for the ordinary Courts of Justice, suppress all meetings, search houses, suspend Habeas Corpus, and punish all persons caught out of their houses between sunset and sunrise. The Bill was passed by the beginning of April, in spite of the eloquent opposition of Sheil and O'Connell.]

of the Government; but I guess that the violence of the debate will induce them, rash and shabby as they are, "*de mettre de l'eau dans leur vin.*"

But to return to the House. For two nights and a half the vehemence and disorder were so great that people began to think the National Convention was begun. Peel told me that it was "frightful—appalling." This induced him to rise late the third night, and read the House a most able, eloquent, and authoritative lecture. While he arraigned the foreign policy of Ministers, he expressed his determination to support their Conservative dispositions, and he deprecated those idle and violent debates. The fate of the Government was, and he knew it, in his hands. If he had chosen to listen only to passion and revenge, he could have put them out. He wisely and honestly took the other line, and the effect was instantaneous and prodigious. The storm moderated, the English Members got time to reflect on the insanity of the Irish, the debate was conducted next night with decency, and the Ministers had 438 to 40; in a second division, on an amendment of their former ally Tennyson, 328 to 60. People now congratulate one another like men escaped from an imminent shipwreck. I do not partake in their hopes, as I see no change in the elements of the case; only I am surprised that the Radicals were not stronger. That is to be attributed to O'Connell's violence, and the shame which Peel's speech produced in some of their minds. Lord Grey is, I hear, loud in praise of Peel. This will give rise to suspicions and rumours; but be assured that Peel is firm and staunch to his principles and his party.

March 10th.

I dined the other day at a small party made at the desire of Burdett, who talked the highest Tory language, praised Peel and his speech up to the skies, and foretold that it would knock off fifty from the Radical minority. He was so *very Tory* that I was obliged to moderate him, and to entreat him not to diminish his ultimate utility by throwing off his popularity too soon; and the Duke of Wellington, to whom I told all this, replied significantly that he had been for some time apprised that Burdett's sentiments did not much differ from his own. Such things as this give rise to the rumours of coalition, but I repeat that it is impossible.

From the beginning of the Session, the eyes of all sections of politicians were turned upon Peel, whose movements and designs no one could fathom. There were some, indeed, who entertained even at that time a strong suspicion that he was preparing to throw over his former friends. This, however, was not the opinion of his political associates; and Mr. Croker clearly foresaw then, as he had always done, that Peel must inevitably rise to the highest place in the Government, and thoroughly believed that he was incapable of the slightest infidelity to the opinions which he professed. The following letter shows how careful and patient was the study which Peel was making of the new House, and how much impressed he was by the fact that the ordinary force of party ties was broken. His reflections apparently had their share in producing the famous Tamworth Manifesto of the following year.

Sir R. Peel to Mr. Croker.

March 5th, 1833.

MY DEAR CROKER,

Thanks for both your letters—chiefly for the first, which drew away my attention from the House of Commons and Irish debates.

It is odd enough that at a large dinner I had yesterday I said that I thought Sir Francis Burdett was the chief Conservative in the House of Commons, and that all I feared was, that he would diminish his efficiency and usefulness in the Conservative line by taking his steps too rapidly in advance. I instanced his doctrine about officers in the army, and the superior, almost exclusive, fitness of gentlemen for a military commission, as a doctrine better suited to the atmosphere of France in 1784 or 1785, than the atmosphere we breathe in the House of Commons. Perhaps he is not far from the truth, but I admired and wondered at his boldness in telling it.

Now for the House of Commons. It is a good one to speak to, but that circumstance does not diminish my fear of it. It is not the suggestion of confidence and vanity, but it is sober truth, when I tell you that on Friday night I could have moved it just the other way. Perhaps not Friday night, but on Wednesday night, if I had chosen to follow Lord Althorp, with his lame accounts of providing for Crown witnesses with good places in the Police; of some man who had actually received a *threat* that his winnowing machine should be burnt; nay, of a clergyman, who absolutely had had panes of glass broken—if I had followed him, given an account of English crimes within the same period, and asked, as Perceval once asked of an excited House of Commons, in the language of true eloquence, "Will you hang a dog upon such evidence?" I could have trampled the Bill to dust. What does this show? That there is no steadiness in the House, that it is subject to any impulse, that the force of party connections, by which alone a Government can hope to pursue a consistent course, is quite paralyzed. Three times already, with reference to three different measures, the Government has said, in the most childish manner, that if not passed they intend to resign.

My belief is, that the Reform Bill has worked for three weeks solely from this, that the Conservatives have been too honest to unite with the Radicals. They might have united ten times without a sacrifice of principle. They might unite on twenty clauses of the Irish Bill.

And what is to happen then? The question is not, Can you turn out a Government? but, Can you keep in any Government and stave off confusion?

What must be the value of that change in the Constitution which rests for its success upon the forbearance and abstinence of parties?—which intended to sacrifice Tories as a party—which appeared to have sacrificed them—and which now appeals to them as a protection, almost the sole protection, from anarchy.

What are we doing at this moment? We are making the Reform Bill work; we are falsifying our own predictions, which would be realised without our active interference; we are protecting the authors of the evil from the work of their own hands. It is right we should do this, but I must say that it was expecting more than human institutions, intended to govern the unruly passions and corrupt natures of human beings, ought to calculate upon.

Ever affectionately yours,

My dear Croker,

ROBERT PEEL.

Three weeks later, it was evident that Sir Robert Peel believed the time to be at hand when his long cherished projects could be matured.

Mr. Croker to Lord Hertford.

March 25th.

I went to Whitehall Gardens (Sir Robert Peel), and found him in much the same opinions; but to my great surprise apparently resolved to accept office and make battle. He spoke with great firmness and spirit, said he would do his duty, and, if necessary, venture to attempt a ministry, though he might think that it could not last a fortnight, but he said he would never give up his principles to that House of Commons; he would be leader, and not led. He would try whether Government could be carried on, and after a fair experiment, he at least would have done his part. I gave him no encouragement, having no hope myself, but I could not deny that what he said was reasonable. He seemed to think there would be an entirely new combination, of which the currency questions would be the basis. On that he was firm, but foresaw that Radicals and Ultra-Tories would unite against him.

The opportunity did not actually arrive till the following year, but the intervening months were not lost. It was noticed that Sir Robert Peel gradually withdrew more and more from the Duke of Wellington, whose views upon reform, and upon other questions which divided parties, were quite unchanged by all that had happened.

The Duke of Wellington to Mr. Croker.

Strathfieldsaye, March 6th, 1833.

MY DEAR CROKER,

I will endeavour to obtain for you the details which you require regarding the state of the representation in the House of Commons. I know none, excepting regarding this county. I have compared notes with others, and I think that all agree in the same story. The revolution is made, that is to say, that power is transferred from one class of society, the gentlemen of England, professing the faith of the Church of England, to another class of society, the shop-keepers, being dissenters from the Church, many of them Socinians, others atheists.

I don't think that the influence of property in this country is in the abstract diminished. That is to say, that the gentry have as many followers and influence as many voters at elections as ever they did.

But a new democratic influence has been introduced into elections, the copy-holders and free-holders and lease-holders residing in towns which do not themselves return members to Parliament. These are all dissenters from the Church, and are everywhere a formidably active party against the aristocratic influence of the Landed Gentry. But this is not all. There are dissenters in every village in the country; they are the blacksmith, the carpenter, the mason, &c. &c. The new influence established in the towns has drawn these to their party; and it is curious to see to what a degree it is a dissenting interest. I have known instances of a dissenting clerk in the office of the agent in a county of an aristocratical candidate, making himself active in the canvass of these dissenters, to support the party in the town at the election.

Then add intimidation and audacity, which always accompany revolutionary proceedings; occasioning breach of promise to vote for the aristocratical candidate, and forcing some to stay away to guard their property, and you have the history of many unsuccessful contests in counties.

That which passed here passed in Northamptonshire and Gloucestershire, but most particularly in the Scotch and Irish counties. The mischief of the reform is that whereas democracy prevailed heretofore only in some places, it now prevails everywhere. There is no place exempt from it. In the great majority it is preponderant.

To this, add the practice of requiring candidates to pledge themselves to certain measures, which is too common even among the best class of electors, and the readiness of candidates to give these pledges, and you will see reason to be astonished that we should even now exist as a nation.

I was aware of Sir Francis Burdett's opinions, and I say the truth is that he is one of the largest and most prosperous landed proprietors in England. He receives above forty thousand a year from his land. He does not owe a shilling; and has money in the funds. He has discovered that they have gone too far, and thinks it not unlikely that the destruction of one description of property, will draw after it the destruction of all.

I happen to know that his opinion upon the state of affairs does not much differ from my own.

Believe me ever yours most sincerely,
WELLINGTON.

Memorandum by Mr. Croker.

March 15th.

Arrived at Strathfieldsaye, and found only the Duke and Mr. and Mrs. Arbuthnot. After dinner, the Duke spoke most despondingly of the public prospects. He did not see what there was to stop, or even check, the revolution, and said that whatever we must think of the Ministers, and the conduct by which they had brought us to this pass, we had nothing to do now, as honest, nay as selfish men, but to endeavour to keep them on their legs; we should not be able to do so long, and that after them would come chaos, but we at least should do all in our power to delay the confusion. Arbuthnot was angry with the Duke for talking so openly, and in so desponding a tone, and begged of me when the Duke returns (for he goes to town to-morrow), and we should be alone, to suggest to him that such disheartening language was the certain way to accelerate the ruin. I said that I doubted whether a false confidence was not more dangerous; that I had in my speeches and writings expressed hopes that I did not feel, because it was thought expedient by my friends, but that I did not think that it did any good; that I did not think anything could do good, but that truth was, I thought, more likely to have some good effect by alarming men who really do not seem to suspect the mine over which they are walking; but I said that certainly I should tell the Duke what he thought. They all went away; the Duke to town to dine with Lord Salisbury. I remained alone at Strathfieldsaye. The Duke came back next day, and when we renewed the conversation, he said that he thought the operation of the Reform Bill though it would probably be slow, was nevertheless sure. The old aristocratical interest has great stamina, and will hold together a long while, but seeing how it has yielded before this shock when in its entire strength, what is it to do in a succession of shocks, each of which will give fresh powers to the democracy? My opinion is that a democracy, once set a-going, must sooner or later work itself out till it ends in anarchy, and that some kind of despotism must then come to restore society. How long we may take in going through that process depends on circumstances, but I myself do not see how the encroaching power of the people out of doors on the House of Commons, and the encroaching powers of the House of Commons on the House of Lords and the Crown, is to be checked and brought back to its fair balance.

Mr. Croker to Lord Hertford.

April 15th.

So Fred. Robinson [Lord Goderich] is an earl, the Earl of Ripon. He wanted to be Earl of Kent and Earl of Harold, but old Lady De Grey would not consent. You recollect that eighteen years ago we made him a Duke of Fuss and Bustle. To see this man, who was our plaything and butt, grown to be an earl, and by such means! A viscount, for insulting Castlereagh's memory by his desertion to Canning, and an earl for insulting Canning's by apostasising to Grey! and the King to submit! Such examples as Stafford, Cleveland, Durham, Western, and Goderich, will have degraded the peerage so much as to diminish our regret for its approaching and inevitable overthrow. The history of this is that Goderich refused to accept Privy Seal, and said that if Lord Grey pressed, he would resign all and break up the Government.* This I should have laughed at as an idle boast, but it seems Lord Grey felt it to be so serious, that he was obliged to capitulate, and accordingly Fred is an earl, and is to have an *extra* Garter. If wonder were a pleasure, we should live in the pleasantest times in the world.

April 30th.

I told you that six weeks ago I dined at Lady Dysart's with Burdett, and that he was talking Conservative lan-

---

* [The story is differently told by C. Greville—'Diary,' ii. p. 367. Lord Ripon was not made a Knight of the Garter.]

guage, and of his own difficulties about the *Assessed Taxes*. In the course of our talk I told him that I saw the chance of an earlier and more dangerous question than the *Assessed Taxes*—the *Malt Tax*. "Some fine evening," I said, "when no one expects it, Sir William Ingleby * will move the repeal of the Malt Tax, and carry it by a small majority, and you will be all astonished next morning to find yourselves with a deficit of five millions and a half in your revenue, and reduced to a Property Tax, or, in other words, confiscation." Such were my very words, remembered by all the parties present; and lo! on Friday evening, no one expecting it, Sir William Ingleby got up and moved the repeal of half the malt duty, carries it by a small majority, and throws the Budget, the Ministry, and the Revenue, on their beam-ends. When the majority was declared, Althorp, with that stupidity which has been called candour, declared that he "*bowed* to the decision of the House;" but his colleagues had soon sense enough to see that the bowing to the decision of the House was no such easy matter; that bowing to the loss of $2\frac{1}{2}$ millions of malt would involve the loss of the whole 5 millions of malt, and the 3 millions of Assessed Taxes, for the repeal of which there is a motion pending for to-night, and that the loss of 8 millions, with great doubts whether a Property Tax *can* be passed, was national bankruptcy. Their first thought, founded on Althorp's silly readiness to bow, was to give up the whole Malt and Assessed Taxes, and to try a Property Tax; their second, I believe, was to resign; their third, was to endeavour to get the House to rescind Ingleby's resolution; and this they have adopted, thereunto, I opine, much induced by an intimation which Peel sent them that he would support them in that course with all his strength.

Accordingly, last night, Althorp backed out of his pledge to bow to the decision of the House, by declaring that he only meant that he would so far bow as not to take a *second* division *that night*. He then stated that he would, on the motion for the repeal of the Assessed Taxes this evening, move a resolution that the repeal of the Malt and Assessed Taxes could not be effected without laying on a Property Tax, and that a Property Tax would be at present inexpedient. You will observe that here again there is trick and juggle, and an attempt to combine in *one* vote, three great questions, viz., to

---

* [Member for Lincolnshire.]

rescind the vote of Friday; to negative the repeal of the Assessed Taxes; and to pledge the House against the Property Tax. Bungling and fraudful as the whole proceeding is, I wish it success, because I am sure that if the Ministers be beaten, we are on the verge of a most alarming crisis. Personal or even political difficulties are not insuperable, but a financial imbroglio would be immediate anarchy and general ruin. Opinions seem much divided as to the result of to-night. I give Ministers a large majority.*

May 6th.

I dined on Saturday at the Academy dinner; a bad exhibition and a very dull dinner. Peel, old Bankes, and I were almost the only Tory commoners, and there was such an overflowing of Whigs that I sat between Spring Rice and the Attorney-General, and opposite the Solicitor. In old times no Government officers used to be intruded into the Whig benches, but now the Whigs push the Tories from even the humblest stools. Old Lady de Grey is, they say, dying. I suppose my Lord Ripon will grow in wealth as rapidly as he has grown in rank. Hobhouse has, in consequence of his pledges upon the Assessed Taxes, resigned, not his office only, but his seat for Westminster. Nobody knows why he resigned both. They say he will be re-elected † for Westminster, though there is a great cry against him; but Col. Evans is such an opponent as may ensure Hobhouse success. The ultra-Tories have set up one of their young lawyers, Mr. Escott, who is said to be more than half-cracked. This will produce nothing but triumph to the Whigs. Those ultra-Tories are certainly the silliest and the wildest party that I have ever seen, and would ruin the country if the Whigs had not been beforehand with them.

A thing however has just occurred which, by giving the Lords an opportunity of doing something, may postpone the necessity of coming into direct collision with the Commons at present. A strange, wild, Navy captain, half mad, of the name of Charles Napier, became a Radical in hopes of being returned for Portsmouth. Failing there, he has turned his

---

* [Lord Althorp's amendment was carried by 355 to 157.]

† [He was defeated by Colonel de Lacy Evans, chiefly through the unpopularity of the Budget. Hobhouse was at the time Chief Secretary for Ireland.]

energies towards Portugal, has engaged with Pedro to take Sartorius's place, and has collected and sailed with a large steamer, a couple of transports, and 1000 men.* He calls himself, I am told, *Don Alphonso de Leon,* or some such thing, and means to pass for a native officer. The Duke asked Lord Grey last night in the Lords if he knew anything of this expedition. Lord Grey said, "No more than he had, like the Duke, seen in the newspapers;" upon which the Duke gave notice of a motion for Monday, of an address to the King to maintain a bonâ-fide neutrality.

June 1st.

The season has been the most sickly ever known. Everybody has had the influenza, as it is called, and though nobody, or very few indeed, have died of *it*, it seems to have disposed those who have it, to take the opportunity of dying of any other disease they may happen to fall in with. I am sorry to say that poor Westmoreland is very ill with it, or some of its consequences, for he had it, recovered, and is now ill again, and worse than before. *That and* 76, and not having an ounce of flesh on his bones, alarms us for our old friend. Lady Westmoreland is in town, dutifully preparing herself for a death-bed reconciliation.

June 14th.

. . . Met Burdett, with whom I flatter myself I am become a great favourite. We dine together twice a week, and rail against Radicals and revolutions, and cry up the Tories and the Irish Protestants. Let me tell you what happened the night before last. We dined at the Bishop of Exeter's. I was talking of Mr. Pitt's error in breaking up the Tory Party in 1801, but I said, "I can't expect you, Sir Francis, to sympathise with me," upon which Burdett made a sign of dissent, and George Sinclair said, "But Sir Francis was a Tory." I replied, "I know he was *born* a Tory, but at the time I was speaking of he had been thrown by circumstances into another line." On which Burdett himself interposed, and said, emphatically, "*At least no one can say* that I was *ever a Whig!*" Is not that capital?

* [The "strange, wild" captain became Admiral Sir Charles Napier. His expedition captured Dom Miguel's fleet, and settled the Portuguese dispute, which had long been raging.]

July 5th.

There was a great assembly at Lady Londonderry's last night. I literally only walked through the rooms, and did not stop five minutes. Overtaking the Duke of Wellington in the hall, he sent away his carriage and we walked to his house together. He says that we are coming to a *dead lock*, that these men cannot work the machine, nor does he believe that any other set of men can.

Peel is now as bad as I am. He thinks this House of Commons is more inveterately hostile to the Church than he had apprehended, and begins to think that its overthrow is quite certain. In the meanwhile the people are quiet, the harvest very promising, fair prices, and a good deal of trade. These favourable circumstances make things go smooth.

From the Diary.

30*th August*, 1833.—Parliament is up. The King closed the session in person. He was received by the people with indifference. The mob observed that he *spat* out of the window of the carriage, as he went along, and said "George IV. would not have done that." Kings are but mortals, and must spit, but I agree with the mob, they had better not do so out the window of the state coach. I believe he is very sick of his *rôle* of reformer, for those about him talk in that tone; meanwhile he gives dinners and makes speeches like a Lord Mayor.

Sir Henry Goodriche is dead of inflammation, at his seat in Ireland, which he had lately inherited with 16,000*l.* a year; and he had nearly as much more before. He has left it all to a friend, Mr. Holyoake, and I suppose the Melton hounds, which he had begun with last season.

The two Buonapartes are still here—rivals for the expected vacancy in France—Joseph as Emperor, Lucien as President. Joseph is a fool, but will show that he is not so great a one as he is supposed, by giving up the game and going back to America. Lucien is fool enough to imagine that *he* has a party in France. 'Tis true enough the movement party would be glad to make use of him, and perhaps will try it, but not a living soul cares twopence about him, and if he were to-morrow to succeed Louis Philippe he would be overturned in three weeks.

7th September.—White's empty. I am alone in the room Crockford's looks equally deserted, and the town itself looks thinner than I ever remember it.

Well, Sutton is Sir Charles. He left town to-day for Dover He says in a note to me " that he is proud of his order, and more proud of the circumstances under which he has received it." The Duke of Wellington gave me a laughable solution of the riddle. He says the Speaker's speech at the bar of the Lords, praising the Ministers and their sessional labours, was so manifestly irony and *persiflage*, that Lord Grey, to prove to the world that it was all *serious*, proposed the red ribbon; at all events, Lord Grey claims the whole merit, but this does not seem quite consistent with Sutton's " pride at all the circumstances."

20th September.—Our King gave on Monday week one of his trumpet dinners to the officers commanding regiments, and made, as usual, a speech, which was all about and *against* Louis Philippe, " They say that I *follow* the Citizen King. So I do *with my eye !* I have my eye on all his movements. I know that our *natural enemy* has not changed her dislike of us. *Sharpen your swords*, gentlemen, for 'tis *you* I must depend upon to uphold the dignity and interests of old England." Such, and even more offensive, was, I hear, his Majesty's allusion to his royal brother. I suppose it *must* be exaggerated, but when he begins to talk after dinner, *il prend le mors aux dents*. They add that Palmerston was by, and said, " Poor man, he means the Emperor of Russia."

Last Monday there was a dinner of the Guards. The first toast after dinner was given by H.M., " the King of Prussia," without any motive that appears, except, indeed, that Bulow happened to be at table. The Duke of Wellington was there; he came up from Woodford on purpose. His health also was drunk with great eulogium.

In the autumn of 1833 a pamphlet appeared which caused a great stir in political circles. Quotations from its pages appeared in nearly all the papers, and the essay itself speedily ran through two or three editions. It was entitled, " The Reformed Ministry and the Reformed Parliament," and its object was to show that all the alarms and predictions to which utterance had been given by the opponents of the Reform Bill, between 1830 and 1832, were rendered ridiculous by the subsequent course of events. It soon became known that the Ministry had practically adopted this *brochure* as their own, and that one or more of their number had even taken a part in the work of compiling it. Lord Brougham had certainly contributed many pages; Lord Althorp and Lord Melbourne, it was whispered, had both had a hand in it. The writer, or writers, ridiculed the "suspicions expressed by the Duke of Wellington" and the "terrors of Mr. Croker." They maintained that the work of Parliament had been done as well as ever—if not better; that the members were "gentlemen," a boast which could not be made of many former Parliaments. Mr. Croker replied to this pamphlet in the *Quarterly Review*,[*] and both the Duke of Wellington and Sir Robert Peel supplied him with copious notes on certain points to aid him in his work. The case of Key, referred to by Sir R. Peel, was that of the Lord Mayor of London, and was thus described by Mr. Croker: "He gets an illegal contract, continues to sit, and vote, and move, and divide in contempt of all law; then asks an appointment for his son, and when the Minister hesitates to appoint a lad of eighteen, asks it for his eldest son, a man of twenty-two, and obtains it; and then it turns out that he has but one son, and the rejected lad is the appointed officer — and appointed to what? To be inspector of the articles furnished under the father's illegal contract."

Sir Robert Peel to Mr. Croker.

Drayton Manor, September 29th.

My dear Croker,

Strange as it may seem, I have not read nor have I seen the Ministerial pamphlet. I saw some extracts from it in the newspapers, which sated my appetite for such reading.

[*] Vol. 50, October, 1833; article entitled "The Reform Ministry and Parliament."

I cannot see much ground for triumph on the part of the promoters of the Reform Bill in the results of last session.

Look how the business was done, and cite the report of the *Times* for the inattention and indecent clamour which marked almost every night's debate after an hour not by any means unusually late.

However, the business was got through. It certainly was, but it was only got through because that which we prophesied took place; namely, that the popular assembly exercised tacitly supreme power, that the House of Lords— to avoid the consequences of collision—declined acting upon that which was notoriously the deliberate judgment and conviction of a majority. I allude particularly to the Irish Church Bill.

With respect to that Bill, it is quite clear that the course taken was taken in spite of the opinions of two out of three branches of the Legislature.

If I were to write on Reform and its consequences, I should take Key's case as my text—the very worst case of which I have any recollection. The man himself, twice Lord Mayor by the voice of the reforming people—the giver of dinners to the Reforming Cabinet—the Baronet of Reform. This fellow, the City member of Reform, getting an illegal contract, procuring the nomination of his son as the inspector of the father's contract articles—the son not eighteen— appointed "in spite of Church," by that very Government which had afterwards the baseness to hold up Church—the Tory appointee—as the delinquent, when they knew that they had rejected his advice and despised his remonstrances.

I should take also the conduct of the Government in the Calthorpe Street affair. I should take the first day's evidence of the Police Commissioners, from which, unless the evidence has been since garbled in publication, it will clearly appear that the Government authorised the dispersion of the meeting, and seven weeks afterwards denied that they had so authorised it, and was ready to sacrifice the Commissioners until it was proved—that a letter written by the Commissioners the day after the meeting, and which had remained unacknowledged and unquestioned for eight weeks, expressly recited the authority of the Home Secretary of State as that upon which the meeting had been dispersed.

When this fact came out, and when the conduct of the Commissioners was shown to be praiseworthy, then did I myself hear in the Committee Room, without communication with the Secretary of State, the Under-Secretary of State tell the Commissioners that their report was admitted to be correct, and that there would be no longer any question about the authority to disperse.

But read the evidence, and see how the matter is stated there, for I know more than one case last session in which the evidence when printed has hardly been recognised as the same by those who heard it orally delivered.

Ever affectionately yours,
R. P.

The Duke of Wellington to Mr. Croker.*

Walmer Castle, September 30th.

My dear Croker,

I don't know that I could have been of much use to you in grappling with the Ministerial pamphlet, if I had not made a mistake, as I find I have, of a week in the time at which you was desirous of hearing from me; as I have here no means of obtaining accurate information from documents, and I am aware that in such cases one's memory is not to be trusted. But having looked into the pamphlet, and considered the subject generally, I am about to give you my views of the mode in which it ought to be answered.

Although the work is a very flimsy one, and is full of exaggerations and falsehoods, it is calculated to make, and has made, an impression in favour of those who certainly wrote it—I mean the Ministers themselves.

I think that the object of the answer ought to be to show that the Parliament which has been formed, and the measures which are applauded in the pamphlet, are equally the legitimate offspring of the dissolution of the 21st April, 1831; and of the King placing himself by that Act, and by the mode of carrying it into execution, at the head of the party whose object had been for nearly two centuries to pull down the institutions of the country, instead of protecting them. It was with such measures in view that the electors of the

---

* [The Duke of Wellington's memorandum is very long, and much of it was worked into Mr. Croker's *Quarterly Review* article. A part of the document only is here given.]

empire were called upon to elect Members delegated for the purpose of pulling down the antient constitution and institutions of the Monarchy. These measures were to be the reward of the parties in the country which enabled the Ministers to attain their purpose.

It is not believed that the Ministers had any immediate object in view, excepting the legitimate one to party men of keeping their rivals the Tories out of power *for ever*. It is extraordinary that the Monarch should not have been sensible of the consequences to himself and his successors, of success in the attainment of even this limited object. The Tories are avowedly the great landed, commercial, and manufacturing and funded proprietors of the country; the Church almost to a man, the Universities, the great majority of the learned professions in the three kingdoms, and of the Professors of Arts and Sciences, of the Corporations of the Empire, &c. This is the party to be excluded for ever from power. This was the object of the Ministers; and it is the repeated boast of their pamphlet that they have attained it.

If they have succeeded, as they have boasted that they have, what becomes of the King? He is either in their hands for ever, or he is delivered over to the tender mercies of a Radical Administration.

The Ministers pretend that they have effected much in the way of economical reform of the Government in all its branches, and particularly in putting down and rendering impossible in future a Government by corruption or patronage. My belief is that we have all done too much in the way of economical reform. We have deprived the King of the power of rewarding those who serve him faithfully, and of relieving the unavoidable distress of the meritorious among his subjects, who by these measures of ours have been thrown upon the bounty of individuals. But they deceive themselves and the public when they tell us that they have put down corruption or government by patronage.

* * * * * *

It is not necessary to enter upon a description of the other measures. They are of the same description, and that relating to education upon the same principle. The Irish Church Bill, together with the measures above referred to relating to Tithes, must destroy the Church of England in Ireland. We must not consider the Church of England, whether in England or in Ireland, as a religious establishment only. It promotes and encourages learning among its ministers, as well as piety, morality, good manners, and civilization. The clergy are composed of the best-educated gentry of the country. They owe much of their influence, particularly among the higher classes, to their education and manners. But deprive the Church of its dignities, its honours and emoluments; pay the clergyman no more than is necessary for his bare subsistence, and to enable him to rear a family in the cheapest and worst way in which a family can be reared, and we shall soon deprive the Church of those ornaments which have given it strength and efficiency as well as credit.

It remains to be seen whether erudition will exist in the country when deprived of its reward and driven from the Church. It is certain that the Church of England, religion, morality, and good manners, will suffer.

The real topic of the pamphlet is the foreign policy of the Government.

The foreign policy of England should be to maintain peace, not only for herself but between the powers of the world. This should be her policy, not only because she can have no interest in a change of the state of possession of the several powers, or in any other change, whether constitutional or other, which could tend to alter their relative strength; but because she has the most extensive commercial relations depending upon peace with each and all the powers of the world, the interruption of which must be injurious to her prosperity. There is but one exception to the existence of such commercial relations, and that is in our intercourse with France; yet it will be seen that that is the power which the existing administration has almost exclusively favoured.

There are two modes of preserving peace; the one by maintaining the existing relations between the several powers, supporting the weak against the strong by the aid of the alliances formed at the period of the settlement of Europe in 1814–1815; the other by submitting to the pretensions and encroachments of revolutionary France, and by rather forcing the advanced guard of revolution than checking the propensity of the consuls of the Tuileries to embark in such projects.

* * * * * *

The great affairs are Holland and Portugal. It is perfectly true that the preceding Government had determined that *they* would not *interfere by arms*, to restore and maintain the authority of the King of Holland in Belgium. They were sensible that they could not maintain this authority without the formation and permanent maintenance in the country of a formidable army; which at that moment of revolutionary excitement might have led to war, in which the extreme opinions prevailing in Europe would have been ranged against each other. We therefore, upon the request of the King of Holland, entered into conference with our allies, France included, upon the best means of putting an end to the contest in the Netherlands; and the first act of the Conference was to make an arrangement for suspending hostilities between the belligerents, taking from each an engagement that the treaty of suspension of hostilities should be carried into execution.

It is not true that the late Government declared that "the two parties should fight no more;" and "established the principle of *separation.*"

That which the late Government did was to settle an armistice unlimited in point of time; and, as usual, the positions to be taken by the troops of each of the belligerents. The principle of the *separation* was not even considered. This is quite clear by the perusal of the first protocols of Nov. 1830.

It is most important to Great Britain that Holland should be in a state of security, independence and prosperity. Belgium is not an object of interest to us excepting for the sake of Holland in the first place; and next for the sake of the North of Europe. It is important that Belgium should be independent of France, not only for the security of Holland and the North of Europe, but because France, even if so disposed, cannot remain at peace if in possession of Belgium. She must extend herself to the Rhine; and when upon the Rhine she would find herself not so secure as she is at present till she should bring her left flank to the ocean.

This is, however, antiquated stuff in these days. I confess that I was disposed to act upon these principles; and having got France into the Conference, and thus under control, I was disposed to wait till the revolutionary fever in Belgium had subsided, and till the King of Holland should have organized the military resources of Holland; and I should then have sought the reunion of Belgium and Holland under a different form, but one which would have equally provided for the security of Holland and the North of Europe, and would have kept Belgium out of the hands of France.

Instead of taking this prudent course, our wise rulers, having allowed France to arm before they had been a week in office, in less than a month recognised the independence of Belgium by the Protocol of the 20th December, 1830. They took this course notwithstanding the protest of the Dutch Plenipotentiaries, who were upon this occasion turned out of the Conference. This last step was a breach of the engagements of the Convention of Aix la Chapelle.

* * * * * *

The conduct of the Ministers towards the Throne deserves attention. Why were the Supplies postponed till the second week in August? But really the time is come when, if possible, we ought to look a little higher, and to warn the King of his own danger. The rights of his subjects are violated, their property is plundered, the interests of the commerce of his subjects are neglected; the allies of his cause are abandoned to the attacks of the ancient rivals of this country or of revolutionists, and the influence of this country in Europe is lost. All this is the produce of three years of a Government of Popularity! I do not much recommend that any notice should be taken of the regulation respecting army punishments. This regulation is very injurious to discipline. I believe that if it is discussed it will be discovered that it is more so than it is now supposed to be; and that the explanation of the ambiguities which it contains will render it still worse. I do not at present recollect other points to be attended to.

Believe me ever yours most sincerely,

WELLINGTON.

In the year 1834 there is, unfortunately, a great gap in Mr. Croker's correspondence. His own letters were no longer copied regularly into his books, and few of the communications which reached him from his friends appear to have been preserved. It is not likely that they were destroyed by Mr. Croker, for in other years, before and after 1834, he saved everything. The probability is that in some way or other the letters were lost after his death. Thus it happens that there is very little in the correspondence respecting some of the most interesting and important events of the year—the resignation of Lord Grey, the accession to power and speedy downfall of Lord Melbourne, the debates in the House on the motion to apply the surplus revenues of the Irish Church to secular purposes, or on the attempt to get a renewal of the Coercion Bill. There is little to fill up the blank which intervenes between the beginning of the year, and the summons to office of Sir Robert Peel in the month of December. One of the few remaining letters relates to a resolution brought forward in the House of Commons on the 6th of March, by Mr. Joseph Hume, for the repeal of the Corn Laws. It possesses great interest, from the fact that it shows how decidedly Sir Robert Peel was of opinion that the landed interest was called upon to bear more than its fair share of public and local burdens, and therefore that it was entitled to some form of protection, in a proportion at least "equivalent to the excess" thrust upon it.

Sir Robert Peel to Mr. Croker.

Whitehall Gardens, March 24th, 1834.

MY DEAR CROKER,

I have not heard the names of any members who specially were reluctant to vote with Sir James Graham against Hume.

The lists were published, and I suppose it may be inferred that those gave the most reluctant votes whose constituencies were most of a manufacturing character.

I dare say that Graham was put forward to oppose Hume's motion partly from his declared opinions on the Corn Laws, partly from the circumstance of his having been Chairman of the Agricultural Committee.

The most striking fact in the debate was one to which public attention has been little called.

Lord Darlington concluded his speech by declaring that his chief motive for abandoning a certain amendment, of which he had given notice, was this, that the highest authority in the Government (I conclude Lord Grey) had sent a message to him, earnestly entreating him to withdraw his amendment; that the pressing of it would create disunion, and that the Government was most anxious to defeat Hume by as large a majority as possible.

Now the Government succeeded in their wishes. The amendment was withdrawn, and the majority was unexpectedly large.* But with what decency does Poulett Thompson—the organ in the House of Commons of a department most intimately connected with the question of the Corn Laws †—retain his office when his colleagues in the Cabinet are united against his opinions, and conspire with his political opponents to defeat those opinions?

I thought the maintenance of the Corn Laws was left in the debate to rest on unsatisfactory grounds—first, a sort of appeal *ad misericordiam* on account of the distressed state of the landed interest; secondly, the invidious and startling argument — the landed interest as the most important, ought to be a favoured class, for the benefit of which the rest of the community may properly be taxed.

In my morning speech I took this line:—I will for the present waive, without abandoning, other grounds; but I will show that restrictions on the import of corn are not restrictions partial and peculiar in their character, but are part of a whole system of restrictions intended equally to favour domestic produce and domestic manufacture.

I will show that you protect your own silk manufacture *more* than you protect certain important articles of the produce of the land, for you raise more revenue on the quantity of foreign butter and cheese that you import, than you do on the whole of every foreign manufactured article into which silk enters as a whole or as a part.

I will show that on the most approved principles of political economy there is no objection in principle to restraints on foreign corn, which does not equally apply to restraints on foreign manufactured goods. Therefore it follows—that you are equally bound to repeal all duties intended not for revenue but protection; and the manufacturers, if they succeed in repealing the duty on foreign corn, must be at

---

* [The majority was 157—312 to 155.]
† [He was President of the Board of Trade.]

once prepared for the repeal of every protecting duty whatsoever

Then I argued: But if the manufacturers would assent to the repeal of protecting duties on manufactured articles, it does not therefore necessarily follow that the Corn Laws must be repealed, because another question will still remain to be discussed. Are not the public and local burdens unduly apportioned? does not the land bear more than its charges? and if it does, the land is entitled at least to a protection equivalent to the excess. I will send you the report of the speech in the *Mirror*, for the newspapers gave no report of it—or, rather, much worse than none.

Morrison, the great retail dealer, said to me that he had always been astonished that the land had not rested its claim for protection mainly on this argument.

Ever affectionately yours,
R. PEEL.

Mr. Croker to Lord Hertford.

West Moulsey, March 17th.

I went up to town to dine with the Duke of Glo'ster, who gave us a great dinner, in the intention, it would seem, of announcing his formal junction with the Tories. Will you have the names of the party? Duke of Wellington, Lords Salisbury, Shaftesbury, Rosslyn, Verulam, Howe, Jermyn, Ellenborough, Limerick, Strangford, Sidmouth, Redesdale, Bexley, Maryborough, Cowley; Peel, Beckett, Goulburn, Baring, Charles Wynn, Herries, Hardinge, Holmes, Kerrison, Howard Douglas, Wilson, and the Bishop of Rochester. It was a fine dinner, and a good and tolerably pleasant one. H.R.H. sees things in a more hopeful light than I do. After dinner he took Peel and me on one side, and appealed to Peel whether he was not right, and that things looked better than I represented them. Peel candidly said that he agreed with me. The truth is, that the Ministers are in extreme difficulties on all sides, and that those who do not look deep into causes and consequences (in which class I include the whole Royal Family) imagine that their difficulties must be our prosperities—a sad mistake, as we shall but too soon discover, but one into which neither the Duke, nor Peel, nor Lyndhurst, nor the Speaker, nor Rosslyn, nor Herries, nor, indeed, any one on whose sagacity I have any reliance, have fallen.

The Chancellor* made last week a strange, mysterious escapade, of which no one can discover the motive; but it must have been one of vital personal importance to him. He wrote to Denman, who is on circuit, to meet him at the first stage out of Bedford. Denman set out in a hack chaise for Hitchin, the first stage on one road. Brougham, in a kind of four-wheeled dog-cart, crossed over from Windsor to Ampthill, the first stage on another road. They played at hide and seek for several hours, and at last met, and came to town together in the dog-cart, and Peel happened to see them come into town, looking, he said, like two fellows coming from a boxing match. They drove to Lord Grey's, and after spending one night and morning in town, Denman returned to his circuit. It is clear that there must have been some weighty personal reason to induce the Lord High Chancellor to go to an assignation with the Chief Justice, and to induce the Chief Justice to leave his circuit (without even telling his brother Judge), and travel in such a strange way to town. The most plausible, or rather the least impossible, solution I have heard is that Brougham, finding he cannot hold where he is, wants to become Chief Justice, and would persuade Denman to vacate for him.

In the month of June, the Duke of Wellington went to Oxford to have the degree of D.C.L. conferred upon him, and to be installed as Chancellor of the University. He invited Mr. Croker, who also received an Oxford degree, to accompany him; and the visit was described in a few letters to Mrs. Croker. The Duke's preliminary arrangements appear to have been soon made.

The Duke of Wellington to Mr. Croker.

MY DEAR CROKER, London, June 3rd.

I am the Duke of Wellington, and, *bon gré mal gré*, must do as the Duke of Wellington doth.

* [This proceeding of Lord Brougham's is referred to by C. Greville, 'Diary,' iii. p. 21.]

I intend to send a footman and coachman and horses to Oxford. But as for magnificent entry, &c., I must enter that city as I have always entered that and others—as an individual.

     Believe me ever yours most sincerely,
            WELLINGTON.

I have not such an article as a post-chaise, or any carriage except my travelling-carriage and a town coach, which it would be ridiculous to send.

Mr. Croker to his Wife.

       Pembroke College, Oxford, June 9th.

Here I am in Ned's den,* which if I had not canvassed an university, would have a little surprised me, but knowing what I had to expect, I really am the reverse of dissatisfied—which sounds something less than satisfied. I came down with the Duke, and we were met out of town by about one hundred young men on horseback, of whom forty passed us in our britscka and pair, not suspecting the Duke to be in such an equipage. At last I saw what was happening, and I stopped and turned the tide, so that we came into town accompanied by about sixty or seventy. I could not make the Duke take off his hat to any one, not even the ladies; he kept saluting like a soldier. I, however, made him show himself occasionally and take notice here and there; but he is a sad hand at popularity hunting.

              June 10th.

Yesterday I dined with the Master, and an almost family party. After dinner we went to take a turn in Christ Church Meadow to see the Beau Monde, but we were rather late and had like to be locked in, and indeed only escaped by a détour. About ten arrived the Bishop of Glo'ster and Mrs. Monk. About eleven we went to our rooms. Mrs. Hall offered me a *cat* as a safeguard against the rats, which, from their long abstinence since Ned's absence, she feared might be very hungry. I declined the cat, however, and saw not a rat, and I doubt whether I even heard one. It was intended that I should have taken an honorary degree, and have been

---

* [Mr. Edward Giffard, who had recently entered Pembroke College.]

exhibited in the theatre as a kind of lion—a *lionceau*; but there having been some demur to granting the Duke of Cumberland his degree, he hit on the device of declining the Oxford compliment, on the ground that he was already a doctor of Dublin. This rendered it impossible for me to take the mere Oxford degree; but I did better, for I was admitted at eight o'clock this morning to what they call *ad eundem*, that is, I was admitted in Oxford to the same rank I held in Dublin. This was doubly agreeable to me; first, because I prefer my own regular degree to one merely ceremonious; and second, because, being thus already a doctor, I had my place in the theatre from the beginning, while the candidate doctors were only admitted after the ceremony had proceeded some way, and then one by one; the public orator making a speech for each, and the *crowd* receiving each name with more or less applause—a ceremony which I was glad to see at my case, and which many of the *candidate* doctors did not see at all. The view of the theatre was certainly the most beautiful thing I ever saw in my life. The sight of the women dressed in all the colours of the rainbow, and with no intermixture of men nor anything to destroy the unity of the effect, was the most surprising thing I ever saw; and the burst of applause from all the benches as the Duke entered the theatre, the shouts of the men, and even the voices of the women were heard, and the waving of handkerchiefs—and all lasted for ten minutes in a degree of beauty and enthusiasm which I had never before seen and which I cannot describe. The ladies were generally in morning dresses, with small bonnets of a thousand colours, and ten thousand varieties of fashions, which looked better than any court dresses I had ever seen. That, in short, was the wonder of the day—everything else I was prepared for, but the effect of this took me completely by surprise. The greatest applause was for the Duke, next, if not equal, for old Lord Eldon, who was looking remarkably well, though he told me in the morning in University College that it was sixty-eight years since he had entered there as a student. There was also great applause for the Duke of Newcastle; but when Lord Winchilsea, who, you remember, had fought the Duke of Wellington about the Catholic question five years ago, came up to the Duke to receive his degree—part of the ceremony being to shake hands—I really was startled by the storm of applause. We then had a dull

Latin speech by the public orator, and a Latin poem and an English essay very ill recited by two of the young men. All this was over by one o'clock, or half-past, and we then went and waited on the Duke at his levée, and at four we are going to levee the Archbishop of Canterbury—which I am now going to do, and I shall finish my letter when I come back. The weather has changed to wind and showers. I hope you have the showers; they rather spoil our gaieties here.

June 11th.

We dined yesterday with the Vice-Chancellor in the Hall of his College, University; we were about 120 at four tables; a very good dinner and very well served, but it lasted till half-past ten. When I came home I found a dance in the College Hall, where I went in for half an hour, but it was dark, and to me dull, so I went into the Master's house and sat with him and the Bishop of Glo'ster till bed-time. Just as I was going to bed, I received a note from Lockhart to tell me that he and Mrs. Lockhart had arrived (I had written to him by the Duke's desire, to offer him a degree). I could not go at that hour, but early this morning I sallied forth to try to get her a ticket for the theatre, which by great good luck I was enabled to do, and so with that passport in my hand I went and breakfasted with them. I then went and heard a sermon in St. Mary's Church, and then went to the assembling of the doctors for the procession to the theatre. It was quite as full as yesterday, but not quite so handsome, for there was an ode to be performed, and the musicians and their basses and kettle-drums broke in upon the ladies in the orchestra and spoiled that *uninterruptedness* (what a word) which was so beautiful yesterday; but all the rest was at least as fine. Before the business opened, the young men in the galleries amused themselves in hooting Lord Brougham, Lord Grey and his cousins, the Whigs and pickpockets, and so forth—it is quite what the Romans called a *Saturnalia*. —and the lads do, or rather roar, what they please. The presentations, however, occasioned less noise than yesterday, till we came to Lord Encombe, old Lord Eldon's grandson, at which there was an enormous shout, but when, after shaking hands with the Chancellor, Lord Encombe went up and shook hands with his grandfather and sat down on the steps at his feet, the seats being all full, the applause was really astounding. Then the ode was performed*—bad music to worse verses. Lord Francis Egerton, who sat behind me, said they should have been translated into Greek to be made in some degree intelligible. The ode was accompanied by a great noise from the crowd in the area, which was so great that we feared some accident would occur. One poor little boy about twelve years old was near stifled, but some of the doctors leaned over and pulled him up into their seat. At last the Duke interfered, and told them that there was room enough if they would only place themselves properly, and showed them how. This restored order, and the stupid ode was finished. Then began imitations, Greek, Latin and English. A Mr. Arnould† repeated some very good verses on the *Hospice of St. Bernard;* and after alluding to Buonaparte's passage of the Alps, and praising his genius, &c., and recounting all his triumphs, he suddenly apostrophised the Duke and said something equivalent to—invincible till he met *you!!!* At that word began a scene of enthusiasm such as I never saw; some people appeared to me to go out of their senses—literally to go mad. The whole assembly started up, and the ladies and the grave semicircle of doctors became as much excited as the boys in the gallery and the men in the pit. Such peals of shouts I never heard; such waving of hats, handkerchiefs, and caps, I never saw; such extravagant clapping and stamping, so that at last the air became clouded with dust. During all this the Duke sat like a statue; at last he took some notice, took off his cap lightly, and pointed to the *reciter* to go on: but this only increased the enthusiasm, and at last it ended only from the mere exhaustion of our animal powers. Some other recitations followed; very good; very clever (particularly one by Lord Maidstone), and very much applauded at every allusion to the Duke; but such a storm as the first it was impossible to create again—indeed, I had no conception of such a scene; but the recitations were all good, and the whole affair went off to our hearts' desire. After this I went to call on Lady Salisbury, and then came home to write to you preparatory to dressing for dinner, which I have barely time to do, as we dine at Christ Church at five.

* [The Installation Ode was written by the Rev. John Keble, and set to music by Dr. Crotch.]

† [Mr. Joseph Arnould, scholar of Wadham College.]

· June 12th.

The dinner in Christ Church Hall was very fine. The members of the college, old and young, dined with us; I suppose we were about 200, rather more, perhaps. The Hall itself is very fine, and the enthusiasm of the young men was as great as in the theatre. We dined at five, and got away by daylight. All the world went to a ball at the Star rooms, which would not hold a tenth of the world. I had the good sense to stay away; so I drank tea with Miss Hall. The Master and his lady had dined at Brasenose, and did not come back till I had come to Ned's rat-hole, where I read till eleven o'clock, and then went to bed. This morning we attended divine service at St. Mary's, and the Bishop of Oxford preached a most excellent charity sermon for the Radcliffe Infirmary. The undergraduate gallery was filled exclusively with ladies. It looked very splendid, and yet the whole was conducted with great decorum. I don't know that I have been more pleased with anything than this service.

The following letter was written after Mr. Croker's return from this visit, and it carried on a correspondence, which was never entirely suspended, with Mr. Lockhart, in regard to various matters connected with the *Quarterly Review.*

Mr. Croker to Mr. Lockhart. Extract.

Molesey Grove, August 17, 1834.

MY DEAR LOCKHART,

Murray well knows that I never was a friend to making the *Review* a political engine; for twenty years that I wrote in it—from 1809 to 1829—I never gave, I believe, one purely political article; not one, certainly, in which *party politics* predominated. Nor, even latterly, did I, of my own free will, write political articles. I did what I was desired to do; and what I was told was advantageous to the *Review.* I insist upon this, that you and Murray may be perfectly aware—as Murray must have been for twenty years —that I am not a friend to a merely political review. To yourself I have more than once hinted that neither *politics* nor *trifles* can make a sufficient substratum and foundation— *solid literature and science* must be the substance—the rest is "leather and prunella." In short, a review should be a *review,* and a review of the *higher* order of literature rather than the ordinary run of the topics and publications of the idle day.

The *Quarterly* has a great name, and has always maintained a rank of composition and information which the *fry* can neither attain, nor, if they for a moment caught them, could maintain. Murray may say to them, as the lion to the hare, "Tis true, *you* produce a litter, and *I* produce but one: but mine is a lion!" After all, the main question is the *sale*. I have stated why that cannot be expected to be kept in its "palmy state" when the party and principles which the *Review* professes, and on which it has thriven for twenty-five years, are in sackcloth and ashes. Murray, therefore, I think, should be prepared for defalcations; and you, if I may venture my advice, should endeavour to counteract that operation by giving the *Review* a higher and more varied scope of general literature. You should embrace *all* subjects, and look out for new *hands*. We grow old. "Our candles burn dim in their sockets." Try to find some link boys with great flambeaux fitter for the dark time in which we live. I am ready to retire whenever you or Murray think that I *twaddle*, as, if I don't already, I soon *must;* and, in the meanwhile, I am willing never to write a line of politics,—but, beware; your sale declines; don't be too sure that "*post*" is "*propter*." It declines with politics; where would you have been *without* them?

As for myself, I am, as long as I may continue in the connection, willing to do what may be considered most useful, and shall always, as you know I have hitherto done, endeavour to do what is wished for; and, above all, when nobody else will. I have of late done some things which were thought desirable, but for which I considered myself as *unfit*, only because those who were *able* were not *willing*. You can't make a silk purse out of a sow's ear, and you cannot make a Southey, nor a Blomfield, nor a Canning out of me.

As to your hint about a series of biographies, I never, I am sure, gave any encouragement to the idea that *I* would or could undertake them; it is essentially against the principle I hold as to the well-doing of a review. If they come in *naturally*—that is, if they arise out of a work under consideration, well and good; but a premeditated series of biography would be, I fear, detestable. Who, nowadays, cares about Castlereagh or Perceval? Murray, it seems, objects to the politics of *the day;* what would those biographies be but the politics of *yesterday*—stale fish!

If I were to advise, I should say the first change you should make would be to say to all your friends without exception that you would, on no subject, nor under any pressure or pretence, suffer any article to exceed two sheets, and of such articles there should not be above two, or three at most, in a number; trifling subjects should never exceed one sheet. There should be never less than a dozen, and more generally about fourteen or fifteen articles in each number, and they should embrace the whole circle of literature—*quicquid scribunt homines*—instead of being a collection of ethical or political essays, very clever, very comprehensive, but having as little to do with the business of the day as Seneca's Maxims or Cicero's Offices.

Yours ever sincerely,
J. W. CROKER.

Several visits were made by Mr. Croker to the Duke during the year, and some notes concerning them, so far as they relate to subjects of public interest, may conveniently be placed together.

Portions of a Diary by Mr. Croker.

The Battle of Vittoria.

Strathfieldsaye, Monday, March 24th, 1834.—The Duke was out hunting when I arrived, but he soon came in. There is a large picture in the billiard-room at Strathfieldsaye, placed since I was here last, of the Battle of Vittoria. 'Tis but a bad picture, but the Duke said was accurate as to the ground and action. He said: "I'll show you how I won that battle. The road on the right is the high road from Madrid to Vittoria, which you see in the right distance; Lord Hill attacked along this road, further to the right on some broken, wooded hills. Into them I sent at first a small force, one battalion; the French thought that was to be our attack, and drew off from the left (their right) and centre to reinforce it. I saw this and sent another regiment (Cadogan's), and by degrees increased the force there. I had the day before sent Lord Lynedoch with his corps to the other side of that little river on our left, and he had been moving unseen behind some hills till he came on that side quite round the French right—that's his fire that you see along there. When I saw that he had begun, and that the French were astonished at having us both on the right and left, I attacked this broken hill that you see in the foreground, and which was the French centre, but they had drained it to support their left, and I carried it and won the battle with great ease and little loss. Those wooded hills on the right were the ground of the Black Prince's victory, and perhaps the French thought that I was ambitious to win a battle on the same spot; but they had a better reason for suspecting that to be my point, for Clausel was on that side, and they believed that I wanted to turn them so as to prevent a junction with him; but my arrangements had been made the day before, as I told you, and took them as much by surprise as anything in a pitched battle can be said to do. I was not at all uneasy about Clausel, for an innkeeper came to me that morning to tell me that Clausel was at his village, in his house, about twenty miles off, and did not intend to move till next day—so that I was quite at my ease about him. It was curious that this innkeeper should have had the zeal and good sense to make so much haste to bring me this intelligence; but so it was."

Long Marches in India.

Tuesday, March 25th.—D. I once marched in India, seventy miles, in what I may call one march—it was after Assaye—to the borders of the Nizam's territory, against a body of predatory natives, whom by this extraordinary march I surprised in their camp. I moved one morning about four o'clock, and marched till noon, when I had rest till about eight in the evening, by which time I had marched twenty-five miles; at eight we moved again, and did not stop till about twelve, midday, when I was in the enemy's camp, distant seventy miles from my first point; and these were not computed miles, nor am I talking by guess, for the whole march was measured by the wheel. I had five regiments, two European and three Native, and two regiments of Regular Cavalry, in all about 5000 men, with a large body of Native Irregular Horse.

C. What sort of troops were these Native Horse? What would they be like in Europe?

D. About equal to the Cossacks. I had before Assaye made another forced march which saved Poonah; but it was not so far, hardly sixty miles, and I took more time to do it, but it was a surprising march; but this was with cavalry alone.

George the Fourth.

C. Who made the King sensible of his danger?

D. Why, he talked very differently to different people and at different times. To his sisters he said he could not recover. On the Wednesday before the Friday night on which he died (I always saw him on Wednesdays and Saturdays) he went through all the business I had to lay before him—all—and when it was over he said: "I think your next visit will be the last I shall receive here, for on Monday I shall go to the cottage, and then to Brighton." And so on with an enumeration of various places which he had.

C. He took leave of Peel three weeks before his death, tenderly, and saying that they should never meet; and I think it was to Peel that on some mention of the cottage he said: "Ah, the poor cottage, I shall never see it again!"

Lord Nelson.

Walmer, October 1st, 1834.—We were talking of Lord Nelson, and some instances were mentioned of the egotism and vanity that derogated from his character. "Why," said the Duke, "I am not surprised at such instances, for Lord Nelson was, in different circumstances, two quite different men, as I myself can vouch, though I only saw him once in my life, and for, perhaps, an hour. It was soon after I returned from India. I went to the Colonial Office in Downing Street, and there I was shown into the little waiting-room on the right hand, where I found, also waiting to see the Secretary of State, a gentleman, whom from his likeness to his pictures and the loss of an arm, I immediately recognised as Lord Nelson. He could not know who I was, but he entered at once into conversation with me, if I can call it conversation, for it was almost all on his side and all about himself, and in, really, a style so vain and so silly as to surprise and almost disgust me. I suppose something that I happened to say may have made him guess that I was *somebody*, and he went out of the room for a moment, I have no doubt to ask the office-keeper who I was, for when he came back he was altogether a different man, both in manner and matter. All that I had thought a charlatan style had vanished, and he talked of the state of this country and of the aspect and probabilities of affairs on the Continent with a good sense, and a knowledge of subjects both at home and abroad, that surprised me equally and more agreeably than the first part of our interview had done; in fact, he talked like an officer and a statesman. The Secretary of State kept us long waiting, and certainly, for the last half or three-quarters of an hour, I don't know that I ever had a conversation that interested me more. Now, if the Secretary of State had been punctual, and admitted Lord Nelson in the first quarter of an hour, I should have had the same impression of a light and trivial character that other people have had, but luckily I saw enough to be satisfied that he was really a very superior man; but certainly a more sudden and complete metamorphosis I never saw.

Polignac and his Ministry.

Walmer, October 2nd, 1834.—*D.* Molé told me years before Polignac's ministry, that if ever he, P., should be made minister, there would be danger of a catastrophe, because he said, that with considerable talents he had a *caractère indomptable*, and that no considerations of expediency would induce him to bate one jot of anything that he thought abstractedly right—such men make great catastrophes.

C. But why did he not show some of his *caractère* in collecting the troops to support his *ordonnances?*

D. First of all, he did not expect a resistance by force; but in the next place he did not know how to go about it.

C. Why, he had himself the *portefeuille* of the War Department.

D. Yes, but that is the very fact which proves my assertion. He did not even understand the returns in the office. Marmont told me his whole story when I called on him at Brunet's Hotel on his arrival here, and one particular of it was that on the morning when Marmont received the command of the troops, Polignac told him that he had 12,000 men. Marmont doubted whether he had half the number. Polignac produced the last return—but it was a return of the whole nominal strength; he made no deduction for 4500 who were absent or on furlough. An economical mode they had at that time of sending a large proportion of their troops on leave of absence, during which they stopped their pay—he made no deduction for the sick, nor for the casualties, so that Marmont was quite right. He had not half 12,000 actual bayonets.

Numbers of Troops engaged in the Duke's Great Battles.

C. What were the real numbers of your army, and the enemy, in some of your great battles?

D. Talavera was the only one in which I had a superiority; but that was only by reckoning the Spaniards. At all the others I had less. At Salamanca I had 40,000, and the French not much more; perhaps 45,000. At Vittoria I had many thousand less, 60,000 against 70,000. At Waterloo the proportion was still more against me; I had less than 60,000, perhaps about 56 or 58,000; Buonaparte had near 80,000. The whole army in the south of France under my command, was considerably larger than the force under Soult at the Battle of Toulouse; but actually employed in that operation, I had less than he. I look upon Salamanca, Vittoria, and Waterloo, as my three best battles; those which had great and permanent consequences. Salamanca relieved the whole south of Spain, changed all the prospects of the war, and was felt even in Russia. Vittoria freed the Peninsula altogether, broke off the armistice at Dresden, and thus led to Leipsic, and the deliverance of Europe; and Waterloo did more than any other battle I know of, towards the true object of all battles—the peace of the world.

C. Did you ever talk with Marmont about Salamanca?

D. It was a delicate subject to allude to. It was brought once on the *tapis;* but all I said to him was that I had perceived very early that he was wounded.

C. That was a compliment. Did he seem to take it so?

D. Oh, yes, and it was true enough. I did not say what was equally true: that his previous movement had given me the opening, for I had resolved not to fight if he had not given me the advantage. He wished to cut me off. I saw that in attempting this he was spreading himself over more ground than he could defend, and I resolved at once to attack him, and succeeded in my object very quickly. One of the French generals said that I had beaten "quarante mille hommes en quarante minutes." Marmont was a great officer and a worthy man.

Fouché's Memoirs.

October 3rd, 1834.—I happened to mention the profuse fabrication of French *Mémoires*, and instanced those of Fouché; the Duke said: "I dare say they were not written by Fouché, and that they are what therefore may be called fabrications, but they are certainly done by some one who had Fouché's confidence or his papers, for there are several passages in them of a secret nature, in which I myself happened to be concerned and which I know to be true. I won't at all answer for the whole book; but as far as my own knowledge goes, I find them tolerably correct, and am therefore disposed to give some degree of credit to the rest; of course they are apologetical, and my evidence can only apply to the short period of the Restoration in which I came into contact with him."

From another Memorandum by Mr. Croker.

I was in Paris in July 1815, while Buonaparte was still lingering at Rochefort, and there was great anxiety on the part of the French Government to get rid of him. We were anxious to take him prisoner; the French ministers, Talleyrand, Fouché, &c., were desirous that he should escape to America. There was held on the evening of the 12th of July, a kind of double Cabinet Council as to what was to be done. As I was Secretary of the Admiralty and knew the state and strength of our naval blockade, I was invited by Lord Castlereagh and the Duke to accompany them to this meeting, where we found Talleyrand, Fouché, and M. de Jaucourt, then Minister of Marine. Measures were concerted for capturing him. I held the pen; Talleyrand took little or no part. Fouché was evidently anxious that Buonaparte should escape, and made all sorts of objections, and particularly as to some strong expressions I used and some strong measures which I suggested. Jaucourt was fair and straightforward. When that affair had been discussed, the Duke turned short round on Fouché about Vincennes, the Governor of which had hoisted the white flag, but would not surrender the fortress. The Duke, it seems, had twice before urged Fouché to put an end to this disagreeable farce; once, I think, that very morning (our present conference was at night), and Fouché had promised that the fort should be surrendered that day; he now put on a penitential air and said that the Governor was *entêté et opiniâtre*, and would not obey the orders, and, shrugging his shoulders, "Que voulez-vous que je fasse ?" The Duke reddened at this question, and stood up and said sharply: "Ce n'est pas à moi, M. le Duc, de vous dire ce que vous avez à faire, mais je vous dirai ce que je ferai, moi! Si la place n'est pas rendue à dix heures demain matin, je la prendrai de vive force. Entendez-vous ?" Fouché hummed and hawed, and hoped he would not be so precipitate, and that a day or two might arrange it *à l'amiable*. The Duke said, No, he had been put off in this same way for (I think he said) two days; much longer than he ought to have waited. "A présent vous avez mon dernier mot, et vous devez savoir que ce que je vous dis je le ferai; si la place n'est pas rendue à dix heures du matin, elle sera prise à midi." He then turned to me, who was sitting at a writing-table, and said: "Croker, you never saw a fight; be with me at 9 o'clock to-morrow morning; I shall give you some breakfast and mount you on a good horse and take you to see the show"—adding gravely—"a show which I shall be very sorry to exhibit, but which such an outrage on good faith and honour forces upon me. The affair," he said, turning to the French Ministers, "is still more insulting to the King of France and his Government than to us; but if you can't arrange it, I must." When he said this, he wished us good-night, and left us. The French Ministers then said a few words to Castlereagh, asking his interposition, who only answered that it was a military point on which the Duke was sole judge; and he assuredly will do what he has told you. M. de Ligny (who was to carry the despatches) was then called in, and was told that he would receive his instructions next day. I sat up late writing my despatch under Castlereagh's instructions, and making a copy for London. I went to the Duke early next morning and found that he had really taken his measures for storming the place; but the fort was given up. I unluckily did not make a note of this at the time, but I have since talked of the circumstance with the Duke, and think that the foregoing is tolerably accurate.

The following despatch may be read in connection with this memorandum, for it was chiefly owing to the navy acting upon Mr. Croker's instructions that Buonaparte found escape impossible :—

Despatch written by Mr. Croker to Rear-Admiral Sir H. Hotham, or the Senior Officer in Basque Roads.

Paris, July 13th, 1815.

Sir,

Lord Viscount Castlereagh, His Majesty's Principal Secretary of State for Foreign Affairs, being now in Paris, has requested me to communicate to you some circumstances relative to Napoleon Buonaparte, and to suggest to you the course which the British Government would wish you to pursue under the new aspect which affairs have assumed. I have therefore (though I have here no public character) undertaken to make this communication, and I have ventured to assure his lordship that you will, under the pressing nature of the case, overlook the want of official form, and will conform your conduct to his lordship's wishes, which would be those of my Lords Commissioners of the Admiralty, if there was time to consult them.

The French Government has received information that Buonaparte has embarked at Rochefort on board one vessel of a small squadron, which the provisional Government had placed at his disposal, and it is understood that this squadron is anchored under the forts of the Isle d'Aix, ready to escape by the first opportunity.

I understand also from the French Minister of Marine that the British squadron in that neighbourhood consists of two or three ships of the line, and two or three frigates, and as in some communications which I had with Lord Keith on this subject before I left England, his lordship assured me that his attention had been directed to Rochefort, I cannot doubt that, except under some very extraordinary circumstance, the escape of Buonaparte's squadron, or of any vessel of it, from the Charente, is impossible ; but as it is, for obvious reasons, of very great importance that the question with regard to this person should be brought to a decision as speedily as possible, Lord Castlereagh wishes you to consult confidentially with the officer of His Most Christian Majesty, who is the bearer of this letter, and to afford him your most cordial assistance in all practicable measures which he may be disposed to recommend, for the capture of Buonaparte.

The plan which has struck his lordship and the French Ministers as most likely to succeed, and which will be suggested to the French officer, is as follows :

If it shall be ascertained that Buonaparte is on board one of the ships in Aix Roads—I say *if*, because, notwithstanding the information of the French Government on this point, I cannot but doubt that he has embarked with any hope of escape from this particular port, which, of all others, is the most susceptible of blockade, and I consider it most probable that he has either not embarked, and spread the report of his having done so as a blind; or he intends to land again, and endeavour to escape by some other means, which he hopes may be covered by his present pretence—I therefore repeat *if* it be ascertained that Buonaparte is certainly embarked in Aix Roads, it may be concluded that he is, as he thinks, sure of the Governor and garrison of the forts which protect the anchorage; and as these forts are very considerable, I entertain little hope that you could think yourself justified in expecting to reduce them or capture Buonaparte, while lying under their full and active protection; but under the present circumstances of France it seems reasonably to be doubted whether the Governor of Aix, if properly summoned by the King's authority, would venture to fire on the ships of His Majesty's allies, in the execution of His Majesty's orders. It is, therefore, expedient that before you proceed to attack the ships, you should send a flag of truce to the Governor of the Isle d'Aix to say, "That by the King of France's express commands you are about to seize the person of the common enemy; that you have no hostile intentions against the ships or subjects of the Most Christian King; but, on the contrary, look upon them as allies, as long as they do not oppose the King's authority; that you do not mean to capture or injure the French ships, or to interfere with them beyond the mere seizure of Buonaparte's person, except so far as their own opposition may render necessary; and as to the Governor himself, that, if after this notice he takes any part with Buonaparte, or permits a shot to be fired at you, you will pursue the most energetic measures in your power, and will hold him responsible in his own person for any mischief that may be done; and you may add that the French Government has assured you that the King will consider the death of any British sailor employed in execution of his commands, as a murder of which the Governor of the garrison from which the shot may proceed will be held guilty." This notice on your part will be accompanied by an order from the King to the same effect, and as soon after they shall have been delivered to the Governor as possible, it seems expedient that you should commence the attack, as it would be desirable not to give the influence of Buonaparte's remonstrances time to operate on that officer's mind.

Your professional skill will be your guide how far in the uncertainty in which you will be as to the conduct of the Governor, you will think it justifiable to pursue your attack. Lord Castlereagh feels that it is of the most urgent importance to seize Buonaparte, but he also feels that the safety of His Majesty's ships ought not to be compromised beyond the ordinary risk of a naval engagement, and he is sincerely desirous of avoiding the effusion of blood, which, however, he is inclined to think may be best effected by bold and decisive measures; and if the ship in which Buonaparte may be, should, by an obstinate resistance, drive you to extremities, he feels that you ought not, for the sake of saving her or any one on board her, to take any line of conduct which should increase in any degree your own risk. The consequences of the resistance will be chargeable on those who may make it.

If, however, you should find it impracticable with any fair prospect of success to attack the ships, or if, having attacked them, you should not find it expedient to continue the engagement, you will of course continue your blockade with the greatest rigour, and if you should require any increase of force you may either draw something from the neighbourhood of Brest, or write to Lord Keith by one of your own cruisers, and send a duplicate of your letter to the Admiralty by way of Paris. I shall remain here till the 24th or 25th instant, and after that time if you should have communications to make to the Board, which seem to require dispatch, you may put them under cover to the English Minister at this Court, or send them by an express.

If Buonaparte for himself, or the Governor of the forts, or commander of the squadron for him, should propose to surrender on *terms*, Lord Castlereagh is of opinion that you should reply, as the fact really is, that you are not authorised to enter into any engagement of that nature; that your orders are to seize the persons of Napoleon and his family, and to hold them for the disposal of the allied powers unconditionally.

It is unnecessary to say anything as to the safe custody of Buonaparte if you should be so fortunate as to take him, as your orders on that head are sufficiently ample; but that particular of your present orders which enjoins you to convey Buonaparte without any delay to a British port in the event of his capture, Lord Castlereagh thinks should not be literally followed under the circumstances in which you would obtain possession of him, and his lordship wishes therefore that you should delay sending him to England, till you shall have had a communication with him on the subject.

Whatever course you may on other points pursue, it must be recollected that your forces are to be considered as acting in concert with those of the King of France within the waters of his kingdom, and it is therefore expedient that as little hostility (as may be consistent with the success of your great object) should be employed, and if the forts and ships should either by force or summons be induced to acknowledge the King's authority, you will naturally feel that (with the exception of possessing yourself of the Buonapartes) the British Government would not wish you in any way to interfere with them.

This letter, the substance of which was settled last night at a conference with the French Ministers, and which has been communicated *in extenso* to M. le Comte de Jaucourt, the Minister of the Marine, Lord Castlereagh and I trust you will consider as a sufficient authority for you to pursue the course therein suggested. I shall this day forward a copy of it to Lord Melville, and I have no doubt that his lordship and the Board will fully approve and sanction all the Secretary of State's propositions.

I request to have the pleasure of hearing from you with the least possible delay, and

I have the honour to be, &c.,

J. W. CROKER.*

The resignation of Lord Grey took place on the 17th of July, and he was succeeded by Lord Melbourne. But on the 15th of November, Lord Melbourne, to adopt the common version, was "dismissed" by the King. Nobody, as

---

* [This letter was referred to by Sir James Graham, so recently as the year 1861, in the House of Commons, as an example of the large discretion which a secretary of the Admiralty might exercise without the express sanction of "my Lords."]

Greville says, had "the slightest suspicion of such an impending catastrophe. The Ministers themselves reposed in perfect security." Mr. Croker's account—derived, as he intimates, from the Duke of Wellington, who was in a position to be made acquainted with all the facts—presents these events in a different light, and leads to the belief that Lord Melbourne's resignation was tendered unsought for to the King, chiefly because he was about to lose Lord Althorp's services in the Lower House. Lord Lyndhurst and the Duke of Wellington gave precisely the same account of the interview between Lord Melbourne and the King, and it is obvious that the version hitherto accepted can no longer pass into history quite without suspicion. There can be no doubt, however, that the King was anxious to get rid of his Ministers, and it is possible that Lord Melbourne may only have resigned to avoid being dismissed.*

Mr. Croker to Lord Hertford.

Sudbourne Hall,† November 24th, 1834.

When I last wrote to you I had not seen the Duke, and could only state matters in general. That evening, however, he wrote to me to call upon him, which I did next day. He put into my hands the copy of his letter to Peel, and original communications between the King and Lord Melbourne. The case is shortly this: when the Melbourne Administration was formed in June last it was avowedly *based* on Lord Althorp, and especially on his weight in the House of Commons. When he was called up the other day,‡ Lord

---

* See Wellington's letter to Peel, in the 'Memoirs by Sir R. Peel,' ii. p. 23. The facts are represented in the same light in Sir Theodore Martin's 'Life of Lord Lyndhurst,' pp. 318–323. "Even before his interview with Lord Melbourne, it is more than probable that the King had come to the conclusion that a change of Ministry was necessary" (p. 321).

† [One of the seats of Lord Hertford. Mr. Croker sometimes went there to look after his friend's interest, at Lord Hertford's earnest desire.]

‡ [He succeeded to the title of Lord Spencer, November 10th.]

Melbourne stated to His Majesty that as the Government originally rested on Lord Althorp, he had always contemplated that Lord Spencer's death must throw the Administration into great difficulties, which apprehension was much increased by Lord Althorp's declaration that whenever that event should happen he was determined to retire into private life altogether. That event has now happened, and the Government, having lost its greatest weight and bond of union, was no doubt in great difficulties, but that he (Lord Melbourne) was willing, if His Majesty should please, to try to go on, and had prepared a proposition for remodelling the Cabinet. This proposition having been made verbally, we only know the points which are noted in a minute made by the King, of his own reply, and of course imperfectly, but it seems that Melbourne proposed to the King the choice of three leaders of the House of Commons—Johnny Russell, Abercromby, and Spring Rice. The King did not think that any of these would do, and particularly thought Johnny, who was Melbourne's first horse, quite incapable.*

From the discussion of *men*, they passed to *measures*, and then it came out that the Cabinet, even if arranged on any of Melbourne's schemes, was to set out with an irreconcileable difference on the first and most important subject that must present itself—the Irish Church. Johnny Russell and the majority of the Cabinet were pledged to act in the spirit of the Commission of Enquiry issued in the summer, namely, to spoliate the Protestant Church in all parishes where the Roman Catholics should be in the majority, while Lord Lansdowne and Spring Rice declared that they must resign if any such measure should be proposed. This, Lord Melbourne suggested, would prevent its being made a *Cabinet* measure, but that when it should be brought forward by any individual, Johnny Russell (the leader) and the other members of his opinions, would vote for it, while Mr. Rice would vote against it. "But," said the King, "I will never listen to such a proposition, and I have to complain of a gross deception practised on me. I signed the Special Commission only as a Commission of Enquiry, and now they would turn it into an actual measure of spoliation." (You will observe that *this*

---

* [This is substantially the same account of the affair as that which was given by the Duke of Wellington to Mr. Greville, November 28th. *Vide* 'Diary,' iii. pp. 162-165.]

was what all the world, except the King, saw and foresaw when he signed the Commission in May last, when Stanley and Graham resigned.) His Majesty went on to state that it was clear that however willing Lord Melbourne might be to get over difficulties, he could not evade this one—that early in the session the Cabinet would exhibit itself in the House of Commons divided on a vital question, and that the leader of the House and the majority of the King's Ministers would take that side which was contrary to His Majesty's fixed opinions. That such a state of things would be a dissolution of the Ministry, and a dissolution at a time and under circumstances which could not but produce the greatest embarrassment. His Majesty therefore suggested that what was eventually inevitable should be done immediately, before the meeting of Parliament should have completed the difficulties. He therefore accepted Lord Melbourne's resignation, and declared the Ministry dissolved.

It does not clearly appear whether the King or Lord Melbourne first suggested the sending for the Duke, but it is certain that Lord Melbourne waited while the King wrote to the Duke—or rather while Taylor wrote—and that he offered to convey the letter, which he did. The Duke was at Strathfieldsaye. He immediately went over to Brighton (Saturday), where he dined and slept. He told the King that the great difficulty would be in the House of Commons; that he therefore advised His Majesty to name Sir R. Peel as First Minister. The King said that Peel's absence was an objection. The Duke agreed that it was, but he undertook to conduct the Government till Peel's arrival, filling up no offices and taking no measures (except when absolutely necessary), so that Peel should be at perfect liberty when he came, and that he (the Duke) would serve *with* him, or *under* him, or not at all, as might be thought best.

The King gladly acceded. The Duke then said, that to prevent the same kind of juggle which had happened before, as well as to avoid the danger of leaving the power of the State in such hands at such a crisis, it would be proper to summon the ex-Ministers to deliver up the seals on Monday, which was done. The Duke was sworn in to the Home Department, as the most central and important, and conducts all the other branches of the public service by the secretaries of the Board and the Under-Secretaries of State. So far you may consider as authentic and sufficiently accurate.

I shall now add some minor matters. When the Duke advised the King to summon the ex-Ministers to deliver the seals on Monday, His Majesty suggested the being prepared with a quorum of other persons to make a Privy Council, "For," said he, "they might all go away as soon as they had given up the seals, and leave us without a council to swear you in!" And it happened just as he had foreseen. I, by good luck, was at Molesey, and so escaped being summoned, which would have been awkward, for I could not have refused to attend on *such* an occasion, and yet my having attended would appear to the public like a pledge to go on with the new arrangements in some official station, which, even under the Duke, I should have been most reluctant to do, and should only have done in the last extremity of necessity. But no power shall ever force me to serve under Peel. We are excellent friends, and shall remain so, which would assuredly not be the case if we sat in the same Cabinet. I know that your partiality and friendship have a hankering to see me in the Cabinet, but I hope and believe you will be satisfied with my declining on *this* occasion, if I should be invited, which, however, I shall endeavour to prevent, because, as I really wish to live on friendly terms with Peel, I think there will be a better chance of that, if I can avoid giving a refusal to what he would consider a kind and complimentary proposition. Nor am I at all swayed by any difficulty about getting into Parliament, for I have been already apprised that nothing but my declaring that I will take the Chiltern Hundreds will prevent the University of Dublin electing me, as I am informed, without one dissentient voice; but neither in office or out will I enter Parliament.

Two messengers have been sent for Peel, with the Duke's letters in duplicate. The first by Mr. Hudson, a young man in the Queen's household. He was to go over the Mont Cenis, by Turin, to Rome. You will know before we shall where Peel is overtaken, and will guess when he will arrive here. I don't expect him much before Christmas, and have some doubts whether the present patience of the public in the provisional arrangement will last five weeks.

When Melbourne came from the King on the Friday night about ten, he, in his usual *poco curante* way, did not think it worth while even to send round a box, to tell his colleagues they were out, contenting himself with summoning a Cabinet for twelve next day. He, however, happened to see our friend the *Bear*,* who is watchful as a *fox*, and the Bear lost no time in sending the news to the *Chronicle* and *Times*, with an addition that it was all the Queen's doing. When Lord Holland† saw the papers next morning, he said, "Well, here's another hoax." Lord Lansdowne equally disbelieved it, and I believe one or two others of the Cabinet also learned their dissolution from the newspapers. How like Melbourne all this is. Personally the King parts with Melbourne on the best terms, and offered him an earldom and the Garter, which he declined. He was at the play on Saturday to see a comedy called 'The Regent' in which there is much talk of turning out a Minister. I am told he laughed and rubbed his hands, and appeared delighted. So, I believe, are Lord Lansdowne and Rice, but the Radicals and Brougham are furious. The Duke has been obliged to take the seals from B. sooner than had been expected, because he had refused to put the Great Seal to the prorogation of Parliament. He also refused to issue Lord Spencer's writ, for the purpose of impeding Sir Charles Knightley's election in Northamptonshire Lyndhurst is full of spirits.

This proved to be the second occasion on which Mr. Croker declined a seat in the Cabinet—for it was well understood that this was the prize held before him by the Duke of Wellington, and again by Sir Robert Peel. As the foregoing letter states, Peel was absent from England when the Ministerial changes took place, and it took a special messenger eight days to overtake him at Rome. Mr. (afterwards Sir James) Hudson, who was Gentleman Usher to the Queen, found him at a ball at the Duchess of Torlonia's, but the King's letter summoning him to return did not reach his hands till he arrived at his hotel. He set out for England on the following day (the 20th of November), and arrived in London on the 9th of December. Almost immediately upon his reaching home he wrote the following letter:—

* [Mr. E. Ellice was usually known by this name (see *supra*, p. 150), but, as a matter of fact, it was Lord Brougham who gave the information in question to the newspapers. See 'Life of Lyndhurst,' p. 323.

† [Chancellor of the Duchy of Lancaster.]

Sir Robert Peel to Mr. Croker.

Whitehall, December 9th, 1834.

MY DEAR CROKER,

Though I have only been one night in bed since I left Lyons, and have found anything but repose since my arrival here this morning, I must write you one line, to certify to you for myself that I am here. Lady Peel and Julia travelled with me as far as Dover; travelling by night over precipices and snow eight nights out of twelve. I shall be very glad to see you. It will be a relief to me from the harassing cares that await me.

Ever affectionately yours,

ROBERT PEEL.

Mr. Croker to Sir R. Peel.

West Moulsey, December 10th.

MY DEAR PEEL,

A thousand thanks for your letter, of which, at this moment, I appreciate all the value, and feel it accordingly. I should acknowledge it in person, but that I am confined by a cold. If I am able I will come to town to-morrow; if not, I trust there can be no doubt that I shall on Friday. If you should happen to dine *en famille*, Friday or Saturday, I should like to dine with you; your mornings will be, I know, so occupied by indispensables, that I should not like to interrupt you.

What a journey! You are near a fortnight sooner than I expected—not only because I fancied you would have been at Naples, but from the wonderful rapidity of your journey. I knew that you would not leave Lady Peel and Julia behind, and I did not calculate on such super-feminine strength on their parts. However, here you are, thank God, neither too soon, I believe, nor too late. Indeed, on the whole, I think the panic, the suspense occasioned by your absence, and the novelty of the circumstances, have been favourable, and that you will have less trouble now than you would have had three weeks ago. The Duke has been standing the whole undivided fire, and it will not be so easy to revive and turn it on *you*. Well may you talk of "harassing cares." The first that I dread for you are the personal *harasseries* of individual pretenders. Except the Duke, and the two or three who dress themselves in his glass, every one that I saw seemed thinking of their own paltry advantage, and not of the great crisis of the country, in which all private interests—nay, all private affections—ought to be merged. One only word of advice I will venture to you: don't suffer yourself to be hampered with the "*veilleurs*"—the Monmouth Street of former administrations. Get, if you can, new men, young blood—the ablest, the fittest—and throw aside boldly the claims of all the "mediocrities" with which we were overladen in our last race. I don't promise that even that will ensure success; but it is your best chance.

Yours ever affectionately,
J. W. CROKER.

Sir Robert Peel's object in seeking this interview was to induce Mr. Croker to accept office, as might be inferred from the letter itself, written at such a time; but some additional particulars concerning the conversation which took place were given by Mr. Croker to his wife.

14, Duke-street. [No date.]

I have seen the Peels; great cordiality; and Lady Peel (with whom I sat an hour before I saw him) reminded me that he had written to me the first on his return. When I went in to him he was exceedingly friendly, and when I was about to ask him a question about his law officers, he said, "But first, my dear Croker, let me ask you whether you adhere to the resolution you stated to me before I went abroad?" I said, positively, nothing could induce me to enter the House of Commons. I thought he winced a little at that, but he said that he would still talk to me in full confidence of all his views. He then put into my hands his letter to Stanley and Stanley's answer (*declining on behalf of self and friends to take office*), and the King's observations (which had just come in) on Stanley's refusal. He then went on to state to me his views and difficulties, &c., but I did not allow him to go far, as I was to see him again in the evening. The only thing that, I think, is settled is, that an offer will be made to Lord Chandos and Sir Ed. Knatchbull —Baring, of course, will be in the Cabinet; but all the rest must be made up of the old *odds and ends*. Peel twice over said, with a querulous tone, that it would be only the *Duke's old Cabinet.* On one occasion he muttered something about the unreasonableness of men not helping in such a crisis, but as this might allude to another person whom we had been speaking of, I did *not take it to myself*, though I own I believe it was a *little* meant for me. On the whole the interview was perfectly satisfactory as to *personals;* I am satisfied that we shall be very good friends, but my fears for the country are greatly increased. I really begin to doubt whether an Administration can be made that will meet Parliament. My particular fear is that the mediocrity of such a Cabinet as is likely to be made will throw difficulties in the way of all the elections. The people like novelty, and would, under present circumstances, like a mixture of new men; and I think that a great many seats will be lost if the Ministry shall assume an entire anti-reform colour. Yet, what can be done? I can't tell. Thank God I have not the responsibility of having advised the attempt, or of endeavouring to execute the details. My cold is better—my cough rather increased. I have seen (by accident) Mr. Jackson,* who will give me something. I mean to come back to-morrow.

Yours,

J. W. C.

Mr. Croker to Lord Hertford.

West Moulsey, December 11th.

The Duke of Glo'ster's death had taken place before I wrote last. He is to be buried privately to-day in *his own* vault at Windsor. Duke of Sussex, stone blind, but led by Sir George and Horace [Seymour], to be chief mourner—very reluctantly, but the King will have it so. The Duke of Glo'ster made a most Christian end. He gave himself over from the first moment, and thenceforth spent his hours in good-nature, charity, and piety. He desired not to be embalmed, and to be buried in the vault with his father and mother, which, after it shall have received Princess Sophia, is to be finally closed. He desired one of the Duchess's rings to be put

---

* [Mr. Croker's medical adviser.]

upon his finger. He has died very rich; they talk of 300,000*l.* He has left legacies to all his attendants, to the total amount of 80,000*l.*; all the rest to the Duchess. Colonel Higgins has 15,000*l.*, besides the remission of 7000*l.* heretofore advanced for purchasing commissions. It turns out that he and the Duchess have *habitually* given above 6000*l.* a year in charity. The complaint began with a bilious inflammation, but ended in the *family* complaint, and the immediate cause of death was the internal bursting of a scrofulous swelling in the head.

Peel arrived on Tuesday morning, after a most extraordinarily rapid journey of twelve days only from Rome, Lady Peel and the little girl* accompanying him. He immediately saw the Duke and the King, and accepted the Government. He has written to Stanley and Graham to come to town; at first it was intended to send Hardinge to *aboucher* with them, but on consideration they have thought it best to invite them to town. It is much doubted whether they (at least, Stanley) will join.† This doubt is chiefly raised by the fact that Stanley has just broken up a party at Knowsley. Graham has gone north to Netherby, and Stanley has come to Trentham, where *Melbourne* has come to meet him, and Melbourne made the other day a second speech in Derbyshire—thoroughly *radical.* I am grateful for your kind wishes about *me.* I regret that so many of my friends differ from me in my view of my duty; but, depend upon it I am right, being convinced that the new Ministry will be forced, *l'épée dans les reins,* to continue the march of Reform. However slowly or reluctantly they may endeavour to go, the smallest advance in that line would be too much for me, and I should probably be obliged to quit the Cabinet before we had agreed on the King's speech.

Sir Robert Peel to Mr. Croker.

December 25th.

My dear Croker,

Ward‡ sent me this morning a proposal to stand for the City, and asked, " What answer shall I give ? " I replied,

---

* [Afterwards Lady Villiers.]

† [Lord Stanley and Sir J. Graham both declined.]

‡ [Mr. Ward was an eminent merchant, who at one time sat in Parliament as a member for the City of London.]

that if I were free from office I might feel it incumbent upon me to come forward at this crisis, but that office and the City were perfectly incompatible. One thing only made me hesitate, the satisfaction I should have in co-operating with *Ward* himself as a colleague in the defence and improvement of our ancient institutions.

I am smiling now when I think of Ward's face on reading the answer which *he himself* is to give from me.

I have relieved *Wynn* from the sad state of suspense in which he was, and given him the Duchy. Haddington goes to Ireland. Major need not be afraid. There is no room for *L'éffroi.**

I write as if I was passing a *merry* Christmas Day.

Ever affectionately yours,
R. P.

By the end of December, Sir Robert Peel had formed his new Ministry,† and the Tamworth Manifesto made its appearance—for the leader of the Tory party felt convinced, and with good reason, that a new election would materially improve his prospects, even if it did not actually yield him

---

* [Mr. Major was a lawyer, an old friend of Mr. Croker's. There is here probably some joke in reference to an Irish lawyer named Lefroy, who may have looked for an office at this time.]

† It was thus composed:—

Prime Minister and Chancellor of the Exchequer	Sir Robert Peel.
Lord President of Council	Earl Rosslyn.
Lord Chancellor	Lord Lyndhurst.
Lord Privy Seal	Lord Wharncliffe.
Home Secretary	Mr. H. Goulburn.
Foreign Secretary	Duke of Wellington.
Colonial Secretary	Earl of Aberdeen.
First Lord of the Admiralty	Earl de Grey.
President of Board of Control	Lord Ellenborough.
President of Board of Trade and Master of the Mint	Mr. Alexander Baring.
Paymaster of the Forces	Sir E. Knatchbull.
War Secretary	Mr. J. C. Herries.
Master-General of Ordnance	Sir George Murray.

a majority. His address to his constituents sounded the keynote of the contest. Mr. Disraeli described it as "an attempt to construct a party without principles," and a more recent writer * has said that "the 'frank exposition' must have been bitter reading to some of the members of the new Cabinet." Assuredly the last statement cannot be true, for we know on Sir Robert Peel's own authority that the document was seen and considered by the Cabinet before its publication. He says: † "Immediately after the completion of the Cabinet, I proposed to my colleagues that I should take advantage of the opportunity which the approaching election would afford, and in an address to the constituent body of Tamworth declare the general principles upon which the Government proposed to act. My colleagues entirely approved of this course, *and of the Address which I submitted to their consideration.*" Undoubtedly, however, the "Manifesto" seriously alarmed a large section of the Tory party,—men of the "old school," like Eldon, who thought that the new leader was going too far and promising too much. He desired to appear before the country in the character of a Reformer; he spoke of the "mere superstitious reverence for ancient usages," and made use of several other phrases which fell unpleasantly on the ears of his followers; he declared that he was ready to act in the spirit of the Reform Bill if that implied "a careful review of the institutions, civil and ecclesiastical, undertaken in a friendly temper." There were many faithful Tories who thought that under such a guide as this they would eventually find themselves pretty much at the same destination as that to which Earl Grey and Lord John Russell desired to conduct them.

Mr. Croker did not take this view. Once more he refused

---

* Mr. Spencer Walpole, 'History of England,' iii. p. 281.
† 'Memoirs,' ii. p. 58.

to share the "general distrust" of Sir Robert Peel. He felt convinced that he would never desert his party. Consequently, he defended the Tamworth Manifesto in the 'Quarterly Review,' and commended Sir Robert Peel for doing what he steadily refused to do himself—that is to say, accepting "as a fact the change which the Reform Bill has made in the practice of the Constitution," and endeavouring "to avail himself of all the good of which its friends consider it susceptible, and to palliate all the mischiefs to which its adversaries may have thought it liable." "There is no other common-sense mode of dealing with any of the fluctuating affairs of mankind, whether they concern individuals or societies. . . . No Minister ever stood, or could stand, against public opinion."* These were the principles which Mr. Croker deemed applicable to Sir Robert Peel's position. He did not see that they were equally applicable to his own.

* 'Quarterly Review,' vol. 53, pp. 261–63. In this article a party was described as a "fortuitous concourse of atoms"—a phrase supposed to have been used for the first time many years afterwards by Lord John Russell.

CHAPTER XIX.

1835.

The Dissolution and the Elections—Combination against Sir Robert Peel—His Letters describing his Position—Lord Stanley's Refusal to join the Ministry—Mr. Croker recommends Mrs. Somerville and others for Pensions—Peel's Reply—The Rev. George Croly—Benjamin Disraeli and Mr. Croker's Speeches—Anticipated Contest on the Speakership—The Ecclesiastical Commission—Church Revenues—Peel's Reply to " Some of Our Tories "—Fears of another Dissolution—Defeats of the Government — The Malt-Tax — Dissenters' Marriages with Church Rites—Letters of Sir R. Peel—The Irish Church Debates—Sir R. Peel's Difficulties—Mr. Croker's Advice—Final Defeat and Resignation of the Ministry—The Premier on his Reverses—Summary of his Measures—The Academy Exhibition of 1835—Sir R. Peel on Wilkie's Painting of Wellington writing a Despatch—And on David's Painting of the Death of Marat—Suggests a History of the Reign of Terror—Illness of Sir W. Follett—The Second Ministry of Lord Melbourne—Corporation Reform—Memorandum of the Duke of Wellington—Sir R. Peel and Dr. Pusey—The " Tyranny of Party "—Amendments to the Corporation Bill in the Lords—Works on the French Revolution in the British Museum—The Duke of Wellington on the State of the Country—And on Napoleon I.

SIR ROBERT PEEL was not deceived in supposing that an appeal to the country would result in making his weakness less manifest and less embarrassing, but it did not turn a minority into a majority. Before the elections, the Tories mustered about 150; when the new Parliament met they were nearly a hundred more. The " moderate men," on whose support Peel largely depended, could not be numbered with any certainty, but there was always a fair proportion on his side. The amalgamation of all the hostile factions readily sufficed to overpower them, and Peel's experience soon proved that a Minister in a permanent minority cannot hope to carry on the government. He was harassed by defeats from the very opening of the Session—defeated on the election of Speaker, on the Address, on every important question that was brought before the House. The Whigs, Radicals, and Irish Members never failed to combine against him, and they refused to accord him even that moderate degree of fair play which is generally conceded to a Minister who shows a disposition to conciliate his opponents. The spirit in which he approached a hopeless task, and in which he afterwards stood at bay, is best described in his own letters.

Sir Robert Peel to Mr. Croker.

Drayton Manor, January 10th, 1835.

MY DEAR CROKER,

Your letter of the 8th* finds me here. I went to bed at two on Friday morning, rose at four, travelled to Drayton, and had the cordial satisfaction of a ball in the evening, at which Lady Peel and Julia, after their journey, danced with a spirit worthy of their Italian fame. The next day I shot eleven wild ducks, twelve pheasants, and I know not how much besides.

I doubt whether the Whigs *can* turn me out on the Address, but I cannot tell you how little all this disturbs or disquiets me. I have done my best. I will leave nothing undone to succeed. If I do succeed, and remain in office (as I mean to make no sacrifice to popular opinion for the mere purpose of gratifying it, at the expense of the real and even remote interests of the country), success will be a compensation to me for all that I must resign of private comfort and happiness. If I fail, having nothing to reproach myself with, no man was ever installed in office with half the

* [Not among Mr. Croker's papers.]

satisfaction to his own mere personal and private feelings as I shall retire from it, and sit with you in the new library at Drayton Manor, after a day's shooting.

I envy not Lord Stanley's *visions* of my place. I would not exchange my position for his.

I should have thought that in such a crisis as that in which we are, almost unconsciously, living, a man might have made up his mind as to some definite course of action; that he might have ranged himself on one side or the other; that if he left his colleagues because they were *Destructives*, to use his own word—that, if he did what he could to ruin them in public estimation, by the grossest and to them most *unseasonable* abuse—if he set the example to his Sovereign of withdrawing from them his confidence—I should have thought, having been one of the main causes of the King's embarrassment, he might, on the highest and most courageous principles, have assisted in the King's defence.

Mind what I now say to you. If he really entertains the principles he professes, he *shall* not be able to maintain them and oppose me.

Ever affectionately yours,

R. P.

Whitehall Gardens, January 26th.

My dear Croker,

It is now six o'clock, and what between letters that I could not possibly postpone, and deputations that I had appointed, I have hardly time to read and return the enclosed by this post.*

I should say that the distinction is not quite sufficiently marked between my position, called for suddenly from abroad, and required by the King to give him my services, and the position in which I should have stood, supposing I had displaced the Government by combination with Radicals, or any sort of Parliamentary tactics.

My address to Tamworth is also, I think, too much referred to necessities imposed by the Reform Bill. I think the necessities rather arose from the abruptness of the change in the Government, and, to say the truth, from the policy of aiding our friends at the election.

---

* [Doubtless the proofs of Mr. Croker's article on the Tamworth Manifesto, published in the 'Quarterly Review,' February 1835, and referred to in the previous chapter.]

I should say also generally, that from the nature of the
returns, our main hope must be in the adhesion of moderate
men, not professing adherence to our politics. Do not therefore discourage their adhesion by an attack on their party,
or enable their leaders to throw scruples of honour and
feeling in the way of their withdrawal from old connections.

Remember Stanley's position, and that he will subscribe
himself a Whig.

Ever affectionately yours,

ROBERT PEEL.

One of Mr. Croker's first wishes on the formation of a
new Ministry was to secure some more decided recognition
of the claims of literature on the State than had hitherto
been vouchsafed. He began by recommending Mrs. Somerville for a pension; and Sir Robert Peel at once advised
the grant to this distinguished lady of 200*l.* a year. The
pension was afterwards increased, by Lord John Russell,
to 300*l.* a year. Mr. Croker also urged the bestowal
of some assistance upon Dr. Maginn, who had frequently
attacked him in various kinds of lampoons; and upon
Moore, whose circumstances were generally in a more or
less disordered plight.

Mr. Croker to Sir Robert Peel.

[Without date; probably January 18th.]

MY DEAR PEEL,

Let me remind you of the pension to Mrs. Somerville.
I never saw her, and have no kind of interest in the matter,
but as concerns the honour of your Administration, and the
cause of science and letters. I have made such enquiries
about her as I could venture to do without exciting suspicion
as to my object, or leading by-and-bye to a suspicion that
I was the benefactor, who, in fact, only ring the bell. She
is the daughter of an Admiral Fairfax, who was Lord
Duncan's Captain in his victory at Camperdown, brought
home his despatches, and was knighted. He is dead about

twenty years. She married first a son of Admiral Greig, of
the Russian service, by whom she had a son, who has all his
father left. She married secondly Dr. Somerville, who is
physician to Chelsea Hospital, with no means, I am told, but
his salary. She has two daughters, who, with herself, are
unprovided for, except by the doctor's situation.

I ought to tell you that I heard a whisper that Brougham
had promised to do something for them, and that they think
he played false with them, but I know nothing of the details,
and did not choose to enquire. 200*l.* or 150*l.* a year would
surely be well applied in this case; or say, 150*l.* to her, and
25*l.* each to the daughters. The child and grandchildren
of Sir W. Fairfax have a degree of merit, exclusive of
Mrs. Somerville's literary reputation.

I urge very earnestly upon you the endeavour to do something for literature. What makes a literary man easy and
happy is often such a trifle as an individual might bestow.
There is a man, whom I am far from recommending for
respectability, or even trustworthiness, one Doctor Maginn,
but he is a powerful, and has been a useful, partisan writer,
though I believe he has libelled both you and me. He is
a zealous Conservative. He has been lately, and I fear long,
in prison for debt, and was released by a subscription of
some of his friends. I could not advise you to do anything
ostensible for him, but 50*l.* or 100*l.* given by a third and safe
hand—Lockhart, for instance, who managed the subscription
that released him—would be well laid out. He is a powerful
writer, and has, I think, some claim to be warmed by the
sunshine, short and wintry as it may be, that now exhilarates
his party.

Moore I before mentioned to you. He is a person to
whom it would be creditable to give any little thing you
might have, but I fear that such little things are very rare,
and it would not do to single out such a Whig or Radical as
he has been, for Tory favour.

Sir Robert Peel to Mr. Croker.

Whitehall, January 21st, 1835.

MY DEAR CROKER,

As far as the *abstract* case is concerned, I have both ample
means and equal inclination to give a pension to Mrs. Somer-

ville; but there are three or four matters connected with this, and with aid to literature, that I should like to speak to you upon before I do anything.

Ever affectionately yours,
ROBERT PEEL.

Whitehall, January 28th.

MY DEAR CROKER,

It is very odd that the same post should have brought under my notice the names of the very persons whom I was trying to recall to my recollection as men of fair literary pretensions, and severe, perhaps unmerited, distress.

Did you ever see a letter which Southey wrote to Brougham, while Brougham was Chancellor, on the subject of encouragement to literary merit? It is a very able and striking letter.

I must be very cautious not to *confine* pensions to Whig or Liberal professors of literature.

Ever yours affectionately,
ROBERT PEEL.

Mr. Croker next appealed to the Lord Chancellor (Lyndhurst) to do something for the Rev. George Croly, author of 'Salathiel,' who once bitterly complained, in a sermon at St. Stephen's, Walbrook, of which he was rector, that he had become "so accustomed to neglect that he had ceased to regard it as an injury."

Mr. Croker to Lord Lyndhurst.

West Moulsey, February 3rd, 1835.

MY DEAR LORD,

If by "Croley" you mean George Croly, D.D., I know him *longer* and *less* than anybody. We were at college together, but very little acquainted, as he was rather my senior, and not in the same society. He was also there what he has been through life, and what I suppose he *still* is, a shy, reserved man. About twenty years ago he published some poems, which I looked over, and I believe touched here and there previous to publication. They possessed great power, but were, "like the father who begot them," somewhat stiff and ungainly. Soon after, Lord Liverpool resolved to set up a weekly paper, and knowing Croly's talents and principles, and having a kindness for him, I recommended him for the editorship, at 300*l*. a year; but his talents did not lie that way, and eventually the thing failed. Even this did not make me better acquainted with this strange, shy, awkward man. I should have suspected that I, in some over-frankness, had offended him, or that I had not handled with sufficient delicacy that over-nice instrument, a poor, proud scholar; but I *am told* that this was not the case, and that his temper is the same to all men. He has latterly been writing a very bad class of books (by bad I only mean visionary and useless) on the Prophecies, and mixing politics and theology. I have not read any of them, but hear that they are ingenious, eloquent, and absurd; but on the whole he has a literary reputation and a character as a clergyman that will justify anything that you can do for him, and I heartily entreat you to do something.

Indeed I should have mentioned his name both to Peel and you as deserving of recollection in the distribution of literary favours, if I had not heard and believed that Brougham had given him a living. Nay, in writing to Peel on a similar subject, I instanced as an example to be followed Brougham's patronage of Tory Croly. It turns out now that, like all the rest of Brougham's merits, all was false and hollow. But I believe the whole literary world is now under an impression that Dr. Croly is enjoying a comfortable preferment *ex dono* Brougham; and if anything about that man could surprise me, your letter would have done so. At all events, I do most strongly urge you to do the thing. It is right in itself, and I should have pressed it had I dreamed of Brougham's roguery; but it is now on every account desirable that the disappointment should be repaired.

As you have given me this opportunity, I would implore you to employ your, I fear, too short-lived patronage, in aid of the Church and literature, at present exclusively. If your reign is to be long, there will be plenty of time to attend to other interests and claims (which I know cannot be altogether neglected), but *now* the great object should be to do whatever may best tend to make us popular with that great and important class, who will be more struck by a judicious and high-minded use of Church patronage than by another circumstance.

I perhaps should not have ventured to give this advice, if I did not know that I speak to willing ears, and that personally as well as politically you are disposed to illustrate yourself and the Government, by giving good things to good men, in preference to any other considerations.

The following letter seems to show that the future leader of the Tory party applied to Mr. Croker somewhere about this time, for information with regard to his speeches in Parliament on the Reform Bill. Mr. Disraeli may have desired to consult them in preparing the 'Letters of Runnymede,' which he published in 1836. His manner of repaying Mr. Croker for the courtesy shown to him on this and other occasions, is known to the public.

Mr. Croker to Mr. Benjamin Disraeli.

[No date.]

SIR,

Absence from home has prevented my receiving and answering your letter of the 30th ult. sooner.

In reply to your question, I have to say that I *believe* that all my speeches were reported in Hansard's Parliamentary Debates, with as much accuracy as the nature of the case allows. One or two of the speeches were corrected by me, at the desire of Mr. Murray, for separate publication; but I rather think that those so corrected and published, were incorporated in Hansard. I have myself no complete set of my speeches, or I should offer it for your inspection; but if Hansard (which, of course, you must have) does not furnish all the information you desire, you may, by using my name with Mr. Murray, obtain a copy of my speeches published by him. He published also a letter to a noble Lord (Haddington) about the Reform Bill, and the resolutions moved by me on the report of the last Bill. But these are in the 'Journals.'

I have the honour to be, Sir,
Your faithful servant,
J. W. CROKER.

On the 29th of January, the Prime Minister wrote to Mr. Croker, "I have done what you suggested as to Maginn." Other and more pressing duties soon called for Peel's attention. It was known that there would be an opposition to the re-election of Sir Charles Manners Sutton as Speaker, the adverse party having resolved to bring forward Mr. J. Abercromby, who was Master of the Mint under Lord Melbourne's Government. Sir Robert Peel expected defeat, and told Mr. Croker that he should regard it as a "mere flea-bite."

Sir Robert Peel to Mr. Croker.

February 1st, 1835.

MY DEAR CROKER,

I think you will be glad to hear that I wrote yesterday to Lady Canning,* stating that I believed her son had formed no political connections, and held no political opinions which could forbid my offer, and that if she would allow me to place him in my own department as a Lord of the Treasury, although he is not in Parliament, I should be proud to give him the means of acquiring the knowledge that might enable him to maintain the lustre of his name, and to have the opportunity of marking that attachment and admiration for his father, which separation from him in public life has never abated.

I have not received an answer yet,† and therefore do not mention the subject.

Ever affectionately yours,

ROBERT PEEL.

I quite agree with you ‡ as to the cause of Abercromby's selection. It must be the hand of Death alone which will prevent *the King's Speech.* I should consider defeat on the Speaker a mere flea-bite, but I must not say this.

* [Peel had offered through Lady Canning, to introduce her son, Lord Canning (afterwards Governor-General of India), to public life by appointing him to a post as one of the Lords of the Treasury.]

† [The answer is published in the 'Memoirs by Sir R. Peel,' vol. ii. pp. 64–5.]

‡ [Mr. Croker's letter is missing.]

Mr. Croker to Lord Hertford.

West Moulsey, February 5th, 1835.

The only interest now existing amongst us is as to the election of Speaker. Johnny Russell having declared himself leader of the Opposition, puts forward Abercromby in opposition to Sutton. I told you last week that [Spring] Rice was to be their candidate, and I had pretty good authority for telling you so, namely, Rice's own; but they found, first, that Morpeth and some other leading Whigs were pledged to Sutton against anybody but Abercromby; and second, that the Irish Mountain would not vote for Rice. They were therefore obliged to change their man.

As to the result, more doubt is entertained by our friends than I could have believed. I thought that whoever the candidate should be, it would be a false step on the part of the Whigs, for certainly, bad as are the elections, and weak as in my opinion the Government is, if we cannot carry *such* a question as *such* a speaker against *such* a candidate, we are absolutely impotent; for my own part I still believe that we shall win, and I *should* have said win easily; but when I find our own friends calculating on a small majority only, I know not what to say.

Peel has issued a Church Reform Commission, and I think it was inevitable; yet, as I told him, I dread a bad precedent from good hands. He will do no harm, and indeed he will do good; but *il n'y a que le premier pas qui coûte*. He means to make a less unequal, but not an absolutely equal distribution of the revenues of Bishops and great dignitaries, and will limit, if not abolish, pluralities and sinecures. From the temper of the elections, I doubt whether without this the property of the Church would not have been in danger of spoliation for secular, or even Dissenting purposes. I believe the view I gave you in my last letter of the result of the elections is pretty nearly correct. It is admitted, even by the most sanguine of the Tories, that all depends upon the moderates—a poor dependence!

The Commission referred to in this letter was designed to prepare a plan of Church reform, in fulfilment of the pledges given by Peel in his Tamworth address. His general views at the moment are clearly explained in the following letter, which was evidently written either in reply to one which has been lost, or to a newspaper letter or article setting forth what "some of our Tories" were saying. No direct trace can be discovered to the allusion.

Sir Robert Peel to Mr. Croker.

Whitehall, February 2nd, 1835.

MY DEAR CROKER,

It is a very harmless occupation for "*some of our Tories*" to keep themselves *in wind* by attacking wind-mills of their own creation.

Whoever dreamed of Equalisation of Livings? of anything but great disparity in their value? of gradations from very low to very high? I am sure I never did. But is this right — that there should be no provision whatever for spiritual duties in some of the largest, most populous, most important, most dissenting districts of the country? Is it right that three-fourths of Nottingham, included in one parish, should have no provision whatever for a clergyman, except what he can collect from dues and pew-rents—that is, from a tax upon going to church?

Is it right that the tithes should be totally withdrawn from many important vicarages and paid over to prebendaries whose duty it is to preach a sermon once a month? Is the Church to be a provision for men of birth, or for men of learning? or is its main object the worship of God according to the doctrines of the Reformed faith?

That worship is promoted by inviting men of birth and men of learning into the Church; but if the time shall ever arrive when it can be shown that to this object, important as it may be, you have sacrificed other and more important objects; you have left hundreds of thousands to become Dissenters or, more likely, infidels, because you would not divert one farthing of ecclesiastical revenues from this Deanery, or that great sinecure. If the time shall come when a strict scrutiny shall be made by unfriendly inquirers into the *principle* on which great preferments have been given by politicians, "*some of our Tories*," who now profess their exclusive friendship to the Church, will find their friendship the severest measure of hostility from which the Church ever suffered.

This is the old cry. The Bishop of London is an enemy, and the Archbishop, it seems, cannot be depended on. Very good. But if such opinions as those which "*some of our Tories*" deprecate do prevail in the highest authorities of the Church, can there be a more conclusive proof that our position is an unsafe one, and that there is a demand from *within* as well as from *without*, which had better be carefully considered in time?

Adhere to principle, say "some of our Tories." Very good; then, if laws have passed enabling Cathedral tithes to be reattached to vicarages, appropriating the revenues of stalls at Durham to the foundation of a College, the revenues of prebends at Lichfield to the repair of the Cathedral, what violation of principle is there in considering whether, for instance, a Dean of Durham with 8000l. a year might not be advantageously placed at Manchester or Liverpool, relieving possibly the Bishop of Chester from some part of episcopal duties which no human strength can perform?

Is it perfection of principle to make Lord Liverpool's cousin a Bishop in Wales, and also Dean of Durham, and an utter abandonment of principle to bring the Dean or his revenues nearer home, not equalising livings, but making high dignitaries perform with sufficient and very liberal emoluments (for they ought to be liberal) effective spiritual duties? For God's sake don't let pretended friends of the Church provoke the statement of the case which can be made out in favour of a temperate review of the present state of the Establishment. Is this right—that in a parish of 10,000 acres, overrun with dissent, the whole tithes go to an ecclesiastical corporation, to the amount of 2000l. a year; that there is only one service in the church, and cannot be two, because the said Corporation will only allow 24l. a year as a stipend to the Vicar?

Ever affectionately yours,
ROBERT PEEL.

The Bishop of Lincoln, in consequence of past spoliations of the see, has *thirty-six* impropriate rectories. If I returned the tithes to the rectories, and gave him a Cathedral preferment instead, would this be violation of principle?

What think you of *Kingston* and *Richmond* being united

in one benefice, because *King's College*, Cambridge, cannot *afford* to endow the two out of the tithes.

Parliament assembled on the 19th of February, and Sir Charles Manners Sutton was defeated for the Speakership, as had been anticipated. He was raised to the peerage under the title of Viscount Canterbury. There was a majority of seven against the Government on the Address, and it was thought that this double defeat would induce the Ministry to resign. But the fear began to spread that instead of resignation, Sir Robert Peel would try another dissolution. He kept the idea before the House, though in a covert manner, and it would appear that this course was suggested to him by Mr. Croker.

Mr. Croker to Sir Robert Peel.

February 22nd, 1835.

Dear Peel,

In talking of " the sense of the people " in the first paragraph of the Speech, you must take care of two points. First, not to concede that this Parliament does speak the sense of the people; secondly, not to foreclose yourself from another dissolution. I myself do not at all doubt that the House of Commons does speak the sense of the constituent body, nor do I foresee the possibility of another dissolution; but it may be inexpedient to bind yourself on those two points, and you should therefore be cautious in the choice of terms. I shall be in town to-morrow, but shall not call upon you, as this note contains all I have to say. I have, ever since I saw you, been thinking of the position of affairs, and I am sorry to say that I see no extrication. If the House votes that it has no confidence in you, I cannot discover any other eventual course but a new Ministry, for if it votes *that*, is it possible that it should not *also* negative " that a supply be granted " ? for, surely, nothing could be more absurd and unconstitutional than to grant a supply to those in whom you have no confidence, and the day is not yet arrived for *coups d'état*.

J. W. C.

The next difficulty was created by one of Sir Robert Peel's own followers, the Marquis of Chandos, who brought forward a resolution for the repeal of the Malt Tax. In this instance the Ministry triumphed, for the opposition to the repeal of the tax was not confined to the Tories. The majority against the resolution was large enough to encourage the young, but already declining, Government—138.

Mr. Croker to Lord Hertford.

West Moulsey, March 10th.

Peel is resolute, and so I may say are his friends, while his enemies are not very stout, and are united only on the one point of opposing him. His immediate and pressing difficulty is the Malt Tax, the repeal of which at least 150 of his minority are pledged to support, which two at least, members of his Cabinet, are bound to [defend?], and which prevented Chandos being of the Cabinet. Peel had a great meeting of his adherents on Saturday—above 200—in which some leading men—Hall Dare, for instance, member for Essex—manfully said that they would forfeit their pledges, and balk their constituents, rather than risk the existence of the Government, and this is, I have heard, so general a sentiment that they now talk—first, of Chandos not pressing the question; and secondly, if he should, of beating him. Whatever may be the result, how fortunate it is that Peel supported the late Ministers on this question, though he earned great obloquy from our friends for doing so. I recollect particularly the Lowthers, who voted twice over against the Malt Tax, and are now very much embarrassed what to do. Those votes, however, were so confused and complicated in the form of putting them, that our friends will find a loophole. In short, the Tories are quite sanguine, and mean to eat all their words and their votes rather than risk the Ministry.

But will it do? Between you and me I should say no! They are like shipwrecked men on a raft, and as long as the sea is smooth, that is, the people quiet, they may hold on their precarious existence, but the least little breeze will send them all to the bottom.

The country is for the moment with Peel, but it may shift

with the wind, and his power has no solid basis to enable it to stand against a shift of wind.

This was the only ray of light in the sky. Every other event turned out unfortunately for the Ministry. The appointment of the Marquis of Londonderry (the brother of the late Lord Castlereagh) to the post of Ambassador at St. Petersburg raised a storm, and the Marquis had to withdraw. Scarcely a day passed without inflicting some humiliation upon the unfortunate Government. The Irish Tithe Commutation Bill was introduced, with the "appropriation clause" taken, as the Whigs declared, from their own measure. Lord John Russell then made ready to inflict what he believed would be the *coup de grâce* upon this hapless Administration. He gave notice of a resolution to apply the surplus revenues of the Irish Church " to the general education of all classes of the people, without distinction of religious persuasion." But before this question came forward, Sir Robert Peel introduced a Bill permitting Dissenters to be married, with the usual rites of the Church, when they were so minded, or with any religious ceremony they pleased, provided notice was given, and the marriage registered.

Lord John Russell's resolution was opposed most persistently by Sir Robert Peel, but upon this, as upon other questions, the House was prepared with its decision beforehand. This position of affairs had given rise to many serious questions in the Minister's mind ; he had but a dreary choice before him,—between " discreditable defeat " and still more " discreditable concession."

Mr. Croker to Sir Robert Peel.

MY DEAR PEEL, [Without date.]

I have been anxiously thinking of our conversation of yesterday, and of all I afterwards heard about the views of parties in town ; and I am convinced that you cannot go out until you are actually *forced* to do so by some positive practical measure ; for instance, if the Irish Church resolution of Monday (which, I hear, is to be carried by 30) should be *only* a *resolution,* I think it would be much of the same nature as the amendment to the address, on which you might have retired ; but not having done so, it seems that you are pledged not to be driven out by a vote of the same *abstract* nature. When anything shall be *done* which you disapprove, and which yet requires your concurrence for its execution, then will come the time to consider of refusing to do or suffer to be done an improper *act,* and (if you cannot evade the practical difficulty) of resigning. That crisis will, I have no doubt, soon arrive, but, depend upon it, the terms under which you took office and the spirit in which you have expressed your determination to hold it, oblige you not to give in till you find the wheels of the Government actually clogged. In the meanwhile I would insist on the doing of the *public business,* and I should not now be deterred from dividing by the fear of being beaten, and should let the country see, when you do resign, that you were forced to do so by the suspension by the House of Commons of the routine of the public service. Quarter-day is at hand, and I don't believe you have a money vote to enable you to pay the pay, wages, salaries, half pay, or the other usual quarterly payments. Let this be known, and let the country see, *on a division,* by whom, and how it is, that this class of business has been impeded. I never for a moment have had a doubt that you must retire, and I now think it only a question of a week sooner or later, but I foresee such utter *despondency and prostration* of the Conservative party, and so much consequent sourness and injustice in their future feelings towards you, that I shall regret your going before *every man* shall be convinced that you had expended your last cartridge, and could *physically* resist no longer.

I heard from some quarters a kind of expectation that Stanley ought *now* to join you openly, if it were only to go out with you; and I even heard that he was not disinclined from some such course. This seems to me a strange conjuncture—like old Wycherly's marriage on his death-bed. I repeat it only because I heard it, and because if Stanley has the magnanimity to take such a course, it might, even now postpone the general ruin.

I *believe* Burdett's opinion is that you ought not to be driven out by the vote on the Irish Church—such, at least, is the language of *his* small *tail.* I did not hear whether he will have the courage to come down on Monday to support you.

Yours affectionately,

J. W. CROKER.

Sir Robert Peel to Mr. Croker.

MY DEAR CROKER,   Whitehall, March 30th, 1835.

We shall resist Lord John Russell's motion to-night on principle and by direct opposition. We shall consider it not with reference to words, but to things, to the time at which it was brought forward, to the ground on which alone it can be supported (namely, want of confidence in the Government), and to the men by whom it will be supported.

Lord Stanley approves of our course, and will cordially act with us on this discussion. The resolution is no abstract one. It means the destruction of the Church in Ireland. It is the most *practical* resolution that ever was proposed; for it will utterly prevent the levy of tithe in the South of Ireland, if the tithe is to be appropriated to the Church. Of what avails public opinion among the *non-voting* part of the people of England, of what avails a counter-resolution of the Lords, or a rejection by the Lords of a Tithe Bill, when the question is this—Can you enforce the payment of a charge which has been discontinued for three years in the South of Ireland, if a majority of the House of Commons be ranged on the side of the payers, or, I should rather say, the non-payers of tithe?

Shall we undertake the responsibility of this state of things—being in a minority not only on the tithe question, but on every other contested question? Again, have we a hope of bettering our condition? If we have not, how long shall we continue habituating the House of Commons, through our weakness, to act without the control of the Executive Government, and to assume functions which do not belong to it?

They will assume such functions whether we are Ministers or not. They will; but in one case we are consenting, or at least, conniving parties; in the other not. You see the course I have taken, I am sure the right one, to prefer discreditable defeat to more discreditable concession.

Ever yours,

ROBERT PEEL.

Mr. Croker to Sir Robert Peel.

MY DEAR PEEL, March 31st, 1835.

On general principles, and in ordinary circumstances, no one can deny that you should go out if beaten on the Irish Church or on any other great question; but you have accepted, or at least have continued in, your post on different conditions. You did not resign on the Speaker—on the address—on all the other defeats; so that we have your *practice* against your principle. I, you know, have *always* wished to see the Church chosen as the stand or fall question, both of the administration and of the House of Lords; and I have no doubt that it will ultimately be so; but after the most deliberate consideration, I am forced to think that you have pledged yourself to a perseverance and tenacity as obstinate as the circumstances are unparalleled. I know it is but the question of a week; that you *must* go out. I thought so in November last, in December, ever since—*now*. I think this a fitting and adequate occasion; but as I know that the public in general, resting on your former pledges and practice, does not consider the precise moment as yet come, I am anxious that you should not retire till all men are satisfied that a longer resistance would be improper, even if possible.

If you, on the spot and in the centre of knowledge, think that the world is agreed that the time is actually come, I have not a word more to say, and my only desire is that you should appear firm and consistent to the last—*servetur ad imum*. I cannot but think that if it were possible, it would be better to try a new combination with Stanley, than to throw up the whole game at once; but that, I suppose, cannot be, nor would it save us long—perhaps not a day—but it would make the Conservative party so strong in opposition, as to afford us some little hope of security for persons and property.

A few more uneasy days, and the fate of the Ministry was decided. On the 2nd of April it was defeated by 33, on the 6th by 25, on the 7th by 27. On the 8th Sir Robert Peel was obliged to acknowledge the uselessness of the struggle, and he resigned. It is now generally admitted—as indeed it was at the time—that he deserved a better fate, and that, in despite of the incessant discomfitures he had sustained, his position as a public man before the country was, upon the whole, improved. Mr. Croker defended him most zealously, not only in the 'Quarterly Review,' but wherever he could make his voice heard, and the fallen Minister took his reverse with a good heart.

Sir Robert Peel to Mr. Croker.

Whitehall Gardens, April 13th, 1835.

My dear Croker,

I received a note from the King about seven yesterday evening, requesting me to facilitate an adjournment until Thursday next, for the purpose of promoting the arrangements connected with the formation of a new Government. I understand that Lord Melbourne is to be at the head.

Lord J. Russell is to be in town at three to-day; and until his arrival I presume that the cast of parts will not be finally settled.

They talk of Sir George Grey for Ireland, Lord Granville as Lord Lieutenant; he failing, Carlisle. Lord Morpeth to have some office or other.* I presume the Government will be as nearly as possible that which was dismissed in November last.

We dine at Oatlands to-morrow. Peradventure, as Brougham says, we shall meet.

"My bosom's lord sits lightly on its throne." †

I do not know why Shakespeare should remind me of an attorney; but I have this morning received a wonderful address—the strongest expressions of approbation and confidence from 1100 *solicitors* resident in the metropolis. I had no idea there were so many; less that they were so nearly unanimous in the support of Conservative principles.

Ever affectionately yours,

Robert Peel.

* [He was made Chief Secretary for Ireland.]
† [Thus in the original. The true text is, "My bosom's lord sits lightly in his throne."—*Romeo and Juliet*, Act V., Scene I., line 3.]

April 14th, 1835.

MY DEAR CROKER,

My measures were Irish Tithe—*English Tithe*—which you omit—English Church—Dissenters' Marriages. These were opened to the House of Commons.

I made a promise of settling the Church Rate Question (which I could not have settled), and of relief to land from certain local charges. I protected the Malt Tax—this was resistance to a serious attack on public credit.

We found nothing done on the Canada Question—not a trace of a line written between June or July, when the House of Commons Committee reported, and the 15th of November, when the late Government went out.

Rice says he was going to write a most voluminous dispatch —of course the very next day. He was, he says, labouring with it, when he was met in Regent Street on the Saturday and told he was out of office. Aberdeen has laid the foundation for a complete settlement of the Canadian question, or a complete conviction of the Canadian party of the intention to rebel and separate.

The pensions—the only pensions—I gave were to a Mrs. Temple, whose husband, an African traveller, died, I think, at Sierra Leone. She had 100*l.* a year. Professor Airy, 300*l.** Mrs. Somerville, 200*l.* Sharon Turner, 200*l.* Robert Southey, 300*l.* James Montgomery, of Sheffield, 150*l.*

The Chancellor gave Crabbe a living. I gave Milman the only preferment I had to give, that of St. Margaret's and the Prebend of Westminster. I will tell Clerk and Venables to send you what you require.

Ever yours,

ROBERT PEEL.

In Mr. Croker's next letter there was very little about politics, and a good deal about the Royal Academy Exhibition of 1835, in which "young Landseer" had a picture of "Horned Cattle," which did not escape notice.†

---

* [Professor (now Sir G. B.) Airy was appointed Astronomer Royal in succession to Professor Pond, in 1835.]

† This picture was probably "The Drover's Departure," first exhibited this year, and now in the Sheepshanks Collection. But "*Horned Cattle*" would be but a sorry description of so fine a work.

Mr. Croker to Sir R. Peel.

West Moulsey, May 4th.

I dined at the Academy on Saturday. A bad exhibition; several tolerable pictures of what the French call *de genre* but all the large ones (almost exclusively portraits) are infamous. There are three of the Duke, each worse than the other—Wilkie and Pickersgill vying in the art of sinking. I forget the author of the third. "Horned Cattle," by young Landseer, attracts some notice. "Columbus explaining his Project," by Wilkie, is an imitation of, or I should rather say a *cento*, from Titian; yet not good, and he has made a bolder anachronism than his oysters in June; he has introduced the telescope full 100 years too soon. Leslie has painted Gulliver at the Court of Brobdingnag, a total failure as to the story (though the parts are good), for the Brobdingnagians all look like ordinary men and women, while Gulliver looks only like a toy. A young man of the name of Say has painted Follett very well—nearly the best in the room. The very best, I think, is a large one of a woman by a woman—one Mrs. Robertson—a picture that no *man* in the exhibition has approached. There are a few pretty little things.

We had Grey and all the Ministers, except Palmerston and my Lord Glenelg. Brougham, they said, was not invited. I rather think he did not choose to come in so dubious a position as he occupies at this moment. The places of the Dukes of Wellington, Northumberland, Newcastle, and Buccleuch were vacant—this is not right at such a dinner. I hope you sent your excuse in good time. Pozzo and Esterhazy also absent. Bulow returned thanks for the Foreign Ministers in a written English speech, so unintelligible that I should have thought it German, only the German has a strong affinity to English, to which this did not seem to have the least resemblance.

Sir Robert Peel to Mr. Croker.

Drayton Manor, May 5th.

MY DEAR CROKER,

I date this from Drayton Manor, but am in truth writing from what we call Mr. Hill's house. That is a respectable brick messuage, just situate at the point where the road to Drayton Church and village turns from the Coleshill road. We are, however, very comfortably lodged, and convenient, as they say in Ireland, to the new house.

My chief interest in your letter is in that part which relates to the exhibition of the Royal Academy. This is the first occasion on which I have been absent from the dinner. I will, however, profit by your experience, not in the eatables, but the visibles of the ceremony at which you assisted, and go with you to Somerset House on my return to town.

I think Wilkie quite wrong in painting the size of life such subjects as Columbus, and the interviews of the Pope and Buonaparte. If he had been present at the interview, and had painted the room in which it took place, the portraits of the two parties to it, with their identical dresses, the picture would have been really historical and really valuable.

But two portraits by a contemporary who never saw either of the personages he represents, and made up their likenesses from busts and the pictures of others, and who represents a scene quite unintelligible and indescribable by painting alone, and which has no other peculiarity about it than that which must belong to the act of every man who refuses to sign a paper offered to him by another for his signature, can never excite much interest.

Wilkie had always a fancy for painting the Duke of Wellington writing the report of the Battle of Waterloo, and to put a trumpeter or some such messenger standing by the table waiting to convey the dispatch as soon as it was sealed.

I told him that trumpeters did not so wait; that dispatches after Waterloo were written very much like other letters on ordinary business; that the only way in which he could attach interest to the representation of such an act would be, not by drawing upon fancy, but by really drawing the room in which the dispatch was actually written, the portrait of the pen with which it was written, the state of the Duke's dress at the moment, if with a night-cap on, introducing the night-cap—in short by a perfectly faithful record of that truth which was possibly within his reach, and the deviation from which in a contemporary would be a fraud upon posterity.

Believe me ever affectionately yours,

My dear Croker,

R. P.

Sir R. Peel to Mr. Croker.

MY DEAR CROKER, [Without date.]

When you come to town, go to Leicester Fields, and see a picture, which will interest you, and repay you for your visit if it makes half as much impression upon you as it did upon me.

It is by David, and I dare say you have already *mentally ejaculated*, that you would not give a farthing to see any picture by so bad a painter, and so great a scoundrel. But this picture, which is by far the best he ever painted, represents with horrible fidelity Marat dying in the bath after his assassination by Charlotte Corday, and was exhibited by order of the Convention.*

There is the pencil sketch of his countenance by David, in the agony of death, made in the bath-room on a piece of paper that David found there. The picture itself is very powerfully painted.

Ever yours, R. P.

MY DEAR CROKER, [Without date.]

I wish you would think seriously of the History of the Reign of Terror. I do not mean a pompous, philosophical history, but a mixture of biography, facts, and gossip: a diary of what really took place, with the best authenticated likenesses of the actors.

French writers treating of the Revolution have very much slurred over this part of the eventful scene, influenced perhaps partly by the feeling which De Thou expresses with regard to St. Bartholomew's Day in his very appropriate quotation:—

> "Excidat ille dies ævo, neu postera credant
> Sæcula. Nos certe taceamus, et obruta multa
> Nocte tegi nostræ patiamur crimina gentis."

There would be many advantages in selecting this subject for a historical record.

---

* [This painting was finished by David immediately after Marat's assassination, and presented by him to the Convention on the 14th November, 1793. The voice of the people, he declared, had called upon him to take the work in hand. "David, saisis tes pinceaux, s'écriait-il, venge notre ami, venge Marat!"]

First, the period is a definite one, and well defined, and the events are a beautiful practical commentary on the maxim:

> "Nec lex est justior ulla,
> Quam *necis* artifices arte perire suâ."

It would show that with the day of success in popular insurrections begins the punishment of their authors. That chapter which detailed the fate of every actor in the bloody scenes, would be written for our learning.

I suppose you have got the five volumes of letters *concerning* Mirabeau, lately published.

Turn to a note in the fifth volume, which attributes to the Parliament of Paris a great share in preparing the minds of the population of Paris for resistance to authority by physical force. The connivance at mobs collected round the building in which the Parliament sat; the denouncement of officers and soldiers who tried to suppress the mobs; the public exhortation to all those who should hereafter be employed *against the people*, to be very humane and moderate, and the inference that the people naturally drew from such exhortations are well described.

Ever yours,
ROBERT PEEL.

The family of Lepelletier lately bought the picture which represented his assassination.

The showman tells the monstrous untruth that David had been offered 3000*l.* sterling for the "Death of Marat."

Lord Melbourne entered into office for the second time as Prime Minister on the 18th of April, and on this occasion Lord John Russell was made Home Secretary, and entrusted with the duty of bringing in the Corporation Reform Bill. The measure was founded upon the report of Commissioners who were appointed in 1833, and whose method of proceeding provoked great complaints in many different directions. The principle of the Bill was, however, in accordance with public opinion, for it transferred the control of boroughs from wealthy landowners to the people themselves. It was a change which could not have been deferred much longer, and which was imperatively called for by the spirit of the time.

Sir Robert Peel to Mr. Croker.

July 2nd, 1835.

The Corporation will fulfil my prophecy—that the first proposal for altering the Reform Bill would proceed from the authors and supporters of that Bill.

After reviewing the returns, they find the freemen vote in the Conservative interest more frequently than in the Radical, and forthwith it is proposed to abolish freemen. And this is done not manfully, not directly, but under the pretence of improving Corporations. Lord John Russell says, that though the right of voting on the part of freemen was reserved in the Reform Bill, yet it was not necessarily a permanent arrangement, that the intention of improving Corporations was declared at the time, that the reservation of the right of freemen was therefore provisional and contingent upon the future reform of Corporations.

This is not true. In the first Bill the right of freemen was destroyed; in the second Bill it was reserved; but it was not reserved generally; it was not reserved upon the principle that corporate rights constituted a separate question to be thereafter decided on. The right was modified and regulated, and limited to those who should reside within seven miles of the borough; the arrangement had all the character of permanency; the abuse of the right, namely, the pouring in of non-resident voters, was abolished, and residence was made the condition of its exercise.

See what the Corporation Bill does. It assumes that the right of voting for municipal officers ought to be co-extensive with the payment of rates; it gives a franchise much more popular than the Parliamentary franchise; nay, it sanctions universal suffrage on the part of householders, subject to certain conditions of continued residence and actual payments.

It rejects with scorn the doctrine that poor men are not fit to exercise political power—when that doctrine aids democratic influence—but this same Bill disfranchises other poor men who have been guilty of the crime of supporting Conservative principles.

It assumes that the Irish pauper, who has resided three years in Manchester and Liverpool, and can get an active democrat to pay up for him his shilling rate, is well qualified for electoral trust; but the man who has served an apprenticeship of seven years; the Englishman by birth; the native of the town; he who has acquired no capital perhaps in money, but the more valuable capital of mechanical skill, experience in his handicraft, who has the testimonial of his master founded on seven years' personal knowledge—he is to be dispossessed of an ancient right, held from immemorial usage, confirmed and regulated and purified by the second Magna Charta—the Reform Bill. Contrast these two acts of power—the devolution of a new trust on the mere ratepayer who may be a pauper, with the extinction of the ancient franchise held by a man who, in nine cases out of ten, gives to the State greater evidence of fixedness of residence and the qualifications of citizenship, and can any one doubt the animus, the bounty on Radicalism, the punishment of Conservative principles in humble life?

The Bill leaves ecclesiastical patronage in the hands of the new Common Council. That Common Council may be occasionally either composed entirely or in great part of Dissenters. These Dissenters are to select for the most important cures the ministers professing another faith. What a universal outcry would there be from every Dissenter in the land, of whatever denomination, if in the case of a bequest for the maintenance of a Dissenting minister, Parliament were to sanction an arrangement by which the selection of that minister might be confided to members of the Established Church!

Among the few other letters of 1835 which have been preserved, there are two of importance from Sir Robert Peel. In the first he shows the cordial sympathy which he felt for Mr. Philip Pusey * under the attacks then, and long afterwards, showered down upon him. The second letter refers to the Municipal Corporation Bill, which had been subjected to many alterations and amendments in the House of Lords, under the advice and direction of Lord Lyndhurst. Peel had from the first been desirous of accepting the Bill from a higher motive, doubtless, than that ascribed to him by Charles Greville, who insinuates that his object was "to convert the new elements of democratic power into an in-

* [Brother of Rev. Dr. Pusey, and M.P. for Berks; first President of the Royal Agricultural Society. The occasion was probably his having voted with Peel and against Lord Chandos on the Repeal of the Malt Tax.]

strument of his own elevation, partly by yielding to and partly by guiding and restraining its desires and opinions" ('Diary,' iii. p. 263). The differences between the Lords and the Commons on the Bill were very serious, and for some time they threatened to bring the two Houses into dangerous collision; but ultimately a compromise was adopted.

Sir Robert Peel to Mr. Croker.

British Museum, August 1st, 1835.

MY DEAR CROKER,

Your letter has followed me here. I returned to town on Thursday evening.

There is no pretext for the attacks on Pusey and Young, and they are equally unjust and impolitic. Pusey came to me after his speech, and I said everything to console him, and earnestly advised him not to resign. There is nothing more intolerable than the tyranny of party, and nothing more insane than the excommunication of a man, because he differs on some one point from those with whom he is disposed generally to act.

Every section of a party is a little disposed to act upon the same principle, each expecting *an impossible* conformity with its own views—impossible, because the views are frequently contradictory.

Ever affectionately yours,
ROBERT PEEL.

Drayton Manor, August 26th.

MY DEAR CROKER,

My absence from town is partly owing to the earnest and repeated advice of Sir Henry Halford that I should leave it on the ground of health; partly to sheer mental fatigue, after the life I led from the day of my landing at Dover on the 10th of December last, up to the middle of August; and partly because I do not concur in the policy of the course taken by the Lords with respect to the Corporation Bill.

Collision with the Commons was inevitable. It was inevitable on a great principle, and a measure of great practical importance—the Irish Church Bill. It was inevitable also, so far as the refusal to entertain a measure at present was concerned, on the Irish Corporation Bill.

Collision on the Irish Church Bill, from the importance

both of the principle it involved, and the practical consequences that must flow from the assertion of it, saved the honour of the Lords, manifested their independence, and selected for the field of battle the best that could be chosen—that on which the Conservative party in the Commons was the strongest, the most united, the most in harmony with Lord Stanley and his few adherents.

I would not have provoked collision—nay, I would have done all I could to avoid it—on the English Corporation Bill. At least, the last course I should have taken would have been to receive evidence without intending to abide by it, and to condemn altogether in debate the principle of the Bill, and yet to adopt it.

What is gained by it? It proves that a vast majority of the House is against the Bill, dissatisfied with the reports of the Commissioners, desirous, if they dare, to reject the Bill; and yet the Bill is accepted, the main essential principles admitted; but speeches made and amendments moved, which speeches are not acted upon, and many of which amendments, without taking any effectual security against danger, are just sufficient to irritate, to afford the pretext for rejection, and to keep the question unsettled.

The manner in which the Bill has been treated in the Lords, is more important than the changes made in it. Some of the changes, that particularly of forcing by law—not the whole of the existing aldermen or burgesses (for that rested at least on some intelligible principle), but forcing a fourth of the body on the new Council—respecting vested interests and self-election in the degree of one quarter of the whole extent of the principle—are to me quite unaccountable.

But I look not to this or that amendment, not to this or that enactment of the Bill; I look to results; and if I do not reject the Bill on principle, or on the ground of imperfect evidence, I would, if possible, avoid a collision on details, or at any rate I would confine amendments to those points on which the same party in the House of Commons had offered them, and would therefore continue to act in concert.

Another course has been taken. Do I personally complain of it? No. But I will not be necessarily made responsible for the consequences of it.

I have a right to speak upon this point; no right to dictate to others what course they shall take, no inclination to complain if they take a different course from mine, but a perfect right to say, "If you do take a different course, if you disregard my advice, look to ulterior consequences; consider, if no great principle be involved, what may be the bearing of your course upon still more important matters than that to which it has immediate reference, and know beforehand that I will not assume the responsibility for acts to which I am not a party, and of which I do not approve?"

I went to London. I had two meetings with the Peers, who were members of the late Government in the Lords. I explained to them fully my views, my inability to be a party beforehand to amendments in the Lords, going far beyond the amendments which I had either moved or supported or suggested in debate in the Commons. Under no circumstances would I have done so; in the position in which I stood with regard to Lord Stanley on the particular measure, it was impossible with honour.

Another course being taken, I blamed no one, but certainly believed that no public interest could be advanced by my remaining in London, when it was every day necessary to consider the conduct of a line of policy in the Lords, to which I was not an assenting party.

I believe that many of those who were parties to it viewed with the utmost apprehension the possible result of it—namely, the breaking up of the present Government on such a question in the present state and relations of parties, and in their relations to this particular question.

Ever affectionately yours,
ROBERT PEEL.

Mr. Croker to Lord Hertford.

West Moulsey, September 30th.

Peel is at last thoroughly—I will not say *frightened*—but convinced that the Revolution is inevitable, and talks of *resistance.* I am by no means so loyal and stout. I hear that neither the Duke nor Lyndhurst, and particularly the latter, are pleased with him. I have long thought that it would be impossible, and if possible, not desirable to keep an innovating Conservative party together. A Tory Opposition is a contradiction in terms and spirit, and never can last—an Opposition which does not outbid the Ministry for popularity is a bubble.

Mr. Croker to Sir Robert Peel.

MY DEAR PEEL,　　　　　West Moulsey, October 7th.

I am glad you like Robespierre.* It is only an essay, which you put me upon, and which I wrote at the seaside without a single book but the 'Liste des Condamnés.' When I came home I spent a couple of days in verifying, as far as I could, my recollections; but it is miserably short of what it ought to have been, and even of what it would have been, if I had written it at leisure and amidst my books.

You ask about the Revolutionary Library of the *Athenæum*. They have, I believe, little but a few duplicates, which I gave them. If you mean the Museum, they have a noble collection of *at least* 50,000 separate publications, which are arranged in about 4000 volumes or portfolios; but they are in three rooms, and there is no catalogue. Mr. Panizzi had begun a catalogue, and had arranged and had bound about one-third of the whole; but the Trustees took him off that work; and when I went to the Museum the day before yesterday to look at their 'Liste des Condamnés,' to verify a name, they were obliged to show me into the room in which the greater part of my *ci-devant* library is placed; and I was obliged to find it by my own recollection of the back. Neither the librarian nor any one else alive but myself could have found it; and while I was looking for it Mr. Panizzi was indexing a collection of French farces, literally; but I must beg of you not to mention this, nor, indeed, to know it —as *a Trustee*, for poor Panizzi, though he could not help letting me see what he was about, and lamenting that he was not allowed to go on with the Revolutionary catalogue, entreated me not to say anything about it, lest he should be blamed by his colleagues and *masters*, one of whom you are. I don't believe there is, amongst all the Trustees, one single person who ever visited the Museum for study, or even to consult the library; nor, except Aberdeen and yourself, is there any one who *practically* knows anything about the requisites of such an institution.†

* [An article on Robespierre, published in the *Quarterly Review*, September 1835, No. 108.]

† [Mr. Croker's collection of books, pamphlets, and broadsides, relating to the French Revolution are now included in the "New General Catalogue." Most of them have been carefully bound and lettered, and

The Duke of Wellington to Mr. Croker.

London, October 26th, 1835.

MY DEAR CROKER,

I am very much embarrassed respecting the information which you require on the Corporation Bill. I could not give it to you and be of any use to you, unless I should do it accurately and in detail, nor give it without the assistance of the different copies of the Bills and amendments which were made. All my printed papers of the last Session are gone to be bound; and I could not easily, if at all, get them out of the hands of the bookbinders.

I will, however, turn the matter over in my own mind, and see what I can recollect of what we proposed, what we carried, and what we gave up. How soon do you require the information?

I am not surprised that Sir Robert Peel should be alarmed. All that I hope for is, that the change in the position of the country may be gradual, that it may be effected without civil war, and may occasion as little sudden destruction of individual interests and property as possible. We may all by degrees take our respective stations in the new order of things, and go on till future changes take place *ad infinitum*.

All that will result from such a state of things will be shame and disgrace to the public men of the day. And I confess that I, for one, look back with no satisfaction to the events from the year 1830 to the present time. It is true that I would have improved them if I could; but I am not certain that the course which I took was the right one.

Believe me, ever yours most sincerely,

WELLINGTON.

The next letter expresses in plain language the private opinion of the Duke on some points in the character of his great opponent Buonaparte. It is possible that Buonaparte himself would not have been inclined to dispute the sub-

---

rendered easy of reference. The work is not complete, but it is far advanced. The great interest and value of the collection are, however, but little known. They were consulted by M. Louis Blanc.]

stantial accuracy of the Duke's judgment, for he always maintained that a general—a French general at least—could not afford to tell the truth about his campaigns. Prince Metternich records that when Napoleon was reproached one day with the palpable falsities with which most of his bulletins swarmed, he laughed and said, "Ce n'est pas pour vous que je les écris; les Parisiens croient tout, et je pourrais leur conter de bien autres choses encore, qu'ils ne se refuseraient pas à admettre." * His hatred of the Duke of Wellington is well known; he would not even admit that he had any military talent. "Ah," he said one day to Las Casas, at St. Helena, "qu'il doit un beau cierge au vieux Blucher: sans celui-là je ne sais pas où serait *Sa Grâce*, ainsi qu'ils l'appellent; mais moi, bien sûrement, je ne serais pas ici. . . . La fortune a plus fait pour lui qu'il n'a fait pour elle." † Upon the whole, the verdict of Wellington is that which the world has confirmed.

Apethorpe, December 29th, 1835.
MY DEAR CROKER,

I have received your letter of the 26th of November. I have not got here any means of refreshing my memory with such details as would be necessary in order to be of much use to you. Buonaparte's whole life, civil, political, and military, was a fraud. There was not a transaction, great or small, in which lying and fraud were not introduced; but one must have a perfect recollection of facts, and must be enabled to correct one's memory by reference to documents, in order to be able to write of them with authority.

Of flagrant lies, the two most important in the military branch of his life that I can now recollect are—first, the expedition from Egypt into Syria, which totally failed, and yet on his return to Egypt was represented to the army there as a victory; there were illuminations, &c.

The next was the battle of Preussisch Eylau. This he

* Metternich's 'Mémoires,' i. 282.
† 'Mémorial de Sainte-Hélène,' vii. 275-7.

represented as a great victory. It is true that the allied army retired after the battle. So did Buonaparte. You will find the details of the Syrian affair in Bourienne, where you likewise find Buonaparte's lies about the defeat of the fleet.

I cannot here tell where you will find the details of the affair of Preussisch Eylau. I should think that Spain would afford you instances of fraud in his political schemes and negotiations. Cevallos will give you the detail of the frauds by which King Ferdinand was coaxed into a departure from Madrid, and afterwards from one town to another by a fresh lie, till he arrived at Bayonne, where he was seized as a traitor towards the Government of his father. In the meantime St. Sebastian, Pampeluna, Figueras, Barcelona, Spanish fortresses, were seized, each by some military trick or fraud, and held by the French troops till deprived by us.

Buonaparte's foreign policy was force and menace, aided by fraud and corruption. If the fraud was discovered, force and menace succeeded; and in most cases the unfortunate victim did not dare to avow that he perceived the fraud.

He tricked the King of Spain, Charles IV., by the concession of the kingdom of Etruria to his son-in-law. He afterwards forcibly deprived the said King in order to put in his brother-in-law. In short, there is no end of the violence and fraud of his proceedings.

I believe that the Government will meet Parliament. They will go on as well as they can, as long as they can; and I believe that their majority will adhere to them.

In my opinion Ellice has been called home in order to enable them to reconcile the Grey family, and possibly some discontented Whigs and Radicals, to taking Brougham again into office.

They will begin by a plan for the reform of the Judicature in Chancery, the House of Lords, &c. They will appoint Brougham Speaker of the House of Lords. In the meantime the House of Lords will throw out their Bill. They will then appoint him Lord Chancellor.

I don't think it will signify. We shall only have to watch the proceedings in the House of Lords a little more closely. We shall then have to contend with weakness and fraud, instead of, as heretofore, with strength and fraud.

Believe me, ever yours most sincerely,
WELLINGTON.

CHAPTER XX.

1836–1838.

Mr. Croker's Literary Work in 1836—Article on Wraxall's 'Memoirs'—Letters from Lord Wellesley and Lord St. Helen's—Lord Aberdeen on Wraxall's Blunders—Sir Robert Peel on Lord Stanley's Position—Doubts as to his future Course—The Duke of Wellington on the Stamp Act—Sir Robert Peel as a Sportsman—Conversations with the Duke of Wellington—The Battle of Talavera—The Retreat from Burgos—His Power of Sleeping at Will—Opening of 1837—Death of William IV.—First Appearance of the "Bedchamber Question"—Sir Robert Peel on the Functions of the Monarch—Two "Coincidences"—Retirement of Mr. Walter from Parliament—Sir Robert Peel on Secular Education—Mr. Croker's Correspondence with the King of Hanover (Duke of Cumberland)—Lord Durham's Mission to Canada—The Duke of Cumberland on English Politics—The Wellington Memorial at Hyde Park—Disputes concerning a Site—The Duke on "Rheumatism" and "Libels"—An Enquiry after Shakespearian Relics at Wilton—Mr. Sidney Herbert's Reply—Lady Peel's Apiary—Sir R. Peel suggests a Cyclopædia of the Revolution—His Remarks on the State of the Country—His Pictures at Drayton—Notes of a Visit to Lord Sidmouth—Anecdotes of Burke, Pitt, &c.

No copies of Mr. Croker's letters during the year 1836 appear to have been made; or, if any were made, they have since disappeared. Of his literary activity we have abundant traces in the *Quarterly Review*, for which he wrote ten articles, three of them on events in the French Revolution, three or four on books of the season, and one only on English politics. Having now no office work to make demands upon his time or attention, and taking no active part in political affairs, he devoted himself with greater assiduity than ever to the *Quarterly*. "It really is my life," he wrote to Mr. Murray, in 1835; "I should stagnate without it." But he was seldom without literary work of another kind in his mind's eye, and at this particular period he appears to have been thinking much of that long-acknowledged defect in English literature —the want of a good dictionary. Mr. Murray had submitted to him a few pages of a work which was intended to fill up the vacant place in the Englishman's library, and Mr. Croker sent them back with a little commentary of his own.*

Mr. Croker to Mr. Murray.

In every work of this kind there are two main considerations—the design and the execution. The distinctive design of this dictionary seems two-fold; first, that on which Scapula's Greek Lexicon is founded, of making rather a dictionary of roots and families than of individual words. Secondly, of tracing each root back to its etymological origin, and forward to its various successive derivations and uses. As our language has already so many and so copious wordbooks in strict alphabetical order, there can be no objection, and there is a manifest advantage, in having one radically arranged, though it will often turn out that words will be thus brought together which have really no other connection than their alphabetical alliance, as, for instance, when Mr. Burke's phrase "bottomless gulf" is placed in the immediate company of "bottomry—the mortgage of a ship," or "Lapland witches bottle air" with Marlow's "bottle-nosed knave." But that is a trifling disadvantage, if it be one at all. It shows, however, that the arrangement by roots is not of such great value as the author seems to think, for of what use can it be to tell us that words of such dissimilar meaning have wandered from the same origin? It can only be, in most cases, a matter of curiosity. But, as I have said, having abundance of dictionaries in the mere alphabetical form for ordinary use, I should be glad to see one in the radical arrangement for the benefit of philologists. This plan has

---

* The work referred to was 'Richardson's English Dictionary.'

also the advantage of giving more of the history of the language, and the variations both of meaning and orthography, than could be given under the strictly alphabetical plan, without a vast deal of repetition and confusion.

So much for the general design. Now for the execution, which, after all, is the main point; for in works of this kind the plan is mere matter of form, and the execution is really the substance, but the execution again has a two-fold aspect. 1st. The literary skill. 2nd. The mode of exhibiting it. On the first point I would not presume to speak without a much deeper examination than I can give to the specimen you have sent me, and without consulting authorities, I myself being none. I will, however, venture to suggest one or two points which have struck me. I find sometimes the Gothic language referred to, and sometimes the Danish and the Swedish, but I do not find, in the preface, any account of the distinction between the " Gothic " and those languages which I have hitherto supposed to be nearest allied to the " Gothic.' I observe very frequently the "Anglo-Saxon " quoted, which in a dictionary of roots seems hardly sufficient; for the roots should be traced either to the Angles *or* the Saxons; and I do not observe that there is any reference to the *Angles*, or, what seems still stranger, to the *Saxon*, and I even observe in óne place (voce *brine*) that a distinction is made between Anglo-Saxon and Old English. Perhaps in some introductory chapter the author may have intended to explain and define his terms; but looking at the specimen before me, I cannot discover why he calls a particular word " Old English," while every page contains twenty words just as old or older, which are not so designated. ⁻I do not observe any reference either to the Celtic or the Erse, which surely must have had some influence on our language; nor do I find any derivations from the Eastern tongues—Hebrew, Syriac, Arabic. I am well aware how fanciful some such etymologies are, but the author has admitted some etymologies from other languages at least as fanciful, and some of our words are certainly derived from Eastern roots, as for instance " abbot," " abbey," " alchemy," " algebra," &c., &c. But, I repeat it, of the author's learning I should be, in any circumstances, a most incompetent judge; but even the most competent would be unwilling to pronounce an opinion in so loose a way, and on so small a specimen.

I now come to that part of the subject on which I am the

least reluctant to give an opinion—I mean the mode in which the materials are arranged and employed; and which is, after all, the main point in a dictionary, for as the materials must be, for the most part, borrowed from other books, the value of the individual work consists: 1st, in the copiousness of the vocabulary and the facility with which every word can be referred to; 2nd, in the clearness and unity of the system of etymology; 3rd, in the clearness and precision of the definitions; and 4th, of the judicious selection of the examples given. Now, in all these points it seems to me, judging from the specimen, that the author has a great deal to correct before he can be said even to have executed his own declared purpose. I shall give you a few examples from the pages before me.

1st. In a dictionary radically arranged how does it happen that "crown" and "coronation" are not found in the same place, nor "crowner" and "coroner." Why are "cross," "cruciate," "crucify," and "crutch" under four separate heads?

2nd. The etymologies seem to be presented to us without system or much selection; for instance: "*Crown*—Dut. *Kroon*, Ger. *Krone*, Fr. *Couronne*, Ital. and Sp. *Corona*, Lat. *Corona*." Now the derivation of all these is the Latin *corona*. It may be useful to see, as in a polyglot, what *crown* is in all these languages; but its derivation is from the Latin *corona*, and that itself is derived from the Greek κορώνη. Again under "cross, crucify, cruciate," &c., we have the French and Spanish, and even some Latin derivations, but not the real root of all, *crux*, which is to be found as the root of *croisade*, which is mediately from the French *croix*. Again, *croisant* and *crescent*, why are not they stated to be, the first from the French *croître*, to grow, and the second from the Latin, *crescens*, growing? And why are not the languages always cited in some settled order or on some principle?

3rd. As to the definitions, sometimes none at all are given, or you must infer them from the derivations; as "cress," "crape," "broth," "both," "cow," &c. Sometimes the definition is erroneous, as *crapula*, which is not "a giddiness of the head," but a sick headache, and is so to be understood in the example given; or "cubit," which is not merely the bend of the arm, but also the elbow, and thence, its most common use, a measure, and all the examples given are of the measure, which is omitted from the definition. Of the chief use of "crest" in relation to a helmet and armour, there is no mention in the definition, and no mention of anything else in the examples.

4th. The examples seem to have been selected with great diligence and some taste; and are certainly the best part of the specimen, but they exhibit a great want of order and system. 1st. The examples do not follow the order of the words and meaning—as, for instance, the word "cramp," which is first given as a verb, and secondly as a noun, and thirdly as an adjective; but the first example is given, not of the verb, but the noun, and no example of the adjective. 2nd. They are repeated uselessly, as seven instances of the noun "cramp" are given without the slightest variation of one from another. Six examples of "crime" in the selfsame sense are given; four similar examples of "bridge;" of "bridle," the noun, five instances, and of "bridle," the verb, as many as eight or nine. Most of these quotations are excellent, but in a dictionary are of little use, and they swell the bulk enormously. It seems to me that one, or at most two, examples of each distinct sense of the word would be enough, and one example of each mode of spelling. As, for instance, I would have given one example of a bridge; one or two of to bridge—bridging; one of brugge; and one of brigge—five examples instead of ten.

This superabundance of examples is the greatest merit of the specimen as a repertory of choice quotations, but it would be a great, and I fear fatal difficulty in the work itself, which it would carry to an inconvenient extent and bulk; but moreover all quotations should be made on some principle, and that principle should be to give one or two of the best illustrations of each meaning of a word, and no more. All after is mere curiosity and amusement, and the dictionary becomes a kind of Elegant Extracts.

These are my candid opinions on the specimen, and all my objections may, I think, be reduced to one, namely, the want of order and principle. The author should fix the order in which, and the principle on which, each word and variation of a word should be treated, and to that he should adhere. I would advise him to give in all cases, as he does in most words, the articles from Junius, Skinner, Minsheu, Cotgrave, &c., in an abridged form, and with contracted marks; as, instead of "Skinner suggests so and so," or "Cotgrave is of opinion that," I would advise him to give the word from

Skinner or Cotgrave with Sk. or Cot., and no verbiage at all, printing his own suggestions with some distinctive mark. This would make it a dictionary of dictionaries.

I fear I have stated all this imperfectly and confusedly, but you gave me a task which could not be done well in my present circumstances, and I am unwilling to detain your proofs any longer.

In an article on Wraxall's Posthumous Memoirs, published in December 1836, Mr. Croker was materially assisted by the Marquis Wellesley, who contributed many interesting notes on his personal friend, William Pitt. This communication was printed by Mr. Croker as he received it, in the pages of the *Quarterly*, and it is not, therefore, reproduced here. Two other notes of Lord Wellesley's contained anecdotes or facts which were only briefly referred to in the article.

The Marquis Wellesley to Mr. Croker.

I knew Wraxall only by sight. He was held in no estimation. Before I came into Parliament he had made a speech which obtained for him the title of "Travelling Tutor" to the House of Commons, and gained him the honour of one of the Probationary Odes, in which he declares :—

"On Norway's foam, with nerves unshaken,
I saw the Sea-snake and the Kraken."

When Mr. Pitt recommended him to George Selwyn as a candidate for Ludgershall, George Selwyn went about town exclaiming : " Does anybody know who is this *Rascall* that Mr. Pitt insists on my bringing in for Ludgershall ? I wish Mr. Pitt could find some man with a more creditable name. It is very hard on me to be forced to bring in a man who calls himself *Rascall*."

Hurlingham, November 3rd, 1836.

MY DEAR SIR,

In reply to your obliging letter of the 1st, I beg leave to inform you that Lord Grenville (himself an excellent

Grecian) has often told me that he considered Mr. Pitt to be the best Greek scholar (not professional) of his time. Mr. Pitt was perfect master of Demosthenes, of whose orations I have repeatedly heard him recite whole pages, dwelling on all the grand bursts of thunder and lightning.

You have imposed a most delightful task on me, which I will undertake with all the zeal and ardour which the warmest affection, admiration, and gratitude can inspire. It will require a little time to discharge such a duty (in any adequate manner) to the memory of so transcendent a character, and so cordially beloved a friend. I think it had best be attempted in a letter to you, to be published (if deserving) with my name.

From the year 1784 down to 1797, I was constantly in Mr. Pitt's society (with the interval of 1790 and 1791, when I was in Italy for my health), and I never observed Mr. Wraxall in that society. He may perhaps have been at some of the crowded Parliamentary dinners; but we certainly knew him only by name, and by his very ridiculous exhibitions in the House of Commons. His knowledge, therefore, of Mr. Pitt must have been collected from the rumours of the day, and from Mr. Pitt's appearance in Parliament.

The disputes between the Government of India and the Nabob of Arcot had not commenced in Hastings's time, and therefore the "Member for Arcot"* might have been at liberty to take Hastings's part. I do not remember any accusation against Hastings of being connected with the corruptions of the Nabob of Arcot's Durbar.

No person was more in Mr. Pitt's society or confidence than Lord Harrowby, and I am certain that he would be happy to lend his aid. If you are acquainted with him, I recommend you to apply to him; if not, I will apply, if you desire it.

The Duchess Dowager (Countess) of Sutherland was the great ornament of Mr. Pitt's society, and much admired by him. I believe her to be greatly attached to his memory. I have frequently met her at Dundas's, at Wimbledon, and have observed that she was delighted with Mr. Pitt's conversation in his gayest hours. If you approve, I will wait

---

* [The "Member for Arcot" was a phrase applied to Wraxall, who "had submitted to be brought into Parliament by the Nabob of Arcot, to advocate his jobs, and had, even while affecting the character of a British senator, accepted the office of agent to Mohammed Ali."—*Quarterly Review*, vol. 57, p. 464.]

on her, and I will endeavour to obtain her testimony to this proposition: "That a more social spirit, or a gayer heart than Pitt's, never existed in the world."

I see you are with Sir Robert Peel. Pray present my kindest regards to him. I was happy to hear at Windsor Castle, where I passed the last week, that he had returned from France in such good health and spirits.

Yours, my dear Sir, sincerely,

WELLESLEY.

Another interesting letter was sent to Mr. Croker by Lord St. Helens, then in his eighty-third year. This old diplomatist was ambassador in Spain from 1789 to 1794, and had also served in Russia and at the Hague. From first to last, he was upwards of five-and-twenty years in the diplomatic service. He was Chief Secretary in Ireland (then Mr. Alleyne Fitzherbert) from 1787 to 1789. Fortified by such authorities as these, it may well be imagined that Wraxall's Memoirs came forth in a much discredited state from Mr. Croker's hands. The work has been republished, but there has never been any defence attempted of the incredible blunders exposed by Mr. Croker.

Grafton-street (Saturday), October 29th, 1836.

I shall feel great pleasure, my dear sir, in complying with your request, the more so, as I have been lamenting this long suspension of our intercourse.

And, moreover, I am glad to learn that you have so generously undertaken the uninviting task of exposing and refuting this fresh outpouring from the late Sir W. Wraxall's storehouse of calumnious impostures, since I am told that, though certainly entitled to no better treatment than that of silent contempt, it is in a fair way of reaching a second edition. Such is the *fames accipitrina* of the reading public for gossip and scandal.

But a week or so must probably elapse before I can transmit to you the remarks that occurred to me in looking it through, because they were consigned to the margin of a copy of the book which was lent to me by my friend

Sir John Osborn, and which I shall endeavour to get back; but am not sure as to the time, as he lives out of town.

I was but very slightly acquainted with the late Sir W. N. Wraxall, but well remember my having met him one morning at the late Lord Walsingham's, soon after the publication of his former memoirs, and my having pointed out to him the utter incredibility of some of the scandalous stories which he had picked up abroad, and which, though grossly injurious to the parties concerned, he had not scrupled to set down, with the names at full length—an expostulation which he seemed to take in good part, and without attempting any reply, yet showing no signs of contrition, but, on the contrary, exhibiting a certain air of triumph; like a monkey, grinning and chattering over the havoc which he has been committing in a china-closet.

Yours ever, my dear Sir,
Very sincerely,
ST. HELENS.

Grafton-street (Wednesday), November 2nd, 1836.

MY DEAR SIR,

The anecdote related by Wraxall concerning the Equerries of King George III. is certainly true, though, as you rightly suppose, they never dined at His Majesty's table when in residence at Windsor. They had a table of their own, denominated "Of the Equerries." But, being also that of all the *male* visitors at the Castle, it was served a full hour later than that of their Royal Master. And, consequently, it often happened that the good old King, who used to dispatch his solitary and scanty meal in a very short time, had sallied forth on his afternoon's walk, ere his Equerry-in-waiting, who was always summoned to attend him forthwith, had had time to swallow his soup. A most unwelcome summons, therefore, as may well be supposed. And accordingly, I recollect an instance of the kind, when the said Equerry, a splenetic old General, afforded us a good laugh, by saying, as he left the room, "Well, thanks to Heaven, my waiting will finish to-morrow, and I shall take care to order *two* pounds of rump steaks for my dinner, and to be *two* hours in eating it."

The late Mr. Joseph Ewart was a person of considerable note in his day, having been Minister to the Court of Prussia at a very important and stirring period, commencing with the Dutch Counter-Revolution, accomplished by means of a Prussian army, towards the end of 1787.

And, as respecting that military expedition, in the success of which Great Britain was so deeply interested, I can confidently say (having been at Berlin at the time, on my way back from my first mission to Russia) that in all likelihood it would not have been even undertaken, far less completed, but for Mr. Ewart's strenuous exertions, and the extraordinary degree of influence which he had acquired over some of the leading members of the Prussian Cabinet— acquired, too, not by address or insinuation, but by a certain peremptory, authoritative, and overbearing language, which it was really quite diverting to witness, in a little raw, red-haired Scotch youth, who was invested too at that time with no higher character than that of *chargé d'affaires*.

But he was uncommonly clever, and a perfect master of the French and German languages, and had the advantage of having married a daughter of one of the Prussian State Ministers. He had afterwards a leading share in settling the terms of the peace between Austria and the Ottoman Porte, concluded at Reichenbach in 1790, under the mediation of England and Prussia. And, lastly, in 1791, he planned and conducted the negotiation, which in its issue was so fatal to himself, being that of our engagement with Prussia for enforcing, by means of a joint armament, the acceptance of our proffered joint mediation of a peace between Russia and Turkey—a favourite measure also with Mr. Pitt, but which he was ultimately forced to abandon, partly by the disapprobation and falling off of many of his own friends and supporters in the House of Commons, and partly by the factious, not to say treasonable, manœuvres conducted without doors, by a certain late celebrated leader of the Opposition party, through the means of a certain individual who is still living. And the effects of this disappointment preyed so deeply and severely on poor Ewart's fiery and irritable feelings and temper, that it actually turned his brain, and he died before the end of the year (if I rightly remember), at an early age, in a state of absolute insanity.

A warning to all over-eager politicians, to which class I cannot be said to belong, having nearly completed my *eighty-fourth* year, after having sustained many much harder *rubs* in the course of my long diplomatical career.

* [Compare with this account of Mr. Ewart the statements in the Memoirs of Sir J. Bland Burges, pp. 145-146 and 181-2.]

I send you these particulars, my dear sir, in reply to your two especial queries, *en attendant* the transcript of my *marginal* annotations, because, notwithstanding what you are so obligingly pleased to say as to the supposed unabated vigour of my intellectual faculties, they are in truth most wofully on the decline—a few pages of this 12mo size being the very utmost that I can achieve, and that only when in the vein; so that there is not much likelihood of my troubling my neighbour with any packet beyond Post-office weight.

Most sincerely yours,
St. Helens.

One other letter on the same subject may be given, from Lord Aberdeen, afterwards Prime Minister.

The Earl of Aberdeen to Mr. Croker.

Haddo House, Aberdeen, October 30th, 1836.

My dear Croker,

The subject of your letter is certainly rather delicate, but I write to you without any hesitation or difficulty, and I think that I am able to give you all the information which the nature of the case admits of. I have read with indignation the statements to which you refer. Wraxall insinuates that Mr. Pitt received money from Lord Abercorn, both for making him a Marquis, and for obtaining the precedence of an Earl's daughter for his cousin, Miss Hamilton. If Mr. Pitt received money for one, he certainly might have done so for both these favors; but, in truth, they are both to be accounted for in the same manner, if, indeed, they require any explanation at all. To those who know Lord Abercorn and Mr. Pitt, it must appear equally impossible that the one should offer, or the other receive, money for any such purpose.

The great affection entertained by Mr. Pitt for Lord Abercorn is by no means generally known. The intimacy commenced at Cambridge, where they were together at the same small college; and notwithstanding the difference of their pursuits, it continued through life. Mr. Pitt had the very highest opinion of Lord Abercorn's talents, which he expressed on all occasions. You may possibly be aware of my opportunities of early intercourse with Mr. Pitt. He died in less than a year after my connection with the Abercorn family, but he has frequently spoken to myself in such terms of Lord Abercorn as it would be difficult to exaggerate. I know that on one occasion he said to Mr. Wilberforce, as an early friend of both, that if Lord Abercorn had chosen to take to public life, "as a speaker, he would have beaten us all."

With these opinions, and with his early affection undiminished, it is not surprising that he should have done everything in his power to gratify Lord Abercorn's wishes. So early as the year 1786, Lord Abercorn, at that time Mr. Hamilton, obtained for his uncle, who was only a Scotch Peer, the rank of an English Viscount. After succeeding to his uncle's title and estate, Lord Abercorn's pretensions to the rank of Marquis, I apprehend, were equal, if not superior, to those of any other person. He was the male representative of the Hamilton family, as may be learnt from all the Peerage-books, and as Wraxall himself mentions. It is doubtful whether he might not have made good his claim to several of the Hamilton titles; at least I am in possession of the very elaborate opinions of eminent Scotch counsel, decidedly affirming his right to the Marquisate of Hamilton, the Earldom of Arran, and to various ancient Baronies of the family. Such a position, in addition to his large fortune, and personal talents, rendered his creation as a Marquis simple enough. But the pretensions of Lord Abercorn were much higher than a Marquisate, and these were fully admitted by Mr. Pitt. I have seen a letter from Mr. Pitt to Lord Abercorn, and which is still in existence, in which he gives his reasons for not making him a Duke,* and employs various arguments to induce him to accept the rank of Marquis, which it appears that he was reluctant to do. Mr. Pitt assures him that it shall be a step to the Dukedom, and refers to the only obstacle which prevents his having the higher rank at that time. The obstacle alluded to was the promise made by George III. to the late Marquis of Buckingham, that no Duke should be created without his elevation. As the King subsequently repented of this promise, he determined to make no Dukes at all—a resolution to which he adhered to the end of his reign. In all this, Mr. Pitt exhibits the anxiety of a friend to gratify his

* [The title of Duke was conferred upon his grandson in 1868.]

own quite as much as Lord Abercorn's wishes, by conferring the Dukedom. The style is far enough removed from the notion of any bargain or sale. I have often heard Lord Abercorn refer to this subject, always doing justice to the warm friendship of Mr. Pitt, but always greatly undervaluing the rank which he actually possessed.

As some proof of the great personal influence Lord Abercorn was supposed to possess with Mr. Pitt, I may mention that when some one asked how he came to be created a Marquis, a mutual friend, who knew them both well, replied: "It is well he did not wish to be Emperor of Germany, for Pitt would certainly have done his best to make him so." This was just about the time of the death of the Emperor Joseph.

The precedence of an Earl's daughter given to Miss Hamilton was certainly a more unusual and less accountable act; but I have not the least doubt in the world that, so far as Mr. Pitt is concerned, everything is to be explained in the same manner. If a bargain was made, it must have been truly expeditious, for the rank was conferred in about a fortnight after the death of Lord Abercorn's uncle, whom he succeeded; before which time, he was in no condition to bribe a Prime Minister, or any one else. This was about two years before he was made a Marquis.

Lord Abercorn has occasionally mentioned this subject to me; and of all the men I have ever known in my life, his regard for truth was the most strict and scrupulous. The desire on his part may perhaps appear extraordinary; but Miss Hamilton was by birth an Earl's grand-daughter, and his own first cousin. She was living as an inmate in his family; and although she was greatly admired and beloved, of course he had not the most distant conception of ever marrying her; his own wife being then alive, and not having died until two years afterwards. I know that he subsequently regretted having made this request; but this regret was in consequence of the unhappy termination of his connection with Lady Cecil. I believe it is true that the King was at first reluctant to comply with the proposal of granting the precedence, not from its being unusual, or improper in itself, but because he gave some credit to the report which prevailed, that an intimate personal connection already existed between the parties. Mr. Pitt, who knew Lord Abercorn's truth as well as I did, was perfectly satisfied that this was not the case, and accordingly pressed the matter still more earnestly with the King. My impression is, that if this report had not existed, the precedence would never have been asked for.

Having said so much about Lord Abercorn, I will now say a few words respecting Wraxall's insinuation as it affects Lord Carrington. You are aware that Mr. Pitt has often been reproached for having been too prodigal of peerages, and Lord Carrington's has often been referred to especially, as introducing into the House of Lords a new description of person. I never heard Mr. Pitt speak on this subject himself, but I have heard the late Lord Melville say that Mr. Pitt always defended this creation on principle, and that he maintained the time was come when, for the sake of the House of Lords itself, it was desirable that it should not be closed against commercial eminence, any more than other well-founded pretensions. No doubt Lord Carrington's political support was valuable to Mr. Pitt, and he had also a personal regard for the individual himself.

Ever, my dear Croker,
Most sincerely yours,
ABERDEEN.

The session of 1836 was comparatively uneventful, for the Tory party was gathering up its strength for future struggles, and the Whigs and Radicals were disposed to take a little repose before exploring still further the wide fields of reform. Sir Robert Peel was intently studying the position, and considering well the men who were likely afterwards to be of use to him on the one hand, or perhaps a source of danger on the other. No one gave him more uneasiness than Lord Stanley (Derby), whose power in debate had already caused all eyes to be turned towards him, and whose assistance Peel had so much coveted, and coveted in vain, in his first efforts to form a Ministry. "What will Stanley do?" was evidently a question which was always uppermost in his mind at this period. It was certain, as it seemed to him, that Lord Stanley would not join Lord Melbourne, but it was almost as unlikely that he would act with the Tory party. No reader will need now to be reminded that when the time came for Sir Robert Peel to frame another Administration, on much more solid foundations than his first, Lord Stanley accepted office as Colonial Secretary, and remained in it until the new policy on the Corn Laws drove him, with so many others, from Peel's side.

Sir Robert Peel to Mr. Croker.

Drayton Manor, January 12th, 1836.

MY DEAR CROKER,

Your letter * puzzles me; parts of it at least.

I never heard of this pamphlet of which you speak, that is attributed to Lord Holland. Is the name of it 'Parliamentary Talk'? I see a pamphlet advertised by that name, but, profiting by your successful example, I have directed application to be made for Lord Holland's pamphlet.

What simplicity and ignorance there is in a country life! You will think such stupidity little calculated to give any hints for an article. I should have thought one on the House of Lords, and the necessity of maintaining its privileges and independence, very appropriate to the time. It would open the whole question of the movement; the tendency of one change to beget another, less from any necessity than from sheer restlessness, or, more probably, from the failure of the first change; the unwillingness to admit that failure, or the desire to account for it on the ground that it was not carried far enough, and that there must be a second revolution to grease the clogged wheels of the first.

Shall we have an amendment to the Address? And if so, what shall it be?

These are two grave questions which press for deliberate consideration, which cannot be disposed of in the flippant way that most of my correspondents dispose of them; all those who look on a party as a pack of hounds which must have blood, or, at any rate, must not be brought to the cover side without the certainty of a run.

* [The letter referred to is not now to be found.]

The amendment is the bag-fox, to guard against the possibility of disappointment.

I do not disregard altogether their views. It is important to keep a party in wind; but in these times the points on which amendments—amendments as indications of principle—must turn, are too important to be treated even like wild foxes, let alone (as Burdett has it) bags.

First, will Stanley and Co. (the firm I apprehend is diminishing in numbers) support any amendment? I doubt it. An amendment is a movement in advance; at least a preconcerted amendment is. There may be, I think there probably will be, some passage in the Address to which we cannot assent. Perhaps Stanley cannot. But there is a material distinction between an unavoidable, unpremeditated protest against opinions to which you cannot subscribe, and a premeditated amendment to an address, the purport of which is unknown.

The one is a necessary act of self-defence; the other an offensive and, almost necessarily, a party proceeding. Acquiescence in the latter, concerted acquiescence at least, implies party union. Stanley's junction with Lord Melbourne may be impossible. I have no reason to think his junction with the Conservative body, I mean avowed and decided junction with them as a party, much more probable.

Suppose an amendment were moved embodying his own sentiments on the Irish Church, and nothing more, how easily he might decline joining in it. He might say, "I am ready to unite in defence of the Church. I shall be forced to unite, but I think the position of resistance more favourable than that of attack. I will not march out of the entrenchments with you." He might also say, and probably would, if his inclinations are what I suspect them to be, "This is a rash and unwise proceeding. It is converting a great question of public principle, on which men of different political convictions in other respects are agreed, into a mere instrument of party attack. It is acting over this session, by Conservative performers, the successful but disgraceful drama of the last, in which Whig automata, moved by Radical wires, dressed and walked the parts. I cannot be a party to the proceeding."

We thus lose Stanley. It may be said, if the bond of union is so very weak, it must very soon be severed; and the remark is just. But would it not be better that it should be severed by an act of his than by an act of ours, unless for that act there be a clear and intelligible necessity?

I am not meaning to argue against, at least not to decide against, an amendment, but scribbling on carelessly. I may assume unconsciously the appearance of a decided advocate for one or other course.

We must not carry complaisance for Stanley too far. If he is not with us or inclined to be, it will be of no avail. Let us make the declarations of principle, at the time, and in the manner we think *bonâ-fide* best calculated to serve, not party, but the public interests, and let others agree in them or dissent from them as they please.

My own present impression is (assuming that there ought to be an amendment) that one in support of the House of Lords would be the best.

There is ground for it in the hostile notices on the book of the House of Commons, and in the open menaces of members of Parliament in the confidence of the King's Government.

Lord John Russell professes to be with us in defence of the Lords. Will he vote with us? If he does, we divide *pro hac vice* the Government party. If he does not, he agrees in the sentiment, and can only justify opposition to it on some questions of fitness of time or form.

But, on the other hand, we may, and probably shall, appear by a voluntary and gratuitous act of our own to put the House of Lords, its privileges and authority, in an actual minority of the House of Commons.

People judge, not by speeches and explanations, but by actual numbers on a division. The question at issue in debate would not be the maintenance of the House of Lords as at present constituted, but five people out of six would only read the purport of the amendment, see that it was negatived, and believe that the division took place on the main question.

Now see the effect of *ventilating*, as Sir Charles says, any revolutionary proposal. It sounds preposterous at first, but it is wonderful how soon repeated discussion familiarises the public to the proposal, and takes off the edge of their antipathy to it.

The plausible, superficial arguments, intelligible to superficial minds, are perhaps apparently in favour of the suggestion, and silence in matters of faith is sometimes better than argument, even where argument to a patient, and deliberate, and impartial mind is conclusive.

Now is it wise in us *to provoke* lengthened discussion on the existence of the House of Lords as a constituent branch of the Legislature, and to provoke it with a tolerable certainty of defeat? Or, on the other hand, do we diminish the danger if it be real by confronting it at once, by declaring that we will not, so far as we are concerned, tolerate the insertion on our pages of menacing and insulting notices directed against the Lords?

That we will force the Government into a declaration of sentiments, it being better to have their shuffling excuses, or even their open and avowed hostility to the Lords, than a treacherous silence, and apparent acquiescence with the Roebucks and O'Connells? What think you of all this?

Ever affectionately,

R. P.

Whitehall, April 14th, 1837.

My dear Croker,

The real state of affairs I apprehend to be this.

The Government was dying to die, and looking out for the rope by which they might most gracefully terminate their existence.

Advice of dissolution, and that advice rejected, was their chief resource.

You never saw men so confounded as they were, at being taunted, not with pertinacious adherence to office, but the contemplation of its cowardly abandonment. Their course has been changed.

I told them distinctly that they were scared by the dangers which threatened the country, and were preparing to run away.

It is not surprising that it should be difficult to keep them where they are. If one wicket is opened, if one old ram escapes, the rest will follow in a herd like the frightened bullocks at Ballinasloe fair.

Take last night, for instance, as a specimen of their sufferings.

We had about a dozen notices of motion given by Radicals, which they must oppose, which they could not successfully oppose without our support.

Among the rest: one by Roebuck and Wakeley for repeal of the Penny Stamp.

One by Codrington for revising naval dismissals of half-pay officers.

One by Hume for Household Suffrage.

To-night we have Canada, we supporting, the Radicals violently opposing, the Government. We are, in short, in this state of things.

All the convictions and inclinations of the Government are with their Conservative opponents.

Half their actions and all their speeches are with the Radicals.

Μὴ γένοιτο indeed! but, alas, what is the alternative? Their remaining, after a crisis, and our acquiescence in their measures. For why oppose if you will not abide by the result, when there is no point of honour to forbid it?

Ever affectionately yours,

R. P.

The Duke of Wellington to Mr. Croker.

London, August 12th, 1836.

MY DEAR CROKER,

Things are taking their course. We had last night a free conference with the House of Commons.* Nothing could be more ridiculous than the whole proceeding; but in due time it will produce its mischief; particularly as we have nobody in the House of Commons to expose the folly, inconsistency, and wickedness of such proceedings.

I quite agree with you about the Stamp Act.† But what can you do when leading men in the House of Lords connect themselves with the gentlemen of the Press? They cannot leave them in the lurch; at least, they will not.

I must protect those who support the good cause in the House of Lords or give it up. But I am tired of the trade.

Believe me ever yours most sincerely,

WELLINGTON.

* [On the Appropriation Clause of the Irish Tithe Bill. The whole Bill was afterwards dropped.]

† [By which the Newspaper Duty was reduced from fourpence to one penny. Mr. Spring Rice was Chancellor of the Exchequer.]

Sir Robert Peel to Mr. Croker.

Longshawe Lodge,* Bakewell, August 13th, 1837.

My dear Croker,

Being tired of trying what repose would do as a remedy for sciatica, and having, in fact, exhausted all other prescriptions, I bethought me of *grouse shooting*, came here to dinner on the 11th, and took the field yesterday, if that can be called field, which is made up of tremendous rocks, bog-holes, and everything else formidable to an inflamed nerve.

With the aid of a pony which Sir Richard Sutton lent me, I killed thirteen and a-half brace of grouse, got twice wet through in a deluge of rain, went to bed quite lame, and awoke more free from lameness than I have been the last three months. So puzzling are speculations about disorders and their remedies.

I am certain Brodie would have pronounced me insane if he had seen me wet through, stumbling over great stones concealed by heather three or four feet high.

I propose that you should come to Drayton with Follett to dinner on Saturday the 9th of September, and stay till Monday the 18th, or as much longer as you please.

Ever affectionately yours,

Robert Peel.

In the early part of 1837, Mr. Croker was once more a guest of the Duke of Wellington at Strathfieldsaye, and occasionally he resumed his habit of making notes of anything interesting which occurred in the course of conversation. The Duke appears to have been induced to talk more than was usual with him of incidents in his own campaigns.

Memorandum by Mr. Croker.

The Duke. When I advanced upon Burgos the second time, and had taken my measures for driving back all the French posts and attacking the place, I was very much surprised by a loud explosion; they had blown up Burgos.

* [The Derbyshire shooting-box of the Duke of Rutland.]

Gurwood. Did they not blow it up rather too soon, sir?

Duke. Why, yes; we were even told that there was a whole battalion which in their hurry they blew up with the place. When I heard and saw this explosion (for I was within a few miles, and the effect was tremendous), I made a sudden resolution forthwith—instanter to cross the Ebro, and endeavour to push the French to the Pyrenees. We had heard of the Battles of Lutzen and Bautzen and of the armistice, and the affairs of the allies looked very ill. Some of my officers (he said, I think, including the two next in command) remonstrated with me about the imprudence of crossing the Ebro, and advised me to take up the line of the Ebro, &c. I asked them what they meant by taking up the line of the Ebro, a river 300 miles long, and what good I was to do along that line? In short, I would not listen to the advice; and that very evening (or the very next morning) I crossed the river and pushed the French till I afterwards beat them at Vittoria. And lucky it was that I did so, for the battle of Vittoria induced the allies to denounce the armistice, and then followed Leipsic and all the rest. The way it reached the allies, who—that is, the Emperor of Russia and King of Prussia, and Count Stadion on the part of Austria— were in a château in Silesia, was this: Buonaparte was at Dresden when the account of the battle reached him in an extraordinary short space of time, and he immediately resolved to send Soult to take the command in Spain (Buonaparte telling Bubna, *c'est la meilleure tête militaire que nous avons*). Bubna soon after found out the extent of the victory, and as the armistice was on the point of expiring, he sent off a secret messenger to Stadion, who arrived at the château in Silesia in the middle of the night. Stadion, as soon as he had read the letter, went immediately along the corridors of the château, knocking at the doors of the King and ministers, and calling them all to get up, for he had great news from Spain. They soon assembled, and seeing that it was a blow that in all probability would free Spain, they resolved on their part to denounce the armistice.

Massena and Soult.

Croker. You thought Massena their "*meilleure tête militaire*"?

Duke. Yes, I did. While he was opposed to me I never

could make an attempt on his line but I was sure to find him in force opposite to me. I should say, as far as my own experience goes, that he was their best.

Croker. What sort of man is Soult?

Duke. A tallish man, and stout—something in size and air like Beresford—bow-legged—indeed, one of his legs is completely bowed by a wound, so that he makes a kind of roll in walking.

Gurwood. He is very much shrunk of late. I saw him this year in Paris, and he was so much diminished in height and bulk that I could hardly believe that it was the same man.

The Battle of Salamanca.

Croker. What do you say about Marmont and the battle of Salamanca?

Duke. Why, Buonaparte was furious against him, and it certainly seems that he ought to have waited for the reinforcements under Joseph, which would have so much increased his army; but as to the battle itself, I saw not much to criticise beyond his having spread himself too much in endeavouring to get round me. Buonaparte was, as I told you, in a furious rage at first, but when he received our gazette with my account of the battle, he said: "This is true; I am sure this is a true account, and Marmont, after all, is not so much to blame;" and he restored him, or pretended to restore him, to favour. This I was told by Barbedel (the Bayonne banker, a kind of partner of Perrigaux, and Madame Marmont's father), who dined with me long after at St. Jean de Luz, and surprised me very much by telling me, with true French civility, that I had done Marmont an essential service. I thought I had done quite the contrary; and asked how? "Why," replied he, "by writing that dispatch, which was so honest and clear that Buonaparte saw the thing in its real light and forgave Marmont."

A Narrow Escape.

My general order after the retreat from Burgos was much complained of—I'll give you one instance of the conduct which I was forced to censure. During that retreat, I was with two divisions of the army—Sir W. Stuart's and Lowry Cole's; the French were following me in force, and I was in considerable apprehension that they would turn me and get into the rear, and perhaps take those two divisions. At the end of a day's march I halted these divisions on a high road, and ordered Stuart and Cole to march by daylight along the same high road to a little village two miles forward, whither I was going to sleep as more central. Stuart, on receiving my order said, " Sir, don't you think we had better march so and so," a direction which, he said, was a short cut, and would save time and fatigue. I told him no, and that that route was not practicable; that there was a river in the way; that I desired him to come along the high road, and to march along that till he had further orders. So I went on to the village, did my other business, and went to bed; but I was very uneasy, for the French had a great superiority of force at this point, and our situation was exceedingly ticklish; so I was up again before day, and kept looking out and listening for the advance of the two divisions; but half-hour after half-hour elapsed and they did not appear. I became very anxious, for I had left them but two miles off; so I rode back in some alarm, which was not diminished when I could see nothing of my army, nor could I guess where they were gone. So I pushed on my reconnaissance towards the enemy, and whether they had recognized me personally and thought I was advancing to attack them, or from whatever motive, I can't tell; but I was delighted to find that they were not pressing after us, but seemed rather concentrating themselves. This was quite a relief to me, and I set out again to look for my divisions, which I found had taken the route proposed by Stuart and forbidden by me the night before; and they were brought to a full stop by a deep little river which they could not get over, and which I had mentioned to Stuart when I rejected his proposal to take this route. If the French had known our circumstances they might have caught these two divisions in this trap, and the whole army would have been, in consequence, irretrievably lost. Stuart knew nothing of the country, and, above all, of this river, and, it seems, did not believe what I had told him about it. These sort of things, of which no one but the general can guess the mischief, oblige him to say and do things that to bystanders and critics may seem harsh.

The Power of Sleeping at Will.

Wednesday 18*th* (at breakfast). The Duke had hunted yesterday, and had ridden above fifty miles (æt. 68). Gurwood hoped he had slept well after his long ride. This brought on some talk about sleep. I said that I believed the power of sleeping at will went further towards making a great statesman or general than was commonly supposed, for without that power the mind would wear itself out; and the greater the genius the quicker it would go, if not duly repaired by sleep. I instanced Buonaparte and Mr. Pitt, as having the power of going to sleep at will, and Mr. Perceval.

Gurwood. Sir, you can sleep when you will. Did you not sleep during the battle of Talavera?

Duke. Oh, I know what you mean. I had a nap before the battle, but it was thus. I had appointed to meet Cuesta at a redoubt between our two armies, in order to concert our operations. Cuesta did not come at the appointed time, and I lay down in my cloak and slept till he came. Once when I had advanced with a couple of divisions close to the enemy in the neighbourhood of Salamanca (not at the time of the great battle), the French army was manœuvring, and I was tired and not sure but that I should be obliged to bring them to action, so I had a mind to get a little rest while I could. So I pointed out one of the enemy's corps to my staff, and told them that that corps was going in such a direction, and would be seen by-and-bye on such a point of the horizon, and I desired that when they should be seen there I should be called; and I then wrapped myself up in my cloak and slept soundly until I was called and told that the French had reached the designated point. I luckily have the power, very generally, of going to sleep when I please.

Charles the Tenth.

January 20th. I was once going with Charles X. to shoot at Vincennes with the Duke of Fitzjames; as we passed through the Rue de la Ferronière, Charles X. pointed to the spot where, he said, Henry IV. had been killed; this brought on a conversation between them about Henry IV., who changed his religion to preserve his crown, and James II., who lost his crown to preserve his religion. Charles insisted on it that Henry had done well, and the Duke insisted that James had done still better. You may judge that I did not enter into the dispute, which, however, soon ended in the common accord of the parties, that as both the courses ended in the glorification of the Roman Catholic faith, both the monarchs were objects of veneration. In the meanwhile it never occurred to either of these polite gentlemen that a Protestant gentleman, the representative of the Protestant King of England, was in the carriage with them. Charles talked with so warm a bigotry on the duty of restoring the privileges of the Church, that I could not help thinking to myself that he was very likely to do something that might lose, or at least risk, his crown.

Mr. Croker to Lord Hertford. Extract.

West Moulsey, February 8th, 1837.

Our influenza, which *kills nobody*, continues somehow to people the churchyards. Last Sunday there were between eighty and ninety funerals in the little church near you in Regent's Park, and as many in proportion in all the other churches in town. In Dublin, on the same day, there were 1000 burials. Of course you know that you have lost your uncle, Lord William. They had persuaded him some months ago to give up his peripatetic life, and to *fix* himself in lodgings at Egham, where he died last week and was buried on Monday. You have heard also of old Mitchell? Some one at White's said, " I am sorry for poor Mitchell; but it is a kind of consolation to think one will never be obliged to *dine* with him again." Our old friend Lady Cork is also gone, and leaves one something of the same kind of consolation.

In politics I hardly know what our state is. The Duke and Stanley met for the first time at Peel's on Tuesday, to consult and concert, and it was all very cordial; Stanley and Peel sit together as closely as Peel and I used to do—I hope with better auspices. The Conservatives certainly gain ground in England and Scotland, and the Renfrew and Evesham elections have had a good deal of effect, enough, I think, to deter Ministers from a dissolution. But they have some internal difficulties in addition to those that every one sees.

On the 20th of June, William IV. died, Queen Victoria ascended the throne, and in the following month Parliament was dissolved. Between February and August there are no letters from Mr. Croker of any public interest; but of letters written to him, a few have been preserved, and among them are two or three of Sir Robert Peel's. Mr. Croker's letter of the 15th of August foreshadows the beginning of a controversy which was destined two years later to assume, for a brief period, the proportions of a question of almost European importance—the portentous "Bedchamber Question," now lying deep beneath the ashes of extinct controversies, but possessing vitality enough in its day to stir hot strife among all sections of parties. In the *Quarterly Review* for July 1837, Mr. Croker appears to have been the first to indicate the importance which this dispute was likely to attain. The facts are too well known to need recounting at any length. Lord Melbourne had placed in personal attendance upon the young Queen—then, it will be remembered, just past her eighteenth year—a number of ladies who were nearly related to his colleagues, the wives, sisters, and other near relations of the Cabinet Ministers. The impolicy of this proceeding was urged by Mr. Croker, but the Queen was satisfied with existing arrangements, and did not desire to change them. The question, however, did not become serious till 1839. At this time (July 1837) Mr. Croker dealt with the general circumstances:—

"But though we express this confidence in Lord Melbourne's fidelity to Her Majesty's essential interests, there are some points on which, we confess, we think the country has already had reason to complain, and of which it has complained. We mean the decided political bias, and the marked political position, of some of the ladies selected to compose Her Majesty's household. It would be absurd to complain of the household appointments being of the same political colour as the Ministry itself—they should in general be so. The men may be reasonably expected to vote with the King's Government, and the ladies to be of the same class and connection; but there has been in all times a marked difference between that party eagerness, that flagrant zeal, which may be pardoned in those who are exposed to political conflict, and the more moderate and measured deportment desirable in those who form the private society of the Sovereign—who, it must never be forgotten, is not the Sovereign of one party, but of all—who expects to see at his or her court the various shades of political opinion testifying one common sentiment of respect for the station, and affection for the person, of the monarch. But this intercourse and interchange of courtesy and duty can never be as free and impartial as it ought to be, if the constant and inevitable attendants on the Court are to be hot, and therefore offensive partisans. We know to what unhappy and scandalous scenes a departure from this wholesome understanding gave rise in former reigns, and we trust there is no danger of their being repeated; but we must say that the appointment of the wives and daughters of Cabinet Ministers to household offices is, on these as well as on other accounts, highly objectionable. The first in rank of those attendants is the daughter of one, and the sister of another Cabinet Minister; the second is the wife of the Lord President of the Council; a third and fourth, and, we believe, half a dozen more, are daughters* of the Lord Privy Seal, the Chancellor of the Exchequer, and their political colleagues. It is impossible to make the slightest objection to the personal character of any one of these ladies; but we do say that the accumulation of political and household offices in the same family is liable to serious inconveniences. It is neither constitutional in principle, nor convenient or becoming in practice, that the Sovereign should be enclosed within the circumvallation of any particular set, however respectable—that in the hours of business or amusement, in public or in private, she should see only the repetition of the same family faces, and hear no sound but the different modulations of the same family voices; and that the private comfort of the Queen's interior life should be, as it inevitably must, additionally exposed to the fluctuations of political change, or what is still worse—that political changes should be either produced or prevented by private favour or personal attachments. The Sovereign should not be reduced to such a state of unconstitutional dilemma as not to be able to change the Ministry without also changing the Mistress of the Robes or the Maids of

---

* [This was a mistake: there were *relations* of the Lord Privy Seal (Lord Duncannon) in the Household, but no daughter.]

Honour—or, *vice versâ*, the Mistress of the Robes or Maids of Honour, without also changing her Ministry."

Sir Robert Peel's first letter appears to have been intended to supply some suggestions for this article, although it does not directly touch upon the household arrangements of the Court.

Sir Robert Peel to Mr. Croker.

Whitehall, July 5th, 1837.

My dear Croker,

The two divisions are, I think, fairly selected—Ballot and the Spanish Question.

The best text, I think, is this—the great influence of the personal character of the Sovereign. The theory of the Constitution is, that the King has no will, except in the choice of his Ministers—that he acts by their advice, that they are responsible, &c. But this, like a thousand other theories, is at variance with the fact. The personal character of the Sovereign, in this and all other Governments, has an immense practical effect.

His opinions and natural prejudices are most probably in favour of the monarchical element of the Constitution—in favour of that which is established, of the old usages, of that prescription to which, in nine cases out of ten, he owes his throne.

There may not be violent collisions between the King and his Government, but his influence, though dormant and unseen, may be very powerful.

Respect for personal character will operate in some cases; in others, the King will have all the authority which greater and more widely extended experience than that of any single Minister, will naturally give. A King, after a reign of ten years, ought to know much more of the working of the machine of Government than any other man in the country. He is the centre towards which all business gravitates.

The knowledge that the King holds firmly a certain opinion, and will abide by it, prevents in many cases an opposite opinion being offered to him. If offered, it will be withdrawn (witness the admission of Roman Catholics to the Army and Navy in 1806-1807). Take the case of George III.

in fifty other instances. He saw plenty of changes of opinion. He did not become a Parliamentary Reformer with Mr. Pitt in 1784 and 1785; and had no recantations to read in 1794 and 1795.

The personal character of a really constitutional King, of mature age, of experience in public affairs, and knowledge of men, manners, and customs is, practically, so much ballast keeping the vessel of the State steady in her course, counteracting the levity of popular Ministers, of orators forced by oratory into public councils, the blasts of Democratic passions, the ground swell of discontent, and "the ignorant impatience for the relaxation of taxation."

> "Luctantes ventos, tempestatesque sonoras
> Impèrio premit, ac vinclis et carcere frænat."

This is the proper function of a King—a function important in other times, when there were other weights incumbent upon popular violence, when its disturbing influence was hid in deeper recesses, and less capable of excitement into sudden explosion. The genius of the Constitution had contrived this in time gone by.

> "Speluncis abdidit atris
> Hoc metuens, molemque et montes insuper altos,
> Imposuit, *Regem*que dedit, qui fœdere certo
> Et premere, et laxas sciret dare jussus habenas."

If at other times this paternal authority were requisite, the authority to be exercised *fœdere certo*, by the nice tact of an experienced hand, how much more necessary, when every institution is reeling, when

> "Excutimur cursu, et cæcis erramus in undis."

But at this crisis of our fate we are deprived of this aid.

Where is the jury-mast?—the good sense of the constituent body; of all that portion of it that has intelligence, property, love for the Constitution, settled feelings of loyalty towards the Monarchy. Real attachment to the youthful representative of it must supply it.

What stuff I have been writing. Perhaps it is not legible.

Ever affectionately yours,

R. P.

Mr. John Walter to Mr. Croker.

Bearwood, Wokingham, July 20th, 1837.

MY DEAR SIR,

It was a gratification to me to receive your letter, in which you rejoice in "my escape from Parliament," inasmuch as, in almost every other quarter, my friends assail me, if not with reproaches, at least with expressions of regret. It was certainly at a period of disgust and dissatisfaction with the now defunct House of Commons—and, not the least, with the Conservative powers in it—that I determined upon retiring; and this threw away the fruits of a victory obtained with much exertion in the county, because I found they were not such as I expected them to be—neither goodly to the sight, nor pleasant to the taste. Whether you will think these public reasons satisfactory, I know not; they drove me from Parliament. Others, perhaps more cogent, drew me to my own nest. My health requires attention, and so do my domestic and rural concerns. Both one and the other suffered by my public labours; indeed, I was sacrificing very much. However, I can tell you more upon these subjects when we meet, which your letter gives me reason to hope will be ere long.

I wish you had kept your Duke from any declaration on the Poor-law. Sir Robert Peel, under the feeling of extreme candour and liberality to his antagonists, has thrown away other chances as well as that which I afforded him of beating up their quarters.

I see no reason for expecting that the next House of Commons will be better than the last. If it so prove, I should have the stronger inclination to make one of it; but having relinquished the county, I have declined every proposition which was offered me for boroughs.

Can you not look in upon us on your return from the Isle of Wight, in which case we shall also have the pleasure of seeing Mrs. Croker? This place is fifteen miles from Basingstoke, and I shall be at home the whole of next month.

Believe me, my dear Sir,

Most faithfully yours,

J. WALTER.

Mr. Croker to Sir Robert Peel.

West Moulsey, August 15th, 1837.

MY DEAR PEEL,

We came back last week from the seaside, and I at least am not sorry to be in my own garden again, albeit burned as brown as Bagshot Heath. I have been twice in town, and have picked up some news, which I may as well tell you. I will say nothing to you about the elections (which I suppose you understand by your various correspondents better than any one else), except that they are better than I could have hoped; and, except Beckett, Clerk, and Graham, I do not see that there is much to regret. It will be a grave inconvenience to *you* not to have Graham with you, and I really don't see how he can be brought in, for *we* have no Kilkenny, and it would be madness, even if it could in other respects be arranged, to open any of the Tory close boroughs. Some accident may make a vacancy. I presume all thoughts of disturbing the Speaker are abandoned. It would fail; and failing, would consolidate them. I can even imagine *your* seconding his nomination, in a sarcastic contrast with the conduct of the Whigs to Sutton. I take our case to be this. We are strong enough to protect the House of Lords and the Constitution in great points, but neither to conduct a Government ourselves, nor even effectually to prevent small radical and dissenting innovations. The danger is that the Government will become so despised as to be incapable of maintaining itself, before we are strong enough to make any permanent arrangement.

I had heard ten days ago, what I looked upon as a very silly rumour, that the Ministers were to become Conservatives. I neither saw the object nor the possibility of any such change; yet, strange to say, one or two things have occurred that give a colour to this improbable report. One is this. A Cabinet Minister and I have a common friend, who is not in public life, but of Conservative opinions, and known for his connection with me. To him his Ministerial friend said, last Friday, "Well, we shall never differ again on politics;" and this was said in apparently the serious earnestness of friendship, and was certainly meant to reach me. What can it mean? The second indication was that I was at White's on Saturday, where there were only two or three other people. One asked me my opinion of the elections.

I gave, of course, a favourable one as to the result, and I pointed out the essential difference from the old Parliaments, that there were no neutral or individual men—no floating party to be swayed by future considerations—so that it was clear that the Government could not hope to better itself, and that every election would make it worse. I then said that we had all foreseen that the Reform Bill must tend to a system of delegation and dependence, but that no one ever expected to see it so soon, and so marked, as that there should not be one unpledged member in the new House. While this was going on, up rises from a table, where he had been writing, a man whom I had before never spoken to; nor had we ever looked at each other but with a party scowl —Henry Cavendish, the Queen's first equerry, who came over to me, with a Tory good-humour in his countenance, and said "that all I had said was quite true, and that the system of delegation was so tyrannical that they (the radical constituencies) not only insisted on their votes, but that they actually watched their Members (and himself amongst the rest) in and out of the House, to see that they not only voted in the division, but attended the debate." I cannot give you the air and manner in which this was said, but I never was more surprised in my life, for the man is a shy, distant, dogged fellow as ever I met, and I should have as soon expected such a *sortie* from Joe Hume. I hear that there has been in the newspapers some allusion to the change of opinion in the Ministers. I have not seen it, but these two facts happening to myself seem to corroborate what else appears a mere vision.

Those who are personally interested for the young Queen complain that she is overworked, and teased with needless details. They send her all manner of things in the various official boxes for signature, and she, not yet knowing what is *substance* and what *form*, reads all. It is suspected that this is done to give her a disgust for business. I don't suspect any such deep design; but certainly the proper way would be that once or twice a week one of the Secretaries of State should attend her with the papers that require her signature, and explain what was important and what not. Lord Melbourne sees her every day for a couple of hours, and his situation is certainly the most dictatorial, the most despotic, that the world has ever seen. Wolsey and Walpole were in strait waistcoats compared to him. His temper and feelings lead him to no great abuse of this enormous influence, nor would his political position out of the palace permit him to do anything essentially wrong in it; but as between him and the Sovereign he is a perfect *Maire du Palais*. He himself is under the guidance of Duncannon, who, however, is just now away in Ireland.

Ever affectionately yours,
J. W. C.

Mr. John Walter to Mr. Croker.

Bearwood, Wokingham, September 20th [1837].

MY DEAR SIR,

I am glad to learn that the health of Sir Robert Peel is thoroughly re-established. The appointment which the Government has bestowed upon his late antagonist really carries with it the appearance of a reward for insolence. But after the proofs of personal courage which Sir Robert has afforded upon various occasions, is it necessary for him to resist the impertinences of such opponents as —— and ——?* He has always appeared to me particularly careful not to give offence to any one; and his life is too valuable to be risked against petty adversaries. Lady Peel and his family, too, must be kept in constant apprehension for his safety by the frequency of these occurrences. I would not wish him to "register a vow," after the O'Connell fashion, but should nevertheless be glad if means could be devised whereby he might avoid incurring those hazards, to which he has been more exposed than any other public man of his day, and to which he will be yet more exposed if he returns to office.

With regard to my retirement, it was as much influenced by disgust as any other cause. With due deference to your judgment, I doubt whether it *is* regretted by any considerable number of those whom you designate as "our friends." From our leader I constantly experienced all the attention which I could in reason claim. I never expected to make him at once a convert to my opinions—pressed, as he must be, by the aristocracy; but it is clear that my particular line of policy was regarded with disfavour by the great body of

---

* [These names have been omitted by the Editor.]

the Conservative party. At the commencement of the Session they gave me their support, but at the close of it they utterly deserted me.

Faithfully yours,
J. WALTER.

Sir Robert Peel to Mr. Croker.

Drayton Manor, September 26th, 1837.

MY DEAR CROKER,

On Saturday night, after shooting at Fisherwick with Dawson, I had a return, not of *sciatica*, but of *lumbago*—the complaint which, with me, preceded the inflammation of the sciatic nerve. I also felt a dull pain, very slight however, along that nerve.

I am convinced my attack arose from *champagne*, from derangement of the kidneys, &c. I abstained from everything stronger than water for the last two days. Shot all day yesterday, and am perfectly free from pain this morning, from every vestige of either lumbago or sciatica.

Depend upon it, Brodie is right. These things do not arise from external influences. The enemy is within, and continued systematic abstinence is the remedy.

Hardinge and I shot thirty-eight brace on the ground that you shot over the second day; and Dawson and I shot twenty-six brace in Fisherwick Park.

Grant took the field yesterday, and the moment we left the phaeton and joined the keepers we were attacked by an *infuriated wasps' nest*. Now, is not this a ridiculous coincidence? The moment he appeared, Ballard* called out to us, "Walk down the road quickly, if you please, for here is a wasps' nest that must have been disturbed."

Grant's whiskers have been recently dyed black; *possibly* with some redolent mixture; but this will not account for the assault, which was impartially directed against all.

We still talk of our continental trip for a month, but the season is so far advanced that I think we must not linger a moment after our arrival in town, and must therefore deny ourselves the pleasure of seeing you and Mrs. Croker at Molesey.

Another coincidence. I was telling the story last night of

* [Probably the head keeper.]

my persecution by Haydon, and his eternal correspondence. I said, I may venture to talk now, for I believe the devil has ceased molesting me, and will not reappear. There was at that moment a letter travelling down to me, which was duly delivered this morning.

Ever affectionately yours,
ROBERT PEEL.

Sir Robert Peel to Mr. Croker.

Drayton Manor, November 12th, 1837.

Education is the great question to which the public attention should be called. We are to have agitation on that now. It was tried on Church Rates—that failed. It was tried on appropriation of Church Revenue—that failed. One is absolutely abandoned, the other sent to sleep in a Select Committee. Now the trial is to be made with education.

Two material points. First, if there is to be a national system of education, excluding the direct intervention of the National Church (at least only tolerating its intervention), there is an end of the Church, and probably an end of any religious feeling at all ultimately.

But secondly, there is no ground on which the members of the Church, if united (lay and clerical) can so confidently and successfully defy agitation. They have it in their power to act independently of Sovereigns, Ministers, and Parliaments; to institute a system of education, based on instruction in the doctrines of the Church, which, if worked out with moderation and discretion, shall command much more of public confidence than any Government system founded on a different principle.

It won't suffice to abuse the Government plan.

There must be a cordial concert between the clergy and the laity, and a determination to undertake a duty which probably can only be well performed by voluntary exertions, unaided by Government or by

Affectionately yours,
R. P.

From the year 1838 a new correspondent of Mr. Croker's appears at intervals upon the scene—the King of Hanover, with whom Mr. Croker had a slight acquaintance of many years' standing. When the Queen ascended the throne, the Crown of Hanover devolved upon the next male heir, the Duke of Cumberland, fifth son of George III. Before the Duke left England, he requested Mr. Croker to correspond with him, and it was in compliance with this request, rather than from any high regard for the Duke, that his first letter was written. A part of it relates to the very serious aspect of affairs in Canada, where, in consequence of mismanagement of one kind and another, the colonists seemed likely to follow the example of the Americans in another part of the Continent, and repudiate all connection with England. Hostilities had broken out, and the whole country was in a ferment. The Earl of Durham was sent out to accommodate the various differences which had produced all this ill feeling, but unluckily he only succeeded in making bad blood worse. His conduct was bitterly attacked by Lord Brougham—who, like Sir F. Burdett, had become a Conservative, in reality if not in name—the Ministry turned their backs upon their own official, and Lord Durham came home in disgrace, first issuing a manifesto to the Canadians attacking the Government. These troubles left one good result behind them, in the union of Upper and Lower Canada, which took place little more than a year after Lord Durham's exploits. This amalgamation put an end at once to most of the feuds which had prevailed among the French and English colonists.

Mr. Croker to the King of Hanover. Extract.

Lord Durham is coming home in dudgeon because forsooth he was protected from the consequence of his own indiscretion and his self-confessed illegal proceedings; but before he came away he published a manifesto, appealing from the Queen, his mistress, and arraigning the British Parliament, his masters, at the tribunal of the Canadian public—a public which his very mission proved to be unworthy of even the lowest privileges of freemen. He will come home, and place himself at the head of the Radicals, who will receive him as a martyr of liberty, though the cause of his disgrace was, in fact, a tyranny too despotic even for a dictator. Some very well-judging people think that he will fail here, and be only ridiculous. I am not of that opinion. The Radicals want a mouthpiece in the House of Lords, and if Lord Durham takes that position sincerely and boldly, he will, in my humble judgment, accelerate the dissolution (already pretty certain) of Lord Melbourne's Cabinet.

I am not in the secret of any party, but it seems to me that the Conservatives are very little inclined to force themselves into office—nay, that they will rather require some force to induce them to accept. The difficulties are very great. The country seems prosperous and contented, because a Tory Opposition never wishes to make mischief or to operate on the natural bad passions of the multitude, but if they were in power and the Whigs in opposition, there would be raised a storm of complaints and a host of grievances and miseries which would render the reformed House of Commons perfectly unmanageable.

The Duke of Wellington is in excellent general health and spirits, but the rheumatism in his neck—though mending—gives him a disturbed air, and has, I think, produced an actual distortion of the neck and shoulders. He is going to Bath to try the hot waters.

I spent a week in October at Sir Robert Peel's. He also is very well, but I cannot see that either he or the Duke have any better hopes of public affairs. They are both happy at the comparatively tranquil state of the country, but I do not think they attribute it to any real and permanent causes.

The King of Hanover to Mr. Croker.

Hanover, November 30th, 1838.

DEAR SIR,

Yours of the 22nd reached me the day before yesterday, and I was the more agreeably surprised, as I have been, as it were, *dead* to all my old political friends in England, at least so I must judge from their utter neglect of me. The only political friend that never has forgot me, and writes to me, is London-

derry;* but all the rest have completely laid me aside, even
that gentleman who for a series of years when out of England,
used constantly to write to me, and when I was in England
was daily with me, Billy Holmes.† *Conceive*, since last October
twelvemonth, when he announced to me his being returned
for Berwick, I have never had *one line* from him; I am told
he has received supreme orders not to communicate with me.
This rather amuses me, for till now I never was considered a
dangerous man; I believe there never existed a fairer, more
candid, or determined man in his politics than myself, never
acting from sordid or personal views, but from the deepest
and liveliest attachment to my country and its dearest
interests. Such I was, and such I remain, for no one can
feel a deeper interest than myself in all that is going on in
old England. I am not given, nor ever was, to croak or be
desponding, but I do own that now I feel very, very uneasy as to
the state of affairs there, and hardly can imagine what will be
the end; the more I consider the present position, the greater
the dangers appear to me. You are now in this position—
Ireland ripe for rebellion; Canada completely so, or will be so;
your affairs in India anything but *couleur de rose*, and you
have neither troops to send, nor, what is as bad, a fleet to
transport them if you had; and all this owing to the desperate set now in office. It may appear to you very presumptuous in me to give an opinion, and I agree in this so far that
what is actually the state of things I cannot possibly be supposed to know; first, from not being upon the spot, and
secondly, from the determined neglect and abandonment of
my old political friends, who have cast me off. All my intelligence therefore is derived from the public papers, and those
you know are so full of lies and falsehoods that there is no
dependence upon them. Why last session the leaders of the
Conservative party chose to lose the opportunity of turning
the Ministers out, is to me inexplicable. The old song, I
suppose, "We are not able to form a Government; we are not
strong enough in the House of Commons." All this I have
heard over and over again, but let me ask this question: Is not
in the meantime all sorts of mischief going on? Are not the
present people demoralising the country in every way? are

---

* [With whom, and the Duke of Newcastle, the Duke of Cumberland
had tried to form a new Tory party.]

† ["Black Billy," the Treasury Whip of that day—as before explained.]

not all the situations in the country filled up by Radicals? is not the magistracy of the country totally changed? Believe me the *first* shock we met with was in the year 1828, the repeal of the Corporation and Test Act; this led to the second in the following year, the Catholic Emancipation; and that to our ruin, the Reform Bill. *This* is my firm belief; our downfall therefore began *ten* years ago. The mischief being, alas, once done, and not able *now* to be recalled, we can only lament past follies, and profit from dire experience. You will say to me, How remedy it? My reply is short and concise. *Those* who must see that they were mistaken in their views, and expected very different consequences from the sacrifices made, let them boldly and openly avow this, all the difficulty is at an end; and let me ask you, is there any shame for a man to say, " I have been mistaken in my expectations; had I foreseen that my endeavours to secure the peace and tranquillity of Ireland would have been thus cruelly disappointed, never would I have done what I have done"? *This* would be a manly and fair line, and would gain the respect and confidence of every one; but to abide by such opinions after the experience we have had, this it is that creates this sort of mistrust. Excuse my thus speaking freely my opinion, but I cannot say one thing and mean another. Depend upon it, *this* is the sore point. Another fatal point has been, and I remark still continues, namely, that the leaders come always to the aid and assistance of Ministers when they are in difficulties. I cannot tell you all the bile I made last year when reading the speeches of our great leaders upon the Canadian affairs; it absolutely made me sick.

However, I have always one hope, and that is, that as Great Britain has somehow or other always managed to get out of her difficulties, so I still *hope* and *believe* she will, though I frankly own I believe that she never had more to combat with than at this precise moment.

I am going on quietly but steadily; have already been able to reform many abuses; but where no master has been for upwards of 120 years, many irregularities have crept in, which can only by degrees be corrected. You must not believe all the lies that are daily heaped upon me in the papers.

Believe me, dear Sir, yours faithfully,
Ernest.

It was in 1838 that the public first began to hear of a colossal equestrian statue to the Duke of Wellington—the statue which, from the first, was doomed to have so unfortunate a history. Mr. Matthew Wyatt was commissioned to execute the work, and no sooner was this decided than all kinds of unpleasant controversies sprung up on every side. The newspapers were filled with angry letters, and as the work proceeded, the Committee—of which Mr. Croker was a member—found itself completely bewildered by the remonstrances and complaints which poured in upon it. One of the first of these remonstrances was sent to Mr. Croker, who, as he said, did not suggest the appointment of Mr. Wyatt, but merely acquiesced in it.

Sir Robert Peel to Mr. Croker.

The Anniversary of Waterloo, 1838.

MY DEAR CROKER,

How could you consent to such a job as selecting Mr. Matthew Wyatt—a bad architect and worse sculptor—for the *Duke of Wellington's* trophy?

I so shrewdly suspected that the whole affair was intended from the first as a memorial in honour of Matthew, that I refused to subscribe, and stated my reasons for it to Trench. It throws ridicule on the whole affair. I doubt whether fifty pounds besides Trench's and the Duke of Rutland's subscriptions would have been raised, if the real object had been avowed at the commencement.

George III. trotting up Cockspur Street would have been fatal.

Let the Committee compensate Mr. Wyatt by giving the sum he required for Lord Dudley's Newfoundland dog in black and white marble (5000*l.*, I think), and wash their hands of him.

Erect the dog in front of the Treasury as a perpetual memorial of a defeated job.

The selection is bad, the principle worse. The cut-and-dried resolutions anticipating *unanimity* in favour of the *protégé* of two or three rich men, the said *protégé* being really the

laughing-stock of everybody else, so far as art is concerned—
are a bad precedent—a retro-active precedent, if such a thing
can be, justifying the selection of Wilkins for the National
Gallery, of Soane for this folly, and Nash for that, and every
job which immortalizes its own disgrace from the durable
materials in which it is recorded.

Et tu Brute! who subscribed 10*l*. to be able to defeat
the job.

Ever yours,
R. P.

Year after year these bickerings went on, while the statue
was slowly brought to completion. When it was finished,
a more furious contest than ever arose over the question
where it should be set up. Mr. Decimus Burton's arch at
Hyde Park Corner seemed to be a tempting site, and indeed
the statue had been modelled expressly for it. The Committee were for placing it there. The Government thought it
a very inappropriate place, and many persons who had seen
the statue were strongly of opinion that, if possible, some spot
should be found for it where it could not be seen at all.
Lord Aberdeen wrote to Mr. Croker (Nov. 22nd, 1846):—" I
am no great admirer of colossal statues, and doubt if much
can ever be gained by increased dimensions. We had too
much money, and we are a little like the artist who gilded
his Helen. Not being able to make the Duke grand, we have
made him big." On the other hand, Mr. Wyatt defended
his work vigorously, contending that, as it was " in honour
of the greatest man, it should be the largest statue in
existence." He declared that this was " truly an unhappy
country for the Arts, since it is not only upon the successful
artist that envy or detraction falls, but also upon his noble
and disinterested patrons," an allusion intended specially for
the Duke of Rutland, chairman of the Committee, who always
remained faithful to Mr. Wyatt's cause. The artist went on

to compare his own hard fate with the rewards which had been given by more enlightened communities:—

"From the moment of his [Charles I.] death the palladium passed away, and the blight of discord has fallen upon the Art from that time. Amongst the Ancients it was natural they should look up to those who made their Gods. When Phidias placed his Jupiter in the temple, the multitude fell down and worshipped him; and to relieve him from all worldly cares his children were made children of the State. In other countries Arts and Artists are still honoured, rewarded, and distinguished. When the statue of Louis Quatorze was completed, both the Sculptor and the Master Founder were made Barons, and even in our own time Bosco was made a peer of France for the mere copy of the four Venetian horses, which still surmount the Arch in the Place du Carrousel."

So far from the State adopting Mr. Wyatt's family, the artist seems to have had great difficulty in getting the money which was due to him. At last, in 1846, the statue was hoisted up on the arch—a party of twelve having previously gone through the ceremony of dining inside the horse—and as soon as it was there, everybody but the great Duke himself seems to have wished it down again. The Duke told the Committee that he was "indifferent as to the fate of the statue excepting on account of the feelings of those by whom this honour to him had been conceived." But it soon became generally understood that he wished the statue to remain where it was, and his wishes prevailed; the statue remained on its arch, a favourite mark for every comic artist and satirical writer down to the year 1883, although even then it did not cease to be a sore burden to the Government of the day. Its ludicrous appearance in the summer of 1884, stranded in the middle of the road, decapitated, covered with dirt and mud, would have occasioned no little mortification to the Great Duke. In the early days of the statue, the

Duke took it, as it were, under his protection, and Mr. Wyatt eventually received his money, and turned to other work, with, it is to be hoped, a somewhat better opinion of the age in which he lived.*

The Duke was at this time beginning to feel some of the effects of age, although he was but sixty-nine, and lived till he was eighty-three. He was occasionally made the object of slanders in newspapers and books, but, as it will be seen from the second of the following letters, he received them with composure, and justly regarded an attack of rheumatism as a far greater evil than all the libels ever written.

The Duke of Wellington to Mr. Croker.

London, May 9th, 1838.

MY DEAR CROKER,

Gurwood is gone, and I believe that he has determined not to publish his volume till after the coronation.

I am very sorry that you are so deaf.

I have been very bad lately. The cause is a deficiency of secretion in the ear. I suffer torments in the House of Lords, at meetings, &c., &c., where I am obliged to talk after listening, and endeavouring to hear and understand what others say.

I should not mind it, if I had only to understand the bawling of the children.† However, I hope that I am getting better.

Ever yours most sincerely,

WELLINGTON.

London, July 2nd, 1838.

MY DEAR CROKER,

I have not heard of the person whom you mention. He is not announced here as a part of the suite of the Duc de N——.

But I conclude he is one of the worthies so announced, and

---

* [The Duke's feelings on the proposed removal of the statue will appear from the correspondence given in chapter xxv., 1849.]

† [Alluding to his grandchildren.]

who is received here with smiles in all our houses, and bows and smiles and makes fine speeches in return, and then writes the letter to which you refer under a feigned name—that is to say, feigned to those who are the objects of his observations, but clearly indicating the writer to the public in France, and eventually to ourselves.

As for my part, I consider such an affair not worth the trouble of writing even this note. I have been abused, vilified, slandered since I was a boy; and I don't believe that there is a living creature who thinks the worse of me for all the horrible crimes of which I have been accused, and which to this moment remain unanswered.

I would much prefer to get rid of the rheumatism in my shoulders and neck than I would of all the libels of all the Jacobins, Republicans, Bonapartists, Radicals, Reformers, and Whigs in all Her Majesty's dominions, including her ancient kingdom of France, and her colonies in N. America.

Ever yours most sincerely,
WELLINGTON.

Strathfieldsaye, December 15th, 1838.

MY DEAR CROKER,

After Lord Durham's proclamation, the dinner given by the Guards was very improper.

He ought not to have accepted it; Sir John Colborne* ought not to have allowed it to be given; General McDonnell ought not to have been a party to the giving it.

He was just the sort of man to suit Lord Durham, and he called him to his council as a member! His speech at the dinner was the more improper.

Having the rheumatism, and not being able to do *comme les autres*, I have made my excuses to the Duke of Rutland for absenting myself from Belvoir Castle. I am a great deal better, and, excepting that I am not very comfortable on

---

* [Sir John Colborne, G.C.B., had just been appointed Governor-General of Canada in succession to Lord Durham. Lord Durham, on the eve of his departure, was entertained by the officers of the Guards at a farewell dinner at Quebec. Sir James McDonnell, who commanded the brigade, made some remarks which were flattering to Lord Durham, but not altogether judicious under the existing circumstances.]

horseback, I am as well as ever. But I am obliged to take care of myself, and it is better to stay at home when that is the case.

Ever yours most sincerely,
WELLINGTON.

Mr. Croker to Mr. Sidney Herbert.*

West Moulsey, November 1st, 1838.

MY DEAR MR. HERBERT,

Allow me to recall your attention to an interesting subject which I some time ago mentioned to you in conversation. I mean the possibility of discovering some traces of Shakespeare in the library or muniment room, or even the lumber room, at Wilton. I need not, I suppose, tell you the extreme interest which the discovery of one or two documents (meagre in everything except the mere mention of Shakespeare's name) in Francis Egerton's Bridgewater paper,† has produced in the literary world. If anything should be found at Wilton, it would probably be of much greater value. The dedication of the first folio edition of the immortal plays proves the favour and patronage with which Earls William and Philip honoured Shakespeare and themselves; for, allow me to say, that the world counts that patronage as amongst the highest honours of your name. It is hardly possible but that Wilton must have at some time possessed something from Shakespeare's hand—letters, verses or presentation copies of his printed plays. The little value set on mere private letters would probably have doomed them to destruction; and however the "two noble brothers" may have estimated Shakespeare, they could not have foreseen the extreme curiosity that posterity would feel about their then humble and little known correspondent. Yet it is possible that something may have been accidentally, or even intentionally preserved—any congratulatory verses, or such like, might be in this latter class. But it is highly probable that some of

---

* [Created in 1860 Lord Herbert of Lea. His attachment to his ancestral seat was well known. When seized with his last illness, in August 1861, he desired to be taken there, and as he was carried into the hall his eyesight suddenly failed him. He died three days afterwards, at the comparatively early age of fifty.]

† [This refers to a letter signed "H." found among the papers of Lord Ellesmere, and published by Mr. Payne Collier.]

the early editions of the separate plays were preserved at Wilton, and may be still found there. One would be curious to know whether the first folio, which, no doubt, was presented by the editor to both the Earls, is to be found in the library. Wilton escaped, I believe, pretty well during the Civil War, and you, of course, know whether there has been any fire or other disaster to diminish the natural hope which *à priori* one cannot but indulge. But if there has been no such accident, I would entreat you not to be too easily satisfied with a general notion that there *is* nothing because nothing happens to be apparent; such treasures may exist by the very good luck of having been hidden away and forgotten, and I confess I should look with more expectation to the lumber garrets than to the muniment room, and to cupboards and closets, and old trunks, rather than to the shelves of the library. I would press upon you not merely the general anxiety of the world on this subject, but the distinguished honour to yourself, your ancestors and your family, if anything shall be recovered. You seemed to me, when I spoke to you on the subject, to be alive to all the feelings which ought to inspire a Herbert on such a question, but I have fancied that you might be waiting some fresh application from me on the matter, and I therefore take the liberty of troubling you with this reminder.

   Believe me to be, my dear Mr. Herbert,
      Very sincerely yours,
         J. W. CROKER.

Mr. Sidney Herbert to Mr. Croker.

Wilton House, November 4th, 1838.

MY DEAR MR. CROKER,

I can assure you I by no means forget the conversation we had at Drayton on the subject of the possible existence of papers in this house; but I fear there is little chance of any being discovered. The whole of this house underwent such a thorough ransacking during the immense and unfortunate alterations made by Wyatt, that there is no *terra incognita* where anything remains undiscovered. All the papers connected with the estate, title-deeds, &c., are *sorted and arranged*, and kept in London. In the lumber-room I have found nothing but some chests of chain armour, the refuse of the collection which is arranged in the entrance hall here, and which is interesting as having belonged to De Montmorency, the Grand Constable, and to the Dukes of Montpensier and Longueville, taken prisoners by Lord Pembroke at the battle of St. Quentin.

Strange to say, we have not in the library even the *first edition* of Shakespeare, and as it must originally have been here, it very probably disappeared through the knavery of my worthy grandfather, who had but little respect for entails, and, when in money difficulties, appropriated and sold pictures, and probably other things belonging to the Wilton collection.

The only things which have been found here in my collection are: first, a sort of wooden book consisting of five or six leaves in which are set precious stones. The inscription on the book states that it was the property of Cardinal Mazarin. The other discovery was a packet found among the leaves of Sir Philip Sidney's 'Arcadia,' containing a lock of Queen Elizabeth's hair, presented by her to Sir Philip Sidney, and a copy of verses from him in return, expressive of his gratitude for the gift. The hair is of a bright yellow, and she must have had a good deal of it if one may judge from the quantity she gave away in this one present.

It is odd that there had been a tradition from housekeeper to housekeeper that this packet existed; but none knew where it reposed.

This house has been injured by fire to a considerable extent on two or three distinct occasions; so much so, that the great Vandyke and some other pictures are very much blistered by the heat. Some papers may have been destroyed in that manner; but still it is strange that there should be no papers at all in a house where so much has been preserved in the way of art.

I leave this place on Tuesday for some days, on a visit to my sister, Lady Anne, at Savernake Forest, and when I return I should be very much delighted if you would come and spend a day or two here. I think you would find a good deal that would interest you, and I should be only too happy to have you as my guest; if you should agree to this I would let you know when we shall be here, in order that you could choose the time that would suit you the best.

Pray believe me very sincerely yours,

SIDNEY HERBERT.

Sir Robert Peel to Mr. Croker.

Drayton Manor, October 29th, 1838.

Lady Peel is about making a flower garden, and told a country neighbour not skilled in derivation, that she had a great mind to have *an apiary.* " Lord, ma'am, where will you get your *apes* from ? For my part, I could never 'bide a monkey."

November 1st, 1838.

I have a new thought—at least new to me—with respect to the French Revolution, or rather to publications on that inexhaustible subject.

I have just been reading Thiers again, and I think, considering his position, and the advantages it must have given him, there will be no call for a new history for some time; with the exception of his evident partiality towards the Gironde, and particularly Roland, I think his work is well done. He makes good use of the records of the Jacobin Club.

But what do you think of a ' Revolutionary Encyclopædia ' ? That is, a work containing the biography of all the most eminent men who were thrown up to the surface of the boiling caldron, and whose memory is interwoven with the chief events—An account of many things that are very imperfectly understood (as I believe, by writers on the Revolution); *the Commune; the Sections ;* their constitution, functions, &c.—Local details; the *places* where the Constituent and Legislative assemblies, and the Convention met—The best description of them that can now be given—The date of each event, ascertainable at once, would be a great assistance to all but Frenchmen, who care nothing about dates nor much about facts. Then the places where the executions took place; a detail of what passed.

Many of these things could hardly be introduced into a regular formal history; they would interrupt the march of it just as a biography of Louvet or Chabot, or some subordinate villain would; but how interesting and how useful to turn to the letter J and the word *Jacobins,* and find all that is recorded or can be preserved as to localities and details. If a ground plan could be had, so much the better, and a little map showing the position of the Convent.

Ever affectionately yours,

R. P.

Drayton Manor, December 13th, 1838.

What say you to a reference to the present internal state of the country; to the burnings, atrocious outrages, murders, that fill the columns of every newspaper, and to a question to Her Majesty's Government, How they account for these things?

We ought to be tasting the blessings of Reform; at least we ought to be beginning to whet our palate for the future feast.

In 1830, when this country had been convulsed by the example and consequences of the three glorious days, and some disposition to tumult and insurrectionary violence existed, mal-administration and the denial of Reform were, among Whig authorities, the unquestionable causes of all disorder; and the specific was Reform.

It cannot be said that the present turbulence is the heaving of the old storm, for the Reformers have been doing nothing else but rejoicing in their success; exhibiting the contrast between the former state of the country, and the latter; attributing the improvement to Reform—to the influence of the popular will, the contentment and satisfaction of the people.

Whence then the present disorders? When the Whig papers say that the country is in a fearful state, why do not they tell us why?

We had no torch meetings even in 1830; no threatenings of physical force half so undisguised as we have now.

What makes the people discontented?

It will be said, and most falsely said, that the attempt to remove the evils of the old Poor Law has made the Government unpopular, and *that the party opposed to the Government has tried to inflame public discontent with that law.*

This shameful falsehood ought to be contradicted. It was *our* support of the Poor Law that enabled the Government to pass it without fearful resistance. It was *our* co-operation in practically working the Law; in becoming Guardians, Chairmen of Unions, &c., that has reconciled, where it is reconciled, the rural population to it. The defender of the Poor Law on the Poor Law Committee was Sir James Graham, not the Government.

But it is said, and repeated every day, that the Leaders of the Conservative party maintained silence; they encouraged some members of their party to declaim against the Poor Law at the time of the general election, and basely took the advantage, for political purposes, of the excitement thus fomented.

There could not be the opportunity for a more favourable contrast between the conduct of a Conservative and a Whig, or a Whig-Radical Opposition, than the history of the Poor Law Bill would present.

The Duke of Wellington, in the Lords, has been uniform in his support—open declared support—of the Poor Law Bill.

What course have I taken upon it? Is there the slightest foundation for the charge that the Conservative *leaders* maintained silence with respect to the Bill in order that they might derive *some political advantage at the General Election from its popularity?*

What are the facts?

In the session of 1837, that is, the session preceding the dissolution and general election, a motion was made in the following tempting form; tempting, at least, to any one who wished to evade the unpopularity of supporting the Poor Law Bill:—

"That a Select Committee be appointed to inquire into the operation of the Poor Law Amendment Act, and to report their opinion to the House."

Lord John Russell opposed this motion, though he gave a committee. I supported him; not silently, but actively by my voice and vote. The amendment he moved on the original motion was this:—

"That a Select Committee be appointed to inquire into the administration of the relief of the poor under the orders and regulations issued by the Commissioners appointed under the provisions of the Poor Law Amendment Act."

Was there ever such an amendment moved by a minister who objected to the original motion and yet conceded a committee? Was there ever such an opportunity for an opponent to observe: There is no intelligible difference between the motion and the amendment, and therefore I will vote for the motion?

Was there ever a Whig in opposition who would not have taken this course?

I did not take it. I supported Lord John Russell and his amendment, and said in my place "that I have given to the measure of the Government, when first introduced, my cordial support, and that I had heard no facts which could induce me to regret the course I had then taken, or incline me to prejudice the operation of the Bill." The debate was 27th February, 1837.

But it will be said "that I did not foresee that the King would die, and that a General Election would take place. What language did I hold at the hustings? What opinions about the Poor Law did I then avow?"

I was taunted on the hustings, at the day of nomination, with my support of the Poor Law. The inclosed will show whether I shrunk from its defence.

My nomination, being for a borough, was among the earliest Did I try to profit by discontent with the Poor Law? I doubt whether any minister took upon himself more responsibility for the passing of the Poor Law than I did, or more frankly avowed upon *his* hustings the course he had taken in its support. Now I release you,

A propos de bottes. When the next edition of your Boswell is called for, do correct the error there is in the account of the portrait of Johnson by Sir Joshua Reynolds. The portrait which Mrs. Thrale had, and which I now have, is *not* the portrait which is described as hers.

I have got the Wycherley, by Lely, and the Arthur Murphy, by Reynolds, and am greatly pleased with my acquisition. I am glad to have *the picture* of which Pope said, "That is a beautiful picture of Wycherley, by Lely." It is close to Pope's bust.

What a strange letter I must have written.

Ever affectionately,

R. P.

Notes by Mr. Croker of a visit to Lord Sidmouth (æt. 82.)

On the day that the coalition members dined with Pitt— Duke of Portland, Lords Spencer and Fitzwilliam; Burke, &c., I also dined. After a little, or rather a good deal of wine, we got up to go to coffee, when Burke addressed us his parting advice in a loud voice:

> "Illic fas regna resurgere Trojæ.
> Durate, et vosmet rebus servate secundis."

Old Lord Chatham made his five children, three boys and two girls, act a play. I was present. After the play, Lord Chatham said to my father with some disappointment, "Did you observe how superior Pitt (Lord Pitt) was to William; how much better he felt and spoke the speeches," and seemed mortified at thinking that his little favourite did not promise to be an orator.

Some one—a man of some consequence—came to attend George III. on some occasion, but happened to come rather late. The King was not pleased, and the other said gaily, "Better late than never, sir." "I don't think so," said the King, "I would rather have the proverb, better never than late."

I asked whether the Catholic question was not rather the colour than the cause of Pitt's resignation, and whether his real object was not to have *peace* made, and then to return to power. Lord Sidmouth said no; that the Catholic question was the real, and he believed, sole cause of Pitt's retirement. "In fact, I cannot call it retirement, for the King *positively dismissed* him," when Pitt in the closet declared that he could not recede from his proposition for emancipation. He added some details (from the King) of Pitt's last interview on this occasion, and concluded by saying that the King's dismissal of Pitt (though kind in manner) was decisive in tone, and took him (Pitt) quite by surprise.

Pitt is said never to have had a female attachment; it is not true. He had, I believe, more than one. One I know of; it was to the present Dowager Lady Buckinghamshire, then Miss Eden. Some of the letters seem to allude to this.*

Pitt supervised Addington's King's speech.

The King writes to Mr. Addington, December 17th, 1802, that he had signed the warrant creating Mr. Dundas a Baron and Viscount, and hopes it will keep that gentleman quiet, and that he will not enter into that captious opposition that does no credit to some members of the House of Lords.

* [The Hon. Eleanor Eden was Lord Auckland's elder daughter. Lord Stanhope has shown, in his 'Life of Pitt' (chapter xxiii.), that Pitt was strongly attached to her, and that he refrained from pressing a proposal of marriage on the ground of his embarrassed circumstances. Miss Eden married Lord Hobart, afterwards Earl of Buckinghamshire, and died in 1851. It is said that Horace Walpole once tried to arrange a match between Pitt and Necker's daughter (afterwards Madame de Staël). An income of £14,000 a year was to have been settled on the lady. Pitt replied, "probably in jest, that he was already married to his country."—*Vide Quarterly Review*, vol. 97, p. 568.]

CHAPTER XXI.

1839-40.

Difficulties of Lord Melbourne's Government—Defeated on the Jamaica Bill—The Bedchamber Question—The View taken by Sir Robert Peel—Opinions of Mr. Croker—Letters from the King of Hanover—His Estimate of English Parties—Correspondence with Lord Brougham—Renewed Overtures to Mr. Croker to stand for Parliament—Lord Brougham on Public Affairs—Letters from the Duke of Wellington—Dr. Hook on the Tractarian Movement—Sir James Graham's Fears of Democracy—The Queen's Marriage—Louis Napoleon's Raid on Boulogne—The Eastern Question in 1840—The "Bloated" Armaments of Europe—Hostile Feeling in France towards England—Prospects of War—Letter to Bishop Philpotts on the Church Service for Sundays—Reply of the Bishop—Particulars concerning Mr. Perceval's Character and Opinions—Sir Robert Peel on the Events of 1830-32—A misdirected Royal Letter.

It was not very difficult to perceive, even at the outset of the session of 1839, that the Government was not likely to remain much longer in peaceable possession of power. The mistakes of Lord Durham in Canada, and the divisions of opinion which existed in the country concerning the treatment he had received from the Ministry, tended to render Lord Melbourne's position precarious; and if the Conservatives had been stronger in the House of Commons, the end would have arrived very soon after the delivery of the Queen's Speech. "I have little doubt," wrote Mr. Croker to the King of Hanover, in the middle of January, "that the present Ministry will break up, and that perhaps very soon;

but I do not think that anything like a Conservative Government could last a session." But no serious reverse occurred until May, when the "Jamaica Bill"—by which it was proposed to suspend the constitution of Jamaica for five years—was opposed by Sir Robert Peel as well as by Mr. Hume and the Radicals. Ultimately the second reading was carried by a majority of five only—a result which the Government justly regarded as equivalent to defeat. Lord Melbourne at once resigned, and Peel was called upon to form a Ministry.

Then again arose the Bedchamber question. Sir Robert Peel insisted that the ladies who held high offices in the household, and who were connected with the outgoing Ministry, should be superseded. There has never been any question that he was within his strict constitutional right in making this demand, but it was doubted at the time, and it has been still more seriously questioned since, whether he was wise in pressing it. It has generally been considered that he might have yielded, without any important sacrifice of principle, to the young Queen's natural desire to retain in her service the persons to whom she had already become accustomed. Sir Robert Peel, however, took a very decided view of the matter, and declined to go on with his attempt to construct an Administration. The result was that Lord Melbourne returned to office; and with this Peel was no doubt well satisfied, for he had some experience of the responsibilities of carrying on a Government with a minority, and he had little desire to incur those responsibilities again. His opinions on the main question at issue are stated in the following memorandum:—

Sir Robert Peel to Mr. Croker.

The declaration by a Cabinet that household offices held by ladies ought to be exempt from change—that is, exempt from the control of the minister. If exempt from that control on a change of Government, why not subsequently? Surely the principle equally extends to future vacancies—equally extends to a claim on the part of the sovereign to fill up certain household offices, without reference to the opinion or advice of her minister. Is it possible to maintain such a position consistently with the first maxim of the British constitution, that the sovereign can do no wrong; that she is presumed in every public act to be guided by the advice of a minister whom Parliament can make responsible?

Is not every appointment constituted by the Civil List Act, paid by the Civil List Act, a public Act?

Could it be tolerated that a Queen might appoint a Mistress of the Robes, without reference to her minister, whom her minister might *know* to be perfectly unfit to be about the person of the Queen.

Take other times and other sovereigns, and other characters, and test your position by a reference to them.

What, in a constitutional point of view, had the country to do with the youth of the sovereign, or the sex of the sovereign? No more than with the nature, or the beauty. A great public principle is under consideration.

Those pay a compliment to the Queen who consider her the sovereign, with the plenary rights and authority of sovereign, but subject to the principles and maxims of the constitution. It is a real insult to the Queen and to the sovereign authority, to mix with constitutional arguments any appeals to the special circumstances of youth or sex.

Would a minister be justified or tolerated if he were to make compromises—not of his personal dignity or authority—but compromises of the public interest, of the public honour, of the first principles of the constitution, by consenting to stipulations in respect to the responsibility for public acts, because the sovereign was only twenty years of age and was a lady?

What would be the inference, if the minister were right? that ladies ought not to be sovereigns, but especially not at the age of eighteen. What does the constitution know of sovereigns, or ministers with mutilated authority, or privileges conceded through deference, and deference not to superior experience and political sagacity, but to youth and inexperience. Either the minister would have grossly misconducted himself or the law of succession ought to be changed.

Suppose a minister had consented to such conditions as the Cabinet minute recommends, and to the principles involved in it, is it not clear that the most grievous injury might be done.

The paid spy of a foreign enemy might be introduced into the household—might have access to every Cabinet secret.

Remember Lord John Russell's declaration that the quarrel was not about the extent to which a certain authority might be exercised by the minister; it was upon the principle of the existence of the authority.

He said expressly, that the Queen resisted the claim to make any change whatever, and that her resistance would be as strenuous against *a single change* as against the removal of the whole household.

What did Lord Grey and Lord Granville contend for? The very same *principle* that is involved in the present discussion.

What was their professed object? The very same. Not patronage *quâ* patronage, but patronage as a mark of confidence.

Lady Normanby will not abuse her right of access to the Queen—will not control Cabinet decisions? Did Lord Grey and Lord Granville contend that the removal of old Lord Cholmondeley was through the fear of his superior political cunning and astuteness, through the apprehensions that their schemes for the public good would be counterworked by the Lord Chamberlain?

Where is the assignable difference in principle between the two cases?

Then Queen Anne's reign.

Read with the utmost care chapter lviii. in the 3rd vol. (8vo. edition) of Coxe's 'Life of the Duke of Marlborough.'

Every sentence almost is *à propos*. For instance:—" Mrs. Hill had not, however, long filled her confidential office, before she likewise aspired to a higher degree of consideration, and the plots of the Cabinet and parties offered a temptation which overcame her sense of gratitude.

"The bedchamber woman found a skilful counsellor and abettor in Secretary Harley.

"She became the channel of a constant communication between the Queen and the Secretary, more dangerous as it was less suspected."

Read also with equal care chapter lxxxvi. of vol. v. (8vo. edition) of the same work; and, above all, see how the embarrassments of Godolphin, and Marlborough, and Somers arose from not acting with decision.

When Marlborough wrote to the Queen, "I hope your Majesty will either dismiss Mrs. Masham or myself," did the Whigs of that day talk about "friends of the Queen's youth," and the harmlessness of ladies, and the hardship of subjecting ladies' appointments to ministerial control? Did they write Cabinet ministers enforcing the *constitutional* principle that ladies ought to be irremovable?

There are *twenty-five* ladies of the household.

The Queen clearly did not understand that any proposal was made to remove the *whole* of them *or any of the sixteen.* Her Majesty's words are to remove *the ladies of her Bedchamber.*

The whole number is nine out of the twenty-five.

Mr. Croker's theory was that the Queen had unconsciously entered into an alliance with the Radicals, and that the cause of the Constitution itself would be injured by the repulse which Sir Robert Peel had received.

Mr. Croker to Lord Hertford.

London, May 29th, 1839.

I admire your asking me to write for you.

"*You*, who in one line can fix
More sense than I can do in six,"

as Swift said of Pope, but you desire my opinion, here it is.

Six years ago I said that if King William were to give me a *blanc-seing*, countersigned by the Duke of Wellington and Lord Grey, I should not know what programme to write on it. Still less can I derive any hope from anything the Queen can do, even supposing her well disposed. The short and real state of the case is this; the Reform Bill has thrown the whole power of the State into the House of Commons, and has, moreover, given a predominance in that House to the Anti-Monarchical party. I know not whether it be possible to place that Anti-Monarchical party in such a minority as to enable the Tories to carry on the Government on the old principles of the constitution. I think not, for any length of time; but the attempt must be made, for the Conservative power is too strong to be finally subdued without another trial.

What do the Duke of Wellington or Sir Robert Peel care for *place?* They both detest it, and would gladly never see Downing Street again. Why, then, would they accept office? Only to protect the Queen and to save the Monarchy, for, under many different disguises and pretences, it is the *Monarchy* that is really attacked.

The Queen by her late unfortunate rejection of the Conservatives (her natural allies) has become popular with a large party in the country. But what party? Why the same, identically the same that for the last 150 years have been the, at once, violent and steady enemies of the Crown— the old leaven of Cromwell and the recent leaven of Tom Paine; the Scotch traitors, the Irish rebels, the British Jacobins. I don't say that *every* man who now supports the Queen is of these extreme classes; but there is no man of those classes who does not now affect an extravagant loyalty to the Throne, because they see the Throne undermining itself.

Our old Constitution had foreseen and provided against every disturbing cause, except the unimaginable one of a junction between the Crown and the mob. If anything to avert, or even to suspend, a democratical revolution can now be done, it can only be by the Queen giving her whole and zealous confidence to the *real* friends of her person and her power; or, to express it all in one word, by adopting implicitly the councils of the Duke of Wellington.

Yours ever,

J. W. C.

Mr. Croker to the King of Hanover. Extracts.

London, May 11th, 1839.

There is but one point which I think it worth while to notice beyond what they say, which is, that the mission of

Sir Robert Peel failed upon what I may call an abstract principle—the right of the Minister to interfere at all in the female household. No lady's name was mentioned by Sir Robert, for on his saying to the Queen "As to the ladies of the household," her Majesty is said to have interrupted him at once by saying, "Oh, I do not mean to make any change among them." This is the sum of the whole affair. Sir Robert Peel could not admit that broad principle that all were to remain. Lady Normanby (whom the Queen particularly wishes for), for instance, the wife of the very Minister whose measures have been the cause of the change, two sisters of Lord Morpeth, the sisters-in-law of Lord John Russell, the daughter of the Privy Seal and Chancellor of the Exchequer. Your Majesty sees that though Sir Robert might, and I have no doubt would, have left the great body of the female attendants, he could not possibly have submitted to have the hostile party thus in possession of the personal favour, friendship, and confidence of the Queen. The general opinion is that this scheme was prepared even before the resignation, and that the whole has been a trick, though for my part I cannot see how it betters the position of the Whigs.

Be all this as it may, I cannot suppose that Parliament or the country will acquiesce in the present state of things, in which there is no change from that which produced the crisis, but the new pretension of having a Ministry of one colour and a Court of another—a proposition which alone would be sufficient to bring on a crisis, if one had not already existed. These are the speculations of a private man who has given up all thoughts of public life, and who is imperfectly informed on the subject; but I have thought that your Majesty might not dislike to hear what an observer who may almost call himself impartial—for I look with more fear than hope to a Tory Ministry—thinks of this very strange but important conjunction. Her Majesty's ball last night was, I am told, rather dull, though she herself seemed in high spirits, as if she were pleased at retaining her Ministers. She has a great concert on the 13th, but to both, as I hear, the invitations have been on a very exclusive principle—no Tories being invited who could be on any pretence left out. These are small matters, but everything tends to create a public impression that her Majesty takes a personal and strong interest in the Whigs—a new ingredient of difficulty!

West Moulsey, January 16th, 1839.

I think the Conservatives have committed a great *party* mistake, and neglected a great constitutional duty, in not having had a direct trial of strength with the revived Cabinet, on their Cabinet minute. Why this has been so I cannot explain, but I apprehend that it must be from the fear that if Melbourne were to be displaced, her Majesty would throw herself into the arms of the Radicals—that I think is no excuse for abandoning a great constitutional duty; but, on the other hand, I feel that Sir Robert Peel and the Duke must have good reasons (though I do not see them) for their forbearance. The last division on the Jamaica Bill gave for a moment great spirits to the Whigs, the majority was swelled by the negligence of some of the Tories, and by the caprice of some of the Radicals, but it will have no real effect. The Bill cannot pass the Lords, and it will be contested again in the Commons on the third reading, and it is expected the majority will not exceed twenty, unless the Radicals come back to us (which is not expected), and in that case the majority would be brought down to six or seven; but in any case I do not think the Bill can pass the Lords.

We are now in the middle of the Education debate.* It is expected that on Lord Stanley's amendment they may have their usual majority of from twenty to thirty, but on the main question the majority will be much smaller, and it is confidently supposed that they will be forced to give that up also. The Ministers have made the ballot an *open* question, and it is thought that this will produce about 230 votes for it —the last time there were under 200, and I myself should incline to put them next division no higher than 210 or 220; but depend upon it, Sir, that question, as well as any other democratical innovation, will be finally carried. It is the nature, in a representative Government, of the Monarchical principle to recede, and of the Democratical principle to advance, and that law of political nature will bring us to a Republic, out of which the equally natural spirit of aristocracy, which it is at the bottom of the human heart, will redeem us again. Such, I am sure, will be the *course* of events, but about the *time* I can prognosticate nothing.

* [A Bill to increase the Education Grant from 20,000*l.* to 30,000*l.*, to place the fund at the disposal of a Committee of five of the Privy Council, and to establish a system of inspection of schools. It was carried by a majority of two only.]

The King of Hanover to Mr. Croker.

Hanover, May 11th, 1839.

DEAR SIR,

I have this moment learnt the great event of Government having resigned, and am persuaded that this step does not arise from the late division, but I have a strong suspicion in my mind that what I prophecied some weeks ago is the real truth, namely, that things have come out in Roden's Committee which they could not face, and in a letter I wrote at the time I said that that Committee would be the death-blow to Melbourne's Administration. I may be wrong in my surmise, knowing so very little what has been going on, and therefore little capable of judging with that exactness as I was enabled formerly to do. My letters say that a messenger had been dispatched to Lord Spencer, but I scarcely can believe he will accept office; first, he has, from the very moment he resigned office under Lord Grey, declared he never would take office again, and he has, I believe, refused since once, if not oftener, forming a part of any Government, and now, when certainly affairs are more *embrouillée* than ever, I never can imagine he will undertake so arduous a task. You know my faithful and zealous attachment to my mother country, and therefore you may easily imagine how deeply my mind is occupied at this moment with all going on in London, for after all, England must and ought to be the pivot for Europe; it was once the Protector of Europe, and alas! how fallen is she since the last ten years. Whether she can ever recover her old state of dignity is more than I will venture to pronounce, and all this owing to the 'many and many false steps she has taken, giving up solid principles and venturing on new. That infernal word expediency has been our ruin. May Providence be merciful to her, and save her, is my most earnest prayer; but I fear you will have still many difficulties to encounter previous to the formation of a Ministry.

With very deep and sincere concern I have heard of poor Follett's recent attack; what a public and private loss he would be, for I look upon him to be now one of our first-rate men, both as a professional man and a senator. It was hearing that he was so ill at your house, that I first learnt of your return to England. In Paris things appear to be in the same state of uncertainty, and the sullen calm there alarms me I own. Let me hear from you, and

Believe me, ever yours very truly,
Ernest.

Frequent temptations were again held out to Mr. Croker, in the course of 1839, to permit himself to be placed in nomination for Parliament, but to every offer he returned the same answer. His political friends always strongly disapproved of his decision, but, for his own part, he never seems to have been for a moment discontented with it. He sometimes complained in his letters that since retiring from office and Parliament he could not find a moment to spare, and that occupation of all kinds accumulated upon his hands. But all who knew him wished to see him back in the House of Commons, and Lord Hertford once more offered to open the door for him. The note was brief, for in these days Lord Hertford seems to have written very rarely, and to have summed up what he had to say in the fewest possible words. The following is the entire letter, bearing no date, superscription, or signature :—

Tell me; you know that telling a quiet friend is like telling a dead wall or a brick-bat.

Do you persist in being the only person of your own way of thinking, of not coming into Parliament any how? I saw a man to-day; it might be quite easy; no one knows anything. Do you persist in Nolo?

Good bye.

P.S.—I only know what everybody knows. All calm and settled.

Several letters signed "H. B." (Henry Brougham) make their appearance in the correspondence, for the first time, in 1839. After this year, Lord Brougham and Mr. Croker were on terms of great intimacy one with the other, for

Lord Brougham was by this time as Conservative in feeling and thought, if not in name, as Mr. Croker himself. They corresponded on all sorts of subjects, and Brougham's letters were so numerous that Mr. Croker must involuntarily have wished that it had been a little easier to read them. The handwriting was almost the worst ever seen; every word was condensed, and every letter destitute of form or shape, so that it was scarcely possible for any human being to make out with certainty all that was written. Sometimes Mr. Croker amused himself by giving a sort of interlinear translation of Brougham's letters, but he was generally obliged to leave numerous blanks. It is worthy of notice that Mr. Croker endeavoured this year to interest Lord Lyndhurst in Brougham's fortunes.

Mr. Croker to Lord Lyndhurst.

West Moulsey, May 8th, 1839.

MY DEAR LYNDHURST,

I am now in perfect ignorance of what is going on, and I do not volunteer showing myself on a theatre on which I have no part to play; but I cannot help urging on you, though I dare say it is needless, the necessity of dealing somehow with our friend Brougham. He volunteered to tell me in Paris, as he said he had told you, that if he was likely to be in the way, he would go abroad for a year or two. This would be a poor device, and could hardly, I think, be carried into effect. [I do not know*] though whether if he were got into legal harness it would not do all that we want, for as a judge he could not, I think, take any inconvenient part in politics; and it would be the happiest and most creditable thing for himself, and what I think all his wellwishers, of whom I am, and I think you are also, would desire. Such talents as his must have employment, and a given direction, and if not either in legal or political office, he must inevitably be in Opposition. I believe that he is, or at least seems to

---

* [These words are not in the MS., but they appear to be necessary to make sense.]

be, not very fond of the idea of legal office, even if we had one vacant to offer him; but he told me that he would like a special mission to treat the slave trade question with his friend Louis Philippe. This might do *en attendant*. Pray don't mention me as having ventured to meddle in such high matters.

Mr. Croker to Lord Brougham.

West Moulsey, March 14th, 1839.

MY DEAR LORD BROUGHAM,

I am amused with, and in many leading points concur in, your characters, and dissertations on parties (at least in the specimens you sent me), though I don't agree with you in details. The contact of party produces a warmth of feeling towards those who sit around us; while the eye is a cold and jealous scrutiniser of those that are opposite to us. We felt towards Canning, and you felt towards Romilly, as contiguity alone can make one feel. You saw in Canning, and we saw in Romilly, defects which it required a certain distance to observe. We should therefore never entirely agree on the minuter merits or defects of our quondam political friends.

Poor Canning's greatest defect was the jealous ingenuity of his mind. He, like an over-cautious general, was always thinking more of what might be on his flanks or in his rear, than in his front. His acuteness discovered so many tortuous by-roads on the map of human life, that he believed they were much more travelled than the broad highway. He preferred an ingenious device for doing anything, to the ordinary processes. In lifting a coalscuttle to mend his fire (as I have been just doing), he would have preferred a screw or a pulley to his own arms. He could hardly "take his tea without a stratagem." I said of him "that his *mind's-eye squinted*;" but this was altogether a mode of his *mind*, of the busy and polyscoptic (may I coin such a word?) activity of his intellect, for his heart and spirit were open, generous, and sincere.

Then there is something in personal appearance and manner, which, like the setting of a precious stone, imparts to, or detracts from, qualities with which they have no real connection. I have no doubt that Fox was as highminded as

Pitt, and Perceval as Windham; but Pitt and Windham had an *air* which improved their natural highmindedness into (in the eyes of the world) a personal characteristic.

In your estimate of party, I venture to think that your scale is too short. You are right to a certain extent, and indeed as far as you go, but you don't (in my humble judgment) go far enough. Your scale is like that of the common thermometer, graduated as high as is necessary for the ordinary uses of life, but not calculated for the philosophical extremes of political science. You reduce all party to a common or antagonist "desire of power and plunder." I don't like the word plunder, and place would, I think, better express your meaning; but I differ from your definition altogether. It is, I think, a definition of the accident, and not of the essence; of an accident, inherent, I admit, in all parties, under a representative system, but not more essentially necessary to party than, to use Molière's comic illustration, the form of a hat is essential to the necessity of a covering for the head. There are two great antagonistic principles at the root of all government—stability and experiment. The former is Tory, and the latter Whig; and the human mind divides itself into these classes as naturally and as inconsiderately, as to personal objects, as it does into indolence and activity, obstinacy and indecision, temerity and versatility, or any other of the various different or contradictory moods of the mind, which, without believing in Spurzheim's occipital or sincipital bumps, one may be satisfied are inherent in human nature. Burke's intellect was Tory, Lord Chatham's Whig, and neither place, nor power, nor Opposition, nor Ministry, could have destroyed, though they often did restrain and modify, the original disposition. I don't believe that any circumstances could have made you a Tory or me a Whig. We might very easily have been thrown into those parties. You might have attached yourself to Pitt, and I might have been a humble follower of Fox, but amongst our more homogeneous associates, we should have been considered as "crotchety, troublesome fellows," always hankering after the opposite doctrine. Look at Canning; look at Windham. What an unsatisfactory Tory was the former; what an imperfect Whig the latter. And this, I take it, was the cause of those anomalies in Burke's character which Goldsmith (unconsciously as to their cause) so admirably sketched:—

> "Tho' equal to all things, for all things unfit,
> Too nice for a statesman, too proud for a wit,
> For a patriot too cool, for a drudge disobedient,
> And too fond of the right to pursue the expedient."

But besides those innate predispositions which your scale does not include below, there are other motives which it does not include above — I mean acquired principles, personal convictions. These are generally the fruits of the natural predisposition (but they may be occasionally, though rarely, independent of it). How many honourable instances could I give you, and you, I dare say, give me, in which party, place, power, have been sacrificed to the pure sense of right and justice. Depend upon it, bad as we are, your views of party make us blacker than the reality. Why was I desirous of resigning my office on Mr. Canning's speech in December, 1826, and was only dissuaded by Peel? Why, in April 1827, did I remain in office when Peel resigned? In both cases I acted against my interests and my feelings, but I acted from a conscientious sense of what I thought right. But the bottom of the eighth page warns me that you are fast asleep, so I steal away without ceremony.

Ever yours,
J. W. CROKER.

The Rev. Dr. (afterwards Dean) Hook to Mr. Croker.

Vicarage, Leeds, April 3rd, 1839.

MY DEAR SIR,

Mr. Murray forwarded to me a copy of the 'Quarterly Review' a few days ago, and he did so, I presume, by your desire, for I conclude that we are indebted to you for the admirable article on the Oxford Divines.* For that article it is impossible to express my thanks in language sufficiently strong. To you we owe entirely the exorcism of that evil spirit of Reform which a few years ago threatened the destruction of all that is sacred in the English Church. The effect of your article in the 'Quarterly' at that time was

---

* [Published in March 1839. The author of the article in question was the Rev. Wm. Sewell. The Bishop of Exeter (Dr. Phillpotts) wrote to Mr. Murray, April 3, 1839: "The article on the Oxford tracts is one of the most valuable your Review ever contained."]

indeed quite extraordinary. Before its publication all kinds of pamphlets issued weekly from the press, recommending all kinds of alterations. I do not think that *one* reform pamphlet has been issued by a Churchman since; at all events, not by a Churchman of any respectability. God grant that the present article may have a like effect. I am not myself one of *the* Oxford Divines, although they are among my dearest friends. Engaged in the duties of a large parish, I thought it would be imprudent for me to render myself answerable for publications over which I could have no direct control. Besides being, what they are not, a practical man, accustomed rather to look at what under given circumstances *can* be done, than at what under the best circumstances *ought* to be done, I have sometimes differed from them in opinion. I have sometimes thought that, by insisting upon a narrow point of detail, they have retarded the progress of an important principle. I have found it necessary to act, too, with a degree of caution which they would hardly approve of. But still I have resolutely maintained the great principles for which they have so nobly fought. I maintained them, indeed, before they wrote; and in former times—when my dear friend Pusey was a Whig and a Low Churchman!—against Pusey himself. Hence the moral persecution raised against them has been also directed against me; and bitter indeed has that persecution been, as raised by the Dissenters, and the few most bitter *Recordites* or "Evangelicals" here. Their malevolence and lies exceed belief. But by resolutely pursuing my own line, by returning good for evil, and taking no notice of them, I had succeeded beyond all expectation, when an article in 'Fraser' did me some damage. There are certain Conservatives who defer to 'Fraser' as the Recordites do to the 'Record,' and, finding the Conservative press making war upon us, they were beginning to cool in their zeal towards me. Now these persons will be quite knocked over by the 'Quarterly'; and thus you see that to me personally, as well as to the good cause generally, your article in the 'Quarterly' will be of service.

May I request you to thank Mr. Murray for sending me the Review. I have ordered many copies that I may lend them. I know that it were vain to express a hope of being permitted to print the article as a tract.

Yours,

W. F. HOOK.

Mr. Croker to Dr. Hook.

West Moulsey, April 14th, 1839.

My dear Sir,

I heartily wish I could accept the praise which you give to the author of the article on the Oxford Tracts. We make it a rule not to disclaim, any more than to accept the paternity of this or that essay; but to you I have no reserve in saying truly that I have had no other share in that article than having rung the bell. I will not deny having suggested the necessity of expressing our opinion and the line in which we should proceed, but the article is altogether by another hand, and, I need not add, a much better. I hope it may do good. I have been much alarmed at the prospect of a schism, which, however, I thought could only be produced by a misunderstanding of the Oxford Tracts; and if they are made more accessible to the general reader by the 'Quarterly' article, great good may be done, and still greater mischief prevented.

Very faithfully yours,
J. W. CROKER.

Sir James Graham to Mr. Croker. Extract.

Grosvenor Place, May 22nd, 1839.

I begin to share all your apprehensions and sad forebodings with regard to the probable issue of the present struggle. The Crown in alliance with Democracy baffles every calculation on the balance of power in our mixed form of Government. Aristocracy and Church cannot contend against Queen and people united; they must yield in the first instance, when the Crown, unprotected, will meet its fate, and the accustomed round of anarchy and despotism will run its course:—

"May I lie cold before that dreadful day,
Wrapt in a load of monumental clay."

But it is too sad to pursue this topic, and I will not inflict on you a Jeremiad.

Yours very truly,
JAS. GRAHAM.

The Duke of Wellington to Mr. Croker.

Walmer Castle, November 12th, 1839.

MY DEAR CROKER,

I have received your letter of the 10th. I had understood that it was a matter of indifference at what time you should receive the information which you require, provided that it was at about the period of the meeting of Parliament.

I don't much care for a trot, and I would have gone 160 miles to get the papers for the Committee at the time at which I wrote. But I now am so engaged as to be unable to leave this place, either for the trot or permanently at the time you mention.

General Maitland is the Secretary of the Committee for the construction of the Duke of York's pillar, and has it in his power to give you all the information that you can require respecting the expense thereof.

It is very difficult to form a judgment what will become of Lord Melbourne.

But, as I see that your friends preach up insubordination among the Conservatives, it is probable that Lord Melbourne's Government will endure; and I am not quite certain that its continuance will not give us a better chance of tranquillity than a Government formed by a scramble of Tories!

Ever yours, most sincerely,

WELLINGTON.

Mr. Croker to the King of Hanover.

West Moulsey, November 21st, 1839.

We are at this moment under two excitements, which cannot but interest your Majesty—the Queen's marriage * and the indisposition of the Duke of Wellington. All I know about the former is that Prince Albert has been here for some weeks, and I am told made himself *visibly acceptable* to Her Majesty. He went away last week, and yesterday I, in common with all other Privy Councillors, received a summons to attend Her Majesty in Council on Saturday next (the day after to-morrow), at one o'clock, on " most important business," which of course can be nothing but the announcement of her

* [It did not take place till February of the following year, 1840.]

marriage. I was in town yesterday, when this summons became publicly known. The town had been thrown into great alarm by the account of a serious attack—supposed to be paralytic—which the Duke of Wellington had suffered at Walmer Castle on Monday evening.... The facts are these: the Duke had been uncommonly well for some time, but he had been exceedingly abstemious. He is always very moderate, but of late he had become over abstemious, without diminishing his usual exertions, either of mind or body. Last week he had been what he called starving a cold, but was so well on Monday that he went out to hunt, and on coming home between four and five, he went into his room, when, about five, he was heard to fall from his chair in a fit of insensibility, in which he continued about forty-five minutes, when he spontaneously recovered both sense and speech, and desired that some company that was expected to dinner should not be put off, but that Col. Munro would do the honours for him. Next day he would have got up as usual if the doctor would have allowed him. Dr. MacArthur, when pressed by my friend as to the real nature of the disease, said there was nothing of paralysis in it, but that, if he were forced to give it a name, he would call it epilepsy, though even of that some essential symptoms were wanting. When I recollect that his Grace had a similar attack last February, I cannot see the recurrence of it without alarm.

The position of the Ministry is equally painful to themselves and perilous to the country, and I do not expect they will be able to last beyond Easter. The Queen's marriage may enable them to reach that period, though I know some well-informed people think they cannot meet Parliament. My own opinion is that they will never go out till there shall be an actual vote against them in the House of Commons, and that will probably not be until some question on education in connection with the *Church* shall be brought forward, which I do not expect before Easter.

Mr. Croker to Lady Hardwicke.

West Moulsey, 24th Nov., 1839.

DEAR LADY HARDWICKE,

I have taken a fine sheet of paper in **honour** of the Queen. By ill-luck I did not receive your letter yesterday till after post, or I should, as you desired, have written you an account of what passed in Council;* and I fear that, owing to the intervention of Sunday, my news will now be too late. We had a very full Council, and the great Duke, as you announced, attended. I am sorry to say that a slight twist of the right corner of his mouth, and some constraint in using the right arm, indicated too plainly the nature of the attack.

When we had assembled to the number of, I think, seventy or eighty (two to one Conservative), and as many had taken their seats as could, at a long table, Her Majesty was handed in by the Lord Chamberlain, and, bowing to us all round, sat down, saying, "Your Lordships" (we are all *Lords* at the Council Board) "will be seated." She then unfolded a paper and read her declaration, which you will, before this can reach you, have seen in the newspapers. I cannot describe to you with what a mixture of self-possession and feminine delicacy she read the paper. Her voice, which is naturally beautiful, was clear and untroubled; and her eye was bright and calm, neither bold nor downcast, but firm and soft. There was a blush on her cheek which made her look both handsomer and more interesting; and certainly she *did* look as interesting and as handsome as any young lady I ever saw.

I happened to stand behind the Duke of Wellington's chair, and caught her eye twice, as she directed it towards him, which I fancied she did with a good-natured interest.

After the Lord President had asked her permission to publish her declaration, she bowed consent, handed him the paper, rose, bowed all round, and retired, led as before by the Lord Chamberlain to the outer room, where the attendants, who were not of the Council, had waited. The crowd, which was not great but very decent, I might almost say respectable, at the palace gate, expressed their approbation of the Duke of Wellington and Sir Robert Peel, and their disapprobation of the Ministers very loudly. Lord John and Lord Normanby, they tell me, were positively hooted. I am always sorry for anything that may vex Normanby, whom I really have a

---

* [On the occasion of Her Majesty announcing her intention of allying herself in marriage with Prince Albert. The Queen in her 'Journal' says: "The room was full, but I hardly knew who was there. . . I felt my hands shook, but I did not make one mistake. I felt more happy and thankful when it was over." The number of Privy Councillors present was eighty-three.]

great regard for, and I dare say Lord John owed the disapprobation of the crowd chiefly to those parts of his conduct which I the most approve. Lord Melbourne, who did me the honour of shaking hands with me like an old friend, seemed to me to look *careworn*, and on the whole the meeting had a sombre air.

Give Charles my best regards, and believe me to be, my dear Lady Hardwicke,

Faithfully yours,
J. W. CROKER.

The Duke of Wellington to Mr. Croker.

Strathfieldsaye, December 29th, 1839.

MY DEAR CROKER,

I have written a summons to members and all the Conservative Peers to inform them of the meeting of Parliament, and of the expediency that they should attend. I can neither do nor say any more. If the Government have any sense, they will so make their speech as that an amendment to the address in answer to it cannot be proposed—at least, in the House of Lords. If the House of Lords act wisely, they will not be in a hurry to attack the Government. I can say no more. Lord Hertford, who has, or ought to have, this summons equally with others, must be the best judge what course he ought to take.

As soon as I shall be informed, or can in any manner learn anything more, I will write to Lord Hertford.

Believe me, ever yours most sincerely,
WELLINGTON.

Mr. Croker to the King of Hanover.[*]

February 17th, 1840.

SIR,

The Duke of Wellington has had another—that is a third—attack, which no one can doubt to be paralytic, and I am sorry to have to add that it has been much the most severe of the three. It happened on Thursday afternoon. His grace

---

[*] [This is one of the few letters written by Mr. Croker in 1840 which are now to be discovered.]

had been paying a visit to Lady Burghersh, and seemed quite as well as usual, and he mounted his horse to ride away, but his groom observed him drop the reins, and alighted and ran up to him, and, giving him the reins again, contrived to get him home, where he was put to bed speechless and paralysed on one side. I cannot, however, conceal from your Majesty, my apprehension that the Duke's public life is over. Shaken as he must be by these repeated seizures, it will be dangerous to his existence, even if it were physically possible, that he should be exposed to the worry of a constant attendance and active direction of the House of Lords. I know how unwilling he will be to give in, but I am sure all his personal friends are convinced that the day of retreat is arrived; he may still, if he will spare himself, give us for a few years perhaps, the assistance of his counsels and countenance, but I confess I do not wish him to take an active part.

I have not yet heard any surmise of what is to be done in the House of Lords to supply (not to fill—that is impossible) his place; my own idea is that there is no one to whom less objection can be made as leader in the House of Lords, than Lord Aberdeen. He wants much that a leader ought, in these times, to possess, but I think he would be the most generally acceptable, and the safest of any one that occurs to me.

The Ministry had a majority of twenty-one on the vote of confidence.* This majority is probably not more than a real majority of fifteen on the whole house—some people think not above ten or twelve, but be it what it may, it fails them on individual questions to a degree of which even their former defeats afford no parallel. Since that vote of confidence they have been beaten on three important points; one the other night, on the finance of the year, they admitted to be a vote of confidence, and they lost it—182 to 172. I do not attach any very great importance to a majority of ten in so thin a House; but I believe the ministers felt it deeply, particularly as it was accompanied by the failure of their two new financiers—Baring and Labouchere.

We have had for many weeks a report that when the marriage † should be completed, Lord Melbourne meant to

---

* [A motion of want of confidence in the Ministry, moved by Sir J. Yarde Buller, January 28th, and debated for four nights; in the end the motion was rejected by 308 votes to 287.]

† [Of the Queen.]

retire, and that Lord Lansdowne would also go. That rumour has been revived, but the resignation of Lord Lansdowne obtains more belief; and it is suspected that they have invited Lord Brougham to join them as President of the Council. I think such a junction hardly possible, but there are some small reasons which make me hesitate in disbelieving it altogether. I rather wish it may take place, for I had rather see Lord Brougham exerting his talents in keeping a government together, than in pulling it to pieces; for in doing the latter, he might carry his zeal so far, or rather his zeal might carry him so far, that he might pull the *Monarchy* to pieces with the *Government*.

The King of Hanover to Mr. Croker.

Hanover, March 8th, 1840.

MY DEAR SIR,

I really am ashamed at not having been able sooner to reply to your kind and highly interesting letter; believe me, this omission has not arisen either from idleness or forgetfulness, but honestly it has been out of my power; what with the worry and plague I have had on account of the Precedency Question in England, which seems to me to have been most grossly mismanaged *at last*. I mean not what was done by the Lords, but afterwards, and how such able, clever men as Lyndhurst and Wynford can have given the opinion they have done, is to me really unaccountable, and what is more, unintelligible. I may be deemed very presumptuous to pretend to offer an opinion at variance with such men, but the fact is, though no lawyer nor pretending to that, still I have common sense, and this pointed out to me that the opinion they had given must have been given at a 240 horse-power rate, and thus they omitted considering *two* points; first, the *spirit* of the act of Henry VIII., and secondly, that the Princes of the blood royal, being in the *straight* line of succession, you cannot admit that a Royal Highness (N.B. a *paper one*) can claim precedency to those *born* so, and thus *de jure;* and in the next place, I have been, and am still most eternally on the watch to frustrate all the machinations and tricks of the attorneys in the country, who, knowing they are now reduced to their last efforts, are moving heaven and earth to prevent all the vacant corporations from electing members for the

General States, which are summoned to assemble here on the 19th of this month. However, by patience, perseverance, and going a straightforward, plain line, and neither permitting myself or any belonging to me to manœuvre or do any underhand work, I have, at least, so far succeeded, that they all own I am acting fair and above board, and they *trust me.*

Thank God, at least for the present the life of our hero has been saved, but I fear his whole existence must be very precarious, and two such dreadful and awful attacks, following each other after so short a period, must have shaken his constitution dreadfully; and it is really a shame that he is so careless of his health, and will thus expose himself; he ought to remember that his life is a public one, and it is a duty he owes his country and his party not to strain upon it as he seems to have done. That Aberdeen is to lead, seems to me to be the best choice they could make, considering all circumstances; if the Duke would now only direct the general plan of business, and remain quietly at Strathfieldsaye till after Easter, and thus recruit his strength, then we might hope that his valuable life might be spared us still some years to come. I wonder how M. Guizot will succeed in England? I hear Lord Granville is highly delighted at Thiers being at the head of affairs, and naturally, as he is, I believe, a thorough Republican.

Yours very truly,
E.

Mr. Croker to the King of Hanover.

Kensington Palace, August 23rd, 1840.

I have been in Paris, whither I went both unexpectedly and reluctantly the week before last, and stayed only six days. The fact was that poor Lord Hertford thinks very ill of himself, and fancying that we might never again see each other, was very anxious that I should accompany him as far as I could, which I did to Fontainebleau, where I left him this day week, not in much better spirits but really in mere bodily health as well as I have seen him of late.

We passed through Boulogne the day of Louis Napoleon's

échauffourée.* It detained us for a couple of hours, as they embargoed the post-horses for *estafettes*, but the whole affair was so futile and ridiculous, that even in Boulogne it made no effect. I was almost inclined to think that Louis Philippe had encouraged it, by way of anticipating and blunting the expected enthusiasm on the arrival of Napoleon's bones. If this foolish man, Louis Buonaparte, had landed with the bones, he would have made a different kind of effect; as it is, he has covered himself with ridicule, and the great name of Napoleon has suffered a little also.

Your Majesty can have no conception of the absurdity into which all classes of French have plunged upon the Eastern Question.† To listen to the talk of the salons and cafés, there must be war; and for what object? To prevent the partition of Turkey, which it seems, England meditates. England insisting on preserving Syria to the Porte, and France insisting on severing it. What an age we live in, when such nonsense is talked by a whole people. They say that M. Guizot, who went to England very pacific, is returned rather warlike, and that he says that he found M. Thiers calm and reasonable, and Louis Philippe excited. I do not believe this, though I heard it from a good quarter; if there be any truth in it, it is only that Louis Philippe thinks the popular sentiment very strong, and with his usual art appears to fall in with it; but I cannot believe that he, in his heart, participates in this folly of the day. I am sure that M. Guizot, whom I saw ten days ago, before we went to France, was as rational as any man could be on the subject, and on the whole I am perfectly satisfied that war, on any existing grounds, is impossible. I hear that the actual state of the case is, that the English Admiral has orders to give effect to the quadruple convention, if Mehemet Ali does not accept the proposition made to him, and

---

* [This was the celebrated landing of Louis Napoleon at Boulogne, with a handful of followers, on the morning of the 6th of August, 1840. The whole business was regarded at the time as the freak of a lunatic, and one of the papers described the hero of the exploit as "the maniac, Louis Napoleon."]

† [This resulted in the siege and capture of Acre, in the month of September. England acted with the Sultan against the rebellious Pasha of Egypt, but France was much irritated, and at one time it was believed that she would attack the Allied fleet. The English part in the affair was managed throughout by Lord Palmerston.]

which it was supposed might reach Alexandria about the 10th of August; the English co-operation is expected to be, first a blockade of the coast, which would starve the Egyptian army; secondly the transport of Turkish troops to the flank, or even the rear of the Egyptian army; and thirdly, supporting them by our own artillery and marines, and 20,000 stand of arms for the Syrian insurgents—half supplied by Austria, and half by us; and then the question is whether France will not immediately take opposite measures. I for my own part, do not believe that any definite orders are yet gone; nor do I think the French will venture to take any directly hostile steps. We shall have Mehemet Ali's answer perhaps within the week, and my opinion is that the terms are so fair that he will accept; in which case the whole matter will be settled, not, however, without great dissatisfaction to the French; but if Mehemet rejects the offer, I still think that France will not be so mad as to interfere by actual force.

I am told, and believe that the Duke of Wellington approves the course of the Government; indeed I know not what other course could have been adopted without giving up the Sultan into the tutelage of Russia. Your Majesty will be glad to hear that the Duke is better. He told me that he had never been spoken to about the Canada Bill by any human being, and that it came to the House of Lords without the slightest indication (except from the newspapers) that such a measure was in existence. Peel's conduct on that and other points seems strange; but I attribute it not so much to his own views, as to the exigencies of the Stanley alliance—a powerful auxiliary—for which, however, we are obliged to pay a large price.

We hear, and can easily believe that there are serious differences in the Cabinet; and I was told to-day that Her Royal Highness Princess Sophia, in mentioning the fact had added: "What a pity it is that the Duke of Wellington will interfere." We know that the Duke has been occasionally consulted on public questions, but I can hardly think that he *interferes* to make up any personal squabbles in the Cabinet. The Conservative party is very much dissatisfied at seeing, or fancying, that their leaders do not wish for office, but I think they mistake the matter. In the first place, I don't believe that they *could* have got in; but if they had, could they have stayed? and should we not have had another edition of Peel's unhappy administration five years ago, which did more serious injury to our constitution in the three months it lasted, than the Whigs have done since the Reform Bill? Individual ambition and interests will naturally wish to come into office, but for the sake of the country I prefer the present state of things, as that in which the least mischief will be done; but I am sorry to say that I do not think that things can go on as they are, and I fear the Conservatives will be soon driven to take office, without, I think, the power of executing it on right principles; they will be forced to purchase a precarious existence by disgraceful and dangerous compliances. These are not, I know, our friend Wetherell's opinions, and I admit that there is much to be said on the other side, but in the choice of difficulties I should prefer the present position, uncomfortable and perilous as I admit it to be.

*Mr. Croker to Mr. George Barrow.**

Montreuil, August 6th, 1840.

MY DEAR GEORGE,

I told M. Guizot on Monday, that I expected to meet an *émeute*, but I certainly did not expect to meet it so early as *this morning at Boulogne*. The story is so extravagant that I am almost ashamed to tell what looks so like a fable; but I will relate to you what I heard, and give you my authority.

Our *avant courrier* left Calais about two this morning, and was to order horses for us, but on his arrival at Boulogne about five, he found the town in commotion; Louis Buonaparte had landed on the shore a little to the eastward of *la Colonne*, probably near the little port of Vimerieux, about half-past four A.M., with about sixty-five followers, including a brilliant *état-major*, the head of which was a General, said to be Montholon (but whose description does not agree with my idea of Montholon). They first marched on the upper town, and attempted the barracks, but the troops shut the gates against them; they then assaulted a *corps de garde*, and *the General* shot a *voltigeur* with a pistol; but they failed here too, and then seemed to have given up the attempt very pusillanimously, and to have hastened to retreat to their vessels. It seems that these were a couple of small vessels, and they had boats, in one of which Buonaparte and some others were endeavouring to escape, when, being fired at from the shore, the boat capsized

* [Mr. Croker's son-in-law, afterwards Sir George Barrow.]

and they were all swimming for their lives; some are supposed to be lost, but the *Prince,* as they call Buonaparte, was picked up; meanwhile the boats of *la Douane* got round and captured the whole expedition. 'Tis said that one of the larger vessels had two *fine carriages* on board, and some arms and ammunition. Our courier says that he saw Buonaparte, the General, and several others brought up and lodged in the jail of Boulogne. During several hours an embargo was laid on post-horses, but it was taken off about one P.M., and we passed at two, with as little symptoms of an insurrection as you can imagine; but you know the post road only skirts the lower town; all we observed was that some windows were closed with their shutters, and that people ran to the upper windows to stare at us as we passed.

The common people and a mob of boys were ready enough to cry *Vive Napoléon,* but the troops, the National Guards, and the better classes, were staunch.

Sir W. Follett to Mr. Croker.

Paris, Hôtel de Douvres, October 6th, 1840.

MY DEAR MR. CROKER,

What are you thinking, saying, or doing about the war, in England? Matters here are really assuming a very serious aspect, much more so than, judging from the English papers, you can have any conception of in England.

In the first place, all the newspapers of all parties, Bonapartist, Carlist, Liberal, Moderate, are unanimous in their abuse of England, and for war. The *Journal des Débats* is the only paper that still preserves anything like a moderate tone on this subject, and even that paper does not venture to take the side of peace. It is impossible that this constant excitement of the Press could fail to produce a considerable effect upon such an inflammable people as the French, even if they were not before well disposed for some violent course; and I hear now that the war party in the country and in the army is gaining such strength, that the Government begin to be afraid they have not the power to control it. The Ministers, I was told, and I think from something like authority, are in the greatest perplexity and distress; all of them, even M. Thiers, desire to avoid war; the King decidedly opposed to it; yet apprehensive that unless something like concession is made by England, they will be forced by the popular cry to take some steps that must lead to hostilities. I understand that they have come to the determination not to interfere so long as the operations of the allies are confined to Syria; but that there is a difference of opinion upon the point whether they shall order the French fleet to sail to Alexandria, with directions to protect the Pasha, in case of any attack on the Egyptian territories. It is said that Thiers is desirous that this should be done, but that the King will not consent to it.

I presume that such a step on the part of France would necessarily bring on a European war. Thiers, they say, tendered his resignation on Sunday, but was prevailed on by the King to remain, and to try the effect of another overture to the English Government to modify the treaty so far as to preserve Egypt to Mehemet Ali. If *some* concession be not made to France it is impossible to say what may be the consequence in the present state of men's minds here, but in the meantime what is thought of this treaty in England? The Duke of Wellington's authority is quoted in its favour; I know not with what truth. I do not profess to be able to comprehend this subject in all its bearings, but I cannot help doubting both the policy and the justice of this interference by force in the dispute between Mehemet Ali and the Porte. If all the Powers of Europe had united, it might have been justifiable and politic as being a sure mode of preventing war; but I cannot conceive anything more likely to lead to war, than a treaty of interference between some of these Powers, while the one most likely to disturb the peace was left at liberty to oppose and take part against them, if it thought fit to do so. No one, however, seems to have attacked Lord Palmerston for this treaty, and therefore I suppose I am wrong about it. In the midst of all this excitement the populace here is perfectly tranquil; no incivility of any sort or kind is offered to the English, either here or in the provinces; and I cannot help thinking even now that with the shopkeepers and a very large portion of the people, a war with England would not be popular.

We saw in *Galignani* yesterday that George Giffard[*] had been wounded in this affair on the coast of Syria. His mother and

---

[*] [A ward of Mr. Croker and brother-in-law of Sir Wm. Follett, now (1884) Admiral Sir George Giffard, K.C.B.]

Jane* are, of course, anxious and uneasy about it, and will be so until we have the real truth about it. I should hope, however, from the way it is mentioned in the paper, that his wound is not very serious. We are expecting the despatches from England.

We talk of leaving this towards the end of this week, and I hope to be in England about the 18th. All unite in kind love to Mrs. Croker and Nony, and believe me, ever most sincerely,

W. FOLLETT.

Mr. Croker to Lord Brougham.†

Alverstoke, near Gosport, October 31st, 1840.

Thanks for your speculative letter, to which I have neither speculations nor facts to return, except, indeed, the facts of two great three-deckers lying before my windows waiting for a wind to sail, I know not where, but assuredly to do no good at all equivalent to the expense and scandal of such uncommon armaments. A few days will tell us whether the French Deputies representing the [people] are to be swayed by them or the Press, and whether they will encourage the system of ruining our respective finances in these hostile demonstrations. The Eastern Question is *per se* nothing. It matters not a fig whether the Sublime Porte spells its name Mahmoud or Mehemet, but it does signify a great deal whether the European world is to be spending its money and irritating its temper on every paltry excuse which a faction may create. Formerly, you are well aware, no Power [increased] its peace armament without notice to or remonstrance from other Powers, and, in fact, they [criticised] each other's budgets more strictly than Mr. Joseph Hume ever did ours; and this foreign jealousy tended to domestic economy. Our peace, I grieve to say almost our whole peace, has been war in disguise. The words of peace, the arts and expenditure of war—the voice of Jacob! the hands of Esau! Where is this to end? We have now a larger and more expensive

---

* [Sir Wm. Follett married Miss Giffard, daughter of Sir Hardinge Giffard, Chief Justice of Ceylon.]

† [There were several words in this letter which the copyist was unable to decipher, and he therefore left them blank. In the absence of the original, the editor has conjecturally filled up these blanks.]

fleet and army than we used to have in our old-fashioned wars, and the system that was to control the belligerent propensities of kings, turns out to be more extravagant than anything that mere kings could have ventured upon. Thank God, I am a private man. You all, of all sides, who have public duties, are (or at least I should feel myself to be) in the miserable plight of not knowing what to do but to fear and tremble. Poor Louis Philippe lives the life of a [mad dog ?], and will soon, I fear, suffer the death of that general object of every man's shot. Guizot [is] a unit—a nullity—Soult a *plastron*. There is no man in France who has any legitimate authority or commanding influence over the public mind. *Our* Ministry is a company of second-rate actors, who might all be buried in poor Lord Holland's grave* without being missed. Ward and W. Villiers, and Buller, and Bulwer would do just as well, and command the self-same majorities. The Tories have more station and following, but not enough to enable them to govern.

Yours ever,

J. W. CROKER.

Mr. Croker to the Bishop of Exeter (Dr. Phillpotts).

Gosport, 15, Anglesea Terrace, October 6th, 1840.

MY DEAR LORD,

I take the liberty of asking you, as the most likely of all my friends to be able to afford me the information, what the meaning is of a paragraph towards the conclusion of the Archbishop's recent Visitation charge, about the "quantity of service" required by the Rubric for the Lord's day? I know not what rubric specifies "the quantity of service" for the Lord's day; nor have I ever known in any church any curtailment of the usual quantity. The Archbishop seems to say that the Rubric requires two full services every Sunday (though his Grace says, I know not why, that weekday service is, of course, not to be required), and on Sundays, Wednesdays, and Fridays, the addition of the Litany, and on Sunday I presume, though I find no rubric for it, the Communion Service, or a part of it, though for the division of that service I find no rubric. It seems to me that the rubric

---

* [Lord Holland had died on October 20th, at the age of sixty seven.]

requires three services on the Lord's day, and not two as his Grace seems to say, and that it is by a convenient abridgement of labour that the Morning Service is, on the Sunday morning, conjoined to the Communion.

I confess also that I do not understand what his Grace's drift or object was. Surely this whole passage (under the pressure, he tells us, of such important matters as were pressing for notice) did not mean that there should be morning and evening service on the Sunday; for, as I have said, there are few, and these few generally excusable exceptions, and probably not one in the diocese of Canterbury, in which the "rights of the parishioners" are so "infringed" on. The only precise object I can collect from the whole passage, is to say that attention to the Rubric on week days is, of course, not to be expected, but that his Grace submits very humbly and hesitatingly whether it would not be an infringement on the "rights of the parishioners" to abridge the Sunday "complement;" and he further ventures to suggest that a second pulpit discourse would be rather desirable, which if not contrary to, is at least not specified by, the rubric. This, then, where the rubric is clear, it is *of course* not to be followed, but something that it does not require is recommended to universal adoption.

Is it Hibernian dulness that mystifies all this to my mind? or is there some rubric or rule not printed in our common liturgies? or, finally, has his Grace some esoteric doctrine on the subject which is not yet reached the laity? Can you, my dear lord, enlighten my ignorance?

Ever very sincerely yours,
J. W. CROKER.

The Bishop of Exeter to Mr. Croker.

Staffordshire, Himley Hall, October 28th, 1840.

MY DEAR SIR,

Since the receipt of your first letter, I have been in a state of incessant occupation—I might almost say of *locomotion*—except the time occupied by an Ordination. A tour of Confirmations has filled up part of the time—a journey hither, on the business of the Dudley Trust, has claimed an entire ten days.

Without my books I cannot write as accurately as I wish on the subject on which you enquire.

I apprehend, however, that you are quite right in your supposition that the Communion Service is a distinct office altogether, and was wont to be performed at a separate time from either Morning or Evening Prayer.

I apprehend, too, that there is no rule, and no principle, which connects it more with Morning than with Evening Prayer.

On Easter Monday or Tuesday, I forget which, but the day on which the Spital Sermon is preached before the Lord Mayor at Christ Church, the Communion Service (without the Sacrament) is performed *alone*—i.e., neither Morning nor Evening Prayer precedes it.

If my memory does not fail me, this is also the case at Lambeth, when the Bishops dine with the Archbishop as a body. On public days the Litany is the service performed; but on the Bishops' day, if I mistake not, it is the Communion Service.

As an excuse for my uncertainty on the point, I must tell you that the Bishops' day has ordinarily been in Easter week, when I am never in London. It is now altered, but I know not that I have dined on that occasion more than once. I am confident that the Litany was not then the service, and am almost confident that the *Communion* was the service.

Respecting the demand of a second sermon from every minister on every Sunday, though the recent statute empowers the Bishop to make it, my own judgment is very far from being that it ought to be generally made. In *rural* parishes especially, I should much prefer the public catechizing of the children, with an effective explanation of part of the Catechism, or a familiar, but grave, and avowedly or manifestly premeditated, though not written, comment on one of the Lessons of the day—to a second sermon. In truth, the more we elevate the Liturgy, the *intelligent* reading of Scripture, or the different offices of the Church (the Baptismal and Burial Service especially), and render them by explanation familiar to our people, even if this be done at the expense of what is called *preaching*, the better in my opinion it will be. By the bye, *Hooker* calls all these things *preaching*.

Yours most faithfully,
H. EXETER.

The following, from a son of Mr. Perceval, was evidently in reply to a request from Mr. Croker for some particulars concerning the early life of his old chief.

Mr. Perceval to Mr. Croker.

My DEAR Mr. CROKER, Sunday, September 6th, 1840.

I wish it were in my power to furnish you with accurate information upon the subject on which you have kindly referred to me, but I fear I have not much to say that will be available for your purpose.

My father was educated at Harrow; he was pupil to Dr. Drury, who afterwards, but not (I believe) during my father's time, was head master. Lord Harrowby and Mathew Montague were among his most intimate friends, and the prize books which he brought away from Harrow, and a number of old exercises of his which I have, together with others by his contemporaries, bear witness that he gave his mind to the studies of that place. He was afterwards a fellow-commoner at Trinity College, Cambridge. His private tutor was Mathias, author of the 'Pursuits of Literature;' but I do not think that I ever heard any one speak of his studies there, one way or the other.

I have heard that Mr. Pitt first saw my father when at Cambridge, upon some occasion when he, Mr. Pitt, came down there after he had ceased to reside; that they met at a supper, and that Mr. Pitt was very much struck by him. This anecdote I am pretty sure I had from Mr. Ryder. I may as well add here what, perhaps, you have heard, but which is undoubtedly true, that Mr. Pitt, when he went to fight Tierney,* named my father to Lord Harrowby as the fittest man in the House of Commons to take his place. These facts are, I am afraid, not much to the point as direct answers to your questions, though they have a general bear-

---

* [On May 25th, 1798, Mr. Pitt introduced a Bill for the more effectual manning of the navy. In the course of the debate high words passed between him and Mr. Tierney, which led to a challenge from Tierney the next day. On Sunday the 27th they met on Putney Heath; two shots were fired with no effect, and the seconds then interfered and put a stop to the quarrel.—Stanhope's 'Life of Pitt,' 8vo., vol. ii. pp. 277–279.]

ing upon the enquiry of how far he cultivated or neglected his talents during the period of his education. I have seen many years ago books of notes and extracts belonging to this period, and to the early part of his law life, which bear a general testimony to painstaking and diligence, but I have not so accurate a recollection of them as I could wish, to enable me to bear witness as to the direction or extent of his reading. He took an honorary degree of M.A.

He never wrote anything *that I know of* (except a very short pamphlet on part of the eleventh chapter of Daniel) that was not written in the way of business. His defence of the Princess of Wales you probably have. I think I remember hearing Lord Denman on the Queen's trial, characterize it as one of the most beautiful writings in the English language; and I have always felt that, independent of the skill, and discretion, and dignity, and boldness manifested in the conduct of the case, the letters, as mere specimens of writing, are worthy a place among the best English classics, and my filial vanity has often longed for a legitimate occasion to publish them. If you have not a copy I will ask my mother to send one to you, which I am sure she will do with great pleasure.

Besides the little pamphlet on 'Prophecy,' which I have mentioned above, I have heard my mother speak of papers in the *British Critic* upon prophetical subjects, and among my father's books I have observed more marks of study in some prophetical works than in any other; and I have no doubt that his steadfast resistance to the Roman Catholic claims was very much owing to his mind being imbued with views of the Papacy obtained from the study of prophecy.

I am, dear Mr. Croker,
Yours faithfully and affectionately,
J. W. PERCEVAL.

The Duke of Wellington to Mr. Croker.

Strathfieldsaye, December 31st, 1840.

MY DEAR CROKER,

I will not deny myself the satisfaction of telling you with what delight I have perused your article in the *Quarterly Review* on the Foreign Policy.*

* [In No. 133, December 1840.]

I believe that there are few persons who know so much of what is called the Eastern Affair as I do, even of Ministers, and I must say that I have not seen any statement of the case of the country, including that of Ministers, half so clear or strong as you have made out.

Thiers has not a leg on which he can stand. The French can only sing the 'Marseillaise,' and talk of *la perfidie Anglaise.*

I see but bad accounts of Lord Hertford. It is said that he is coming home.

Ever yours, most sincerely,
WELLINGTON.

Sir Robert Peel to Mr. Croker.

Drayton Manor, Saturday. [No other date.]

MY DEAR CROKER,

I would willingly give you, if I could, the information you want as to the date of Lord John Russell's speech; but I do not very well recollect the speech. I think it could not be a very recent one, for it would have been too impudent to take credit for much improvement in the social condition of England within the last five or six years.

I will look, however, and try to find the speech. The whole system of government in 1830 was condemned because there were some incendiary fires, and because the mob was so maddened by the three glorious days and the praises bestowed upon them by such men as Lord Brougham and Lord Denman, that it became unwise to let the King visit the Lord Mayor on a November night, for fear mischievous people might provoke a disturbance, from which innocent ones would suffer.

If *we* had been so profoundly ignorant of the state of the country as to let 8000 or 9000 men march upon a town, without a suspicion that such a thing was possible, and had then shot dead with the military fifteen or twenty rioters, what would the Whigs have said of such culpable negligence? and how they would have inveighed against the defective principle of institutions with which great masses of working men were dissatisfied! They would have considered a rising of 10,000 men a conclusive proof against the whole constitution of Government, assuming, as they always have done *till they were in power*, that every turbulent fellow or seditious meeting must have a cause of complaint *fully* justifying the turbulence or sedition.

A day or two before we went to Gopsall, Lord Howe received a letter addressed to *Lord How*, the envelope of whitey brown, with an inscription, "per railroad." He thought it one of a dozen letters addressed to him from people who wanted money, or a subscription, or the permission to dedicate, or work for a bazaar, or anything else than from Queen Adelaide, and was very nearly throwing it into the grate. However, he fortunately opened the envelope, and discovered *the letter from the Queen*, announcing to Queen Adelaide her intended marriage, addressed in the Queen's own hand to Queen Adelaide, and written in very kind and affectionate terms—as full of love as Juliet.

I suppose some footboy at Windsor Castle had enclosed and directed it to Lord *How*.

If it had been disregarded, and had thus remained unanswered, what an outcry there would have been of neglect, insult, and so forth—and not unjustly.

Ever affectionately yours,
My dear Croker,
ROBERT PEEL.

CHAPTER XXII.

1841–1842.

Fall of Lord Melbourne's Administration—Dissolution of Parliament—Great Tory Gains in the New Elections—Sir Robert Peel's Second Administration—The Corn Law Agitation—Peel's Sliding Scale—His Account of the Debates upon it—Foreshadows a Tax upon Property—The Income Tax imposed in 1842—Mr. Croker again defends Peel's Policy—Peel on the Necessity of a Liberal Tariff—England's Commercial Policy "on its Trial"—England must be made a Cheap Country to Live in—Peel's Defence of the Income Tax—Sir James Graham on the Corn Law Agitation; and on the Local Disturbances—Sir R. Peel on High Prices and Landed Property—Public Distress at Paisley, &c.—The United States' Boundary Question—Sketch of the Dispute—The Mysterious Map—The "Strong Red Line"—Lord Ashburton's Account of the Map—His Defence of the Treaty—The Second Map—Letters from Mr. Goulburn, Lord Aberdeen, Lord Ashburton, and Sir Robert Peel—Conversations with the Duke of Wellington—Last Letters from Theodore Hook—Birth of the Prince of Wales—The Queen's Attention to Business—Remarkable Duels—Church Music—The Prime Minister in Former Times and Now—Letter from Sir R. Peel—Visit to Windsor—Peel on the "Voracity" for Titles—The "Distinction of an Unadorned Name"—The Tractarian Movement—Mr. J. G. Lockhart on the Rich and the Poor in England—Sir R. Peel on the Price of Bread—Death of Lord Hertford—His Latter Days—Mr. Croker's Account of Lord Hertford's Death—Suspicions of Lord Hertford's Insanity—The Missing Packet of 100,000 Fr.—Nicolas Suisse—Probable Nature of his Duties—Mr. Croker's Prosecution of Suisse—Suisse Retaliates—Trial and Acquittal of Suisse—Letter from Lord Hertford's Son—The Attacks on Mr. Croker by Macaulay—Their Manifest Injustice—Mr. Croker's Character in Private Life—Slanders published since his Death.

It is to be regretted that the greater part of Mr Croker's letters for these two years is missing. Some few notes of a private or business character were found after diligent search, but comparatively little of public interest was left relating to 1841. This is the more unfortunate from the fact that 1841 was a year of some importance in politics; the Corn Law agitation began to show signs of greater vitality than heretofore, the Government had become unpopular, and Sir Robert Peel saw, in the month of May, that the moment had come for dealing it a fatal blow. He brought forward a direct motion of want of confidence, and it was carried, on the 4th of June, by a majority of one vote; the defeated Ministers advised a dissolution, and the new elections were held in the midst of great excitement. The famous big loaf and the little loaf made their appearance, apparently for the first time, at least in election contests; but the effect produced was not so great as had been expected, even Lord John Russell, who was identified with the big loaf, barely escaping defeat in the City of London. Two of the Whig seats were lost, and Lord John was at the bottom of the poll. The total gain of the Tories was reckoned at eighty votes on a division.

Lord Melbourne had now no alternative but to resign, and Sir Robert Peel was called upon to form his second administration. Lord Stanley and Sir James Graham joined him, and Mr. Gladstone accepted office as Vice-President of the Board of Trade, afterwards becoming President, as successor to Lord Ripon. Mr. Gladstone, in his address seeking re-election at Newark, declared that the British farmer might rely upon two points: "first, that adequate protection would be given to him;" secondly, "that protection would be given him through the means of the sliding scale." The principle of the Melbourne Government, it is scarcely necessary to say, had been that of a fixed duty of 8s. on corn ; and the question of a total repeal of the Corn Laws was not first brought forward by a recognised leader on either side, nor by Mr. Cobden, who sat for Stockport, but by Mr. Villiers, whose name has almost slipped out of later histories of the Free Trade controversy.

As the new Parliament did not meet till September, 1841, no step could be taken either in reference to this or any other important question; but during the winter the great struggle between Protection and Free Trade was continued throughout the country, and Sir Robert Peel saw that no time was to be lost in endeavouring to devise terms of settlement which might be satisfactory alike to the agricultural and manufacturing classes.* As soon as possible after the opening of Parliament in 1842, on the 9th of February, he brought forward propositions, which comprehended a sliding scale varying with the price of wheat, but involving also a substantial diminution of the duty. Thus he found a duty of 27s. 8d. on corn, when it was at 59s. and under 60s. the quarter; he proposed to make it 13s. At 50s. the duty was 36s. 8d.; he proposed to reduce it to 20s. He laid much stress upon the importance of deriving the "main sources" of the supply of corn from "domestic agriculture," and he expressed the hope that England would "in the average of years," be able to produce a sufficiency of wheat "for its own necessities." It is needless now to point out how delusive was this hope. England does not grow much more than a third of the quantity of wheat which it requires for its "own domestic necessities."

Mr. Cobden protested against the scheme, which merely professed to be a revision of the Corn Laws of 1828, as "an insult to the Government," and Mr. Villiers brought forward his motion for immediate repeal. But there were only 90 votes for Mr. Villiers, and 393 against him, while a proposal to make an increase in the duties, proposed by the Ministry,

* "The great question of Protection and Free Trade was at no time really a question between the Conservative and the Liberal parties." These are the words of a very high authority, in the *Quarterly Review*, vol. 99, p. 502.

encountered a defeat equally decisive, though not so large. The Bill was passed through both Houses before the end of the first week in April.

During the progress of the debates, Sir Robert Peel and Mr. Croker were in frequent correspondence, but, as it has just been stated, none of Mr. Croker's letters can be recovered. In February, 1842, after Lord John Russell had moved an amendment to the Ministerial measure, condemning the principle of a sliding scale, Sir Robert Peel addressed the following to Mr. Croker:—

Whitehall, February 21st, 1842.

MY DEAR CROKER,

The debate on Villiers' motion has been hitherto unexpectedly flat. I attribute this to two causes: first, the failure of the Anti-Corn Law League to get up much excitement, excepting in the cotton manufacturing districts; secondly, to the mistake of the Corn Law Repealers in permitting Lord John Russell to invert the natural order of proceedings, and take the discussion on his motion, which (coupled with the known sentiments and with the speech of the mover), implied a duty on corn, before the debate on the question whether there should or should not be any duty whatever.

The Repealers were in an uneasy position during the whole of the first debate, and they could only relieve themselves from it (as Roebuck did) by anticipating the discussion on their own motion.

Our measure is taken very well upon the whole, much better than any one could, *à priori*, have anticipated.

The true line for the *Quarterly* to take is to dwell upon the enormous difficulties to which we have succeeded; to show that the Whigs attempted nothing for the furtherance of the principles they profess, until they were *in extremis*, and then they did what they could to embarrass. They were hanged, like Charteris, for offences which they could not commit. Either they had in 1835, 6, 7, and 8, the confidence of Parliament and the country, or they had not. If they had, why did not they review the commercial, legislative and financial position of the country?

If they had not, why did they drag on, not for months, but for years, a miserable existence, powerless for any good purpose?

What excuse have they to offer for trying their miserable

expedients of 5 per cent. on Custom duties, and 10 per cent. on Assessed Taxes?

When they remitted the Post Office Revenue, they made Parliament promise to repair the deficiency, if there were one; and the promise has never been redeemed.

Their whole financial policy may be summed up in one sentence.

They burned the candle at both ends, increasing expenditure and diminishing revenue. Their policy here has been faithfully copied in India. They began with a surplus; they ended with a frightful deficiency.

My own private opinion is that the country is in that state, that the property of the country must submit to taxation, in order to release industry and the millions from it; that the doing so voluntarily and with a good grace, will be a cheap purchase of future security.

Three *good* appointments in the English Church, indicating the sense of the Government, would do more to allay the fever of Puseyism, than 3000 controversial tracts with a Chillingworth for the author of each of them.

The sense of the Government must be marked in favour of that which is reasonable and just; in favour of Church of England Protestant principles, as they have been understood for the last hundred years, the *via media* between Popery and Dissent.

I suppose it must have been beautiful weather by this glimpse of the sun which I sometimes catch. I wish they would give me a ten hours' bill.

Ever affectionately yours,
ROBERT PEEL.

In this letter it will be seen that the Prime Minister makes an allusion to the necessity of placing a tax upon property, and this idea he carried out in his Budget—introduced on the 11th of March, 1842—by proposing a tax of seven-pence in the pound on incomes of 150*l*. and upwards, limited in duration to three years, with the power reserved of extending it to five years. The duties on various articles entering into British manufactures were reduced; the timber duties were brought down to 25*s*. a load, and Canadian timber to 1*s*. a load. The Prime Minister was still dissatisfied with the amended tariff, believing that it ought to be carried much further in the direction of concession. It seems to be evident, indeed, from his letters, that his mind was working slowly round towards moderate free trade principles, although it is equally clear from the support which Mr. Croker consistently extended to him that his intimate friends did not realise the truth. In September, 1842, there appeared an article in the *Quarterly Review*, by Mr. Croker, vigorously defending the whole "Policy of Sir Robert Peel," including the income tax. But it was assumed that the tax could and would be remitted at the end of three or five years "without any derangement of other interests." Mr. Croker was disposed to regard the income tax as in the "nature of a temporary advance, made by wealthy capitalists to relieve and facilitate certain branches of industry, which, though now suffering, will by this timely assistance be enabled to recover themselves, and to repay at no long interval, their debt to the general fund." In a word, Mr. Croker still retained that unbounded faith in Sir Robert Peel which has been shown throughout this correspondence, from the early days of Peel's career, when scarcely anybody else reposed any confidence whatever in him. He therefore accepted Peel's own views, however much they may at times have startled him. As for the belief of both Peel and Mr. Croker that the income tax could easily be done away with in the course of a few years, no comments can be necessary.

Sir Robert Peel to Mr. Croker.

Whitehall, July 27th, 1842.

My dear Croker,

I can assure you that the difficulty will be to prove that we have gone far enough *in concession*—that is, relaxation of prohibitions and protections—not that we have gone too far. Something effectual must be done to revive, and revive permanently, the languishing commerce and languishing manufacturing industry of this country.

France, Belgium, and Germany are closing their doors upon us.

Look at the state of society in this country; the congregation of manufacturing masses; the amount of our debt; the rapid increase of poor rates within the last four years, which will soon, by means of rates in aid, extend from the mixed manufacturing districts to the rural ones, and then judge whether we can with safety retrograde in manufactures.

The declared value of the exports of cotton manufacture fell off above a million last year, compared with the former. Seventeen millions in 1840; sixteen millions in 1841. If you had to constitute new societies, you might on moral and social grounds prefer corn fields to cotton factories; an agricultural to a manufacturing population. But our lot is cast; we cannot change it and we cannot recede. The tariff does not go half far enough in the direction in which it does go. If we could afford it, we ought to take off the duty on cotton wool, and the duty on foreign sheep's wool.

I repeat that the man who pays £2 18s. per cent. on his income, may make that saving in his expenditure in consequence of the tariff.

I am confident of it, and yet in the same breath I say to the agriculturists, Your apprehensions about fat pigs and fat cattle from Hamburgh are absurd. There will be no reduction in the price of meat or cattle which need terrify you.

Where is the inconsistency of this?

I never said to the consumer, you will save three per cent. a year expenditure by the reduction of the price of meat. I said to him, and said most truly: By the reduction in the price of timber, of coffee, of fish, of oil, of all articles of furniture, of corn, of everything in short which you consume, there will be a saving of three per cent. There may be a saving of 1d. a pound in the price of fresh meat (I sincerely hope there may). There will be *a guarantee* that meat shall not be at an extravagant price of tenpence or a shilling a pound.

Ham and bacon will be reduced in price. But if there is no reduction in the price of beef and mutton, the calculation of 3 per cent. saving in expenditure will remain unaffected.

When farmers were stupidly selling their stock at 30 per cent. abatement, and were whimpering over advertisements offering fresh meat from Hamburgh at 3d. a pound, which ment costs 5½*d.* in the Hamburgh market, I said the alarm is groundless, you, the farmers, will receive no such injury as you stand in dread of. But again I say, where is the delusion or inconsistency in this language, compared with my promise of general reduction in the cost of living?

I have made no abatement in the Tariff or in the Corn Law in deference to repealers of the Corn Laws. There is nothing I have proposed which is not in conformity with my own convictions. I should rather say, 1 have not gone, in any one case, beyond my own convictions *on the side of relaxation.*

Experience will prove that nothing but good will result from the extent of relaxation.

Ever affectionately yours,

ROBERT PEEL.

The Income Tax and Tariff Bills were passed through both houses before the end of June, but the prospects of the Ministry were darkened by the distress which continued to increase throughout the country, especially in the manufacturing districts. The Free Traders began to talk of using "force" as a "remedy," and bitter attacks were made in all directions upon Sir Robert Peel. Some of the conditions in this grave state of affairs are touched upon in the next letters, and Peel expresses many striking views on principles much discussed in his own day and at a later period.

Sir Robert Peel to Mr. Croker.

Whitehall, August 3rd, 1842.

MY DEAR CROKER,

I hardly know what to send you in respect of the tariff and our commercial policy.

They are on trial, and a much more satisfactory judgment will be formed in respect to them from facts which must be known a short time hence, than from *à priori* reasonings.

1 have taken from the papers of this day the enclosed paragraphs.

They are very important as indications of *improvement.*

Without improvement we are on the brink of convulsion, or something very like it.

For thirty weeks in succession, not less than 10,000 human beings on the average have been supported in one town—*Paisley*—on charity.

Some decisive effort was necessary to terminate, if possible, such a state of things.

The new Corn Law has, so far as we have had experience (but the experience is too short to enable us to judge satisfactorily), worked well.

There has been a *weekly* import of foreign corn since it passed, and a weekly payment of duties on taking out the foreign corn for home consumption.

The trade, foreign and retail, has been steady and regular.

The duty will not fall below eight shillings, and very probably we shall receive 600,000*l*. or 700,000*l*. of revenue during the quarter for corn.

I heard a great corn merchant make a bet last night in the lobby of the House of Commons that, before the 1st of November next, the weekly average of wheat would be so low as forty-five shillings a quarter.

He repeated the bet once made.

Three months hence we shall see the working of the law, the effect on the American market, and many other particulars which will determine its character and probable permanent operation and tendencies.

The Anti-Corn Law League determined, as soon as we had passed our financial and commercial measures, to make one desperate effort at the close of the session to bully us into further alteration of the law.

Hence the deputations and interviews; the system of lecturing; the gross exaggerations; the detail of individual cases of suffering; exhuming buried cows, &c. See the circular of the 1st of August: the observations on the falling off of the receipts of railroads as an evidence of depression.

We must make this country a *cheap* country for living, and thus induce parties to remain and settle here.

Enable them to consume more, by having more to spend.

The argument that people must pay more for the articles they consume *because* they are heavily taxed, is absurd.

If you have to pay annually sixty-four shillings a quarter for 24,000,000 quarters of wheat there is a dead loss of 12,000,000*l*. sterling annually.

Comparing the expenditure on one article with that which would be requisite were wheat at fifty-four shillings, how will that 12,000,000*l.* be employed? In consuming more barley, more wheat, more articles of agricultural produce. It is a fallacy to urge that the loss falls on the agriculturist. They too are consumers; they lose almost as much *in increased poor rates* alone, the burden of which, as they contend, falls almost exclusively on them, as they gain by increased price.

Lower the price of wheat,—not only poor rates, but the cost of everything else is lowered.

We do not push this argument to its logical consequences, namely, that wheat should be at thirty-five shillings instead of fifty or fifty-four.

We take into account vested interests, engaged capital, the importance of independent supply, the social benefits of flourishing agriculture, &c.

We find that the general welfare will be the best promoted by a fair adjustment—by allowing the legitimate logical deductions to be controlled by the thousand considerations which enter into moral and political questions, and which— as friction and the weight of the atmosphere disturb your mathematical conclusions—put a limit to the practical application of abstract reasoning.

Ever, most affectionately,

R. P.

My dear Croker,

Whitehall, Aug. 8th, 1842.

Corn Law.

Read page 48 of the enclosed. Read the whole speech if you can, as it is a sort of profession of faith, *before* the last General Election, and out of office.

Read also my speech on the first address, after the passing of the Reform Bill, when I said a new course of action must be adopted by the Conservative party, that they must govern —if they did govern—on principles in harmony with the changes in the Legislature.

Read my letter to the electors of Tamworth *before* the General Election of 1834-5, and the principles which I then avowed on entering office.

Read also the declarations I made on entering office in

August last (1841), and my declaration that I would scorn to hold it on the condition of being the mere organ of a party, or an instrument in the hands of the House of Lords, or on any other terms than those of the freest latitude, to propose what I deemed best for the public interest.

I notice the returns of contract prices for Greenwich, of meat, &c. See how the high price of necessary articles tends to increase the public burdens.

At Leicester—they had a subscription for the relief of distress; they raised about £2700; they have just invested £1200 in the funds to meet future demands, finding the distress greatly exaggerated.

Ever most faithfully,

ROBERT PEEL.

Whitehall, August 13th, 1842.

MY DEAR CROKER,

Surely you have got answers to every query you have sent me? Have you got Gladstone's detailed answer to your queries about copper ore, &c.? I sent them to you myself.

The best thing we have done, without exception, is the reduction of the duty on timber. It is confidently reported in the City, and generally believed, that I have greatly overestimated the loss to the revenue. All species of shipbuilding, all parties concerned in fisheries, all public works—piers, harbours, and coffer-dams; all public buildings, all repairs of farm-houses will be benefited by the free access to Baltic timber.

Landlords with farmhouses out of repair will save their income-tax by the reduced cost of timber for repairs.

I hope you have got the import duty report.

Hume of the Customs said, and said justly, "We have the command of coal and iron, give us the command of timber, and we have every natural advantage." See the evidence about our fisheries.

Our inability to enter into deep sea fishing in competition with other countries, from the dearness of timber and the consequent fragility of our boats.

· I was told the other day that the estimated saving on a new Conservative Club-house that is to be built at the bottom of St. James's Street is 2000*l.* from the reduced cost of timber alone.

The colonies will indeed be burdensome to us if, in addition to the cost of defending them, we are to submit to enormous burdens to encourage the consumption of their inferior timber.

Depend upon it, it admits of demonstration that, by diverting capital and enterprise from the steady encouragement of agriculture in our North American colonies to the lottery of the timber trade, we are injuring rather than benefiting them.

We are going to submit the timber-growers at home, by the removal of the duty on colonial timber, to unlimited competition with colonial growers. This for the first time, and without notice. It would be absurd if the colonial growers were to insist on *extravagant* protection from the competition of foreign growers. We give them a very high one.

The argument in respect to timber is, I assure you, conclusive. There is no one article that contributes so much to comfort and social improvement, to cheapness of production, as low price of timber.

Sir James Graham, who was Home Secretary in Sir Robert Peel's second administration, was in frequent communication with Mr. Croker on the state of the country, and supplied many of the facts which were set forth in an article on the Anti-Corn Law Agitation, published in the *Quarterly* for December, 1842. This article reviewed the history of the League down to the date of its appearance, and showed that the leaders had spent 90,000*l.* in 1841, and were then engaged in raising another 50,000*l.** The existence of such associations was denounced as " incompatible either with the internal peace and the commercial prosperity of the country " or with " the safety of the State."

Sir James Graham to Mr. Croker.

Home Office, August 20th, 1842.

MY DEAR CROKER,

Our accounts are better to-day, but the whole state of society is feverish in the extreme; and it is a social insur-

---

* The expenses of the League, as it has since been authoritatively stated, amounted to about 1000*l.* a week.

rection of a very formidable character, and well organised with forethought and ability.

I wish we could get at the authors. I by no means despair of arriving at this great object.

I am always yours very truly,
J. R. G. GRAHAM.

Whitehall, September 1st, 1842.

MY DEAR CROKER,

You are the most severe of critics, if you are not well satisfied with your own performance. I never read a more able or satisfactory article, and the case of the Government cannot be placed on stronger or safer ground. It is, in fact, a statement of the real truth, and is therefore impregnable. We are greatly indebted to you for this able and complete defence of our policy.

I shall remain here till Saturday. I hope on that day to go to Cowes, and to remain there till the following Wednesday; but my movements must depend on reports from the disturbed districts. The state of affairs is by no means satisfactory. The workmen are sullen and discontented; they return with great reluctance to their employments; they have just cause of complaint against their masters; plunder is their object, and plunder is their weapon; and a state of social disorder is advancing with fearful rapidity, for which legislation can supply no remedy, and against which force is the only safeguard. This is an unhappy view of affairs, but it is the truth.

I shall be glad to see you and to converse with you.

I am, yours sincerely,
J. R. G. GRAHAM.

Home Office, December 1st, 1842.

MY DEAR CROKER,

I congratulate you on the conclusion of your grand outline. You have extracted the marrow from the dry bones with wonderful skill, and I anticipate the best effect from this able article.

If I might advise, I should change the commencement, and begin with Lord Kinnaird, whose happy ignorance of any intention to use physical force, demonstrates the necessity of putting the unwary on their guard, and of undeceiving those who have been wilfully blind.

I shall send you to-morrow some further useful information.

Yours very truly,

J. R. G. GRAHAM.

Hill Street, December 4th, 1842.

MY DEAR CROKER,

You will have heard from Peel.

He is anxious that the last paragraph should be omitted, and he deprecates the admission that law cannot reach these proceedings, as also the threat that it may be made to do so. He thinks that you cannot end better than with the last paragraph but one, which I praised as a most effective summary of the whole case; and on reflection I am disposed to think that Peel's view is quite right. Confessions of impotence excite boldness; threats of rigour beyond the law provoke extreme violence beforehand, and if the necessity should arise, they increase the difficulty of legislation by the resistance which has been organised and prepared in consequence of the menace.

The broth is so good that all the cooks in London cannot now spoil it; and as it is a question of omitting a paragraph and not writing a new one, I more readily press on you this suggestion.*

Yours very truly,

J. R. G. GRAHAM.

[Extract.]

Hill Street, December 5th, 1842.

My confident hope, my fervent prayer, is this—that *we*, the faithful friends of the British constitution in Church and State, may be enabled boldly to do our duty in our respective conditions, and that, forgetting all past dissension and angry discord, we may join heart and hand in the defence of the

* [The suggestion was adopted by Mr. Croker.]

blessings we still enjoy, and of the form of government which the League seeks to overthrow.

I am, yours very truly,
J. R. G. GRAHAM.

Sir Robert Peel to Mr. Croker.

Drayton Manor, October 30th, 1842.

MY DEAR CROKER,

These articles in the *Presse* surprise me from the ability with which they are written, and the knowledge of the subject in detail which they evince. I am very anxious, as you justly suppose, on the subjects to which your letter* refers, but chiefly anxious on account of dangers approaching from an opposite quarter than that in which you are looking out for them.

Tell me what we are to do with the population of a town circumstanced like Paisley. The case of Paisley may be the *most* grievous one, but there are many not very dissimilar.

For the last *year*, there have been supported in that one town of Paisley, (and necessarily supported, unless you choose to run the risk of wholesale death from famine—or a frightful outbreak and desperate attack upon property,) 9000 persons, on a weekly average throughout the year, by charity, exclusive of Poor Rate. There has been an expenditure of 500*l.* a week, from voluntary, or rather forced, contributions.

This is agrarian law. The question asked in my letter from Paisley to-day is, What is to be done for the winter?

Look at the Malt Duty; look at the Sugar Duty for the last year.

The danger is not low price from the tariff, but low price from the inability to consume—from the poor man giving up his pint of beer, and the man in middling station giving up his joint of meat.

Rest assured of this, that landed property would not be safe during this next winter, with the prices of the last four years, and even if it were safe, it would not be profitable very long.

Poor Rate, rates *in aid*, diminished consumption, would soon reduce the temporary gain of a nominal high price.

The long depression of trade; the diminished consumption

* [No letter to be found.]

of articles of first necessity; the state of the manufacturing population; the instant supply by means of machinery of any occasional increased demand for manufactured goods; the tendency of reduced prices to sharpen the wits of the master-manufacturer, and to urge him on in the improvement of his machinery; the double effect on manual labour and the wages of manual labour—first, of this reduction in price, and secondly, of the attempt to counteract it by improvement in machinery; the addition that each day makes of two thousand hands to the unemployed hands of the day before. These are the things about which I am more anxious than about the cattle from Vigo, or the price of pork. Go to the Lothians, and see what skill and industry can do there in the improved culture of the earth. The same things may be done here, and must be done here. If people will grow more weeds than corn, they cannot prosper; but there is a remedy for this by following the example of those who contrive to grow corn instead of weeds, and who have found out that cattle half-frozen to death by cold, will not fatten so fast as those that are kept warm; but where is the remedy for the other evils.

Whether low prices will be an effectual one I cannot foretell. But this I am sure of, that they will be aggravated to a frightful and unbearable extent by continued high prices.

Ever affectionately yours,
ROBERT PEEL.

Whitehall, December 4th, 1842.

MY DEAR CROKER,

I think this is excellent.*

But I was in hopes you would have overwhelmed Lord Kinnaird with ridicule for his letter complaining of the tariff for having *reduced prices.* Do read it with this view. His lamentations over his "lot of Highland wethers which will not pay the summer's keep."

This fellow complains of *hay being reduced from* 1s. 2d. to 9d. a stone.

Above all read this, and flesh and blood will surely not resist the temptation to an addition to your article, to an embalmment of Lord Kinnaird's letter.

* [Referring to a proof of the article above referred to, on the Anti-Corn Law agitation.]

But what is the state of the linen trade in Dundee?

Somewhat better, but only because there has been a demand for *sacks* on account of the abundant harvest.

Show that if you touch these aristocratic leaguers by reducing the price of provisions, and make them lose 14s. on their lot of wethers, they 'are just as clamorous as if you were extracting their heart's blood.

When the Anti-Corn Law manufacturer scents from afar a reduction of the price of corn he reduces his wages, and the Anti-Corn Law lord abuses the tariff for reducing the price of meat.

Ever affectionately yours,

R. P.

There was still another difficult and intricate public question upon which Mr. Croker wrote much at this period, and that was the famous North-East Boundary question, which more than once had threatened to bring about a war between England and the United States. The dispute chiefly affected the interests of the States of Massachusetts and Maine on the one side, and of a part of Canada on the other. It had been carried on at various times, and under various forms, ever since the acknowledgment of the independence of the United States by Great Britain under the Treaty of 1783. The loose nomenclature adopted in that Treaty, in the attempt to define the boundaries of the United States and British possessions, was the cause of all the subsequent bickerings and angry feeling. The "north-west angle" of Nova Scotia was referred to, but there was ample room for endless difference of opinion as to what *was* the north-west angle; the "highlands" which divide certain rivers were mentioned, but no one could decide where they were. In 1833 the arbitration of the King of Holland was sought, and the decision—as usual in foreign arbitrations—went much against England. About two-thirds of the disputed territory were given to the United States. Yet England would have considered herself bound by the award, had not the United States rejected it. The people of Maine thought that as so much had been conceded to them, they might, by dint of pertinacity, obtain the whole, and therefore the compromise was refused. More years elapsed, and gradually the Americans pushed out their settlements to the very verge of the debateable country, the British colonists threatened reprisals, and the dispute once more became dangerous. At last, in 1842, Lord Ashburton was requested to go to Washington, for the purpose of making a new Treaty, and he succeeded in his mission, so far as signing a Treaty was concerned; but to this hour the people on the Canadian side consider that Lord Ashburton permitted himself to be duped, and that their interests were in consequence mercilessly sacrificed. There were stories of spurious maps and false boundary lines, and for many years there was a large party in England, as well as in the colonies, in which the deepest anger could be stirred by the mere mention of the "Ashburton capitulation." To Mr. Croker, however, the new Treaty appeared a reasonable and fair solution of the problem, and he defended it with the zeal which never failed to animate him when he believed that he was right. Seven-twelfths of the territory were given to the United States, and the remaining five-twelfths to Great Britain.

The story of the map appeared in a score of different shapes at the time, and in itself it was very curious. Before Lord Ashburton arrived at Washington, a map of the whole region in dispute was discovered by Mr. Jared Sparks at Paris, and upon this map Benjamin Franklin had marked with "a strong red line" the boundaries of the United States as fixed by the Treaty of 1783. This line indicated precisely the boundary originally claimed by Great Britain—running south of the St. John's River, and between its head waters and those of the Penobscot and the Kennebec. It gave *all* the "no man's land" to Great Britain. "It is evident," wrote Mr. Sparks, "that the line, from the St. Croix to the Canadian highlands, is intended to exclude all the waters running into the St. John's." The difference to the colonies was immense; but the American negotiators kept the map under lock and key, and Lord Ashburton was not allowed to see either that or Mr. Jared Sparks's letter. The Americans yielded a little of their claims, and thus got the credit with the public of acting with generosity; Great Britain thought she had made a good bargain by surrendering seven-twelfths of the territories which she would have obtained had the map been produced. When the facts became known in England, it did not tend to increase the public satisfaction with the Ashburton Treaty; and as to the feeling stirred up in Canada, readers of Judge Haliburton's works may still be able to form some faint idea of it, although he dealt with the subject only from the light and humorous point of view. Even now it would be hard to persuade an old Provincial that the Ashburton Treaty was not one of the most unjust agreements ever entered into between two great powers.

The British Government, it must be added, caused a search to be instituted at Paris for Franklin's map. Strange to say, *that* map was not found, but another was, on which a thick red line had been traced, giving all the disputed territory to the United States. This was, indeed, an "extraordinary coincidence," and to this day it has never been explained.

This brief summary of the question may be necessary to make clear to some readers certain portions of the following correspondence.

Mr. Goulburn* to Mr. Croker.

Albemarle Street. (Monday Morning.) [Without date.]

MY DEAR CROKER,

On looking over my Parliamentary papers I do not find that we ever printed the statements submitted by England and America respectively to the King of the Netherlands, and yet I have a recollection of having seen them. They were probably printed in the Foreign Office. If I can find out I will let you know more precisely.

The difficulty in the way of our view of the North American boundary, is undoubtedly the definition of the north-west angle of Nova Scotia, which was made by the Commissioners under the Convention with America of 1794. That point, in consequence of taking the wrong branch of the St. Croix as our guide, was fixed too far to the eastward. It is a serious question whether after the Convention of 1794 we are at liberty to change that point. I am not satisfied with the reasons given by Messrs. Mudge and Fetherstonhaugh in favour of doing so. But after carefully reading the article in the Treaty of Ghent and the Convention of 1794, I am rather inclined to the opinion that the words of the former imply the previous settlement of the north-western angle of Nova Scotia, and therefore view it as a matter no longer in dispute. But this is a hasty opinion, by which I should not wish to be definitively bound. It is, however, as you observe, the really pinching part of our case.

'Yours ever, my dear Croker, most affectionately,

HENRY GOULBURN.

Albemarle Street. (Friday.) [Without date.]

MY DEAR CROKER,

I am afraid I cannot give you a very satisfactory answer to your inquiries, but such as I can give you shall have. The Treaty of 1783 undoubtedly speaks loosely as to the north-west angle of Nova Scotia, but it does so because both parties to that Treaty conceived that there was a distinct line of highlands running east and west, and when they talked of "an

---

* [At this time Chancellor of the Exchequer.]

angle formed by a line to the highlands and along the said highlands," they meant that a line drawn as described would make an angle at the intersection of the due north line and the said highlands, which angle would be taken as the northwest angle of Nova Scotia. The Plenipotentiaries wished to fix what was before doubtful, the north-west angle of Nova Scotia, and they determined that it should be where the due north line intersected the supposed highlands.

The statements submitted to the King of the Netherlands on behalf of Great Britain and the United States, were never laid either before Parliament or Congress, and are therefore only to be got from the Foreign Office, where I have no access. I asked Palmerston, whom I met incidentally, why they had been kept back from Parliament, and he answered that he thought of presenting them, but as in some parts they appeared to take a ground different from that subsequently taken, he had thought better of it.

I cannot find the names of the Commissioners who settled the source of the St. Croix wrong. In those days papers were not profusely lavished on Parliament, and nothing is to be found in our Journals or papers respecting their decision.

Yours ever, my dear Croker, most truly,

HENRY GOULBURN.

Lord Ashburton to Mr. Croker. Extract.

The Grange, November 25th, 1842.

Upon the defence of my treaty I am very stout and fearless, and they who do not like it may kill the next Hotspur themselves. It is a subject upon which little enthusiasm can be expected. The truth is that our cousin Jonathan is an offensive, arrogant fellow in his manner, and is well represented in the swagger of the enclosed speech. By nearly all our people he is therefore hated, and a treaty of conciliation with such a fellow, however considered by prudence or policy to be necessary, can in no case be very popular with the multitude. Even my own friends and masters who employed me are somewhat afraid of showing too much satisfaction with what they do not hesitate to approve.

Leaving Maine and its boundaries for the county of Hampshire, I congratulate you on having pitched your tent there.

I dare say your little farm is worth the whole pine swamp I have been discussing. If you think well of your purchase do not let your treaty linger, but strike at once and put it in black on white. At the present price of stock there should be an abundance of purchasers of land at the rate you mention. I fear we shall not get to Bay House * this autumn. Stewart writes that the rain beats in worse than ever, and I have written to Burton to say that he should understand these miseries, but if there is no cure for them I must pull the house down. If I did not make to myself a rule never to lose my temper about anything, this would much provoke me. I suppose we shall therefore be fixtures here, and by-and-by I hope we shall see you when you are less in demand, if that ever happens. At the present moment I am suffering the torment of sitting for my picture to a very clever American artist, for my co-capitulator Daniel Webster. We agreed to exchange phizzes with the ratified treaties.

Ever my dear Croker, yours,

A.

The Earl of Aberdeen † to Mr. Croker.

Ury House, February 25th, 1843.

MY DEAR CROKER,

I ought to have written to you before, and I suppose it is now too late to do so, but I will answer your question at a venture, although I hope to have the opportunity of talking the matter over with you at Peel's to-morrow.

1. Your first question is the Dutch award. I answer that it was an honest judgment. It was unfavourable to us, but it proceeded on the principle on which almost all arbitrations are conducted, viz., that of mutual concession. The territory in dispute was not very unequally divided between us. So far from the decision of the King being fairly attributable to any feelings of resentment, in consequence of our political conduct in the Netherlands, the Americans rejected it because he was so notoriously under our influence, and because he had lost his independence with the loss of Belgium.

2. You next inquire about Livingston's proposal.‡ Palmer-

---

* [At Alverstoke. "Burton" was Decimus Burton, the architect.]

† [At that time Foreign Secretary.]

‡ [Mr. Livingston was then the Secretary of State in General Jackson's

ston delayed to notice it for eight or nine months, as far as I can learn, for no particular reason at all. This is the opinion in the office.

When he did reject it, he gave a very bad reason for doing so, when he required the previous assent of Maine. This was the business of the Central Government, and not ours. If we had the Government at Washington committed to the principle, this quarrel with the State of Maine was of no consequence to us; and, indeed, ought rather to have been encouraged.

But I do not think Palmerston was so very wrong in rejecting Livingston's proposal. There is no doubt that he would have carried his N. W. line across the St. John's until he found the highlands, which, according to his interpretation of the Treaty, could only be to the north of the St. John. No doubt, had he diverged from the due north line, he would have found highlands to the south of the St. John; but he would have said that these did not fulfil the conditions of the Treaty of dividing waters, &c., &c.

Ashburton was not instructed to renew Livingston's proposal; but on the contrary, to give no encouragement to it, if it should be reproduced.

3. You must know by this time why I expressed myself greatly dissatisfied with the message of the President. The manner in which he treated the subject of the Right of Search was really scandalous. His mention of the Oregon question was also most uncandid. When he talked of pressing us to enter into negociation, he had in his pocket a most friendly overture from us, which he had already answered favourably.

Ashburton had full instructions upon this subject, and if he had remained long enough in the United States, I have no doubt that it would have been settled. But the pressing

---

Cabinet. He proposed that a scientific survey of the disputed country should be made, and that from the "highlands," when found, a line should be drawn straight to the head of the St. Croix, and that this should be regarded as the north-eastern boundary of the United States. This proposition, it was generally admitted, would have given the whole or the greater part of the disputed territory to England. But Lord Palmerston first "pigeon-holed" it for some months, and then saddled it with conditions which made it impossible for the United States to accept it. This was universally considered a great mistake on the part of England.]

affairs being brought to a close, he was naturally desirous of returning home.

4. I think we have no strict *public right* to complain of Webster in the affair of Franklin's Map. It was most fortunate that it was not discovered by us before the Treaty was concluded; for it might not have been easy for us to proceed, with such evidence in our possession. We must have gone to an arbitration, before the end of which war would probably have ensued. Convincing as the letter and map must be to any impartial man, they have not convinced the Americans, who still maintain their line of boundary in spite of them.

Although we cannot complain of Webster so as to vitiate the agreement, it is a piece of concealment, and of disingenuousness, which must inevitably produce an unfavourable impression against him in all honourable minds.

It is a strange thing that neither letter nor map are to be found at Paris; at least we have hitherto failed in doing so. But we have found *another map* altogether in favour of the American claim. I will tell you the particulars of this curious affair when we meet to-morrow.

Ever most sincerely yours,

ABERDEEN.

Lord Ashburton to Mr. Croker. Extract.

Bath House, February 7th, 1843.

MY DEAR CROKER,

The story of the map is undeniable, and has, I believe, been truly told. I shall have much to say about it when I see you, but it is rather an extensive subject to write about, and in some respects rather a delicate one. Jared Sparks, the American historian, rummaging in the archives of the French Foreign Office, first found the letter from Franklin to Vergennes referring to the map, which he instantly searched for and found in the midst of copies, maps, and charts at the depôt of the office, and, though not doubting that he should find the American case confirmed, to his inexpressible surprise he found the precise contrary. The map was, it seems, used to persuade Maine to yield, and subsequently to persuade the Senate to ratify my capitulation. Mr. Rivers, the Reporter of the Committee of the Senate to which the Treaty was referred, reports that the Committee were unanimously of opinion that the American right was not shaken by this discovery, but nevertheless give their opinion that it would not be safe to go to a new arbitration with such a document against them. The truth is, that *probably* but for this discovery there would have been no treaty, and if the secret had been known to me earlier I could not have signed it. "Ainsi tout est pour le mieux dans le meilleur des mondes possibles." The public are very busy with the question whether Webster was bound in honour to damage his own case by telling all. I have put this to the consciences of old diplomatists without getting a satisfactory answer. My own opinion is, that in this respect no reproach can fairly be made, but the conduct of both President and Secretary is most extraordinary in the other matters relating to my treaty.

Lord Ashburton to Mr. Croker. Extract.

Piccadilly, February 13th, 1843.

With respect to myself, I was clearly acting under such instructions, and with such lights, as my masters could furnish me. If there be blame it is with Palmerston and Co., who looked everywhere for evidence but in the quarter where it was to be found. Large expenses were incurred; commissions established; engineers went out to measure the hills and the valleys of the country for facts of very small importance to the matter in issue, while the very obvious places of inquiry were neglected—left to be accidentally explored by the historian who was searching for other things. I think my responsibility in this matter stands quite clear. But how stands Webster's case? Was he bound to show up and damage his own position? I think not; and when I interrogate on this subject experienced diplomatists, though they make answer somewhat partaking of their character of diplomatists, I rather collect that they are of the same opinion. The only doubt I have surmised is whether Webster did not make something of a personal pledge of opinion as to the intentions of the parties. I can find nothing of the sort; and in conclusion, if I am called upon to say anything in the Lords, it will be in favour of my collaborator on this point. I think him the more justified because the map, though a *very* strong evidence of the intentions of the American negotiators, is by no means conclusive on the whole scope of the argument. The evidence of intention, as understood by Franklin, seems hardly to be denied, but I must say that it is still a mystery to me how such common sense men as they were, and more especially Jay, could think those intentions answered by the words of the Treaty. It is true that they left unascertained what was the *true* St. Croix, whereas our position *now* is unfortunately different. We have determined by treaty which is the St. Croix, or by a second solemn agreement, which is the *head* of that St. Croix. A monument is there set up by common consent; from that we cannot budge, and it would seem that we have nothing to do but to run our line north until we find lands turning their waters into the St. Lawrence. This would be the American argument against alleged *intentions*. Intentions directly at variance with plain facts are inadmissible in argument. If the counties of Surrey and Middlesex were declared to be divided by the Thames, no map showing intentions to the contrary would be for a moment listened to.

Sir Robert Peel to Mr. Croker. Extract.

Whitehall, February 23rd, 1843.

MY DEAR CROKER,

I did all I could to persuade Lord Ashburton that unusual and extravagant reward for the Treaty would be injurious to him, to us, and to the country; to the country as showing misplaced exultation on account of our differences, or rather, some of our differences with the United States having been terminated.

If I had been an intimate bosom friend of Lord Ashburton, or if I had not stood in a situation which made my advice as to public honours have the appearance of interested advice, I should have strongly recommended Lord Ashburton to refuse any mark of royal favour on account of the treaty, and to have reserved for himself the enjoyment of the consciousness that he had sacrificed his ease for the public service, without looking to reward and without accepting it.

Do nothing and say nothing at present about the Treaty. So far as any Paris map is concerned, we are in the crisis of inquiry, and the *present* state of it is extraordinary.

Canning was at Paris in 1826, made search for documents relating to the boundary and Treaty of 1783; could find nothing.

Bulwer can find no trace of a letter from Franklin; no trace of the map mentioned by Jared Sparks. But strange to say, he does find a map, of which he sent us the tracing; a map apparently deposited many years since, which follows exactly with a crimson line, the boundary claimed by the United States!!

Jared Sparks cannot have lied so enormously as this discovery would imply.

Notwithstanding the failure to find it, there must, I think, be a letter from Franklin and a map just as Sparks describes. I tell you all I know at present. Bulwer is a very clever fellow, with great experience in such matters as that which he has been investigating. He writes two letters; one after a short interval; and in the second as well as the first, says he cannot confirm the alleged discoveries of Jared Sparks.

Ever affectionately yours,
ROBERT PEEL.

It is now necessary to return to the general notes and correspondence of these two years:—

From Mr. Croker's Note Book.

Saturday, 30th Jan., 1841.—Called on the Duke of Wellington, whom I had not seen for some time, though I had been in communication with him. His looks were better than when I had seen him last, and his voice and manner very clear and firm. The only symptom that I could see of age or anything like infirmity about him, was the kind of exaggeration with which he stated his perfection of health.

"You know," he said, "I have never been well since that fellow poured liquid fire into my ear, and electricized not only the nerves of the ear, but all the adjacent parts, and the injury extended in all directions, sometimes to the head and then down to the stomach, then to the shoulders, and then back again to the head, and so on; but I outlived it, and have, in fact, worn it out, and I am now, thank God, as well as ever I was, and in all respects. I eat as well, I sleep as well, I walk and ride as well, I hunt and shoot as well as I have done these twenty years." He *fears*, as I do, that the Whigs must go out. Still agreeing that we know not how difficult, how impossible, it will be found to carry on the Government with the reformed House of Commons. "The Whigs, with the help of the Tories, can hardly govern the country. What will it be when the Tories have to make the attempt with a fiery opposition."

I hear that even his particular friends who have any business with him, begin to find the Duke restless and excitable. I daresay it is so, for he seemed profoundly sensitive as to the public prospects, and I observed that while conversing he walked more about the room than he was used to do. He wants just three months of being seventy-two—the only fact which he seems practically to forget.

Strathfieldsaye, 16th April, 1841.—The Duke.—Charles X. was a repetition of James II., as Louis XVIII. had some resemblance to Charles II.

Ashburton.—Who never said a foolish thing or did a wise one.

The Duke.—That is not quite true of Louis, for he acted prudently on many occasions.

Ashburton.—Then Louis Philippe is much in the same position as King William, and is just as dissatisfied with the "principles that placed him on the throne" as William was.

Croker.—Yes, and talks, we hear, as William used to do, of *abdication.*

Ashburton.—William said to Wharton, "After all, I see the Tories are the only party to make a King comfortable in this country." "Yes," replied the other, "but your Majesty must recollect that you are not the *Tory King.*"

Croker.—And when you recollect how close the execution of Charles I. and of Louis XVI., and the intermediate usurpation of Cromwell and Buonaparte seem—the whole parallel—it is certainly a most striking similarity, not to say identity, of events and characters.

The Duke.—Because it is human nature. Human interests and passions will be always the same, and, on the large scale, will always produce like general results; but certainly the resemblance between the personal characters of James II. and Charles X., particularly in their bigotry, was remarkable.

Theodore Hook to Mr. Croker.*

[No date, but marked by Mr. Croker "Answered March 21st, '41."]

Fulham. (Saturday.)

The very sight of your writing, my dear Sir, does me good. Here I am still in my armed chair, having been during the last fourteen weeks three times out of my house—once to call at Dorchester House, once to dine with Sir Francis Burdett, and once on unavoidable business, all of which days were mild and moist. I have by reducing myself to this state of chrysalism, quite escaped cough, and hope now to act butterfly upon the large scale.

In *re* Townshend. I had a long talk with Bentley, who, moderate as the terms were, declined, because, as he told me, much to my surprise, he has experienced a very heavy loss by his Walpole Letters. Colburn, I have little doubt, when I can make him clearly comprehend who Lord Townshend was, will be glad to do them, and I will send to him on Monday about them. The terms you mentioned were fifty guineas for copyright (100*l.* being asked), with your kind help I might for my name get the other 50*l.*, unless you would put your own, in which case my part would be only that of master of the ceremonies to introduce Mr. Townshend to Mr. Colburn. I name no one, but a very popular publisher declined publishing—the book was offered him *gratuitously*—a collection of 'William Spencer's Poems,' with a short memoir of him, and which has already been printed and privately circulated—because, he assured me, that all the later editions of his works, whether expurgated, modernised, or in their original state had failed. *Spencer* pro *Spenser*—perhaps the same Mæcenas might without explanation mistake our statesman for the late highly-respectable Bow Street officer. I return, as you desire, the Babylonian brick.

I hope and trust that you all are well, and that dear Mrs. Barrow is out and about again. I conclude Alverbank is concluded; although the long frost must have much retarded your progress.

Believe me, dear Sir, yours faithfully,

T. H.

* [Theodore Hook died on the 24th of August, 1841, in his fifty-third year. The letter to Mrs. Croker, dated the 12th of August, is probably the last he ever wrote.]

Fulham (Thursday), [August (?) 1841].

Many thanks, my dear Sir, for your kind note, and the kind invitation it contains, to accept which would be to me perfect happiness; but I have somehow worried my *small* mind into a state which has affected my once *large* body, and I am not only wholly unfit to make visits, but I do not think that I should be able to endure the journey, even by railroad. I have not been out since last Monday fortnight, and have a dread of moving hardly describable, but I think I *must* make an effort in my little carriage to call on Mrs. Croker while she is at Kensington.

T. H.

To Mrs. Croker.

Fulham (Thursday), August 12th, 1841.

MY DEAR MRS. CROKER,

I have each day this week tried to rally myself sufficiently to get to Kensington in my little carriage, but I am not able. From a kind invitation in Mr. Croker's last letter to me, I fancy you return to Alverbank to-morrow or Saturday, which makes me regret missing the pleasure of seeing you the more, as I fear you will be gone again. I am *exceedingly* unwell, and so weak that I can scarcely cross the room.

I hope that your travellers found benefit from their excursion. I believe *myself* past that, for I have really not the strength to move. This uncongenial wretched weather, I am told, is moreover much against invalids. However, I suppose I am mending, as I can eat three oysters for luncheon, and a little mutton broth for dinner; but for nineteen days I tasted *literally* nothing.

I write because I cannot personally present my regards and compliments to you all, but it is with great regret, for I was most anxious to see you, which, when you get away to your delightful mansion, I shall have no chance of doing. At least, I see none at present.

Do me the kindness, my dear Mrs. Croker, to remember me to all your circle, and

Believe me most truly and gratefully yours,

T. H.

Mr. Croker to Sir W. Follett.*

West Moulsey, 12th Feb. 1841.

MY DEAR FOLLETT,

I send you a few memoranda which I fear will be of little use to you. Duels are seldom matters of record, at least in such volumes as have indexes.

If you find it necessary to parry an attack on the general system of duelling, I would have you strongly to lament that the law connived at it, and that custom, stronger even than law, had so sanctioned it, that one would be dishonoured who should decline. Let the House propose and pass a distinct law against the practice, but not attempt to do it by a sidewind, against one who was a peer, and therefore in a special degree bound to stand, as *they* were all trying *him, on their honour*—against one, too, who was a soldier, and was challenged in his military character by a soldier; and finally against, not the aggressor, but the challenged.

Within the last hundred years, six persons have fought duels who have been prime ministers: Pulteney, Lord Bath, Lord Shelburn, Mr. Pitt, Mr. Fox, Mr. Canning, the Duke of Wellington—I might almost add Peel, who twice challenged —and Castlereagh, who was almost a first minister. Of late years the custom is certainly decreased, and the House of Lords has not now, I dare say, above half a dozen who have actually fought, and about as many who have been seconds.

Yours affectionately,

J. W. CROKER.

Duels of Peers.

Deaths.

Byron and Chaworth, 26th January, 1765. Byron tried.
Falkland and Powell, 17th March, 1802. Powell tried.
Camelford and Best, 10th March, 1804. Best tried.

Wounds.

Lords Paulet and Milton, 29th January, 1770. Milton wounded.

---

* [This letter relates to the trial of Lord Cardigan, in the House of Lords, for having fought a duel with Lieutenant Tuckett on the 12th of September, 1840. The trial took place on the 16th of February, 1841, and failed on a technical point raised by Sir W. Follett in behalf of his client, Lord Cardigan.]

Lords Townshend and Bellamont, 2nd February, 1773.
Bellamont wounded. Offence given while Lord-
Lieutenant of Ireland; seconds, Lord Ligonier and
Col. (afterwards Lord) Dillon.

Lord Shelburn (Lord Lansdowne's father) and Fullerton,
for words spoken in the House, 22nd March, 1780.
Shelburn wounded.

No injuries.

Duke of York and Col. Lennox, 25th May, 1789.
Duke of Norfolk and Lord Malden, 30th April, 1796.
Duke of Wellington and Lord Winchelsea.

Other remarkable duels.

Fox and Adair, 29th November, 1779. Fox wounded.
Pitt and Tierney, 27th May, 1789. Lord Harrowby
Pitt's second.
Castlereagh and Canning, 21st September, 1809. Lords
Hertford and Seaford seconds.
Sheridan and Mathews.

Sir James Graham to Mr. Croker.

Whitehall, October 29th, 1841.

MY DEAR CROKER,

It must be a Prince of Wales who so delays his coming and keeps us in such suspense.* Since Tuesday evening we have expected the summons every hour, and the doctors directed us to be prepared. The public business has not been interrupted, for Her Majesty continues to write notes, to sign her name, and to declare her pleasure with the utmost gallantry up to last night, as if nothing serious were at hand. She possesses beyond all doubt the hereditary firmness and a commanding spirit.

What a dreadful October! Your double glass will hardly have excluded the S.W. gales from your delightful cottage.

I am always, yours very truly,

J. R. G. GRAHAM.

---

* [The Prince of Wales was born on the 9th of November, 1841.]

The Rev. Samuel Wilberforce* to Mr. Croker. Extract.

Alverstoke Rectory, July 23rd, 1841.

MY DEAR SIR,

I assure you that I feel much obliged to you for the suggestions of your note, which has just reached me. So far from looking at it as any boldness, I esteem it as a very grateful mark of your interest in the service of the Church, a thing I hail in any one, and specially in the laity. I believe that I may say that I coincide in *all* your suggestions, with the one exception of that touching the *Amen*, on which I am quite undecided, and as to the variety of tunes. Your words are the substance of a lecture I gave my organist last week, ending with this charge: "Repeat the same tune for the Te Deum until all the congregation join in it"; and I added mentally, "and then you shall continue it *because* they join in it." The tune I have chosen is *Jackson in* F, one not popular with fine musicians, but one which the common ear soon catches, and which to myself and ordinary persons appears to be singularly spirited and apposite to the words. I hope before many months are past to have all the congregation joining in it. I think that an occasional trip in the performance was what threw out you, as it did me also, on Sunday last.

My dear Sir, most truly yours,

S. WILBERFORCE.

Sir Robert Peel to Mr. Croker.

Whitehall, September 20th, 1841.

MY DEAR CROKER,

I think this is excellent.† I wish you could add a paragraph to point out the difference between a Prime Minister in these days and in former times, when Newcastles and Pelhams were ministers.

That now (particularly if the minister is in the House of Commons, and if he is fit to be minister), his life is one of toil and care and drudgery. His reward is not patronage, which imposes nothing but a curse, which enables him to do

---

* [Afterwards Bishop of Oxford, and of Winchester. At this period he was incumbent of Alverstoke, where Mr. Croker had a villa.]

† [An article by Mr. Croker on "The Old and New Ministries," *Quarterly Review*, September, 1841.]

little more than make *dix mécontents et un ingrat;* not ribbons or hopes of peerage, or such trumpery distinctions,— but the means of rendering service to his country, and the hope of honourable fame.

But the man who looks to such objects and such rewards will not condescend to humiliating submissions for mere party purposes; will have neither time nor inclination to be considering how many men will support this public measure, or fly off to gratify some spite or resentment; he will do his best for the great principles that his party supported and for the public welfare, and, if obstructed, he will retire from office, but not from power; for the country will do justice to his motives, and will give him the strength which his party had denied to him.

[I came in as he was writing this, and took it away without his signing.—J. W. C.]

Sir Robert Peel to Mr. Croker. Extract.

Whitehall, November 8th, 1841.

MY DEAR CROKER,

As the man who found a piece of smooth pavement in some country town (Tamworth, it might be) walked to and fro for the purpose of enjoying the pleasure of the contrast, so I, in spite of your injunctions to the contrary, *indulge myself* in the satisfaction of answering a letter which not only does not apply for a baronetage or a peerage, but absolutely dissuades from the creation. The voracity for these things quite surprises me.

I wonder people do not begin to feel the distinction of an unadorned name.

Ever affectionately yours,

ROBERT PEEL.

The Rev. S. Wilberforce to Mr. Croker. Extract.

44, Cadogan Place, January 31st, 1842.

MY DEAR SIR

I do not know who the writer of the letter in the *Hants Standard* is;[*] but I have no doubt that I can easily learn if your curiosity outlives my stay in London. On the general

[*] [Evidently a letter had appeared in the *Hants Standard* on the Tractarian movement.]

question, I am very glad to have the expression of your opinion. It will well exhibit my own, though I never was (and if you had seen as much of the system as close at hand as I have done, you would not think that you ever were) in any degree a tractarian. It is far too cramped, and crotchetty and narrow, and dogmatic a circle for you ever to have been enticed into it. I have always been (before they were warm on the subject) a staunch Churchman. I remember refusing when an undergraduate to go to Newman's then church, because he was too low a Churchman for me. Whilst afterwards he had made such hasty strides, that one of his acts on becoming sole editor of the *British Critic*, was to cut short (in the civillest way possible to me) my future connection with it, he then making it solely tractarian in its tone, on the ground of our irreconcileable difference of views. In truth, from the very first they have been essentially non-Anglican. As they have risen into notice, and younger men have carried out their principles more fully, and their own circle has enlarged, this has become more and more clear; but it was always so. I could not find rest in the narrow views of the so-called strict Evangelicals, and clung to the Church of England, and so far fought with them, and was often classed by the low Church with them; but their hatred of the Reformation, their leaning to a visible centre of unity for the Church, the essence of Popery, their unnationality, for they can have no notion of a national life; their cramped and formal dogmatism; their fearful doctrine of sin after baptism, and many other things of the same cast, revolted me long since. Now these things are breaking out into more visible and dangerous tricks; and should they predominate would threaten all. But I have no great apprehension of this.

Ever, my dear Sir, believe me to be,

Most truly yours,

S. WILBERFORCE.

Mr. Lockhart* to Mr. Croker.

September 9th, 1842.

MY DEAR CROKER,

I have a long letter, *de omnibus rebus*, from Murray, and I enclose the last leaf, as it touches on the subject of the dis-

* [Then the editor of the *Quarterly Review.*]

turbances. After saying he agrees with the Manchester man referred to in a note of mine, which John showed you, he proceeds as you will read.

In a former page of this despatch he says he fears the *tone* of the article may be thought too laudatory, and expressing his opinion that Peel is the greatest Minister we have had, regrets that "he seems to make no allowance for those prejudices which so very naturally arise from such a thorough and sudden change in our national policy, and almost to deprecate any kind of deliberation on this subject."

I think it right that you should know what our sagacious friend thinks on these matters. As for myself, I consider party questions with little interest at present. The only one I really feel concerned about is the improvement of the condition, moral and physical, of the people. I fancy most men of my standing who are not immediately engaged in the sphere of politics, are much of the same mind. I fear there is a cancer at the bottom of our social condition, and with all respect for my betters, doubt if Ministers understand the extent of the danger, or mix enough with men of different orders to learn what is thought by those who live near to the poor.

What a wonderful political writer Southey was. On looking back now to his articles of thirty or twenty years ago, how few are there of the questions now pressing that he had not foreseen the progress of! His views were always for the paternal management of the poor people. He knew how easily they might be kept right if their hearts were appealed to by those above them.

I cannot think that this Government has taken due advantage of the opportunities they had for enlisting the *people* on their side. And on the other hand they are too likely to say, "Sufficient for the day is the evil thereof," and not provide for the certain recurrence of these disturbances.

What has come of the disbanding of the yeomanry? Wherever they had been retained, their usefulness has been conspicuous. Wherever dismissed, their loss has been, and is, felt grievously. Will the Government re-establish that force on the former scale? If not, they should abolish it wholly—for as it is, the duties thrown now and then on the poor relics are such as ought not to be imposed on a voluntary force. Wherever there are yeomanry corps, they have been kept from their farms during the harvest. Why should we not have the old local militia back. If Income-tax may be fitly imposed when peace is as perilous as war, why should not the same argument apply as to the means of security as well as the resources of finance?

These Corn-Law leaguers will, like the Chinese, learn how to fight. A little, but a little, *real* co-operation, and what force have we that could keep the peace? All young men like being trained and drilled. It is the best exercise they can have, and the most innocent amusement. It is idle to argue about the committing of *power* to the middle-classes— we have given them the political power as far as Acts of Parliament can give it. Shall we lean on *them* as to our defence, or take our chances with those who have nothing to defend?*

Ever sincerely yours,
J. G. LOCKHART.

The Rev. S. Wilberforce to Mr. Croker. Extract.

Alverstoke Rectory, October 4th, 1842.

MY DEAR FRIEND,

. . . There is one expression of your letter which makes me suspect that I did not clearly enough indicate my purpose. You speak of "Newman's last work." I meant my subject to be 'Newman's Sermons,' which have now reached to six volumes, and are rapidly leavening the clerical mind; effecting a great change, in very many respects for good, in the style of preaching; as well as reaching the lay mind in a multitude of directions from their power, their beauty, and their real excellence; but which continually *insinuate* principles, and canons of judgment which are the seeds of his whole system in the minds on which they fall.

My view was to take Newman's and some other volume of sermons, and allowing all their excellence, to point out some of the most striking of these insinuations.

I am, ever most truly yours,
S. WILBERFORCE.

* [This was a singular anticipation, as will be noticed, of the volunteer movement.]

In the following letter by Sir R. Peel there are one or two miscalculations or errors. Wheat had often been lower than 40s. a quarter in the " large towns " of the " east coast." In the very year when this letter was written (1842) it touched 83 cents a bushel, or 27s. 8d. a quarter. From 1874 to 1883, the average of *lowest* prices was about a dollar a bushel, or 33s. 4d. a quarter. Sir Robert Peel's other theory, that it would be " impossible to bring any quantity of wheat worth mentioning, and land it here for 30s.," was also fallacious. American wheat, grown immensely in excess of all possibilities of home consumption, could be landed in England, with a handsome profit, at 25s., and some estimates have assigned even a lower figure. It is doubtful whether, taking one year with another, wheat could be grown in England, to pay any profit whatever to the farmer, under from 35s. to 40s. a quarter, according to locality, the price of labour, &c. In August, 1884, new English wheat only brought from 36s. to 38s. A large harvest, therefore, no longer brings with it the great prosperity to the farmer which it once ensured, nor does it even render the bread of the poor much cheaper, the baker's prices being, as a rule, kept up without much regard to the cost of wheat.

Sir Robert Peel to Mr. Croker.

Drayton Manor, October 16th, 1842.

My dear Croker,

I quite agree with you that though we cannot directly interfere in respect to *prices*, we may ascertain and tell the truth and either shame bakers and butchers with proven reductions, or induce private individuals to supply themselves from other quarters.

Societies are in progress—self-bread-furnishing societies—which will soon tell upon bakers' charges.

Have no fear of New Orleans wheat paying a twenty-shilling duty.

Wheat, on an average of years, on the east coast of the United States, in the large towns at least, has not been less than forty shillings. It would be impossible to bring any quantity of wheat worth mentioning and land it here for thirty shillings. But to return to the price of bread.

I have desired Gladstone to ascertain the price of the 4-lb. loaf in each town from which the averages are collected. I have also desired him to ascertain whether there are public baking establishments, in which it might be clearly ascertained what quantity of bread can be made from a given quantity of flour. Having the price of the flour, it may then be determined what price the bread ought to bear—charges and fair profits being provided for.

Ever affectionately yours,
ROBERT PEEL.

A topic of a more personal kind now demands attention. The story shall be told with perfect frankness, though with all due brevity.

From 1830 to 1842, Mr. Croker had devoted a large part of his time and attention to the supervision of the management of Lord Hertford's landed estates, under the circumstances which have been described in a previous chapter. It was perfectly well known to all his friends that he performed this service without any kind of remuneration, and it was equally well known to the friends of Lord Hertford that his intention was to settle a substantial sum of money upon Mr. Croker under the provisions of his will. On the 1st of March, 1842, Lord Hertford died. The following appears to have been the last of his letters to Mr. Croker; it was found in the 1842 bundle, but it bears no date. The wild and reckless spirit of the man makes itself visible even in these few lines:—

I am pretty well, and suffer but little from the influenza, which, I suppose, I have got because I have, like everybody else *a cold*, which I suppose it is. I believe we are going to change, because they say so, but I do not know.

He was not even certain of his own movements; "they" managed everything for him. And who were "they"? The chance favourites of the moment—the parasites who lived and throve upon a diseased mind. He seldom saw any of his old friends in these last days. For some years there had been living in his house the Count and Countess Zichy; but they too had been driven away. The Countess Zichy was one of the three daughters of Lady Strachan, whose relations with Lord Hertford had long been the subject of comment. Once he decided to bequeath her a fortune, but he altered his mind, because, it appears, he disapproved of some one whom he cynically refers to as his "successor." Sir Richard Strachan, knowing all the facts, left his three daughters to the care of Lord Hertford—a strange choice of a guardian; and they lived in Lord Hertford's house till they were married. The Countess Zichy received about £100,000 under the will; the Countess Berchtholdt—another of the Strachan sisters—£80,000.; the Princess Ruffo—the third sister—£40,000. These matters will, perhaps, be best explained by Mr. Croker himself.

Mr. Croker to the King of Hanover. Extract.

March 15th, 1842.

I need not say that he had been long ailing, and that the most prominent symptom was a kind of palsy, which affected the organs both of speaking and swallowing. He had been, it seems, tired of the company of Count and Countess Zichy, whom he had brought over with him, but whose presence in his house interfered with the kind of company he liked to have sometimes to dine with him; so that when he was at all well, he went out to dine at Greenwich or Richmond with this inferior society. At last, however, he seemed resolved to lie in bed as long as the Zichys stayed, and this, and some other broad hints, induced them to go. This they did on Tuesday, the 22nd Feb. They were hardly out of the house when Lord Hertford got up, and, by a strange *inconsequence* did that which he might have just as well have done if they had stayed. He went to dine with his usual company at Richmond, where, being unexpected, there was a room without a fire, much delay, and consequently a very late return, in which he caught a severe cold, and was next day really confined to his bed, where I saw him. Finding him so unwell, I stayed and dined alone in his library; but he grew better, and I saw no immediate danger, and left town late that night (Wednesday) for Moulsey. He mended for a couple of days, and on Saturday got up, dressed, and received company in his library, but that night became so much worse, that an express was sent to me at Moulsey, and I reached him very early on Sunday morning. All this while he would not be persuaded to have a physician, being satisfied with Mr. Copeland, his old surgeon, and Mr. Fuller, his old apothecary; but on Sunday we persuaded him to allow us to call in Dr. Watson, who had formerly attended him—but in vain. The catarrh, which would have been little or nothing by itself, was too strong for organs enfeebled by palsy. He had not power to clear his chest of the phlegm, and he died at fifteen minutes past four in the afternoon of Tuesday, 1st March. The last moments were as tranquil and placid as death could be. At the last moment (which happened as he lay in a *chaise longue* in his library while they were making his bed in his bedroom), Sir George Seymour stood behind the chair, Sir Horace held his left hand, and I was on his right. Mr. Fuller also was present, and his confidential servants.

His will is curious, and even to me, though kindly considered in it, not satisfactory. His own family is mentioned rather unkindly, and little benefited. Horace* has a legacy of 8000*l.*, and Captain Meynell of 4000*l.* A considerable legacy to Sir George is revoked, and given to one Mrs. Spencer. It is one consolation that his son is his residuary legatee, but I fear he will not be so great a gainer as might have been expected, for the legacies to the Strachan family seem on the surface of the will to be very great—not much less than 250,000*l.* or 300,000*l.* As there is a good deal of intricacy in the codicils, I cannot venture to say whether some of them may not revoke others, and so diminish these enormous legacies. To me he has left three legacies of 5000*l.*, 7000*l.*

---

* [Sir Horace Seymour.]

and 9000*l*., and seems to have *intended* still more, but the codicils have not been found. He has also named me one of his executors—the others are Lord Lowther, Mr. Hopkinson, the banker, Mr. Kilderbee, De Horsey, and Captain Meynell. If all the codicils in favour of the Strachans were to be valid, Lady Strachan would have about 700*l*. a year and 10,000*l*. (a *great* reduction from what was at one time left her), the Countess Zichy would have about 100,000*l*., besides, I believe, almost as much more which she has had *de la main à la main*. Countess Berthold * seems to figure for about 80,000*l*., and Louisa, lately married in Naples to Prince Antonio Ruffo, for 40,000*l*.; but, I repeat, it is doubtful whether some of the codicils which give the details of these large sums do not contradict each other. I fear there is room for litigation. He has also given 5000*l*. and an annuity of from 1000*l*. to 1500*l*. to a Mrs. Spencer, whom he had left for some time, and who, it seems, had been a maid of Lady Strachan's before Lord H. knew this lady. He has left large, over large, legacies to his servants, unless some codicils in their favour be revoked by others; and upon the whole, I grieve to say, that it was hardly possible to have made, in every respect, a less creditable will than, if all the codicils stand, this must appear to the world to be. This sounds ungrateful, as he was so good to me, but even my own good luck cannot reconcile me to his negligence of his own family.

Among the legacies to servants referred to in the above letter, there were several to a man named Nicholas Suisse, a valet. In seven different codicils a separate sum was left for his benefit, and altogether he received upwards of 20,000*l*. It may be mentioned that Lord Hertford made numerous codicils to his will; if he found himself on a dull or rainy day in a foreign town, he seems to have amused himself by writing a codicil. A portion of one may be given as an example. It is dated at "Munich, the Inn of the Goldene Hirsch," 13th October, 1834:—

"This is a codicil to the will of me, Francis Charles Marquis of Hertford. I direct in case of my death while

---

* [The name is spelt "Berchtholdt" in the will.]

abroad with Charlotte L. Strachan [afterwards Countess Zichy] that all the transferable securities for money, cash, diamonds, and bankers' travelling notes be given to the said Charlotte L. Strachan as her property. . . . I advise Charlotte to entrust these securities, if I die abroad, with the nearest respectable banker, to be transmitted for her to Sir Coutts Trotter's house, and I warn her to beware of her mother's new connection; and as soon as she can, to marry some respectable English gentleman. Charlotte to open my secrets in carriages and boxes. She knows how and where, and take her legacies. Suisse to have all my clothes and apparel of all sorts. Charlotte to take great care of Belle and Bezuies [two dogs] for love of me."

In another codicil he speaks of "Nicholas Suisse, my head valet, an excellent man." There can be little doubt as to the nature of the work which this excellent man did for his master. But was the master perfectly sane when the orgies of his last years were going on? There is reason to believe that he was not. One of the medical men who had attended him, wrote a letter to Mr. Croker stating that "the brain of the late Marquis of Hertford was a diseased brain, and had long been so—the partial paralysis, speechlessness, and other long-standing direct cerebral symptoms demonstrate it." Mr. Croker was fully convinced of the truth of this view. He wrote to the Marquis Wellesley (who himself died in 1842) a note in which he said, "the lamentable doings of his latter years were neither more nor less than *insanity*. You know, and he was himself well aware, that there is hereditary madness in his family. He often talked, and even wrote, about it to me."

When this misguided and wasted life came to an end, there was a repetition of the scene delineated in one of Hogarth's pictures; the birds of prey gathered together, and swooped down upon all that they could collect. Among the packages missing there was one containing a hundred thousand francs. It was traced to Nicholas Suisse, the valet. He declared that it was a gift from his master. Mr. Croker, as one of the executors, felt it to be his duty to prosecute Suisse, and Suisse tried hard to make the prosecution as disagreeable to Mr. Croker as it was to himself. He brought forward a woman named Angeline Borel, to swear that she had dined at Lord Hertford's in Mr. Croker's society, and Mr. Croker admitted that he had once dined with her at the Marquis's table; it would probably have been difficult to have gone to Lord Hertford's house at any time in those days without meeting some of his peculiar associates. But Mr. Croker also stated that when the Marquis, on another occasion, expressed his intention to call for the woman in question, and drive her out, "he left the carriage rather than remain in such company." Suisse was acquitted; the character of his master secured that result. It was shown that Suisse and Angeline Borel had long had a good understanding with each other; they were even engaged to be married. Suisse had ordered for his own use a service of plate worth 2000*l*. Man and woman had made the old Marquis their dupe, and their rage was turned upon Mr. Croker for endeavouring to defeat a part of their plot. But it could not be proved that Suisse had stolen the hundred thousand francs, and he was acquitted. Proceedings were taken in the French Courts for the recovery of a packet containing 30,000 francs, which Suisse had stolen, and judgment was at first given in his favour, but on the case being taken up to the Court of Cassation, the decision was reversed, and Suisse was ordered to pay the costs. Mr. Croker did his duty fearlessly in following up these proceedings, and he was not to be deterred by the slanders which were hurled at him. His course was entirely approved by Lord Hertford's son.

Lord Hertford (*fourth Marquis*) to Mr. Croker.

2, Rue Lafitte, August 7th, 1844.

MY DEAR SIR,

Our lawsuit terminated as I expected it would. By this time you have had the details in the papers, so I will not take up your time by making any observations.

Mr. Glandaz desires me to mention to the Executors that he is *convinced* the 100,000 fr. Suisse pretended Lord H. gave him, and that he evidently stole, can easily be recovered. He desires you will not pay him his legacy till all these proceedings are terminated, and he wishes to have the positive proof from the books of the banker of the negotiation of coupons to the amount of 77,000 fr. rentes this Suisse had himself paid in England. I send you Mr. Glandaz's note on the subject.

He considers Suisse so *immense* a scoundrel that he thinks it right to recover as much as possible from him.

Perhaps you will be of the same opinion, and give your directions. It is very important his legacy should not be paid.

I am afraid there is little chance of the 83,000 fr. rentes.

Yours, my dear Sir, most faithfully,

HERTFORD.

Mr. Croker to Lord Hertford. *Extract.*

Alverbank, Gosport, August 11th, 1843.

Thank you for your kindness in my defence. I had neither motive nor interest to prosecute Suisse until the discovery of the robbery. We had no suspicion of him; though I now begin to suspect much more than I did at first. I believe that there was a more extensive spoliation of papers than we imagined, and Suisse's guilty conscience thinks that I have discovered this, and he is actuated by peculiar enmity on that account. As to the fellow himself, I never used to interchange a word with him, except on the score of your father's health, now and then.

Mr. Croker received about £23,000 under the will. A much larger sum was bequeathed to him by a codicil, but in consequence of an informality, the intentions of Lord Hertford could not be carried out. Sir Robert Peel remarked to Mr. Croker, in a letter dated the 3rd of March, 1842, "My chief interest in respect to Lord Hertford's will, was the hope that out of his enormous wealth he would mark his sense of your unvarying and real friendship for him."

The reader has now before him the circumstances which Lord Macaulay deemed sufficient to warrant a broad and sweeping attack on the moral character—not of Lord Hertford, but of Mr. Croker. No one was ever more devotedly attached to his home and kindred than Mr. Croker; no one could possibly be more free from all cause of reproach in his own private life. But he happened, in common with most of the leading men of England, to know a peer who kept bad company, and therefore Lord Macaulay chose to speak of him with some of the flourishes which were ordinarily reserved for his special favourites, such as Barère. Macaulay's biographer—writing, as it must be presumed, under a total misconception of all the facts—improved upon the text which was left for him by throwing out a dark allusion to "certain unsavoury portions" of Mr. Croker's "private life," which "had been brought into the light of day in the course of either parliamentary or judicial investigations." Charges of this kind, going to the very root of a man's whole life and character, were put forward without a word of proof, and without anything to justify them which deserves the name of evidence. Nothing whatever that was injurious to Mr. Croker's private character was ever "brought to light" in a "parliamentary investigation," or any other investigation. To the last he was held in the highest esteem and honour by men who were not less punctilious on the score of morals than Lord Macaulay. Everybody knew that his private life was absolutely irreproachable. The only imputation cast upon Mr. Croker was that which was prompted by a dishonest valet whom he was seeking to bring to justice. What it amounted to, even at the worst, we have just seen. Macaulay took the utmost pains that it should *not* be seen. It was this peculiar method of treating public men which led Mr. Croker to predict that whatever else might be thought of Lord Macaulay's history, it would never be quoted as an authority; a prediction which has yet to be disproved.

END OF THE SECOND VOLUME.

www.ingramcontent.com/pod-product-compliance
Lightning Source LLC
Chambersburg PA
CBHW051737300426
44115CB00007B/608